European Intellectual History Since 1789

fourth edition

ROLAND N. STROMBERG
University of Wisconsin - Milwaukee

Prentice-Hall, Inc., Englewood Cliffs, New Jersey 07632

Library of Congress Cataloging in Publication Data

Stromberg, Roland N., (Date)
    European intellectual history since 1789.

    Bibliography: p. 318.
    Includes index.
    1.   Philosophy—Europe—History.   2.   Europe—
Intellectual life—19th century.   3.   Europe—
Intellectual life—20th century.   I.   Title.
B803.S85   1986   001.1'094   85-3646
ISBN 0-13-292046-8

Editorial/production supervision and
   interior design: Barbara DeVries
Cover design: Lundgren Graphics, Ltd.
Manufacturing buyer: Barbara Kelly Kittle

Printed in the United States of America

10   9   8   7   6   5   4

ISBN 0-13-292046-8   01

Prentice-Hall International (UK) Limited, *London*
Prentice-Hall of Australia Pty. Limited, *Sydney*
Prentice-Hall Canada Inc., *Toronto*
Prentice-Hall Hispanoamericana, S.A., *Mexico*
Prentice-Hall of India Private Limited, *New Delhi*
Prentice-Hall of Japan, Inc., *Tokyo*
Prentice-Hall of Southeast Asia Pte. Ltd., *Singapore*
Editora Prentice-Hall do Brasil, Ltda., *Rio de Janeiro*
Whitehall Books Limited, *Wellington, New Zealand*

All human history is fundamentally a history of ideas.

H. G. Wells

The drama of Europe is a spiritual drama, a drama of the mind.

Georges Bernanos

Contents

Preface

For this fourth edition of a book first published nearly twenty years ago, I have made some changes while trying to preserve the features that made it a successful textbook in modern intellectual history. Reasons to revise are found in both the volume of recent research and the inevitably changing patterns of interpretation. In an interesting way, these changes mirror the continuing development of thought in the years since this book was first conceived. Karl Marx once said that he would ideally have liked to change what he had written every day, never being content with anything he wrote upon re-reading it. Every writer and scholar must have had similar feelings, for we constantly add to our knowledge and alter our perception of what is important. I have continued over the years to teach the courses in nineteenth- and twentieth century European intellectual history, to learn something in this process, and to attempt to keep up with the reading in it, in the form of the scores of admirable monographs produced every year—these days, one often feels, every month. This proliferation of books and articles is a tribute to the almost frightening productivity of modern scholarship, in an era of far more professional scholars than ever before, a by-product of the explosive growth in higher education during the last several decades.

I hope that this edition is a "new and improved" version of the same product. I feel that it is. I would like again to thank all those including students as well as colleagues who have read the book, made useful criticisms, or bestowed encouragement.

The preface to the first edition spoke of the need for a basic textbook in modern European intellectual history, combining adequate coverage with relative brevity, a nucleus around which one might build a course by adding source readings and other supplementary reading. Such a book "should be fairly concise, well-informed, attractively written, well-organized . . . full enough to raise the issues and introduce the topics that need to be introduced, above all able to stimulate the student to more exact investigations, and supply him with the references he needs to carry on these; yet not so long as to become tedious, and to drown the beginning student in detail." This goal has not been basically altered.

The earlier preface made the obvious point that this book rests on the labors of many other scholars working in the history of ideas who must supply the building blocks for any such synthesis. "The average citizen wants to know about his heritage of civilization, which is contained in a fabric of thought so old and complex that guides are urgently needed," the first preface observed. The citizens want to know about the world in which they live, we might add, a confused and churning world concerning which one observation at least would not be challenged: Ideas are in ferment. And some of them, alive and vital today, are very old ideas. Radical youth, for all its "nowism," seems to thrive on the thoughts of those early Victorian thinkers, Marx and Kierkegaard, while neoconservatives resurrect Burke and Tocqueville. Debates about the role of science in cultural life are as fresh in the era of Snow and Leavis as they were in the time of Huxley and Arnold or Newton and Swift. Freud is as relevant and controversial as Darwin.

Whether or not it is true, as H. G. Wells urged, that all history at bottom is a history of ideas, certainly there are those to whom intellectual history is the most exciting kind of history, combining as it does, or should do, the special excitement of Man Thinking with an attempt to show this thinking in its connections with the realm of fact and action and as part of a larger cultural unity. For bewildered moderns trying to make sense of a world of consciousness so vast, diverse, contradictory, frustrating yet exciting as our postmodern one, this attempt can be not only interesting but therapeutic.

Roland N. Stromberg

Introduction

To "trace the history of the human mind," said Hume, is the task of the historian, as distinct from the chronicler. Voltaire added that "it is better to know how men thought in former times than how they acted." A great deal of intellectual history has crept, willy-nilly, into history, it being impossible to keep out the men and women of ideas. A current collection of readings offered to students of the beginning college course in Western civilization includes selections from Plato, Aristotle, the Bible, Cicero, Augustine, Aquinas, Machiavelli, Rabelais, Luther, Calvin, Bodin, Descartes, Locke, Bossuet, Rousseau, Burke, Tocqueville, Marx, Nietzsche, Sartre, and Camus. Obviously it would be difficult to justify their exclusion from such a course. One wonders, though, to what extent most first-year students are equipped to grapple with these formidable adversaries.

We no longer restrict history to politics or public events, if for no other reason than that these cannot be "understood" without reference to the climate of opinion in which they took place. The deeds of Charlemagne cannot be understood apart from the peculiar mixture of ideas and values that made up the mind of his age, a mind quite different from ours. Nor, to come closer to home in both space and time, can the deeds of Thomas Jefferson be understood except in the context of the Enlightenment—a "lost world," as one Jefferson student has cogently argued. Some men and women of ideas "made history" directly—Luther, for example. Others, who did not, contributed so much to those who did that we cannot leave them out: Robespierre had his Rousseau, Lenin his Marx. "If ideas in politics more than elsewhere are the children of practical needs," J. N. Figgis has written, "none the less is it true, that the actual world is the result of men's thought. The existing arrangement of political forces is dependent at least as much upon ideas, as it is upon men's perceptions of their interests." "Not ideas, but material and ideal interests directly govern man's conduct," Max Weber held, but he added, "Yet very frequently the world images which have been created by ideas have, like switchmen, determined the tracks along which action has been pushed by the dynamics of interest." Nothing is falser than the view, often associated with a kind of vulgar Marxism (Marx never held it), that ideas are merely the mechanical reflection of some supposedly nonintellectual material interest. There is nothing mechanical about an idea. Created in the mysterious ways of individual genius, it will then be acted upon in the realm of social reality and can partly decide the nature of that reality. Or, as Lord Acton observed, if people are stimulated by the hope of material gain, they can also be stimulated to action "by political or religious motives with no hope of material profit, and a certainty of material loss." Nothing is greater than the power of an idea; if greatest "when its time has come" (that is, when it agrees with the direction of social evolution), the idea yet remains an indispensable part of the recipe for meaningful action; even if it runs against the main flow of social evolution, an idea can be important.

Here is not the place to go into the troublesome question of just how *ideas* and *interests* act together in history. It is enough to observe that they do interact, that they are the "two faces of reality," in Jean Lhomme's expression, which one sees in all the great issues of humankind. Ideas are quite commonly found first in the mind of some unwordly person, a recluse like Bentham, an obscure refugee like Marx, a poor vagabond like Rousseau; then they are taken up by men and women of affairs, who, as John Maynard Keynes observed, snatch them from the air, perhaps without knowing that they came from some scribbler of yesterday.

The interaction of historically important ideas with the social milieu from which they emerge and which they in turn influence—this is, broadly, the domain of intellectual history. The separate disciplines, such as philosophy, the sciences, or political theory, insofar as they study their past ideas tend to do so unhistorically, treating them substantively and as if they arose in a vacuum. It must remain for the intellectual historian to show how these ideas interacted with social reality, with past ideas, and with each other. At any particular time and place there is a specific set of influences on the human mind, which includes (1) the legacy of past ideas available to people at that time, (2) a social context, consisting of all sorts of phenomena prominent in the environment of the times, political, economic, and so forth, and (3) other contemporary strains of thought and expression. If, for example, we wish to grasp the thought of Nietzsche, we have to know the older thinkers who influenced him (a great many reaching back to the Greeks), some more than others, such as his immediate predecessor Schopenhauer; also his social atmosphere of nineteenth-century bourgeois culture, together with such events as the Franco-Prussian War and the Bismarckian supremacy; and finally other significant intellectual movements of his time, among them French estheticism, Darwinism, socialism. A recent European scholar has remarked, "There is room for a disciple whose aim is to assess the factors which influence the human mind in one period or in one region," this being his definition of the realm of intellectual history.

What validates or testifies to the importance of intellectual systems? Few of them, if any, can stand the test of absolute logic: The great philosophies have all turned out to be postulates at bottom, mere assertions, fiats, resting on something assumed to be true without proof. This is quite as true of allegedly "scientific" structures such as Marxism, Newtonian physics, or logical positivism as it is of more patently "metaphysical" ones. The reason they appear and are adopted, become popular and influential, is related to factors other than the merely immanent laws of thought. These factors, it may be suggested, are historical and social; historical, in that ideas evolve in time as one generation hands down its thoughts to others who take them up and use them as a point of departure—the endless dialectic of intellectual history; social, in that the selection of some ideas rather than others for emphasis and discussion has to do with the structure of social reality at a given time—the issues, atmosphere, and great events of the day. Even genius must create with reference to the external social world it finds at hand; it cannot just create in a vacuum.

Clearly the subject matter of intellectual history is intensely interesting, for those with a flair for ideas. Defined as the study of the role of *ideas* in historical events and processes, intellectual history is admittedly a difficult art. In this connection one scholar observes that historical writing of the usual sort "often fails to apprehend the slow subterranean movements which minds inclined to be too matter-of-fact find intangible"[1] —those movements of the mind, of ideas and ideologies and tides of taste, which never appear overtly in history until one day, perchance, they explode in a French Revolution. While the details of politics and administrations and wars are studied in the most minute detail, because they are neatly documented in archives and can be grasped by the matter-of-fact mind, the role of ideas may be dismissed in a vague phrase or two. The need for careful and precise studies in intellectual history is now recognized and is being met. There is much recent research.

Writing some years ago, that philosopher so celebrated in the "history of ideas," Arthur O. Lovejoy, noted the unnatural fragmentation of the study of ideas, apportioned out among at least twelve "disciplines."[2] While students of literature, of the arts, of science, theology, education, social thought, and so forth, each cart away a portion of the body of Western thought, to dissect it minutely in the privacy of their chambers in isolation from each other, the whole organism perishes of this process, and there is no one to restore it to life unless a discipline called "history of ideas" can do so. The specialist work done by the various departments of learn-

---

[1] Henri Peyre, "The Influence of Eighteenth-Century Ideas on the French Revolution," *Journal of the History of Ideas,* January 1949.

[2] Arthur O. Lovejoy, "The Historiography of Ideas," in *Essays in the History of Ideas* (1948).

ing is extensive and valuable, but badly needs to be collated. And a service may be rendered to these various departments themselves, for Milton's poetry cannot be understood apart from the poet's store of general ideas, nor can Darwin's science be fully grasped without this context. That sometimes disparaged entity, the *Zeitgeist,* the "spirit of the age," assuredly does exist. Coleridge, perhaps, put it best: "Such as is the existing spirit of speculation, during any given period, such will be the spirit and tone of the religion and morals, nay even of the fine arts, the manners, and the fashions." (Nor is this the less true, he added, "because the great majority of men live like bats, but in twilight, and know and feel the philosophy of their age only by its reflections and refractions.") Later culture historians have attached much importance to the *generation* as a key to the discovery of that mysterious but omnipresently real set of the mind which permeates all aspects of the thought and expression of an era.

Introductory textbooks are intended for the important function of introducing the as yet fairly unsophisticated student to fields which it is hoped he or she will further explore, with the aid of the suggestions for additional reading supplied. This book should of course also be supplemented by outside readings in the sources of intellectual history. Asked what to read, Walter Pater advised students to "read the great authors whole; read Plato whole; read Kant whole; read Mill whole." Excellent advice, but a little impractical for many students. This textbook is not meant to substitute for the reading of the great thinkers, but rather to prepare for or supplement that task. It has arisen from a number of years of experience in teaching such a course in modern European intellectual history. Intellectual history, as it seems to us, should provide an introduction to the most important—from a general cultural viewpoint[3]—"ideas" (intellectual systems, movements of the mind) in the cultural heritage; it should relate these ideas to the social and political background so far as possible; it should show the continuity and lineage of thought; it should indicate the relevance of the ideas to general culture.

Most especially, perhaps, as a *history* of ideas, a presentation of this sort should provide a sense of history. That means a sense of the living context of reality, and it means a sense of the flow and movement of things. Too often the great thinkers and the great ideas are drained of life by being presented as disembodied abstractions. The historian wants to see Kepler's unhappy childhood and restless adolescence, he wants Voltaire's misspent youth and Rousseau's neuroticism and Marx's proud poverty, Locke's bourgeois prudence and Nietzsche's madness—all the human story of the great thinkers.

---

[3] Philosophy students, attuned to the analytical mood, often do not find the intellectual history course satisfying because it is not much interested in the truth or falsity, consistency or inconsistency, of intellectual systems or philosophies and is therefore prone to linger over some not interesting from this point of view, while ignoring others that are. Rousseau and Marx are not great philosophers and the essentially analytical mind soon grows impatient with their cloudy terms and vague ideas; they are historically and existentially of the highest importance, that is, they posed questions relevant to their age and of deepest significance for the human situation of modern times. It has been noted that specialists in whatever field, from economics to theology, will choose figures different from those selected by historians for their general cultural interest.

Perhaps it should be added that the ideas we study are mainly those that belong to serious, "high," or "elite" culture. Popular culture especially in the most recent period is a subject in itself, akin to social history in bearing on the way people live—and think. It is Guy Lombardo or the Rolling Stones rather than Beethoven or Stravinsky; it is astrology and yoga rather than Science and Philosophy. At times—in serious jazz, say, or for some writers who lurk on the fringes of both academic and popular thought—the two things can draw rather close together. This is commoner today than a century ago when in Britain, for example, the high culture of Oxford and Cambridge and the low culture of the music hall and the pub were worlds apart. The latter hardly counts as intellectual history. A democratic and syncretic twentieth century has undoubtedly brought the two modes in sight of each other. Without denying the interest of popular culture, we confine ourselves almost entirely to the realm of serious thought—of which, in fact, the popular is often an echo or caricature.

Nor should they, intellectual historians feel, deal only with the great thinkers, for Croce was right in observing that the spirit of an age is sometimes better found in the second-rate thinkers, and the spirit of the age must always be close to what historians of ideas seek. It is the general direction of the movement of thought that concerns them. From earliest times to the present, the great army of thought has marched—some individuals ahead, some in the rear, a large straggling army—steadily past one milestone after another, leaving behind some ideas, fashioning new ones, transforming old ones. We do not know the ultimate destination of the long trek, if it has any. But where we have been and what we have learned is worth knowing, for each of us is a part of the army, anxiously searching for signposts and wondering where, in the endless chaos of things, we are. History orients us.

It also equips us to live. To understand the past is to be able to live fully in the present. To be acquainted with the intellectual heritage of our long and rich Western civilization is to be a civilized person and to be prepared for constructive thinking. The object of this book is to present the most important general ideas in modern European history, not in isolation but as part of the stream of history. As Dr. Johnson said, "There is no part of history so generally useful as that which relates to the progress [?] of the human mind, the successive advances of science, the vicissitudes of learning and ignorance, the extension and resuscitation of arts and the revolution of the intellectual world."[4]

[4]Some additional references on the definition and methodology of intellectual history are Franklin L. Baumer, "Intellectual History and Its Problems," *Journal of Modern History,* September 1949; John C. Greene, "Objectives and Methods in Intellectual History," *Mississippi Valley Historical Review,* June 1957; Peter Burke, "Ideas Have a History," *The Listener,* February 9 and 16, 1967; Sir Isaiah Berlin, Introduction to Marc Raeff, *Russian Intellectual History: An Anthology* (New York: Harcourt Brace Jovanovich, 1966); Hayden White, "The Tasks of Intellectual History," *Monist,* Vol. 53, 1969, pp. 600-30; Leonard Krieger, "The Autonomy of Intellectual History," *Journal of Historical Ideas,* October–December 1973; Roland N. Stromberg, "Some Models Used by Intellectual Historians," *American Historical Review,* June 1975; Quentin Skinner, "Meaning and Understanding in the History of Ideas," *History and Theory,* Vol. 8, 1969, pp. 3-53; Dominick LaCapra and Steven L. Kaplan, ed., *Modern European Intellectual History: Reappraisals and New Perspectives* (Ithaca, N.Y.: Cornell University Press, 1982).

THE MODERN EPOCH

Few deny that the French Revolution ushered in the specifically modern epoch of history. The Revolution in some measure looked to the eighteenth-century "philosophers," to Rousseau and Voltaire and Montesquieu and Diderot, for its inspiration and ideas; but it soon swept beyond their prescriptions (which were hardly in agreement with each other) to explore political frontiers previously unheard of. Examinations of the role of Rousseau's and Voltaire's ideas in the Revolution impressively document both the extensive nature of this role and its amazingly chameleon-like character: The revolutionaries constantly quoted the Enlightenment giants but just as constantly made these words mean entirely different things. Apart from its specific content of novel political ideas, including equality, individualism, democracy, nationalism, and socialism, the Revolution was so massive that people could not help thinking of it as ushering in a new epoch in every department of life. Then the reaction to its violent excesses entailed opposition to all those ideas that had presumably inspired it, and a kind of intellectual counterrevolution against the Enlightenment, associated with Edmund Burke, took place. The titanic struggles of the twenty-five years after 1789 left the entire civilization forever altered, socially, politically, and intellectually. This era of revolutions dominates the early part of the nineteenth century.

The nineteenth century falls rather naturally into three parts, from the viewpoint of *Zeitgeist* and history of ideas. The morning is the Romantic and Revolutionary age, lasting from about 1789 to 1832 or perhaps 1848. It is marked by convulsions both political and moral, an intellectual revolution, and a great deal of creativity emerging from its storm and stress. Its heroes of thought are Kant and Fichte and Hegel; Burke, Chateaubriand, Saint-Simon, Fourier; the Romantic poets; the renovators of political philosophy; the creators of new social doctrines. It is an age in which people felt old moorings give way and wondered where the storm would blow them.

Then, during the noonday of the century, calm returns and there is time to take soundings. Doubts and tensions remain, but this Victorian period is marked by relative stability and by the undertaking of extraordinary efforts at synthesis. This is the time of Comte, Marx, Darwin, and Mill. Realism replaces romanticism in literature and the arts; science, the ultimate realism, mounts the pedestal as the modern god; visions of utopia in politics and society suffer a severe blow with the failure of the revolutions of 1848. There is disenchantment, but there is also success, on solid if pedestrian foundations, the kind of success and solidity the adjective "mid-Victorian" conveys.

The evening brings its gloom and uncertainties; unquestionably a darker mood strikes Europe late in the century, from about 1885 down to the stunning collapse of 1914. If the average man remained complacent and hopeful, post-Darwinian and post-Marxist Europe produced a crop of amazingly insightful thinkers who were exploring domains never heretofore much known, zones of fearful nonsymmetry. The unconscious irrational, or the prerational, interested those who dominate this epoch—Nietzsche, Freud, Bergson, Sorel, Max Weber. In part, this mirrored the experiences of an epoch which brought vast movements of population from farm to city, vast increases in population with the accompanying problem of "mass," almost terrifying technological "advances." In this period artists and intellectuals became increasingly estranged or alienated from society, yet were creative as seldom before. The "modernist" mood and movement began. It was marked by a breach between private and public realms which brought the search for personal identity to the front as a prominent theme. Sociologists and psychologists joined a new kind of literature in exploring the frontier between the individual and society, now highly problematic.

Of all watersheds, 1914 is rivaled only by 1789 in the modern world; nothing after the terrible World War—to the coming of which intellectuals had actually contributed strongly—could be the same. Shattered visions of infinite progress littered the postwar landscape, and Western civilization suddenly found it had no other values to fall back upon. It tried to invent new ones, tried even to restore old ones, but watched the world descend into even lower depths of war and degradation. The response of thought to the challenge of "decline and fall" was at times nothing less than heroic. If this was the age of Hitler and Stalin, it was also the age of Toynbee and Sartre, as well as of Le Corbusier and Picasso, Lawrence and Joyce. From the awful devastation and slaughter of World War II, Western civilization made a remarkable recovery. And its thought has been dazzlingly prolific—too much so, perhaps, an embarrassment of riches, an excess of self-consciousness which explodes and fragments into an urban society losing all intellectual as well as social unity. Surmounting one crisis of depression and war, the civilization met new crises of order and legitimation.

Throughout this period of the nineteenth century and beyond, powerful forces were at work transforming the social structure in which ideas operate—vast processes of population growth, urbanization, technological progress, and new social stratification. "The concentration of population in cities," a British student of urbanization, A. F. Weber, noted near the end of the nineteenth century, had been "the most remarkable social phenomenon" of that century. Yet by present standards it had hardly begun. These teeming urban masses were uprooted from their traditional folk cultures to become consumers of ideas and values supplied by urban intellectuals. "What bonds link the two million inhabitants who crowd into Paris?" asked Baron Haussmann, the redesigner of Paris, in 1864, "For them Paris is a great consumers' market, a vast workshop, an arena for ambitions." A place of marvelous stimulation where keenness of mind fed on rapid communications and the competition for prizes, the metropolis, growing toward megalopolis, was also a place of restless discontent. And it was a place where an essentially new class, the intellectuals, specialists in ideas, sellers of ideological wares, arose as never before. (The term *intellectuels* was first popularized in France at the time of the Dreyfus Affair in 1898.[5]

---

[5] T. W. Heyck finds the idea of "an intellectual life" emerging in England in the 1870s, with the first recognition of the noun "intellectual" coming in the Oxford English Dictionary edition of 1888. See Heyck, *The Transformation of Intellectual Life in Victorian England* (1982), pp. 234–35.

This volume, then, tries to take the Europeans from the French Revolution through the tumultuously changing nineteenth century and into the tragic, turbulent, creative twentieth. It begins with them emerging from an aristocratic into a democratic society, from an agrarian and commercial era into an industrial and technological one. It observes their thinking as they are carried on a tide of modernization that leaves them confused and buffeted creatures, victims in part of too many ideas that escape their control. Alienated, they need to rethink and put to constructive use this remarkably rich inheritance of thought and expression.

chapter 1

Romanticism and Revolution

1789-1815

What is the good of curbing sensuality, shaping the intellect, securing the supremacy of reason? Imagination lies in wait as the most powerful enemy.

Goethe

At least three revolutions—the French, the Romantic, and the Kantian—occurred in the 1780s, with their direct impact carrying on through the next several decades to leave a deep mark on the entire modern world. To these, general history must add the Industrial Revolution. Contemporaries were prone to regard them as but different aspects of a single revolution. Thus the conservative Francis Jeffrey in 1816, discussing "the revolution in our literature," attributed it to "the agitations of the French Revolution . . . the hopes and terrors to which it gave occasion." Some recent scholarly students of romanticism have been inclined to endorse this verdict. And the German poet Heine, speaking of Immanuel Kant, remarked that "with this book [*The Critique of Pure Reason*] an intellectual revolution began in Germany which offers the strangest analogies with the material revolution in France" and, he added, to the reflective mind is of equal importance. This judgment was endorsed by Karl Marx, who observed that the Kantian revolution in philosophy was the intellectual counterpart of the French Revolution in politics. It only remains to connect Kant with romanticism, and of course, that is a common juxtaposition—not that the two things were quite the same but that Kant's successors and disciples, Fichte and Schelling, provided philosophical grounding for the romantic poets.

Clearly these three important developments, in politics, literature, and pure philosophy, respectively, did interact and sometimes blend. It is not clear that they were of similar origin. Kant was working on problems bequeathed to philosophy by Locke, Berkeley, Leibniz, and especially Hume; he wrote his chief books before the Revolution, and his basic position does not seem to have been affected by that event, though it stirred him deeply, even in his ivory tower at Königsberg. (But Jean-Jacques Rousseau demonstrably influenced both Kant and the French Revolution.) The Revolution, needless to say, owed nothing directly to the German philosopher on the shores of the Baltic, whose abstruse speculations were known in 1789 to only a few. As for romanticism, which also can be traced back to Rousseau, it most clearly announced its arrival in Germany around 1781, with the writings of Schiller and the young Goethe, in a context that seems neither politically revolutionary nor at all interested in technical philosophy. The young Goethe was mostly interested in mystical religion. Schiller's *William Tell* was to inspire many a revolutionary, but it was not written until 1804.

Causation in history is a tricky problem, never simple. Monistic dogmas that assert the invariable priority of one factor, such as technological change or the rise of a social class, do not stand the test of careful criticism. Material, social, and intellectual factors continually interact on each other. It is not clear that they do so within the matrix of a single system, so that one can speak of the unity of an historical epoch. Any historical period contains within itself many processes and themes, not necessarily all knit together in a seamless web; there are always loose ends.

One can say with assurance that there was restlessness and malaise in the 1780s. The American Revolution, an event of the profoundest significance for Europe, not least France, concluded successfully. The French monarchy was in deep trouble before 1789, reeling toward bankruptcy, apparently unable, since the failure of the Turgot reform effort in 1776, to install necessary reforms. In Great Britain, a political organism weakened by the American defeat faced impending great changes, as reformers demanded a more democratic and representative Parliament. At just that moment, a silent but immensely important "revolution" had begun, for most economic historians date from the 1780s the era of sustained economic growth in Great Britain that marks the crucial moment in the rise of modern industrialism. But few can have appreciated this at the time.

In the realm of literature and thought, there were some equally disturbing signs. The German drama of *Sturm und Drang* (storm and stress) was a strong reaction against Enlightenment classicism, while the turn toward mysticism and religion expressed itself in France in such figures as the popular *Philosophe inconnu*, Saint-Martin. Hamann, Swedenborg, and Blake are other examples in diverse quarters of Europe.[1] The 1780s was a glorious decade that gave us Mozart and the

---

[1] Robert Darnton, *Mesmerism and the End of the Enlightenment in France* (1968), interestingly recounts another reaction against rationalism that appeared in the 1780s, becoming almost a mania for a time. Darnton points out that mesmerism had a distinct radical component, being adopted as a kind of anti-Establishment gesture by a number of the future leaders of the Revolution.

American constitution as well as Kant, in many ways the climax of the Enlightenment. But the leaders of the great *philosophe* era were falling away. Voltaire died in
1778, Rousseau in the same year, Hume in 1776, Diderot in 1784, d'Alembert in
1783, Condillac in 1780, Frederick the Great in 1786. Buffon and Franklin were
octogenarians. These illustrious passings signaled the demise of an age. Many sensed
change in the air—even before the French Revolution arrived to confirm it.

Though Enlightenment strains continued on, to be seen in such prominent
schools as British utilitarianism and political economy, the Revolution ended by
discrediting much of it. It was accused, by the important conservative manifesto of
Edmund Burke, of having led France to disaster through its simplistic and abstract
conception of people, its utopian quest for a perfect social order. It was now said to
have been metaphysical, a charge it had once itself leveled at the past. It had invented fantasies and called them Reason. It had thrown out the really important
things in life, such as religion and tradition and concrete human ties, in favor of
slogans about human rights which, in practice, only invited the godless to slaughter
each other. Europe, the conservative foes of revolutionary France believed, would
have to purge itself of this disease which, erupting in the Terror, had its roots in the
sick cynicism of Voltaire, the wild dreams of Rousseau. In Burke and his numerous
followers strains of romanticism interacted with the reaction against the Revolution
that affected most of Europe's major intellectual figures by 1798, continuing on
through the Napoleonic wars and into the post-Napoleonic Restoration.

THE FRENCH REVOLUTION

Some historians of the French Revolution tell us that we should not speak of a
French Revolution. Jacques Godechot states, "In fact, the French Revolution was
only one aspect of a Western, or more exactly an Atlantic revolution, which began
in the English colonies in America shortly after 1763, extended through revolutions
in Switzerland, the Low Countries, and Ireland, before reaching France between
1787 and 1789." From France it bounced over to Germany, Switzerland, Italy, and
other parts of Europe. One might object that it is foolish to compare the rumblings
in Holland or Ireland with the French Revolution for significance and scope and
that the later revolutions came about precisely because France's had done so. But it
is certainly true that the French Revolution from the beginning exerted a worldwide influence, and, if this was because of French prestige and influence throughout
Europe, it was also because the Revolution produced ideas for which the whole
Western world was ready.

What were the great ideas of the Revolution? Some of them seem self-evident
and therefore pedestrian today, but they were not so familiar then, and they were
given vibrant new meaning by the marvelous events of 1789: popular sovereignty,
self-determination of peoples, equality of rights. And nationalism. The French
joyously toasted *la patrie* of which they were all, equally, the children now: no more
Bretons, Angevins, or Dauphinards, any more than nobles and commoners. The
whole conception of the political society changed. The king could no longer be King

of France; he must (if he stayed) be King of the French, for he owed his power to the people. The special privileges and rights of the nobility, renounced by the nobles themselves in an orgy of ideological altruism, were no more; all citizens were equal before the law, with equal access to office, equal liability to taxation. Much of the Revolution's mystique went into that word *citoyen*. The Nation, then, was born—a community of citizens sharing equally in rights and duties, not a class hierarchy. If people did not like the government they had, they should have a right to change it. And they had a right to speak up freely, according to the Declaration of the Rights of Man and Citizen, that great manifesto of the Revolution.

Those who alleged a certain vagueness and utopian character in the ideology of the Revolution would, of course, be right. It was an apocalyptic moment, and all kinds of millennial ideals came forth. Universal peace was one of them, ironically enough in view of what the Revolution, in fact, soon brought to Europe. Numerous orators repudiated the very right to make war, and the Assembly solemnly adopted a resolution of this sort in 1790. Two years later, France was at war with the monarchies of Europe, and only that incurable ideologist, Maximilien Robespierre, was still (for the time being) a pacifist. It had been expected that all mankind would be brothers. In fact, "popular sovereignty" or "self-determination" entailed war, because Europe's political order did not correspond to this principle. Nor would it have been possible to decide what this slogan meant exactly, in practice, in many parts of Europe.

Faced with the need to transform the largely negative character of the initial revolution (the first Constitution resounds with *il n'y a plus*—"there no longer exists"), eighteenth-century ideas were called upon. Rousseau especially was to be quoted incessantly by leaders of the Revolution. Enlightenment political theory tended to be vague and utopian. Nor was it all of a piece. Montesquieu disagreed with Voltaire, Voltaire with Rousseau, and Rousseau, if not with himself, at least with some of his followers. It is easy to identify at least three major strains in the Revolution, perhaps more. The first period of the Revolution was in the hands of the moderates, who did not wish drastic change; the intellectual idol of this phase was Montesquieu, the goal a limited, constitutional monarchy on the English model. Then, in terms of the chief Revolutionary factions, came the Girondin, Jacobin or *Montagnard,* and *sans culotte* or perhaps Babeuvist forces—in broader ideological terms, roughly liberal, democratic, and socialist.

The Girondins admired Voltaire, his disciple Condorcet being one of their brain trust. Not lacking in revolutionary zeal, the party of Brissot, Condorcet, and Mme. Roland was anticlerical and antiaristocratic, and inclined to a doctrinaire liberalism based on Montesquieu and Locke along with Voltaire (though Mme.Roland also admired Rousseau, an ambivalent figure). These were the upper bourgeoisie, insofar as a class label might be roughly pinned on them. They believed in natural rights of the individual and were suspicious of excessive state power. Constitutional government with "checks and balances" but not too much democracy appealed to this group, who perhaps betrayed their bourgeois outlook as much in their deistic anticlericalism as in the law against workers' associations passed in 1791. Anglophile admirers of the British constitutional system, they bequeathed much to nineteenth-century French liberalism, always weaker than in Britain but not without its influence. They lost out in the struggle that developed, were destroyed, and sent to the guillotine by their enemies on the Left. It is significant that under the impact of events they moved toward democracy. Initially hostile to universal suffrage, some of them came around to it. Condorcet's constitution of 1793, which never went into effect, included universal suffrage and a single legislative assembly, ideas approved by the American friend of this group, Benjamin Franklin. But executive and judicial checks on the will of this assembly were to exist. If the Gironde moved close to a type of democracy under the pressure of events during the Revolution, its position should be distinguished from Jacobin democracy. One of the important grounds of dispute between the two great Revolution factions, as it seemed in 1792-93 (the situation was complex), was that the Gironde stood for devolution of political power while the left-wing Jacobins favored centralization. The concrete issue on which they broke apart—and which in the end broke the Girondists—found the latter unwilling to send King Louis XVI to the guillotine (1792-93) because they shrank from the implications and consequences of so drastic a deed.

The left-wing Jacobins developed an unusual conception of democracy based on Rousseau's social contract and general will, or their construal of these concepts. Their goal was equality, and the idea of the general will together with the mass or mob action on which their power often depended caused them to glorify the people *en masse*. Robespierre and Saint-Just accepted a dictatorship of Reason, with themselves representing the "people." This strain of thought had relatively little regard for individual rights or parliamentary institutions, which seemed to it selfish and corrupt. The Jacobin constitution of 1793 provided for no separation of powers, no limit on the power of the state, no guarantees of individual liberties. It sanctioned a plebescitary or democratic dictatorship, based on the popular will but with power delegated to a small number of people. Jacobin democracy with its frank worship of the mob spirit is difficult for Anglo-Saxons to grasp, but it has been a potent tradition in France. Democratic in a deep sense, with a feeling for the common man *en masse,* a desire to bring the people directly into government (Robespierre wished to build a stadium holding twelve thousand people to allow the crowd to watch the legislators), and a passion for equality, its disregard of legal processes and individual rights may have been reflected in the Reign of Terror, though that abnormal episode ought not to be charged to ideology alone. (Later Jacobins showed a keen concern for individual justice: Consider the glorious fight of Georges Clemenceau, a century later, on behalf of Captain Dreyfus.)

Robespierre was the great ideologist of the Revolution and leading personality during the hectic bloody days of the Republic of Virtue. It is significant for his love of Jean-Jacques that he believed in the worship of a Supreme Being; atheism, he declared, is aristocratic. He was a believer, but his true God was a kind of abstract embodiment of the People. Effective mass orator, he was coldly unhappy in most of his relationships with concrete, real people. With a sensitivity that caused him to tremble at the sight of blood, he could order the death of thousands in the name of humanity. All that Edmund Burke meant when he accused the Revolution of abstract theorizing and a want of practical judgment is embodied in Robespierre, the man of austere principle who hated the intrigues of practical politics and became a bloody dictator because he would not compromise.

Robespierre was not the most radical product of the French Revolution. Jacobinism was not socialistic though it accepted the supremacy of community over individual in the spirit of Rousseau's social contract. Danton, Robespierre, and Saint-Just assumed a right to regulate property in any way necessary, but the social order they believed to be best was one in which every citizen held a little property, as Rousseau had suggested. This might well be designated as a petty bourgeois or artisan-worker utopia.

Socialism did appear in the French Revolution though it did not get far. Babeuf and Buonarrotti, revolutionary socialists, attempted an insurrection in 1795 (the Conspiracy of the Equals) but failed badly. Nevertheless they began a powerful tradition. Somewhat inarticulately they hated property, commerce, luxury, while extolling the virtues of poverty, equality, honest labor. They, too, took their inspiration chiefly from aspects of the writings of Jean-Jacques, which partially articulated their natural class feelings. Morelly, an obscure writer, had developed Rousseau's thought in a more socialistic direction just before the Revolution. Mably and Holbach also wrote in a similar vein and reached large audiences. These were mostly poor men and their words are significant as among the first sounds from the lower depths. Like the Levellers and Diggers of the English Revolution, the left-wing Jacobins and the Equals spoke briefly for classes hardly yet represented at all in literate thought; the Revolution had stirred the pot sufficiently to bring them momentarily to the top, then they subsided. But this time their voices were not forgotten. Buonarrotti survived to become a link with the socialism of the 1840s, and Parisian revolutionary radicalism lived on in other firebrands such as Blanqui. This *sans culotte* socialism spread over Europe quickly, making an appeal to doctrinaire representatives of the poorer classes. It was, after all, close to elemental Christianity. Russo, the Italian Babeuvist, echoed Savonarola's medieval call to the rich to throw away their jewels.

These extremes tended to discredit the Revolution. The initial joy with which it was greeted all over Europe turned to disillusionment as the 1790s wore on, and the Revolution led to civil war, persecution, terror, international war. At first all the intellectuals of Europe were enchanted by it, including dozens who later became its bitter foes. "Bliss was it in that dawn to be alive." Not only Wordsworth but Maistre, Chateaubriand, Kant, Fichte, Novalis, Goethe, Coleridge, Southey, and many others felt this. Rousseau had passionate admirers in England, like the father of Thomas Malthus, who asked only to be known as "the friend of Rousseau." Gilbert Wakefield, a Rousseau disciple, was imprisoned in 1799 for allegedly expressing a wish that the French would invade and conquer Britain. Everyone at this time, too, was reading Gibbon, whose *Decline and Fall of the Roman Empire,* which he had finished in 1787 after more than twenty years of labor, radiated a republican spirit—or did it only seem so in the atmosphere of 1789? The Roman state had begun its collapse with the very first emperor, and Christianity had finished it off, the great historian seemed to be saying.

But the Revolution seemed to lose its way and turn to violence, rapine, and injustice. It ended with the Reign of Terror and the awesome spectacle of the revolution devouring its own children. The result was a reexamination of the premises of the Age of Reason and a rejection of them that aided the turn toward romanticism.

The Revolutionaries had seemed to cling to eighteenth-century rationalism. It was not the romantic Rousseau they worshipped, but the utopian rationalist of *The Social Contract*. Before his suicide in a revolutionary prison, Condorcet, the disciple of Voltaire, wrote a hymn to unlimited human progress under reason. The Republic of Virtue and of Terror paraded the Goddess of Reason through the streets of Paris. Volney (*The Ruins,* 1791) theorized that empires fall from an insufficiency of natural religion and too many priests. Robespierre, in his meteoric path upward to grand inquisitor and then downward to victim of the Terror he had instituted, carried Rousseau's words with him everywhere. Little wonder that some who watched turned away in disgust from eighteenth-century thought, holding it responsible for the failure of the Revolution. In actuality, none of the leading *philosophes* had advocated or expected violent revolution.

CRITICS OF THE REVOLUTION

Edmund Burke's great indictment of the Revolution stood out above all others. It was eloquently answered by Tom Paine and others; the conservative reaction did not entirely sweep the field. But it tended to dominate. Historians still debate the element of validity in Burke's charges against the Revolution, but it would probably be generally agreed that he was right in holding that *philosophe* thought on politics was both too vague and too doctrinaire, in an area where these qualities are peculiarly dangerous. A scholar has observed concerning the thought of Helvétius and Holbach that they "must answer for the fact that they ultimately offered nothing beyond pious wishes" for an enlightened despot, ignoring "institutional structure" altogether.[2] One can readily find fantasies in which it was simply assumed that revolution would somehow install good government and do away with all evils—crime, hatred, deceit, envy, lawsuits, prisons, poverty—presumably by a sweep of the pen. No more monumentally innocent thought can be imagined. It would still be found in the Revolution of 1848.

The famous Declaration of the Rights of Man and of Citizen, manifesto of the Revolution, is a case in point. Attempting to reduce the formula for political justice to a few axioms, it revealed considerable confusion and subsequently was completely ignored. It might mean everything or nothing. "Men are born and remain free and equal in rights." "The purpose of the state is to secure the citizen in enjoy-

[2] Everett C. Ladd, Jr., "Helvétius and D'Holbach," *Journal of the History of Ideas,* April–June 1962.

ment of his rights." What exactly were these rights, and how could the state maintain them? They were said to include "the unrestrained communication of thought and opinions" as well as "a sacred and inviolable right to property"; but in both cases there might be exceptions, "in cases of evident public necessity." Similarly equivocal were statements that "the law ought to prohibit only actions hurtful to society" and "ought to impose no other penalties but such as are absolutely and evidently necessary." Would anyone disagree about the principle, but could any two people agree on the all-important matter of just what these actions and penalties were?

Critics of the "natural rights of man" school such as Jeremy Bentham have claimed that such rights are either equivocations or tautologies—meaningless slogans. But clearly they have an emotional value. At that time their concrete referents were real enough. For example, Robespierre in his younger days attacked the law that "inflicted civil infamy upon the innocent family of a convicted criminal" (John Morley) as well as another that denied civil rights to children born out of wedlock. Such remnants of irrational barbarity fell before this wave of political reform. The reforms of the Revolutionary era were real enough, though stated in an abstract way. And had they not been so stated, they might never have been secured. In their attempt to bring about the final perfect state of humanity, the Revolutionary ideologists overstated their case and spoiled it, but en route to its ultimate failure as an apocalyptic movement, the Revolution achieved all sorts of useful changes in the lot of humanity. The old order of inequality, with its relics of the seigneurial system in the countryside, its unequal taxation and denial of equal economic opportunity, its unjust and arbitrary laws, disappeared forever. This is what the Revolution meant and why it has always been celebrated joyously in France.

But it meant something else in England—something suggested by that cartoon in which an ugly assassin armed with faggot and dagger is offering to give "liberty" to Britain. Secure (as most English thought) in their own liberties, the work of history and experience and not slogans and theories, Britain looked with horror on the bloody and turbulent French scene and found itself at war with revolutionary imperialism. From this position it produced the leading works of the counterrevolution, most notably that of Burke.

Edmund Burke's renowned book of 1790, *The Reflections on the Revolution in France,* has been, and probably always will be, the subject of violent disagreement. But its distinction is usually admitted even by those whose ideology forces them to be its foe on principle. Burke claimed that the Revolution went wrong because its leaders tried to scrap an entire political system and put a new one in its place overnight; he related this mistake to the outlook of the *philosophes,* the political rationalists whose method lacked realism in an area where abstractness is fatal and the nondoctrinaire approach is vitally necessary. It is true that the wholesale abolition of an entire order in France in 1789 created immense confusion during the transformation period. "Feudalism" was declared at an end, which meant the dissolution of such institutions as the army, local government, the judicial system, the clergy. As for the *philosophe* political ideology, it did indeed consist in good part of general maxims without careful attention to detail and so was more helpful in tearing down than in building back up.

Whether Burke's analysis of the Revolution was right or wrong, the events in France stimulated him to formulate his political philosophy. A soaring eloquence and dazzling sense of the subtle texture of actual politics lent to Burke's book a memorable quality; as a piece of literature, it is one of the pioneer works of the new school of Romanticism. The leading idea emerging from this eloquence and this subtlety was that society is a vast and complicated historical product that may not be tinkered with at will like a machine; it is a repository of collective human wisdom to be regarded with reverence, and if reformed at all it must be with due respect for the continuity of its traditions. There were other related ideas: that a political community is something made by history, an unanalyzable bond between people which makes free government possible; that the social organism has its "natural aristocracy," which the commoner sort of people must and do, in a healthy society, respect; that general rules and abstract principles are no help in politics.

With a disdain for the "abstract rights" proclaimed by the French, he tried to make clear the real rights of man: Burke certainly believed in rights, but he stressed the degree to which those entering civil society must give up some of their liberties in order to gain the advantages of government. He distrusted the restless innovators who had no patience to search out the wisdom of their ancestors but must draw amateur blueprints for the total reconstruction of society, as if they were the first to think. The science of government is not for these, whose visionary schemes "in proportion as they are metaphysically true, are morally and politically false." These "smugglers of adulterated metaphysics" knew not man—or God. Burke felt that Western political society was sound only on Christian foundations. To Burke two human needs were evident above all: history and religion. The human being is a religious animal who, without Christianity, would turn perforce to some other, and probably less satisfactory, faith—not a bad prediction of what has actually happened in recent times. A social animal, the human being would be no more than a beast if cut off from the sustaining fabric of ancient custom and tradition. Reverence toward God and toward the social order are therefore the two great duties, and they are linked, for history is the revelation of God's purpose.

There is irony, and perhaps confusion, in the fact that Burke accused the *philosophes* of being "metaphysicians," they whose banner always bore the motto "Down with metaphysics." It seems that Burke is right, if we think of some of the cruder post-Rousseau political pamphleteers. But Burke's own empiricism has roots in the better sort of Enlightenment political thought, Hume and Montesquieu especially.

The Irish politician deeply influenced all subsequent conservative political thought. Edition followed edition of the *Reflections,* all over Europe. Louis XVI personally translated it into French. For this popularity, its timeliness and what seemed an uncanny prophetic quality (Burke announced the failure of the Revolution before it had failed, it seemed) were partly responsible, along with the richness and color of the style. Stripped of its rhetoric, Burke's thought may not appear extraordinary.

Perhaps it was not necessarily "conservative" in the most obvious sense of this word. In suggesting an empirical approach to the enormous complexity of human affairs, in place of the vague sloganizing of the *philosophes,* Burke may well be viewed as the founder of a real science of social reform, rather than as a hidebound conservative. He was certainly not opposed to change, if properly carried out, and his own career, that of a person of humble birth, consisted of one passionate crusade after another, on behalf of American independence, Ireland, and India (the Warren Hastings affair)[3] and against the French Revolution. "The most urgent need of his nature was always some great cause to serve—some monstrous injustice to repair." This tempestuous Irishman was temperamentally as little a conservative as it is possible to conceive.

But there was, of course, the conservative Burke—or, since he almost created the school, the Burke traits that came to be thought of as conservative. The feeling of piety for the social order, the mistrust of hare-brained reformers with a one-shot plan, the organic conception of social growth, these were the foundations of the conservative faith. A great deal of Burke has been accepted as essential political wisdom for anyone who wants to participate in politics as it always is and must be, rather than merely shout slogans from a distance. A modern socialist, Harold Laski, declared that "the statesman ignorant of Burke is lost upon a stormy sea without a compass."

Burke's thought was a sort of idealized and conceptualized version of the traditional rural order of society, with roots reaching far back into recorded time. Nineteenth-century liberals and socialists applauded the decline of that society, which they saw as brutalized, narrow-minded, backward, and inequalitarian. "From the village street into the railway station is a leap across five centuries from the brutalizing torpor of nature's tyranny over man into the order and alertness of man's organized dominion over nature," George Bernard Shaw wrote. Writing a few years into the twentieth century, Bertrand Russell rejoiced that "this whole order of ideas has vanished from the civilized world"—ideas of hierarchy and authority, intolerance and subordination, religious dogma and social constraint. Russell, the liberal (despite occasional flirtations with socialism), rejoiced in the freeing of the individual to fulfillment as a creative person emancipated from the tyranny of society. Shaw, the socialist, looked forward to a new and rational organization of society based on science and not superstition. And yet, throughout the nineteenth and twentieth centuries (it was never stronger than in quite recent years), a nostalgia for the country accompanied a horror of the city, of industry and technology and the

---

[3] The trial of the first governor-general of British India on charges of arbitrary and illegal actions against Indian natives stretched over the years from 1788 to 1795, ending in his acquittal; Burke's long and bitter campaign against Hastings was not popular in Parliament and diminished his prestige.

dissolving of human ties. Burke's image of the primeval "natural" order of humanity, before corrupted by commerce and cities, never died.

The *Reflections on the Revolution in France* was a work of genius, written at white heat, blazing with indignation and charged with eloquence—an eloquence that is a bit too much for some modern readers ("Burke never takes the trumpet from his lips"), yet makes a gorgeous effect. It deeply influenced his generation and contributed not only to the anti-Revolutionary cause but to the romantic taste. In his youth, in the 1750s, a struggling young lawyer turned literary man, Burke had written a treatise called *The Sublime and the Beautiful,* which has often been seen as a landmark in the evolution of taste from neoclassical to romantic. He argued that while the realm of the "beautiful" is indeed subject to the familiar classical rules about harmony, proportion, elegance, and so forth, there is another realm, the "sublime," which inspires fear, awe, which does not civilize and socialize us as the classical does but makes us feel alone while exalting and exhilarating us. Burke was always a little romantic, his career was exceedingly so, and his last great work is, perhaps paradoxically, as romantic in style as it is conservative in content. So in a way the great advocate of the counterrevolution was a revolutionary, too.

THE BONAPARTIST ERA

Insofar as he was trying to defend tradition and "prescription" as the "guardians of authority," Burke was swimming against the tide of the times. Despite its excesses and horrors, the French Revolution happened and, as Lord Acton later remarked, "it taught the people to regard their wishes and wants as the supreme criterion of right"; it accustomed men to change and swept away the old order beyond hope of recovery. Even Burke did not imagine, realist that he was, that it would be possible to restore the *status quo ante* in France. Soon the troops of France spread the Revolution all over Europe. The dictatorship of Napoleon (1800 to 1814) turned most of thinking Europe, even thinking France, against the Revolution, but the Bonapartist victories continued to overturn the old arrangements of Europe.

Against the rule of Napoleon, a good many of France's leading men and women of letters protested and went into exile, though some (like Bonald) came back when the anarchy was over and order restored by a vigorous ruler. Benjamin Constant, Mme. de Staël, and Chateaubriand headed the brilliant crowd of refugees, to whom Bonapartism was purely and simply tyranny. There were others, like Goethe, who never lost faith in Napoleon, seeing in him the man of destiny whose mission it was to unite Europe under a single progressive law. In France, beginning in the period just before Napoleon (the Directory), the so-called Ideologues reacted against political failure and disillusion by becoming severely objective, seeking to study the human mind as strict scientists. (They were the ancestors of those antiseptic moderns, the "behavioral scientists.") This was the time of Laplace, Lamarck, Cuvier, and other great French scientists, indicating that the more detached subjects could flourish under Bonaparte. Laplace crowned the "classical mechanics," perfecting

Newton, and was the author of a famous *Système du monde,* which undertook to explain the operations and evolution of the universe without recourse to Newton's *deus ex machina.* ("Sire, I have no need of that hypothesis," he responded when Napoleon asked him about God.) Cuvier and Lamarck began the controversy over evolution. The Italians, Galvani and Volta, were installing the age of electricity. Napoleon did admire the sciences and thought it important to encourage them in every way possible.

Within France, however, political controversy could hardly exist, and freedom of speculation was limited. Not that Bonaparte was, personally, anything other than the most emancipated of thinkers. Enormously cynical, he delighted in shocking people with his atheism in private conversation; but, believing that "only religion gives the state firm and lasting support," he would not tolerate any public irreligion. "You must form believers, not reasoners," he told the teachers of a state school for girls. Since "the stability of marriages serves the interest of social morality," the Code Napoleon was severe on adultery, but privately Napoleon called it "a mere peccadillo, an incident at a masked ball . . . a most common occurrence." Women he regarded as "mere machines to make children," and intellectuals and artists he affected to despise; therefore Mme. de Staël, an intellectual and artistic woman, was his *bête noire.* But many of Napoleon's outrageous opinions were, as they so often are, a kind of defense mechanism of an ego unsure of itself in this domain and cannot quite be taken seriously. He claimed, for example, to be "insensitive to what is called style," but he obviously was not. An omnivorous reader, he missed little that went on in the world of art, science, and philosophy and often commented on it shrewdly. Nevertheless, we feel he was sincere when he wrote that "the statistics of my army are, as far as I am concerned, the most enjoyable literary works in my library and those which I read with the most pleasure in my moments of relaxation!" But one should not be unjust to this remarkable man; in some ways his insatiable curiosity, especially about scientific matters, was hardly less than epochal. On his expedition to Egypt in 1798 he took along two hundred scholars to investigate that fascinating but still largely unknown land of antiquity. He shared and advanced the historical and orientalist interests of the times. He did not, however, admire the new literary fashion of romanticism that belonged to his foes, Mme. de Staël and Chateaubriand. Speculative thought and letters did not flourish in France in the years of Napoleon.

Bonaparte did not see himself as a tyrant and was shocked to find himself so regarded. On his deathbed, an exile on the remote island of St. Helena, he declared that his mission had been to extinguish feudalism throughout Europe, reunite the continent, and "secure the dignity of man" by just and impartial laws. He had organized the Revolution and made it practical, pacified turbulent France, and then exported the principles of equality and liberty to Germany and Italy. The restorer of Polish independence, he always had friends in many parts of Europe; the war he waged almost constantly during the fifteen years of his rule often resembled a European civil war, though most outside France came to see it as French imperialism. Some who had cheered him early, like the poet Shelley, finally rejected him as a betrayer of the cause of liberty. The story that Beethoven first dedicated his great "Eroica" symphony to Napoleon but then tore up the dedication has been questioned. Among other great thinkers, the German philosopher Hegel was a staunch Bonapartist. The jury may still be out on the great man; it always will be, according to the fine historical work by the Dutch historian Pieter Geyl, *Napoleon: For and Against.* Certain it is that this child of fortune expressed and embodied forces far larger than himself and left Europe forever altered in fundamental ways.

But during the long war, British thought turned strongly against the French viewpoint. The mystique of the French Revolution gradually lost what force it had had in England. In 1794, Tom Paine's reply to Burke (the *Reflections* did not lack answers), *The Rights of Man,* sold like hot cakes, and the London Correspondence Society caused a fear of the French Revolution happening in Great Britain. William Godwin's *Enquiry concerning Social Justice* was very much in the French spirit, a rationalist utopia based on the ideal perfection of individuals. Though repeating Rousseau's indictment of existing property relations as theft, Godwin's utopia differed significantly from most of the French in being antistatist. In Britain, the idea of a natural order of society took the *laissez-faire* form: Society will run itself if left free from interference. The Physiocrats also believed this, but the idea took deeper root in the Whiggish environment of England. Tom Paine claimed that "the common consent of society, without government" can perform all the necessary functions heretofore discharged by government. The rest ought to be dispensed with, and would be as men approached perfection: "Government, like dress, is a badge of lost innocence." Laws regulating property and morality are, as Godwin observed, useless if men are not virtuous and unnecessary if they are. Godwin, father-in-law of the poet Shelley and husband of the women's rights author, Mary Wollstonecraft—a group around which much of the political Left in Great Britain revolved—was so suspicious of the state and indeed of all forms of institutional organization that he attacked public education, among other things. "Did we leave individuals to the progress of their own minds," Godwin believed, "without endeavoring to regulate them by any species of public foundation, mankind would in no very long period convert to the obedience of truth." This was the ultimate *laissez-faire.* Godwin believed, as H. N. Brailsford once remarked, that all men are as rational and virtuous as Swift's Houyhnhnms.

England was to be the land of liberalism, and Godwin no doubt is significant for the British bent of mind. But after some initial popularity, he was regarded as a crank and was the only man ever known to have caused Coleridge to lose his temper. British opinion turned away from the French Revolution and all radical thoughts during the long wars with France. Coleridge was among those who, earlier enthusiastic for the Revolution, "threw away his squeaking baby-trumpet of sedition" and combated the revolutionary heresy with all his strength. Coleridge ranks with Burke, to whom he owed much, as a founding father of English conservatism. But the sometime radical journalist, William Cobbett, joined the anti-Jacobin cause too, indicating that this mood was well-nigh universal in Britain. The Evangelical movement within the Church of England, led by William Wilberforce, was a reaction against the deistic laxities of the eighteenth-century church, thus a reproach to the infidel French.

Popularly, there was much millennial excitement in the air. Estimates of the number who followed the alleged prophetess Joanna Southcott in London from 1803 to 1814 ranged as high as fifty to one hundred thousand. Although not the first by any means to announce the second coming of Christ to be at hand, this un-lettered Devonshire countrywoman became a sensation; her message fitted the un-settled times, when fears of a French invasion combined with much economic distress from rising prices and unemployment. Such strange religious outcroppings among the urban poor trying to adjust to urban life were to become familiar in many places thereafter. Thomas Macaulay was amazed: "We have seen an old wom-an, with no talents beyond the cunning of a fortune teller, and with the education of a scullion, exalted into a prophetess and surrounded by tens of thousands of devoted followers; and all this in the nineteenth century; and all this in London." It was the beginning of a career of popular culture in the cities that would often amaze the intellectuals; at this time there was a kind of popular romanticism re-flected in religious emotionalism.

Controversy about Napoleon remained to the end. William Hazlitt, the famous literary critic and essayist, was described by a friend as "prostrated in mind and body" when he learned of Bonaparte's final defeat; "he walked about unwashed, unshaven, hardly sober by day, and always intoxicated by night" for weeks, until one day he awoke as if from a stupor and never touched alcohol again. His friend Haydon, author of the foregoing description, believed that Napoleon had criminally betrayed the true cause; and yet on the great man's death in 1821 he reflected in his diary that "posterity can never estimate the sensations of those living at the time" about Napoleon—how his rise, his glory, and his fall affected men. Shelley found himself warming again to Bonaparte when he saw what followed:

> I hated thee, fallen tyrant! I did groan
> To think that a most unambitious slave
> Like thou, should dance and revel on the grave
> of Liberty. . . .
>
>   I know
> Too late, since thou and France are in the dust,
> That Virtue owns a more eternal foe
> Than Force or Fraud. . . .

These were exciting times. It is not surprising that Romanticism arose in those twenty-five hectic years from the first dawn of revolution in 1789 to the final de-feat of Napoleon in 1815.

Germany gave birth to nationalism in reaction against humiliation by the French. Herder and Fichte, giants of German thought, preached it along with humbler writers and organizers of youth (Arndt, Jahn, Kleist). The Enlightenment had been cosmopolitan. Fichte became convinced that this was another one of the errors made by that now politically discredited era. The Germans were assuming the cultural and intellectual leadership of the world in this time of Goethe, Schiller, Kant, Beethoven. A cultural people should have a great state. Germany must wake up politically, as she had done artistically and culturally, Fichte declared in his popular *Addresses to the German Nation* (1807). In the thought of J. G. Herder Romanticism blended with nationalism. It was a humane and liberal nationalism, by comparison with some manifestations of that spirit; it meant, to Herder, the self-fulfillment of peoples who thereby make their contribution to humanity. He glorified the people, the *Volk,* exaggerating a strain already met with in Burke (there is wisdom in the collective consciousness of the people). Herder went seeking the songs of the people "on the streets, in alleys and fish markets, in the simple roundelays of the peasant folk." He has been compared to the American poet Walt Whitman in this respect, and indeed he deeply influenced Whitman. Mystical adulation of the national genius could lead in dangerous directions, perhaps, but Herder did not suggest them. He simply believed that nations exist, that peoples have their national cultures, and that these should be developed as the source of a valuable literature and art. The democratic element in this romantic nationalism is apparent.

Napoleon I met his downfall during 1814 and 1815, and conservative Europe Europe gathered at Vienna to try, as far as possible, to restore order based on principles of tradition, prescription, monarchy. But forces had been set in motion which could not be halted, though they might be slowed or deflected. Between 1815 and 1830, Restoration France and conservative Europe produced some notable attempts to develop the conservative ideology, but it also saw the elaboration of the liberal, democratic, and socialist political philosophies. These political "isms" will be dealt with in the next chapter. Meanwhile we may note that of all these, the most potent "ism" in the nineteenth century was to be nationalism, affecting even the smaller and lesser peoples of Europe. The English and the French had long suspected they were nations, the Germans were finding it out, the Italians soon would discover it; but we also catch a glimpse of the Danes, who previously had had no inkling of their separate nationhood, seeking to restore the ancient Danish tongue and old Danish customs, while Gothicism in Sweden represents a similar impulse. The Belgians will find that they cannot live under a Dutch king, no matter how beneficent his rule and how logical and beneficial the larger political unit is, for they are different.

Nietzsche was one who felt that Napoleon had tried to unite Europe, but re-actionary nationalism had interfered to botch his plans. It may later have seemed reactionary; but for at least the first half of the nineteenth century, nationalism was regarded as liberal, progressive, and democratic. It meant the right of peoples to be free and self-determined, not merely because freedom in any of its guises is a good thing, but because the idea had been deeply implanted, by such as Herder, that each people has a sacred mission to make its unique contribution to the symphony of nations. And it meant, concretely speaking, the struggle of Germans to escape the dominion of France, of Poland to throw off the tyranny of the Tsar, or Italy to free herself from the Austrian yoke. It thus enlisted the support of idealists and activists, democrats and radicals, all who rejoiced in a struggle for justice against tyrants.

Nationalism was a consequence of the French Revolution. Once the old order of hierarchy had been dissolved, its replacement, the notion of civil equality, found in the nation its natural focus. Men were equal as children of the nation, *enfants de la patrie*. Redeemed from domination by the privileged orders, the state seemed the treasured possession of all and became both the guarantor and the symbol of equal rights. To depose kings and nobles was to deliver the fatherland to the people. *"Freies Reich! Alles gleich!"* sang the German nationalists who followed such figures as "Father" Jahn. The *Volksstaat* or people's state knew no privileged orders, only equal citizens in the one nation. When Napoleon's armies brought the principles of the Revolution to Germany, it directly encouraged national feeling; then the humiliation of Prussia at the hands of the French stimulated a national reaction *against* the French. But nationalism fed also on the ideas that stemmed from Romantic writers and thinkers.

The shaping of a larger community, forged from local, regional loyalties, appealed to many in this historically minded era as a step forward on humanity's road to some future utopia. Indeed, for a while nationalism was almost the common denominator of all ideologies and all social processes in the nineteenth century. For better or worse, Europe was to divide into numerous national cultures in the nineteenth century—a process accompanied by disruptions and upheavals. This vast and epochal process was in part a movement of the mind. More will be said about it later. Certainly that other of our three revolutions, the Romantic, had much to do with it.

IMMANUEL KANT AND THE REVOLUTION IN PHILOSOPHY

Born in 1724, the man who became the greatest of modern philosophers did his most creative work in the 1780s, against the background of the crisis in Enlightenment thought. Rousseau made a deep impression on Immanuel Kant, as he did on so many of this generation. Indeed little that was discussed during the Enlightenment escaped the attention of the omniscient little professor of Königsberg. The young Kant, brought up in the reigning German philosophical school of Leibniz as systematized by Christian Wolff, showed strong scientific interests and entered into some of the typical *philosophe* controversies; thus we find him contributing his bit to the Lisbon Earthquake argument of the 1750s, begun by Voltaire, about the problem of evil. But it was particularly the work done by Berkeley and Hume to undermine the confident certainties of rationalism that engaged his attention. It was only in his middle age that Hume awakened him from his "dogmatical slumber." He found Hume's skepticism most unsatisfactory and, like the Scottish "common-sense" philosophers (but more effectively than those simpler souls, whom he ridiculed), determined to rescue men from it, restoring their confidence and vitality. Kant was an *Aufklärer,* a spokesman of the Enlightenment. But his powerful mind, in attempting to refute Hume, penetrated into ground beyond the frontiers of that movement. He made what he called a "Copernican revolution" in philosophy and was, in later years, compared to the French Revolution in his impact on thought. Heinrich Heine writes, "With this book (*The Critique of Pure Reason*) an intellectual revolution began in Germany which offers the strangest analogies with the material revolution in France, and, to a more reflective mind, appears to be of equal importance. . . . On both banks of the Rhine we see the same break with the past, all respect for tradition is revoked."

One of Kant's major objectives, then, was to rescue science from Humean skepticism. The eighteenth-century Scottish philosopher took his departure from Locke's empiricism, which held that the only real knowledge comes from sense experience and there is nothing in the mind except what comes to it from the senses. He demonstrated—and Kant accepted his demonstration as "irrefutable"— that through the senses alone the human mind cannot encounter reality at all, nor can it have a science founded on anything but "opinion." We have only an unrelated sequence of sense impressions. The principle of cause and effect cannot be derived from experience; we simply assume it arbitrarily; it may only be an accident of our mental processes. How can I say that A causes B, when the "cause" is not either A or B, is nothing empirically observable? (I do not *see* the causing, for example, when A hits B and causes it to move; I see the events, the sequence, but this does not necessarily entail the effect.) To Kant, this raised the question of the possibility of a valid science, and he sought by overcoming this Humean skepticism to ground scientific knowledge on unshakeable foundations. Stated more technically, the problem was the status of "synthetic *a priori* judgments," synthetic being the factual as opposed to the strictly logical or "analytic." Are the observed relationships in nature as certain as mathematical truths, or are they, as Hume alarmingly suggested, accidental, contingent, uncertain?

Kant's reply was roughly as follows: The mind or intellect, far from being passive or negative, contains the organizing principles that *impose order on experience.* The mind contains forms and categories which are the basic concepts that give meaning to experience. These "fundamental conditions of thought itself" are *a priori,* that is, not derived from experience. Kant, in what he describes as the hardest metaphysical work ever done, specified these forms and categories: two forms of perception (space and time) and twelve categories of the understanding (for example, cause and effect).[4] These correspond to the types of judgment of Aristotelian logic, that is, the types of quantity, quality, relation, modality. All

---

[4]Kant's categories are *quantity:* unit, plurality, totality; *quality:* reality, negation, limitation; *relation:* substance and accident, cause and effect, community; *modality:* possibility, existence, necessity. It is usually held today that Kant's categories, too dependent on the logic of his day, do not hold up; but this is not to say that basic categories of the understanding do not exist.

minds contain these categories, thus mind is a fundamental unity—reason is "transcendent."

Thus our minds condition and, indeed, determine knowledge by being as they are. Agreeing with Leibniz, Kant denied that there is nothing in the mind except what the senses bring in; there is the mind itself, which sorts out, classifies, relates this raw material, making it intelligible. We will not here, of course, follow Kant in all his arguments and terminology. From his powerful analysis, it is enough to say, emerged a picture of mind as creative, not passive, and of reason as something *a priori*, thus rescued from the skepticism of an empiricist approach. Goethe interpreted Kant to mean that "had I not borne the world in myself by anticipation, I would have remained blind even with eyes that see." It is not our senses that enable us to experience reality, but a preformed structure within the mind that prepares us to receive and understand sensory impressions. It is not the "solid" data of sense that provide the basic cement of science; it is something given within the mind, something like those "innate ideas" Locke had sought to banish as too mysterious or occult.

Because of a debate that arose, it must be added that Kant was evidently not an "idealist" in the sense that some of his followers were. He does not say that reality is a *creation* of the mind. Things are out there, and in striking our senses, they provide the indispensable, primary data of knowledge. The point is that we could not "understand" them if we did not have minds equipped with a rational structure. Kant is pointing out that the world outside must appear to us in a certain way because of the kind of mind, as well as the kind of senses, that we have. If we put on red-tinted glasses, things look red, though they really are not all red; and we also have our built-in sensory apparatus, so that colors, odors, and so forth appear to us as they do because of the way that apparatus works. Kant adds the important point that things appear rational—classifiable and subject to order, such as cause and effect, identity, comparison—not because of the way *they* are but because of the way our minds are. The mind makes sense out of experience; it would be senseless without mind. But the external world exists; Kant is not denying that, nor that we must have its stimuli for the mind to work on in the knowing process. If percepts without concepts are blind, as someone said, concepts without percepts are empty.

This was only part of Kant's examination of the knowing process, and it must be added immediately that the sort of knowledge we have been talking about—scientific knowledge, taken from experience as worked on by the categorizing intellect—was not, to him, knowledge of ultimate reality. This domain of science is perfectly valid; Kant's goal was to rescue science from skepticism, and to represent him as a foe of science (the view is not uncommon) is a gross error. He himself made some contributions to the sciences, in which he was always interested. But it is a particular sort of knowledge, appropriate to the practical or useful realm only; it is knowledge of appearances, not of substance. In the famous Kantian language, it is the *phenomenal*, as opposed to the *noumenal*, world. It relates to the properties of things, not the "thing-in-itself." Kant's other great objective, the inspiration for which he perhaps derived from Rousseau, was to rescue the realm of *value* from the scientists. Thus he sets up two sharply different categories. The realm of science, which is useful knowledge, deals with the phenomenal world, the world of appearances. The realm of value, of religion, is intuitive and deals with the noumenal world, the world of substantive reality. Kant thinks that the two realms must not be confused. One of his achievements was to riddle the proofs of God's existence derived from the facts of physical nature—arguments extremely popular during the eighteenth century, especially the "argument from design." From ontological argument to argument from design, Kant devastated all these venerable "proofs" with such effectiveness that few dared revive them. The proofs appropriate to science have nothing to do with God, Kant believed, for they can never give us values.

There is nevertheless the noumenal realm. Kant was not quite sure whether we can know it at all. He seemed to think that in moments of moral or esthetic experience we can glimpse it fleetingly, and these hints were to be built upon by the romantics who followed him. The human soul, a thing-in-itself, by quite other roads than the analytical reason, may make contact with other things-in-themselves. Kant seems ambiguously poised between the Enlightenment and romanticism here. On the one hand he said that he "had to deny knowledge to make room for faith," which he clearly much wanted to do. His most widely quoted sentence is that in which he proclaims the equal wonders of the two realms, the starry heavens and the moral law. On the other hand Kant seldom departed from his Enlightenment hard-headedness, was certainly no mystic by temperament, and was not at all sure about our being able to make contact with the noumena at all. Perhaps we are condemned to live in the phenomenal world as far as intellectual activity is concerned, while being aware that there is another world, the real world, which we can never know—at least in this life. Each of Kant's realms is flawed. From the scientific, phenomenal one we can get clear and useful knowledge, but it is knowledge of appearances only. From the spiritual, noumenal realm we could get ultimate truth if we could reach it, but ordinarily we cannot do so.

Kant nevertheless at times put great stress on his rescuing of religion from the clammy grip of science so as to restore faith to its true estate. The existence of God, freedom of the will, the soul, these things cannot be proved by scientific argument. But when we move from "pure reason" to the "practical" or moral reason, we are in a realm which is in its own ways quite valid though different. Pascal's "the heart has its reasons" was close to Kant's meaning. Moral consciousness exists and is entitled to great respect, though its knowledge is not the kind appropriate to science. Though we cannot prove them, we have to assume the existence of some noumena, for example God and human freedom, especially for moral purposes.

Kant's writings on ethics were among his most celebrated. Consistent with his general point of view, he argued that valid rules of conduct cannot be found in experience but must be sought in pure reason. Can we find the "categorical imperative" which reason must recognize as the basic principle of morals? It cannot be found in circumstances, Kant stated in a profound and subtle piece of argumentation, but in the moral agent, the person. That which is good in itself is the Will, when it is good; and a will is good when it is rational. The moral worth of an action is determined by the motive, not the result; it is Duty, the rational resistance to evil impulses, that is the highest moral faculty. In the end Kant reached his famous statement of the "categorical imperative": Act so that your action is one you would want to be a universal law, or, in his other version of it, always treat people as ends, not means. (If you act in a way you would *not* want everybody else to act, you are selfishly using them as means for your ends.)

Beyond Kant's formal arguments, which do not constitute proof that he found the key to ethics, is an assertion of faith in rationality and human dignity that is the main source of Kant's amazing appeal. Many who could not follow his formidable trains of reasoning were captivated by his general spirit. In the last analysis Kant's message is a tragic one. We are finite and imperfect creatures torn by contradiction and unable to plumb the ultimate secrets. We come against ultimate mysteries—"antinomies," such as nature and culture, freedom and authority, the individual and society in conflict—which our reason can never resolve. As soon as we start to learn a little, Kant reflects, we grow old and die. In this respect Kant was not a typical romantic.

It is interesting to compare the dualism of Kant with the other great dualisms of Western thought—Plato's, Ockham's, Descartes's. To Plato, the realm of essences or ideas alone is real and knowable; to Kant, it is alone real, even more so, but it is scarcely knowable, certainly not knowable by the reasoning intellect as Plato thought. To Descartes, there are two realms, the physical and mental, one the domain of necessity and the other of freedom; there is something of this in Kant, but, again, Descartes felt the physical world to be perfectly knowable in a way that Kant could not. Kant is closer to William of Ockham and to Pascal. Science is one thing, religion another; two wholly different kinds of cognition are appropriate to them; we cannot pass from one to the other.

Kant's successors tended to quarrel about what he meant, and it is plain that with but a slight twist his "critical philosophy" might be made the foundation of several different systems. Some Kantians forgot about the thing-in-itself and became either idealists, arguing that the world is completely a mental construct, or positivists (phenomenalists), urging that we do not and cannot know what ultimate reality is and had better remain content with the orderly arrangement of our observations. Others developed Kantian noumenalism in a romantic or mystical direction, stressing the role of the poetic or religious intuition in touching the deepest reality by non-scientific methods. Kant himself, as we have said, was hardly a romantic by temperament; but the romantic era was beginning as he wrote and his immediate followers in Germany tended to be either idealists or romantics, sometimes blending the two. There is no doubt a sense in which Kant is the uncle, if not the father, of Romanticism.[5] But we ought not to forget that the bulk of his work was directed towards clarifying scientific philosophy and that his contribution here was enormous. It is

---

[5] Wilhelm Busch, the jolly children's poet whose *Max and Morris* (1865) is the German equivalent of *Alice in Wonderland,* wrote in his autobiography that he was fascinated by Kant though he could not understand him, and found that *The Critique of Pure Reason* left him with a delighted interest in the secret places of the mind "where there are so many hiding places."

part of the wonder of the Königsberg philosopher that he greatly advanced both of those different domains of the mind which he so sharply separated, the scientific and the esthetic-religious.

Kant's dualism nevertheless was unsatisfactory for many who had been accustomed by the Enlightenment to clear and final conclusions. Phenomena and noumena, pure reason and practical reason, seemed completely divorced, a situation not felt to be satisfactory. Fichte and Schelling, his immediate successors in German philosophy, sought for a unifying principle that would weld the divided self and divided world of thought together. Impressed by Kant's "transcendent" structure of reason, they wished to broaden it so as to bring pure and practical reason together under one roof. Kant stimulated future philosophy by the problems he left, as every great philosopher does.

But in both of Kant's two realms, the "Copernican revolution" is evident: The human mind is creative, not passive, whether it is working as scientist or as seer. It is an active agent, far from the wax of Condillac; it imposes order on nature, even in the scientific process. Kant reminded scientists that Galileo had understood the necessity of hypothesis, asking questions of nature; pure empiricism is poor scientific method. The creative mind is as much a necessity in science as in poetry. This is well understood today; Kant, probably more than any other modern thinker, established it firmly.

Kant made significant contributions to political and ethical thought too. For our purposes it will be sufficient to note the *liberal* implications of these. In making *duty* a linchpin of his system, Kant may have betrayed his Prussianism; but his political thought generally stressed individual freedom, the moral autonomy of the person, human beings as ends. There were even Kantian socialists in the nineteenth century who pointed out that the rule of treating people as ends and not as means, as persons not as things, invalidates the labor system of capitalism, which makes the workingman a commodity. Some attempted to blend Kant and Marx.

These liberal features, along with the attack on rational proofs of God's existence, caused Kant's writings to be banned for a time in his native country. But his political thought also stressed the reign of law, obedience to duly constituted authority; it sought to resolve the dilemma of liberty and authority (a dilemma of which Kant was very conscious) through just and general laws. History is the story of the education of humanity toward freedom under law. Thought should be free. Kant was one of those who "wished to be warmed by the fire of the French Revolution but not burnt up by it"; he was a moderate liberal with a horror of violent revolution. He believed a republic to be the best form of government (not a pure democracy which is irrational). If Kant stresses authority, he also believes in liberty. His political thought is perhaps a little trite; his well-known essay on universal peace does not take us much farther than the usual utopian exhortations. But Kant's deep respect for the individual was rooted in his great Critical Philosophy: One can readily see that he made the human mind and the inner self more important and sacred than did the Lockeans. They would have it determined, passive, dictated to by external conditions; to Kant it is hub and focus of all, it is self-determining and free insofar as noumenal, and even in its phenomenal aspects, it dictates to nature rather than being dictated to. The final purpose of all creation, Kant suggests, is our full realization as moral beings.

Kant came soon to be regarded as the greatest of modern philosophers (Hegel disputed the title with him in the nineteenth century, but clearly Kant made Hegel possible) as well as a notable contributor to moral, esthetic,[6] and political ideas. It seemed that he brought an end to the typical Enlightenment philosophy by rejecting both its empiricism and confused skepticism in favor of a new form of rationalism. The peculiar Enlightenment formula of commonsense empiricism was not tenable after his criticisms and reconstructions. He also gave hints to both the romanticists and the liberals, to whose influence the next generations largely belonged. The intellectual revolution of this era was bigger than Kant, but he was somehow an integral part of it.

There has always seemed something wondrous about the quiet German professor, a pure thinker living in an obscure university town (Königsberg) from which he never ventured, who changed the course of human thought and hence human history. Of his influence Kant himself held no doubt: "my book can produce nothing less than a total change of outlook in this area of human knowledge." This book was *The Critique of Pure Reason,* published in 1781 when Kant was 57; it was followed during the next dozen years by half a dozen others equally original and brilliant. With one of history's most potent all-time minds, fit to be ranked with Newton's and Einstein's, he sounded philosophic depths still being plumbed, of which our brief account has given but suggestions; without question, he is the most influential modern philosopher. Yet his personality with its simple dignity exuded a strange, almost popular, charisma. His was indeed an electrifying influence.

POST-KANTIAN PHILOSOPHERS

The grand lineage of German philosophy in its golden age began with Kant and ended with Hegel a half century later. In between lay several others, most significantly Johann Gottlieb Fichte and Friedrich Wilhelm Joseph von Schelling. Here a very brief summary will suffice. Fichte, brought up on the writings of the French *philosophes,* praised the French Revolution and subsequently wrote much of significance on political, social, and economic subjects—especially his famous *Addresses to the German Nation* (1807), inspired by the Prussian defeat at the hands of Napoleon, which we have mentioned. He also had a good deal to say about religion and was, in fact, dismissed from the University of Jena in 1799 largely because of his excursions into this arena, bringing on him the charge of atheism. (A sort of pantheism would, of course, be closer.) He was not very romantic in temperament; philosophy, he thought, should be a science. But he adopted and preached a

---

[6] In *Critique of Judgment,* Kant sought to establish an objective, transcendental basis for artistic taste, while recognizing subjective elements also.

philosophy of idealism, believing that anything else leads to determinism and materialism, which destroy human dignity. According to the vision of reality that Fichte developed, the universe consists of an absolute Ego which is like our own consciousness, a unique, free activity that strives to realize itself in perfect self-awareness and is the foundation of all nature. Leaving aside the technical jargon, which probably mystified all but a few, this vision of reality dramatized the human will or consciousness as hub and center of the universe, an expression of the absolute spirit of which the universe consists. Spirit or idea makes up reality, and our spirits, represented by our basic consciousness, an indescribable but intuitively certain thing,[7] are the concrete manifestations of this world spirit. One might say without too much distortion that, according to Fichte, each of us is God, or a part of God—if we equate the "absolute" or "world spirit" with God. So, if Fichte was technically not a "romantic," he introduced an intoxicating idea which in the broader sense was very romantic: that the world is spiritual, that we are a part of that spiritual world, and that in moral experience especially we can touch the uttermost sublimities of the universe.

Schelling, a disciple of Fichte and friend and collaborator of Hegel, whom he influenced, produced a stream of writings, especially between 1797 and 1802, which developed the idealist outlook into what he called Transcendental Idealism. He put greater stress than Fichte on physical nature as the objective form of the Absolute and pointed out the road Hegel was to follow in many respects. Perhaps the most striking feature of his thought was its representation of artistic creation, the act of esthetic intuition, as the supreme achievement. In it the unconscious and the conscious forces, representing the two forms of the Absolute, are fused in synthesis; it is in art that the infinite manifests itself in finite form.[8] Coleridge and all the romantic poets absorbed Schelling eagerly, for understandable reasons; he provided a metaphysical basis for the artist such as had never before been known. Romanticism's glorification of the poet as seer, as "unacknowledged legislator of the human race," as discoverer and purveyor of loftier truths than the merely logical, relates closely to Schelling's thought. Much later in his career Schelling opposed Hegel's excessively abstract rationalism by offering a kind of foreshadowing of existentialism; he influenced Kierkegaard, who listened to his lectures at Berlin in the 1840s. He came to reject all abstract, conceptual thinking as "negative philosophy," inferior to concrete, existent realities. He showed a keen interest in the history of religious mythologies, like Jung in our time. In this, his earlier preference for art may perhaps be seen continuing.

Fichte and Schelling may seem to have traveled a long way from Kant, who

---

[7]Consciousness is the foundation of all thought and experience, yet we cannot find it in thought or experience because it cannot be objectified, cannot be made an object of thought or experience, Fichte pointed out. Sartre and the existentialists have made the same point.

[8]To explain further, the unconscious is the real, or objective, physical world, the conscious the realm of the ideal and subjective. Both are parts of the Absolute. Their destiny is to be merged in one, the objective becoming merged in the subjective and vice versa. This happens when the artist shapes nature, or cooperates with it, as Michelangelo carving a statue.

insofar as he lived to meet their ideas evidently repudiated them. But Kant had started them off. This extraordinary spate of German philosophizing concluded with the titanic figure of Hegel, consideration of whom we shall postpone for a moment. The whole of it cut a wide swath in intellectual Europe in the first half of the nineteenth century. It combined keen and searching thought with daring speculation and a good deal of moral sublimity. Later, especially in the non-German world, it seemed excessively "metaphysical" and might be dismissed as empty bombast. From another point of view it revealed about as radical a perspective as Europe had seen. For it may be noted that Fichte, Schelling, and subsequently Hegel offered a philosophical alternative to religion, substituting their Absolute for the Christian conception of God. A prominent feature of this metaphysical faith was man's place in it as almost the equivalent of God. The Absolute was not quite just the individual human Ego writ large, but it came close to being that, at least in the popular interpretation of these philosophies. The human consciousness reflects and participates in the divine. Man's art and moral experience are in effect cosmic forces working in and through him. German idealism united with Romanticism to deify the mysterious forces working in the human soul and so to introduce that theme of "titanism" so marked in the nineteenth century and, according to some, so dangerous. "Glory to Man in the highest," sang the poet Swinburne.

At any rate the lofty and searching inquiries of the great German philosophers of the Kantian age captured humanity's imagination. Near the end of the century, South African General Jan Smuts, having made his fortune and reputation by the age of 30, decided to retire. "I prefer to sit still, to water my orange trees, and to study Kant's 'Critical Philosophy,' " he said. It could have been any thinking person's dream. Kant—together with his children—came close to meaning *philosophy* for the nineteenth century.

The Germans soon found their way to England, chiefly by way of Coleridge. They were less well known in France until around 1850; the Enlightenment carried on more strongly there, represented by Condillac's empirical psychology. But eventually the impact on French thought, and on Italian, was to be strong. Meanwhile France was not without idealist and romantic philosophic strains, as, for example, Maine de Biran and Victor Cousin.

THE ORIGINS OF ROMANTICISM

Romanticism is sometimes said to have begun with Rousseau, and particularly with that amazingly successful novel *La Nouvelle Héloise,* which had all Europe weeping in 1762. Certain romantic affinities can be found in other eighteenth-century writers, notably the English poet James Thomson (d. 1748), while the poets Gray and Cowper are often classified as "pre-Romantics," bridging the gap between Dryden and Pope on the one end and Wordsworth and Coleridge on the other. As a counterpoint to the dominant theme of reason, moderation, and order, the eighteenth century played with the grotesque, the primitive, the mysterious, invoking the

Sublime as a mood to be placed over against the Beautiful.. Rich folk built themselves artificially wild ruins; the Noble Savage whether from North America or the South Seas found himself lionized in European drawing rooms. The Gothic novel with its eerie abodes and its spooks made its debut. One can round up quite a bit of this in the eighteenth century.[9] This has been called "the Romantic Enlightenment," but only in certain ways was it akin to the later Romanticism. Passion, emotion, or wildness, are not the best criteria of the Romantic. The sentimentalism of the age of Julie and Pamela made itself at home in the Age of Reason and had little in common with what later came to be called Romanticism. But at any rate Rousseau strongly influenced practically all the Romantics of the next generation or two; it is hardly too much to say that in France the figure of Jean-Jacques, shrouded in mists of legend, became deified. Before long the German writers Goethe and Schiller took up the romantic manner, the former's *Sorrows of Werther* rivaling *La Nouvelle Héloise* in its ability to reduce all manner of people to tears, while the *Sturm und Drang* plays of the early Schiller were to be showpieces for many years. (*The Robbers* was written in 1781.) The chief disciples of Rousseau at first seem to have been the Germans; in France the influence of the rationalist Enlightenment continued, with Voltaire getting his tremendous triumph in Paris near the end of his life in 1778. But the restless decade of the 1780s, with its Saint-Martin mood, has been mentioned.

Then came the Revolution, which tended to halt literary and intellectual life, diverting all attention to the political melodrama being enacted at Paris. Some Frenchmen for a time suspected Romanticism as too German to be patriotic. But in 1801 to 1805, French Romanticism asserted itself with the powerful figure of Chateaubriand, the leading literary personality of his day. With *Atala* and *René* a new mode of literature had arrived, it was widely recognized. Chateaubriand was the father, as Rousseau was the grandfather, of all subsequent French romantic literature.

Meanwhile in England the young poets Coleridge and Wordsworth were experimenting with a new poetry they rightly felt to be nothing less than revolutionary. They, along with the poet-seer William Blake, began English Romanticism in the years just before the turn of the century, but it remained obscure for some time. Blake printed his own books, *Songs of Innocence* (1789) and *Songs of Experience* (1794), but they were neither noticed nor understood for a number of years. He was known slightly as designer and engraver, but evidently not at all as poet, until well into the nineteenth century.

The Revolutionary and Napoleonic wars were going on; Chateaubriand became an exile from Bonaparte's dictatorship, and even Coleridge and Wordsworth took up political pamphleteering. In Germany Romanticism continued to flourish uniquely: A group that included Frederick Schlegel and his brother August in Berlin, Novalis and Schelling at Dresden, and Jena called themselves romantic and threw out ideas important to the philosophy of the movement, to which it is

[9]Cf. Christopher Thacker, *The Wildness Pleases: The Origins of Romanticism* (1983).

A Romantic poet, Lord Byron in Albanian dress, 1813. (London, National Portrait Gallery. Portrait by T. Phillips.)

necessary to add the theology of Schleiermacher (1799) and the music of Beethoven (1800). All this was in the years from 1798 to 1801—Romanticism's moment of creative fruition. But its popular triumphs lay ahead.

Picking up momentum, Romanticism reached its maximum of influence in the years from 1810 to 1830. Wordsworth and Coleridge began to achieve fame and were joined by Shelley, Byron, and Keats to make up the most renowned group of poets in England's history, all of whom are customarily labeled "romantic." In 1813 the Swiss-born Mme. de Staël, a glamorous figure who wrote, made love, and fought Napoleon with equal verve, popularized the Germans in France with her celebrated work *D'Allemagne.* France succumbed to Romanticism between 1820, when Schiller's *Maria Stuart* (composed in 1801) took Paris by storm, and 1830, when Victor Hugo's *Hermani* caused the wildest tumult in the history of the French theater but emerged triumphant. Hugo and Lamartine, along with the novelist Alexander Dumas, the avowed leaders of the Romantic movement, were the most popular and distinguished writers of their age. At the same time the painter Eugene Delacroix headed a school which called itself Romantic. Add Musset, Stendahl, Nerval, Sand, Vigny, Balzac, with Chopin and Liszt also in Paris, and "the dozen years from about 1823 to 1835 are a cultural apocalypse" in France (Geoffrey Hartman): we should not underestimate the strength of French Romanticism.

In the 1830s a "romantic" influence may be seen in many directions, and indeed for the rest of the century that influence never ceased to exist, being so absorbed into the texture of thought and expression that "nothing after it could be the same." But it became diffused. A partial reaction against it set in. We must not think of romanticism as ever quite sweeping away all opposition. In France, where a strong classical tradition existed, Hugo was denied admission to the Academy five times, the last time in 1836, and warfare between romantic and classic never ceased to enliven the theatrical season, at least. In 1829 the Academy denounced romanticism as that which "puts in disorder all our rules, insults our masterpieces, and perverts mass opinion." Eighteenth-century taste, classical and rococo, remained popular at the high tide of romanticism. In England, embittered literary reactionaries helped bring on Keat's early death, his friends believed. The greatest German literary figure in history, Goethe, who contributed to romanticism early in his career, eventually declared that classicism is healthy and romanticism diseased. Unconverted "classicists" always existed and, indeed, there was something of a classical revival contemporary with romanticism. If we grant that the Romantics had carried away most of the prizes by 1830, they were under attack from the younger generation of the 1840s and 1850s as being too pompous and theatrical. Broadly speaking, this next generation preferred to absorb its romanticism, if at all, in carefully filtered form.

Yet between 1760 and 1840—to take the widest time span (the creative zenith coming then in the middle of it)—Europe had been hit by something new, exciting, and controversial. We have yet to define what this was, having only named its landmarks. What was romanticism? The question has puzzled the more literal minded for a century. A definition is elusive. Someone declared that this inability to define romanticism is the scandal of the century. The word took on many meanings. The romanticism of Chateaubriand was Catholic and, reacting against the Revolution, became Royalist; but the romanticism of Victor Hugo was (eventually—Hugo began as a conservative) republican, liberal, even revolutionary. It was romantic to suffer, to pray, to fight (as Byron did for Greece), to venture on far voyages, to commune with nature, to have a sense of history. It was romantic to love passionately and transcend the conventional moral boundaries, but the eighteenth century, now old hat, had done this too, like all other centuries. It was romantic to read about the Middle Ages and to admire the pseudoprimitive bard Ossian,[10] but also to adore the days of classical antiquity—"fair Greece, sad relic." Fate was romantic; so was soulbaring. What was not, if done with the proper spirit? Romanticism was a mood and a style much more than a doctrine; moods and styles are hard to define. The ambiguity of the term is carried over into everyday speech, in which today the word "romantic" is widely but quite variously used.

As part of the early nineteenth-century revolution in ideas, romanticism "has become a label for half a dozen things that have only an accidental connection" (Christopher Dawson). He instanced the following: expressing one's emotions, love

---

[10] Between 1760 and 1763, the Scotsman James MacPherson published three volumes purporting to be literal translations from the legendary ancient Gallic poet Ossian, a sort of Celtic Homer of the third century A.D. Suspected by a few at the time and confirmed by later scholarship was the fact that little if any of this material really came from such a source, most of it being made up by MacPherson himself. But this "romantic" verse enjoyed wide popularity throughout Europe, much though Dr. Johnson inveighed against it ("Sir, a man might write such stuff for ever, if he would abandon his mind to it").

of nature, intuition as a source of truth, the quest for new experience, the view of society as organism rather than machine. This is not an exhaustive list. In drama it meant departing from the classical "rules," to the great indignation of the tradition-alists; in poetry it meant, to Wordsworth at least, using simple rather than "literary" language and writing about plain people rather than fancy ones.[11] In a clever essay Arthur O. Lovejoy once showed that these various meanings can be made to seem flatly contradictory and suggested that we must speak of romanticisms—not one thing, but a number, that happened to coincide in roughly a single period and have sometimes gotten badly confused. In concluding that "the word 'romantic' has come to mean so many things that, by itself, it means nothing," Lovejoy came near the truth; and yet of course we must not conclude that therefore it did not exist at all. The mood of an age may be nonetheless real for being illogical. Future historians will find it as difficult to say exactly what existentialism was as present ones do to define Renaissance, Enlightenment, or Romanticism. Historical phenomena take on many accretions as they pass through society; they become involved with other phenomena and eventually lose themselves in the common stream. Any major move-ment of the mind inevitably accumulates a crowd of different associations and meanings as it spreads. But we do not for this reason infer its nonexistence or meaninglessness. It is, in fact, possible to argue the reverse: that whenever we find a doctrine that everyone knows about but no one can quite define, we are in the presence of a major intellectual revolution. ("The indefinable word is the essential one," Chesterton noted, terms such as love, good, blue cannot be defined, but only illustrated, because irreducible.)

Without question, Romanticism was such a revolution. We are in danger of losing this truth if we seek too narrow or precise a definition. Behind the *forms* of romanticism, which were various, lay a deep spiritual change, often vague but none-theless mighty. Critics of romanticism, then and later, charged that it was a fever which rejected all discipline and, by being out of proportion with nature, refusing to accept boundaries, became a dangerous malady, "an assault delivered on the modern soul by all the combined forces of disorganization" (René Doumic). To them it was nothing less than the destruction of the sense of balance on which European civilization had rested ever since the Greeks invented classicism with its message of nothing in excess, everything in proper proportion, each element in its due place. On the other side, friends of the new spirit believed that it had for the first time emancipated Europe from a timid orthodoxy and opened minds and hearts to poetry, to real religion, to true philosophy, to sincerity rather than artifi-ciality. It was, said Sismondi, a "Protestantism in letters and the arts," a demand for liberty against authority in style; some have added that it was nothing less than an ultimate Protestantism (without dogma) in all ranges of life—a defiant Promethean rejection of all constraints on the free spirit of the individual man.

---

[11] The word *romantic* derives from the medieval "romances," so named because written in the vernacular (French) rather than in classical Latin. Thus in returning to popular speech, and trying to find folk themes, romantics were loyal to the basic meaning of their movement.

TYPES OF ROMANTICISM

Leaving such sweeping claims aside for the moment, we may try more precisely to state the range of romantic attitudes. First, Romanticism began in *reaction against* the eighteenth century, that is, against rationalism, mechanistic materialism, classicism, all the dominant ingredients of the Enlightenment. Youth looked for new ideas and found them in Rousseau, and subsequently in Kant, Fichte, and Burke. A chief weakness in the Enlightenment was its neglect of the imagination, its externalism and absence of anything inward or deeply esthetic. It denied religious emotion; it ignored the mystery and terror of existence in its effort to make all things clear. All common sense and broad daylight, it became uninspiring and unthrilling. It lacked what the French call *frissons,* or thrills, and its literary style was, or came to seem, flat, conventional, unenterprising. Likewise its ethic of selfish hedonism, along with its mechanical and materialistic view of the universe, could appear as ignoble or dull.

Consequently the Romantic era is filled with cries of rejection. "I, for my share, declare the world to be no machine!" exclaimed Thomas Carlyle, repeating the German idealists. The eighteenth century had said that it was. Burke speaks of reason being "but a part, and by no means the greatest part," of human nature, while Coleridge says that the "calculating faculty" is inferior to the "creative faculty." This rejection of the analytical reason in favor of an intuitive "eliciting of truth at a flash" was very close to the heart of romanticism and represented, in good part, another reaction against the Enlightenment. In literary form, romanticism rebelled against the "rules" imposed on drama or poetry by the classical formula, and against classicism's preference for the general rather than the concrete. "We are not to number the streaks of the tulip," classicism had pronounced. Romantics wanted to do just that. Romantics sought religion—a source of *frissons,* if nothing more—because rationalists scorned it. Chateaubriand declared that nothing is pleasing except the mysterious; the mysterious had been the great common enemy of all the *philosophes.* So, too, with "enthusiasm."

That which had been sensible moderation now seemed like torpor, or worse. The eighteenth century, "soul extinct but stomach well alive," in Carlyle's phrase, became a byword for crass materialism; Thackeray called it an age of gluttony. "The man of Locke" was to be scorned. "I mistrust Locke," Schelling announced; virtually all the Romantics shared this contempt for that earthbound philosophy. (Some Romantics made use of Locke, but if so they read him as meaning that the senses, that is, the feelings, and immediate experience, are to be trusted above the abstract reason.) "Unable to believe but terrified of skepticism," the peculiar "heavenly city" of the eighteenth-century philosophers with its "faith of reason" was now seen to be uninhabitable. Carlyle spoke for the Romantic generations in repudiating its hedonistic ethic or pleasure-seeking spirit as unworthy of humanity: "the pig philosophy" he called it. (It was still vigorously alive in Carlyle's Britain in the guise of Jeremy Bentham's utilitarianism; the two schools could not abide each other.) This reaction against "the pursuit of happiness" as swinish sensualism pushed the Romantics into some very lofty poses: Man was once again to be Promethean hero, world-conquering adventurer, sublime sage or saint—anything except that simpering courtier of the eighteenth century whose only goal in life was satisfaction of creature comforts. Romantics certainly celebrated the sensual pleasures, but regarded them as the doorway to transcendental realms of knowledge, not as ends in themselves.

The Age of Reason had been an Age of Prose; and so romanticism meant poetry, or a new kind of poetic prose such as Chateaubriand wrote. Romanticism was, after all, primarily a literary movement, though it spilled over into all branches of life. Eighteenth-century poetry had become on the whole unsatisfactory. "Crushed by rules, and weakened as refined," this polite literature usually failed to communicate sincere feeling, was overly formalized and abstract; it was Dr. Samuel Johnson, no romantic,[12] who noticed this much:

> From bard to bard the frigid caution crept
> While declamation roar'd and passion slept.

Hazlitt, though not uncritical of the new poets, affirmed that

> Our poetical literature had, towards the close of the last century, degenerated into the most trite, insipid, and mechanical of all things, in the hands of the followers of Pope and the old French school of poetry.

In revenge, the Romantic poets gave full vent to what Locke had disparaged as "the conceits of a warmed or overweening brain." For a later taste as well as an earlier, they often sought too many "grand effects," they bared their souls and gushed too much. Still, few would deny the mighty debt to literature owed to the poets of the romantic generation. They revitalized language, and, among other things, brought poetry to the people. Too vast to be estimated is the force exerted on millions of people, heretofore hardly reached by the printed word, by romantic literature: Think of Musset and Hugo in France, Shelley and Wordsworth in England, Goethe and Kleist in Germany, Emerson and Longfellow in the United States, Bobbie Burns in Scotland. Or think of Pushkin and Lermontov in Russia, reminding us of the universality of this movement in the European cultural world. These and their imitators molded the consciousness of the nineteenth century, it is not too much to say. They made poetry something more than rhymed reason; as image and symbol, haunting the imagination, it shaped the feeling for life in its own unique way.

Mounting "an insurrection against the old traditions of classicism," the romanticists achieved a virtual revolution in the canons of art and literature. One measure of that revolution may be found in attitudes toward the art of the Middle

---

[12] From his famous *Dictionary,* definition of "Romantick":
1. Resembling the tales of romance; wild. . . .
2. Improbable; false.
3. Fanciful; full of wild scenery. . . .

Ages. Ever since the Renaissance, Gothic architecture had been dismissed as crude and barbarous. Gibbon said that the Piazzo San Marco in Venice contained "the worst architecture I ever saw." Ruskin, only a few decades later, pronounced it the most beautiful of human creations (*The Stones of Venice*). Each of us must make up his or her own mind about this, but in general the romantics prevailed: Most people today grant the beauty of St. Mark's and of the Gothic cathedrals in general. The French Revolution started to pull down those "piles of monkish superstition"; the Gothic Revival of the 1830s tried to renovate them and imitate them. Similarly, it may surprise us to learn that the poet Dante had been held in considerable disdain. In the eighteenth century Thomas Warton had spoken of the *Divine Comedy* as "disgusting," and a follower of Voltaire pronounced it the worst poem in all the world. Dante's reputation was made by the romantics, by Blake, Byron, Shelley, and Coleridge, enthusiastically seconded by Carlyle, Tennyson, Browning, and Ruskin a bit later.

A popular product of the romantic revolution, much fancied today by collectors of the unusual, was the Gothic novel, with its eerie atmosphere and supernatural events, its werewolves and ruined abbeys and diabolical happenings. Thus the taste for the medieval could go to extreme lengths. The mysterious, the exotic, the irregular, the sublime and even the grotesque now became appealing.

In a similar way the taste for wild nature, for mountains and deep forests, was largely a romantic reaction; pure neoclassical taste considered the Alps hideously unkempt and would have gone some distance out of the way to avoid them. "Nature" was a word much on eighteenth-century lips, but it did not usually mean the woodlands wild. Rousseau's *Reveries of a Solitary Walker* passed down to Chateaubriand and to Lamartine's *Meditations;* and everyone knows how important nature was to Wordsworth and Thoreau. This attachment to the trees and flowers and hills had, or came to have, a metaphysical foundation which, forming a link to philosophical idealism, is one of the leading ideas of the age. Rousseau believed vaguely that nature soothes and calms us, returning us to fundamentals and reminding us of deeper truths than those of human society. Wordsworth, without much philosophy, felt keenly

> . . . a sense sublime
> Of something far more deeply interfused,
> Whose dwelling is the light of setting suns
> And the round ocean and the living air,
> And the blue sky, and in the mind of man;
> A motion and a spirit that impels
> All thinking things, all objects of all thought,
> And rolls through all things.

In Germany, where philosophy had been stimulated by Kant and where romanticism from the first interacted with it, this pantheistic sense of spirit in nature, "rolling through all things," received explicit formulation. How Kant's critical philosophy created a revolution in philosophy, and how this led on to the other great German philosophers (Fichte, Schelling, Hegel) has already been pointed out. There were philosophers who specifically called themselves "romantic"; and there were idealists, like Fichte, who contributed to the popular conception of romanticism in certain ways. Broadly speaking, the result was to present a vision of reality as basically spiritual, and to suggest in some sense a unity of this world spirit linking us to nature. The post-Kantians in various ways postulated a fundamental knowable unity, spiritual in nature—a mind-stuff underlying and giving form to the appearances, corresponding to the mind-stuff we have in us, and which we contact when we are using our minds creatively. Fichte called it the Ego, adopting an idealist position in which thought is the basic reality and stressing moral experience; Schelling spoke of the Absolute, of the union of object and subject in the human consciousness, and of the paramountcy of esthetic experience. All this might seem rather Teutonically mystifying to most people; on any showing it was difficult and academic, for these worthies of German philosophy were all university professors. But it got outside the classroom, as the poets Novalis and Hölderlin and Richter transformed its abstract words into concrete poetic symbols. And as esthetic doctrine it was tremendously influential.

Many people came to hold, more or less loosely, something like this idealist-romantic position, meaning that we can see God or a higher reality in Nature, actually commune with it, feel its basic kinship to our own souls. Nontechnical, semipopular romantic idealism may be found in Thomas Carlyle's first book, *Sartor Resartus,* wherein this vivid writer gave expression to the idea that "the external world known to our senses and explored by our sciences is mere Appearance. Reality is its divine, unseen counterpart, standing to Appearance as Soul stands to Body" (D. C. Somervell). "Transcendentalism" became a byword among the literary of both France and America from 1820 to 1840; the name of Ralph Waldo Emerson is enough to remind Americans of its potency. This heady doctrine might persuade people that all the appearances, social conventions, for example, are a fraud, and that all of us can be godlike if only we dare to search our own souls. It was close to mystical pantheism, a heresy long known to Christianity, whereby the god intoxicated felt that they might communicate directly with deity. Often it had explicit roots in neo-Platonism; William Blake's mysticism has been traced to this source, and these writings were also prominent in the omnivorous reading of Coleridge, who claimed that he had found mysticism in many of the ancients before he read the Germans. There was also a discovery of the Indian religiophilosophical tradition at this time. "The pantheism of the Orient, transformed by Germany," E. Quinet wrote in 1841, was responsible for what he called a *"renaissance orientale."* (But the discovery and translation of the Hindu classics owed most to an Englishman, Sir William Jones, and a Frenchman, M. Anquetil-Duperron.)

The romantics added the thought that it is above all the artist, the poet, who feels the Infinite Spirit when creating. Working intuitively, the artist "elicits truth as at a flash" (Coleridge), truth deeper than the experimental or analytical. Poetic images are symbols of nature, keys to reality. The visionary-religious element in romanticism is perhaps to be found in its most remarkable state in the works of

William Blake, the English artist-seer-poet. Taking quite seriously the identification of his own thoughts with the soul of the universe.[13] Blake believed it was the mission of the poet and artist to be a religious prophet, endowing the old religious truths with new meaning. A "symbolist" before the French school that was to bear this name later in the nineteenth century, a discoverer of the "archetypes of the unconscious" before Jung, Blake gave new names to the gods and spoke of building a "new Jerusalem" in England. His haunting, childlike songs touch closely on perennial religious and moral experience.

The church called the New Jerusalem was associated not with Blake but with the writings of the eighteenth-century Swedish seer Emanuel Swedenborg (d. 1772), whose visionary writings interpreting the Christian scriptures became popular, especially in England, in the early nineteenth century. There is still a Swedenborgian society in England; there was considerable American interest, too. The German Romantic theologian Friedrich Schleiermacher (*Discourses on Religion,* 1799) sought to transpose Christianity from dogma to interior experience—a faith experimentally true, true to the meaning and purpose of life when its doctrines are transformed into concrete human terms. This idea grew familiar in the nineteenth century and merged with the "liberal" Christianity which dismissed biblical literalism arguing that the "essential" truths of Christianity are deeper and broader. Romantic theology stressed inward emotional experience as a criterion of faith and interacted with a revival of evangelical, pietistic Christianity. Already begun by the Wesleyans in the eighteenth century, this movement was quite popular from about 1780 to 1825. Various fervent if unorthodox sects arose. Alexander of Russia succumbed to one and tried to write it into the Holy Alliance of 1815; the socialist Saint-Simon preached a "new Christianity" to go with his Enlightenment social science. The Evangelical movement within the Church of England, beginning at the end of the eighteenth century, greatly influenced the whole Victorian era. More intellectual, the celebrated "Oxford Movement" produced John Newman and others in England in the 1830s; in rebellion against materialism and utilitarianism, these Anglicans shared with the romantics a poetic and spiritual emotionalism, a sense of history, a medievalism. Some Oxonians stayed within Anglicanism but revived the "high church" tradition; others followed Newman to Rome.

Popular manifestations of the return to religion included the American "great revival" of the earlier nineteenth century on the frontier and the Evangelical movement in Britain which reached the lowest classes. But many of the major writers shared it. Chateaubriand's *Genius of Christianity* was a leading work by one of the most celebrated of romantics; Wordsworth and Coleridge, if not Shelley and Byron, sought Christian piety. Eighteenth-century scoffing at the gods was no longer in vogue. Often unorthodox and verging on pantheist heresy, the feeling for religion was not the less strong for that.

Politically, Romanticism was ambiguous. Coinciding with the French Revo-

---

[13]Compare Gerard de Nerval, the French romantic poet: "The human imagination has invented nothing that is not true, either in this world or the next."

lution, it could not help but interact with it. At first the Romantics hailed the Revolution with delight, joining figuratively with the young Wordsworth as he danced with the French people. Then they turned against it, listening to Burke's great indictment, which is charged with many feelings close to the heart of romanticism. The Revolution stood for eighteenth-century rationalism and failed for that reason; it was, in fact, reactionary. Most romantics distinguished between the French Revolution as a particular historic event and the broader movement of history it imperfectly embodied. They did not doubt that humanity was on the march, seldom wanted to go back to the eighteenth-century "old regime," but agreed that the French Revolution had degenerated in a cynical and vulgar imperialism, because of its false groundings in Enlightenment materialism. In his famed history of the Revolution, Thomas Carlyle regarded it as having failed because it did not (until Bonaparte) produce any "great man." But the advocate of hero worship condemned the old regime also for having failed to provide inspired leadership, a sure sign of decadence. Romantics might, like Wordsworth, retain a rather naive Godwinian faith in human perfectibility, believing however that this utopia would come when we realize our *inner* powers of consciousness, something not to be attained by changes in forms of government.

Coleridge's political odyssey may be taken as typical: Interested in politics and at first enthusiastic for the Revolution, he wrote an ode on the storming of the Bastille; his *Ode to France* (1798) records his disillusion and despair. "In Mr. Burke's writings the germs of almost all political truths may be found," he thought, but he also thought that Burke had gone too far in his hatred of the Revolution. There must be a moral basis of policy; Kant's categorical imperative, that persons are not to be treated as things, is the great foundation. Coleridge was a staunch foe of economic individualism and of the pseudoscience of political economy, which he regarded as "solemn humbug." The mystic bonds that tie people together shape the almost sacred entity of Society, which is a reflection of the divine, as much so as physical nature. This *organic* view of society, opposed to the eighteenth century's alleged atomistic individualism, was a marked romantic trait. Coleridge's political insights are deep, but he failed to communicate any very coherent platform; he had too much awareness of the complexity of things, and felt the great need was not for a program but for human understanding.

The others in the galaxy of great English Romantic poets illustrate the political ambiguity of romanticism. If Wordsworth and Coleridge ended as Tories, Byron, by far the most popular poet of his day, was an aristocratic revolutionary, who defended the Luddites, wrote much about rebels and died fighting for Greek independence; though, in view of Byron's life, we cannot but feel that he more nearly spoke his mind when he asked for "wine and women, mirth and laughter." Shelley, that "beautiful and ineffectual angel," was also full of revolt at times,

> Men of England, wherefore plough
> For the lords who lay ye low?

but more full of poetry and the love of beautiful women. The greatest of these poets, John Keats, simply had no discernible politics; nightingales interested him far more. "Romanticism," the authors of a book about it assert, "fostered sympathy for the oppressed . . . and looked forward to a new social system, a Utopia" (W. V. Moody and R. M. Lovett). So it did, doubtless. But another writer (C. Grana) tells us, with equal accuracy, that "romanticism included a revival of political traditionalism, neofeudal at times, decrying social fragmentation and exalting a sense of unspoiled community, born of spontaneous loyalty to ritualized customs." And we should have to take account of others who, like Keats or Alfred de Musset, were innocent of political convictions altogether.

But the great events of revolution and war wove themselves through the texture of feelings of all the writers. Stendhal, in his essay on "Racine and Shakespeare," remarked that those who had lived through such times, who had experienced the Terror and marched with bloody feet through Russian snows with Napoleon, could no longer be moved by the chaste tragedies of classicism. The blood stirred by these mighty happenings and warmed by revolutionary slogans, demanded stronger meat and drink. The political thought of romanticism was diverse, but whatever it was it demanded and created excitement.

Even after disenchantment with the Revolution set in, a sense of impending apocalypse persisted, through the Napoleonic years and after—a feeling that "Great spirits now on earth are sojourning" (Keats) and some momentous climax must be at hand for humanity. It took a great deal of sobering up to extinguish this exalted state of consciousness, which, at a fever stage between 1789 and 1815, persisted on the whole down through 1848.

Nevertheless the confusion in romanticism is amply evident in its political thought. We have only to observe that an organic view of society is widely regarded as most typical of it, but how are we to adjust this vision of collectivism with the spirit of revolt and individual self-expression, even alienation, which was also a romantic attitude? Between Coleridge opposing the English reform bill of 1832 and Hugo on the barricades, there seems a decided gulf. No doubt German philosophy could provide a shaky bridge between the ego and the cosmos, but there seems little to be gained by trying to cover positions so various with a single term.

THE MEANING OF ROMANTICISM

A century of scholarship and criticism has sought in vain for a single definition of romanticism. From this, some have drawn the conclusion that the term is useless, that no such thing existed, rather a number of different things that somehow got lumped together owing to sloppy thinking. Still, the term *romanticism* survives despite all efforts to kill it. It survives because it *is* a useful term to cover a number of striking if not identical cultural phenomena of the period from 1780 to 1830. The philosophy, literature, and general *Zeitgeist* of this period had enough in common over large areas to justify the use of some general word to describe it. Possibly we should use several terms; but we can, if we like, choose to subdivide the one term, qualify it, mark the exceptions—but retain it.

All kinds of definitions, divisions, and distinctions have been offered. Of these, it seems useful to distinguish the *negative* romanticism, which was a reaction against the Enlightenment, against neoclassicism, materialism, hedonism, and the like, from the positive romanticism, which was largely a gift of German philosophy—the philosophy of subjective and intuitive truth, spiritual nature, and the poet's role in bringing the two realms together in conscious creative experience. It may be useful, too, to sort out things which got interlocked with romanticism but were not essentially of it, such as the political explosions of the times, nationalism, democracy, the reaction against the French Revolution. It is also helpful to sort out things which, while characteristic of numerous romantics, were not at all new, such as Byron's sexual morals. And the careful student will take note of national differences. Thus the English Romantics, despite Byron and Keats, were a more chaste and prudent lot than the Germans, reflecting the stability of English life and its strong bourgeois morality. French Romanticism wore the badge of anti-Revolution with special prominence. Romanticism was weakest in Spain and Italy, especially in the latter, perhaps because of the pervasive influence of classicism on the Italian landscape. (The Gothic had been weakest there too.)

When all is said, the Romantic revolution is linked to Kant and the French Revolution as a vital aspect of what was perhaps the most exciting and creative period of modern times. If one wishes to hazard a definition of the basic factor in this intellectual revolution, it would be *subjectivism* or the participation of mind in shaping reality. It has been said that no one previously had conceived the knowing process except in terms of the object known; now the subject came into the picture. The mind partly creates the external reality it grasps. Coleridge objected that "Newton was a mere materialist. Mind, in his system, is always passive—a lazy looker-on in an external world. . . . *Any system built on the passiveness of mind must be false.*" This was the central insight of the Romantics: The mirror and the lamp, as an important critical study has put it—the mind creates truth rather than simply reflecting it. And in this sense romanticism, though many aspects of it went out of fashion after a time, has left its stamp on the contemporary Western world.

Subjectivism worked itself out in the unique romantic conception of the free individual, freed from the rules, from moral conventions, from all external restraints. In the concept of genius, romanticists found their central literary conception. Bound by no rules, geniuses make their own. By no means is everyone a genius, but conceivably all *might* be. At any rate they do arise—a Homer, a Shakespeare, a Goethe—and they make the pattern for others to follow. In the last analysis we follow and should worship the actions of genius. Carlyle, in his famous *Sartor Resartus,* repeated the message of Goethe as an antidote to skepticism and lethargy; arise, WORK, do what thou canst do. Hero worship, and the gospel of work, affected people in all walks of life in the nineteenth century; they were romantics without knowing it. (The American Westward Movement has been seen as essentially romantic.)

It may be suggested then that romanticism was a literary and intellectual counterpart of the new principle of individualism in society—and this despite the fact that romantics often inveighed against individualism. The old regime had been corporative and organic, a society of estates and classes; after the French Revolution, one had a society of equal individuals. The literature of the eighteenth century was a social literature which sought essentially not to express the personal soul but to communicate the common ideas. Romanticism ushered in the modern fate of loneliness in the crowd, or the modern privilege of individual self-development, as one may choose to put it. The stable order of countryside would soon be challenged and overcome by the city's anonymity. A collection of individuals replaced "society," as Jeremy Bentham and the Utilitarians divined. One stood or fell by one's own unaided efforts. Romanticism was a literary retreat to the individual ego which, seen or not as part of a larger world soul, remained as the one solid basis of life. Nothing, the poet Wordsworth wrote in a characteristically Romantic way, "can breed such fear and awe" as to look

> Into our minds, into the mind of man—
> My haunt, and main region of my song.

Few of the classic works of Romanticism strayed far from this region. Many of the great lyrics use the play of memory across time to narrate the process of growing out of childhood into maturity, a voyage of the self. The *Bildungsroman,* a novel of self-education and discovery, was a Romantic genre. The conflict of the individual with society became the great theme of the nineteenth-century novel. And for the first time, sympathy goes more to the individual than to society. In German as well as French literature of the eighteenth century, the rebel, Molière's "misanthrope," is almost always treated with scorn. The *philosophe* Diderot, in a remarkable work that influenced Sigmund Freud more than a century later (*Rameau's Nephew*), produced a dialogue between the respectable self and the insolent, immoral fellow lurking under the surface—only to reject this talented but absurd *alter ego.* But the Romantics make legends of the poets destroyed by an unfeeling society (Chatterton, Chénier), those whose genius the philistines persecute and who "perished in their pride" but are to be admired for this courageous independence. Schiller's hero proudly joins an outlaw band. The Byronic hero scorns a world that cannot understand him. In brief, in literature the outsider changes from a ridiculous pariah to a heroic rebel from the seventeenth to the late eighteenth centuries—a fascinating index of one of the most significant revolutions in modern history. His age, thought the great philosopher Hegel in his early work *The Phenomenology of Mind,* was one in which "the spirit passes over into another region, the land of the inner subjective moral consciousness."

Arthur O. Lovejoy, that great student of ideas, found the fundamental romantic trait to be diversity, as over against Enlightenment standardization and simplification—the search for unique particulars rather than universals and generals. So stated, the change embraces a great deal of this age of revolution, counter-revolution, and romanticism. Romanticism's stress on diversity relates to some general features of nineteenth-century civilization. That civilization was in many ways more diverse and less unified than the older one. Aristocratic and cosmopolitan, the eighteenth century had *a* style, even though one might note exceptions to it. The nineteenth was to be eclectic in its architecture, pillaging the past for borrowed styles; it was to offer a "generous confusion" of modes in the arts and in ideas; it divided into separate national cultures. It was a much more pluralistic civilization. Man was parceled out in men, as the poet Rossetti put it—which he, looking backward nostalgically, took to be a sign of the decadence of Europe. Unconsciously perhaps, romanticism reflected the atomization of European society.

Despite its occasional lapses into modish *Weltschmerz* or Byronic *Menschenhass,* romanticism on the whole shared the general optimism of the earlier nineteenth century. Romantic writers exhibited a lyric exuberance, a love for life. Nothing today, the great critic Lionel Trilling once remarked, can compare with the exhilarating effect of Keats's letters—destined, as he was, to die a young and tragic death from the great nineteenth-century killer, tuberculosis. Their minds soared, their spirits aspired to ecstatic heights, they escaped earthly bondage. A new inspiration visited poetry and swept into the other arts. "In 1813 music had newly become the most astonishing, the most fascinating, the most miraculous art in the world," Shaw wrote. The marvelous energy of Beethoven would carry into the great romantic composers, Chopin, Schumann, Berlioz, Brahms. Whatever its possible confusions of thought, the romantic generation of European expression saw an outburst of creative energy and inspiration not matched since the Renaissance and seldom equaled since; it fertilized the rest of the century and continues to this day, for all subsequent European literature and music is indebted to it. The visual arts, despite a Blake and Delacroix, seemed less affected, perhaps because painting and sculpture are essentially classical in spirit, depicting repose and equilibrium rather than—as in a Beethoven sonata or symphony—the ongoing rush of powerful feeling.

If we attempt to tie the great writers and artists of the Romantic era to any one social class, we fail; they were a diverse group, in terms of social origins. Keats was the son of a livery stable manager, Blake the offspring of a haberdasher, Tom Moore the son of a grocer, John Clare a farm laborer; Victor Hugo's father, on the other hand, was a general under Napoleon, Lord Byron was of course high-born. Balzac, actually of bourgeois origin, added a "de" before his name to make himself seem aristocratic. "George Sand," offspring of an aristocratic father and a low-born mother, was raised in a convent and first donned her male attire as a farmworker, not a feminist; she married a country squire before fleeing to Paris with her two children to write eighty novels, become world famous, and adopt unconventional views as well as life-style. Her story is a microcosm of the Romantic era. The ability to win fame and fortune in the new urban market for literature was a factor of increasing importance. But the many interesting careers of the hundreds of romantic writers and artists show them coming from all classes and every sort of background, united only by their talent and their credo of the artist's self-expression. Coleridge wrote in *Kubla Khan:*

Weave a circle round him twice
And close your eyes with holy dread
For he on honey-dew hath fed
And drunk the milk of paradise.

chapter 2

The Birth of Ideologies

1815-1848

We preached everywhere and at all times. Exactly what
it was we preached it is hard to say. . . .

Alexander Herzen

THE EUROPEAN SITUATION 1815-1848

The profusion of political and social "isms" in Europe after 1815 was a consequence of the situation people faced in that year. Especially acute in France, the
crisis affected all Europe, for none of it had been untouched by the Revolution and
Napoleon, and much of it had been as profoundly altered as France itself. Bonaparte
had destroyed the old order in Italy and Germany and had brought sweeping innovations wherever his legions marched. Now the Revolution and its great leader were
vanquished. But was it possible to go back to the old regime of 1789 as if nothing
had happened? Even the most reactionary did not really believe that. If one could
not believe in either the old order or the new, what lay ahead? All over Europe the
need was felt to take soundings and mark out some course. Clearly the old Europe
was dead—ten centuries of civilization washed out. The new Europe had failed
morally and now physically from the Reign of Terror to the coup d'état of Bonaparte and so to his military defeat after a terrible war. But Europe was going on,
filled with all kinds of half-understood dynamisms such as democracy and industrialization. Did they portend destruction or creation, rebirth or decadence? "The

people who have gone through 1793 and 1814 bear two wounds in their hearts," wrote Alfred de Musset, attributing to these wounds "all the sickness of the present century." The first had forever destroyed the old order; the second had revealed the problematic nature of the new one. Those who had lived through the wars, the Terror, the Bonapartist regime, and its defeat might land on the shoals of cynicism, with Stendahl's young hero of *The Charterhouse of Parma*. Or they might continue searching for the elusive principles of the new order.

In France the impulse to order showed itself strongly. *Laissez-faire* liberty did not appeal to the rationalist French mind. Both conservatives and socialists shared a desire to define and shape the reconstruction of a positive social order. But this must be done in a new way, and there was widespread realization that science and fact, not metaphysics and dogma, had to form the foundation. In Great Britain liberal individualism was much more prominent. In both countries political and social ideologies constituted the leading intellectual interest. Even in Germany is that true; for while the great Hegel reigned as the last of the classical lineage of German philosophy and produced a system some found too metaphysical, his chief interest was in human history and its political order; his disciples included critical historians such as David Strauss and social ideologists such as Karl Marx.

The greatest need in Europe after 1815 was for political and social reorganization following the destruction of the old order by the French Revolution. The peace settlement at Vienna in 1815 tried to do this in the arena of practical politics; it partly succeeded and partly failed. Popular movements, such as nationalism in Germany and Italy or working-class radicalism in Britain and France, reflected the deep disturbances of a society undergoing rapid economic and social change along with political uncertainty.

Socially, one marked the decline of the old aristocracy and the rise of a new class, an upper bourgeoisie of commerce, finance, and industry. The period of a few years from 1815 to 1830 witnessed a generally conservative spirit, the product of the reactionary victors of the long war against Bonapartism; in France it was the time of the attempted Bourbon restoration, in England, the Tories continued their power, and in Germany Prince Metternich's Austrian conservatism controlled affairs. But the underlying social realities defeated the attempt to preserve aristocratic domination. The revolution of 1830 sweeps aside the restored monarchy in France; the great Reform Bill of 1832 signals the demise of old-fashioned Toryism in Britain.

The middle classes had begun their long reign. There was at this time considerable class consciousness among speakers for this group. Power must be transferred from the landed oligarchy to the "intelligent middle and industrious classes," said Richard Cobden, an oracle of British liberalism. These classes distinguished themselves from the "mob" below as carefully as from the aristocracy, or what was left of it, above—from both of which they differed in possessing the traits of industriousness, sobriety, and morality, they thought. (The upper classes and the lower, someone remarked, were united by the bond of a common immorality in sexual matters—the former having advanced beyond morality, the latter having not yet encountered it.) The new bourgeoisie were serious, frugal, upright, hardworking, and, according to some critics, hardhearted. Certainly they were builders of wealth in this vigorous morning of the Industrial Revolution, very proud of their achievements, inclined to be scornful of those who contributed less, as they believed. Distinctions must be noted within the "bourgeoisie"; the term is too broad to be meaningful. In France, at least, the "grande bourgeoisie," who dominated the Orleanist Monarchy from 1830 to 1848, was a haughty coterie of rich bankers and industrialists who were "political liberals but social conservatives," having little regard for their social inferiors and absolutely no taste for democracy. In France, the 1830 revolution brought a "liberalization" of the suffrage to the degree that perhaps one in forty adult French males voted as compared to one in seventy-five before. In Great Britain, after the great Reform Bill of 1832, one in five had the vote. In the Continental revolutions of 1848 a lower bourgeoisie joined with workers in demanding universal suffrage. Britain escaped that revolution because to a much greater extent its lower as well as upper bourgeoisie were enfranchised.

The word *bourgeois* became an epithet in two circles: the socialists and the literary. It was alleged that the middle classes were indifferent to the arts as well as to the sufferings of the poor. The stereotype of the bourgeois (as depicted in a Daumier caricature, for example) had some basis in reality. It is true, for example, that the Benthamite *Westminster Review* regarded literature as inappropriate to civilization, while the liberal *Economist* along with Herbert Spencer coolly considered it better to starve the poor than to administer public charity. But one must remember the strength of this "industrious and intelligent" bourgeoisie. By and large they *were* in possession of a large share of those not altogether contemptible characteristics, industry and intelligence. They were creating wealth as it had never been created before. If their natural habitat was the *bourse* or the factory rather than university or parliament, they did produce powerful speakers in this age: not merely Samuel Smiles with his propaganda of self-help, but such as Cobden, Bright, Thiers, Guizot.

It is also necessary to keep in mind the point once made by Balzac, the astute French novelist and observer of the "human comedy": If the bourgeoisie destroyed the nobility, a combat would immediately ensue between the bourgeoisie and the people beneath them. The weapons with which the bourgeoisie had brought down the aristocracy—charges of special privilege and unearned income, demands for more democracy and equality—could obviously be turned on them by the others. Coleridge, opposing the extension of the suffrage in 1832, warned the middle class that they would be unable to stop by giving the vote just to themselves but would eventually have to give it to all. Carlyle warned them that by refusing to look after their workers, they would drive them to social revolution; the feudal landlords had at least given protection to their serfs, whereas the new factory owners gave them no human sympathy, only an inadequate wage. So the "social question" arose early and socialism became a factor, though unable to overturn the rule of the bourgeoisie. Few serious thinkers were ever quite happy with the new organization of society, or lack of it, under middle-class industrialism.

RESULTS OF THE FRENCH REVOLUTION

The most basic change wrought by the French Revolution (in principle, for most of Europe) was that which Henry Maine capsulized in the phrase "from status to contract." The Old Regime had been hierarchical, organic, inequalitarian, and corporative. Treating people neither as individuals nor as equals, it had yet contained a place for all within the society. Within fifty years of the French Revolution, Thomas Carlyle could develop a considerable nostalgia for it on the grounds that the serf at least had had a protector, humble though that role was. The Revolution proclaimed equality and freedom. People were free to make their own way; they were also free to starve. The medieval peasants had held land and duties by custom (status); the nineteenth-century workers had lost this security; they could rise, but if they fell there was, in principle, no one to rescue them.

From this enormous change issues a series of nineteenth-century ideological statements. The socialists were indignant that human labor had been turned into a commodity and claimed that "bourgeois freedom" was only a disguise for the greater exploitation of labor. More objectively, historians pointed out that the opposition of classes had been increased, not diminished, by the abolition of the old feudal ranks of society; now all were theoretically equal but marked off from one another by just the possession of wealth, a thing more likely to breed jealousy and bitterness. The gap between rich and poor became greater, not less, and the poor had less protection. In *Past and Present,* Carlyle asked his contemporaries to consider "Gurth, born thrall of Cedric the Saxon," who, though not exactly "an exemplar of human felicity . . . to me seems happy, in comparison with many a Lancashire and Buckinghamshire man, of these days, not born thrall of anybody!" "The Revolution ended one inequality and gave birth to another," as a later French writer summed it up. The new inequality was both more obvious and less tolerable. Plutocracy had replaced aristocracy. Legal, juridical equality meant a rat race in which the weaker or unluckier were ground into the dirt by the more energetic and less scrupulous.

The results of the French Revolution led by and large in the three main directions of nineteenth-century social thought: liberal, socialist, and conservative. Those who were content in the main with the abolition of the old regime and the installation (more or less by default) of legal equality and free competition were liberals; those who pined for a return of the ancient order of things, or what they imagined that order to have been, were conservatives; the socialists, for their part, pronounced the work of the Revolution incomplete—it had established a formal but not a real equality, a political but not an economic one. A new ruling class of the moneyed had replaced the old one and was even worse:

> They have given us into the hands of the new unhappy lords
> Lords without anger or honour, who dare not carry their swords,

as G. K. Chesterton subsequently wrote ("The Secret People"). The germ of socialism had appeared very soon after the Revolution in Babeuf's unsuccessful "conspiracy of the Equals" of 1795. All during the nineteenth century, victory in this three-horse race went to the bourgeois liberals, for while socialism remained a utopian dream of the future, those who dreamed of restoring the past were equally ineffective.

If the new "bourgeois" leaders could sometimes express feelings of disdain for the lower classes, they did not entirely neglect their welfare. Rejecting most plans of state assistance in accordance with their approval of the "night watchman" state that only "prevented crime and preserved contracts," bourgeois liberals could not deny that their maxim of "a fair field and no favors" required some social services. Education was perhaps the leading case of this sort. "The schoolmaster was abroad" in these years, in Europe as well as in the United States, where the name of Horace Mann became a household word. Guizot, who scorned the multitude, nevertheless put through the educational reform of 1833, called the charter of French primary education. It was far from installing free and universal elementary education, but by requiring every commune to maintain a public primary school, it began the movement that led in this direction. Probably the nineteenth-century bourgeoisie have been overly blamed for their alleged callousness toward the poor and the workers. Still, their creed did not allow for much social welfare legislation by modern standards. The political economists, proclaiming the advantages of private property and pure competition, were engaged in developing a highly specialized, formidably exacting branch of knowledge, with rare success; they were arbiters of public policy and beacons of light to the powerful industrial bourgeoisie.

Writing in 1831 on "The Spirit of the Age," young John Stuart Mill remarked that "a change has taken place in the human mind. . . . The conviction is already not far from being universal that the times are pregnant with change, and that the nineteenth century will be known to posterity as the era of one of the greatest revolutions of which history has preserved the remembrance, in the human mind, and in the whole constitution of human society." With the progress of the so-called "industrial revolution," the rise of what Carlyle named the "social question," and a steady trend toward popular democracy, there was to be no stability on the basis of the settlements of 1830 to 1832, which provided for neither a democratic suffrage nor a welfare state. They were in fact political and social orders dominated by the upper classes and offered little to either the workers or the lower middle class, who were to join in making the revolutions of 1848, proving, however, to be incompatible allies. The 1830s witnessed a rise of interest in socialism and related ideas, brought violent insurrection to some districts (for example Lyons in 1831), and then gave way to the "hungry forties," at the end of which major revolutions swept Europe from one end to the other.

An unprecedented ferment of social and political thought prepared the way for the revolutions of the year 1848, a secondary tremor hardly less earth-shaking than the first quake of 1789. Various sorts of socialism, democracy, social democracy, and liberalism mingled in another apocalyptic moment, when many expected the deferred social millenium. Again came apparent failure and disillusion. But in fact 1848 marked the permanent arrival, if not the absolute victory, of both democracy and socialism. The ideas that grew up in the period from 1815 to 1848 are the political and social ideas or ideologies with which the Western world has been living ever since. They are, then, of the utmost importance.

CONSERVATISM

The rise of a conservative ideology began with Edmund Burke, and all subsequent members of this school were basically indebted to his *Reflections on the Revolution* (see Chapter 1). Coleridge, as we have noted, built on Burke's foundations in England, though his political thought was somewhat scattered. Writing under the impact of his own later (1798) disillusionment with the French cause, he did not go as far as Burke in rejecting all rationalism in politics; he joined him in the respect for tradition, the organic sense of society, and the feeling for a moral order in history. His influence flowed down through the nineteenth century as a strong philosophic source of British enlightened Toryism; John Stuart Mill declared that Coleridge and Jeremy Bentham, the utilitarian, were the two opposing seminal figures in nineteenth-century British thought. The contrast must be noted for American students: British and European conservatism has been an enemy of *laissez-faire.* Coleridge believed in government regulation of manufacturers, government aid to education, the duty of the state to enhance the moral and intellectual capabilities of its citizens in all sorts of positive ways.[1] Conservatism abhorred and was set over against the individualism of the "liberals," who preached free competition and no state intervention in the economic order. Related to the rural squirearchy, it was certainly not equalitarian or leveling (Coleridge opposed the Reform Bill of 1832) but was deeply humanistic and more likely than liberalism to support governmental welfare measures for the poor. The leading hero of factory reform and other humanitarian measures in early industrial England was the Tory, Lord Shaftesbury. The Coleridge tradition passed to such writers as John Ruskin, who described himself as "a violent Tory of the old school" and rigorously denounced the materialistic and unprincipled society of industrial England. It also passed to Benjamin Disraeli, with his conception of a democratized Conservative party leading the way to social reform on behalf of the workers.

It was in France, though, that the conservative ideology developed most prominently. There were a few liberals in post-Napoleonic France (1815 to 1830), for example, Benjamin Constant and Mme. de Staël, those old foes of Bonaparte, who stressed constitutionalism, civil liberties, a limited monarchy, parliamentarian-

---

[1] In his later years, Coleridge's important religious thought featured the idea of a new kind of national church which would be led by prominent people from all areas of life and thought. Coleridge's Christianity was liberal in the sense of being based on individual conscience—a legacy of his Romanticism—rather than dogma or ceremony, but it was conservative in seeking to combat anarchic individualism and materialism by a "clerisy" of the best and brightest. His "Broad Church" movement in the Church of England found a few notable disciples but appealed chiefly to intellectuals; his was thus an enlightened or philosophical conservatism.

ism. In this camp, too, one might put Chateaubriand, whose career now turned to statesmanship as he struggled to make the system of parliamentary monarchy work. But even these French "liberals" do not seem to have had much of the spirit of Benthamite individualism, then becoming dominant in Britain. Nor were they the dominant voices, distinguished though the thought of Constant was. France in the 1820s produced two brilliant streams of thought from opposite directions: right and left. These were the conservatives and the socialists. The conservative camp included Joseph de Maistre and the Vicomte de Bonald as its chief ornaments.

Born in 1753 of aristocratic Savoyard family, the first of these was early a follower of Rousseau. In the 1780s he became interested in the occult Christianity pursued in the circle of the Marquess de Saint-Martin, "the unknown philosopher," as he signed himself, but dropped the attachment when the Church pronounced against it. A provincial senator, happily married, Maistre would never have made himself a famous figure in the history of thought had it not been for the French Revolution. Initially he was known as a liberal or even a Jacobin. But he fell afoul of the Revolution in 1793 and went into exile. At Lausanne in Switzerland he frequented the society of M. Necker and his celebrated daughter, Mme. de Staël, and met Gibbon, the historian. At that time he began to put together his thoughts on the origins of the Revolution, the reasons for its failure, and the means of reconstructing France. These were themes to which the thoughts of many turned in these dramatic years.

Bonald was in exile in Heidelberg at the same time, and Maistre wrote to him in 1796 that "your spirit and mine are in perfect accord." They had to wait out the Napoleonic years; Bonaparte, though he read and admired a book of Maistre's in 1797, could not secure the loyalty of the man who had made himself the spokesman of French royalism. Maistre worked as a diplomatist for the King of Sardinia, going to St. Petersburg as ambassador in 1803. The rugged integrity of this Savoyard (a people noted for this trait), who separated himself from his family whom he deeply loved, whose faith in France did not waver through the darkest days, added to the eloquence of his prose and the charm of his personality. He was a writer of genius and a scholar of great learning, as even his foes conceded. In St. Petersburg he wrote his chief works: *On the Pope, On the Gallican Church, Evenings in St. Petersburg.* After the fall of Napoleon and the restoration of Louis XVIII, Maistre returned to France to receive considerable acclaim, and his books, now published in France, earned him the reputation of chief theoretician of the Bourbon restoration; he died in 1821, just as he was gaining this long-deferred but well-earned recognition. Bonald, whose ideas were quite similar (he lacked Maistre's grace of style but was rather more systematic), lived on to reign as the high priest of the monarchists, joined among others, by the youthful and fiery La Mennais, who would later turn to the left. But of these, Maistre's writings are the best known.

Negatively, Maistre's thought was marked by a cold fury against the whole *philosophe* school. He wished to "absolutely kill the spirit of the eighteenth century." Maistre concluded that the *philosophes* had introduced the poison that had caused the sickness of the Revolution; the poison must be purged from France's body before it could be restored to health. Maistre would not even allow Voltaire and company the virtue of common honesty. They were great criminals; to like Voltaire is the sign of a corrupt soul; the very visage of the great satirist bespoke his service of the Devil. Locke, Hume, Voltaire, Rousseau were all evil or at the very least horribly misguided men. Here Maistre was simply a polemicist, a vigorous and eloquent one, turning Voltaire's weapons against himself and assailing the mockers as they had once assailed the church.

However, once the poison had been cast out, these "reactionaries" saw the additional task of reconstructing society and tried to show how it might be done. Here they proved immensely stimulating and influenced many who did not at all share their ideological preconceptions; they notably influenced the socialists, Saint-Simon being the best example. They combined keen intelligence with penetrating insights into the weaknesses of the liberal or democratic order, while also contributing some fruitful ideas about methodology in the social sciences. They were aware that one could not go back to 1789, much though they may have regretted the Revolution, which Maistre could only explain as having been sent by God to punish France for its sins. Maistre was not the "prophet of the past," as a wit dubbed him. It was necessary to establish a new political philosophy; this was the age of ideology, with mere habit no longer sufficing; "the intellectual principle has taken priority over the moral principle in the direction of society," as Maistre put it. Living in a France which had seen the failure of the Republic and then (defeated in frightful war) the collapse of the dictatorship that succeeded it, and which now found itself trying the uncertain experiment of a restored Bourbon monarchy, Maistre and Bonald hoped to explain clearly why republics always failed and only monarchies could provide political security. The task stimulated them to a wide-ranging investigation of political and sociological phenomena.

Their argument made extensive use of the idea that the natural order of society is historical and traditional, while individualism and democracy are diseases resulting in social anarchy. Take away the discipline imposed by church, monarchy, nobility, each in its proper place in the orbit that is natural to France (nations have character; each has a form of government suitable to it; you must not tamper with this truth by an arid rationalistic universalism), take this away, and the result will be disorder, corruption, decay. Written constitutions are crude and artificial; the true constitution of a people is written in the hearts of its people and expressed in its ancestral customs. The school of Maistre, Savigny, and Haller[2] was historical; they held that wisdom in politics comes from experience only, that is, from a discriminating study of the past and from the understanding of national character as revealed in history. Abstract theory had caused much damage, they believed; ignorance of and contempt for history was the prime source of political error.

Their arguments in favor of absolute monarchy may now make tedious read-

---

[2]Savigny was spokesman for the historical school of jurisprudence in Germany, Burkean in its stress on the organic evolution of the law rooted in tradition. Haller, a German Swiss, held similar views. The latter's nostalgia for the Old Regime in its corporate, organic, and inequalitarian aspects was especially strong.

ing, but the conservative school had a considerable influence on nineteenth-century thought. Bonald has been called the founder of sociology; he certainly influenced Comte, who is more frequently granted that title. Alexis de Tocqueville's famous *Democracy in America*, a pioneer work of sociological analysis, was much influenced by these writers. (See La Mennais's comments on democracy in his 1825 book, *De la religion considerée dans ses rapports avec l'ordre politique et civil* (Vol. I.) It looks as if Tocqueville were testing the hypotheses of La Mennais—that democracy leads to despotism, enshrines mediocrity, causes people to be restless, rootless, and godless, and makes money the only idol.) Whereas their recommendations for the good society came to little, their critical analysis of the social changes overtaking France, their investigations of such matters as what effect the loss of religious faith or of social hierarchy will have on politics and society, were truly stimulating. Their appeal from the abstract theories of the rationalists to positive historical facts and careful sociological investigation bore fruit in many students after them, who admired their methods, while not necessarily sharing their political prejudices.

A deep awareness of the tragic aspects of the human situation marks Maistre's thought. In politics he was in a sense not illiberal; he wished to see the monarch checked by tradition and by local institutions in a "pluralistic" society, as in the Old Regime. His editor, Jack Lively, has pointed out how close he was after all to Rousseau, whom he thought he hated. Like Bossuet, Maistre distinguished an "absolute" monarchy from an unlimited or despotic one. In a notable argument set forth in *Du Pape*, he argued that the papacy might mediate between the sovereignty of the state and the liberty of the individual. The argument impressed few, least of all the pope, but it indicates Maistre's desire to mitigate the authority of the state (which he felt necessary) in some way, lest it become tyranny. He did not think democracy the answer, not at least for France (he conceded that England had it in its national character to live as a republic). It would only lead to a new Bonapartism. How accurate that prophecy was the events of 1848 to 1851 would reveal. Too much the polemicist and marred by corroding hatreds, Maistre remains a major figure because of his flashes of rare insight.

A recent writer (Benjamin N. Nelson) has observed that "a society founded on sheer egoism . . . will undergo atomization, anomic loss of a sense of belonging." It then leads to totalitarianism by reaction, modern totalitarianism being an effort to substitute for "subtle and satisfying forms of organic solidarity" by "imposing the yoke of mechanism." In other words, a natural community being absent, there is flight from the intolerable rootlessness and anonymity of modern urban life toward some kind of statism. The case for the conservatives of nineteenth-century France must rest on some such point as this, and it would seem to be one of enduring pertinence.

British Utilitarianism and Political Economy postulated free self-reliant individuals, the "mainspring of social progress" because their energies were released by the knowledge that what they gained would be their own, capable of enriching themselves and thereby also enriching the nation, capable also of enlightening and educating themselves. But an accompaniment of this far from unworthy idea was the loss of a social sense. The market was an impersonal force, though it regulated the relationships of society—impersonal and selfish. Society became only a collection of individuals, and thus something necessary to humanity was lost, for though we like to assert our individuality, we cannot do without membership in a community. The conservatives, whatever their sins in other respects, surely performed a valuable service to modern Europe in defending the community against atomization.

Moreover the conservatives typically disliked commercialism as well as mass democracy, and they had a deep sense of human dignity. Their values tended to be rooted in the stable society of the countryside where the impersonality of the city is abhorrent. In both England and France there were "Tory radicals" throughout the century who sided with the working class against the capitalists on matters of social reform. They produced a strong vein of social criticism. Coleridge, Carlyle, Disraeli, and Ruskin might be put into this category in England—a distinguished heritage of social thought, by no means reactionary, holding up the ideal of a society that was aristocratic, but not plutocratic, socially responsible rather than irresponsible.

Saint-Simon, the socialist, acknowledged his debt to Bonald, who taught him that society is "an organic machine whose every part contributes to the movement of the whole," not a mere collection of separate and unconnected individuals. The conservatives and the socialists had something in common, and that, an important idea: the social principle. But the conservatives saw society as the will of God, favored obedience to political authority, believed religion to be a necessity, abhorred revolution, and could scarcely accept either equality or democracy. Agreeing in the conviction that society must be ordered and organized, wherein they both differed from the nineteenth-century liberals, conservatives and socialists disagreed about the nature of that organization and its source. For the socialists held to an Enlightenment faith that human reason might contrive a new and ideal organization. Conservatives, with a wisdom they thought they had learned from the melancholy experiment of the Revolution, held this to be impossible and disastrous. No opinion lay closer to the heart of conservative doctrine than a mistrust of what Burke called "the fallible and feeble contrivances of our reason." It mistrusted political theories and believed that we must fall back on existing rooted institutions which represent a kind of collective wisdom of the ages. The liberals and radicals believed that people could do better; the conservatives feared that they might well do worse. They would rely on the allegedly natural social order, which seemed to mean just the *status quo.* Their defect was that the age was seething with change, and there was no stable order of things.

LIBERALISM

Though conservatives tried to put down an anchor against the currents of change, no task was less promising in this first half of the nineteenth century. It was the most revolutionary half-century in history up to that time. Everyone felt whirled away by the pace of change; "We have been living the life of 300 years in 30," Matthew Arnold's father, the famous schoolmaster, remarked. "Can we never drop anchor for a single day, On the ocean of the ages?" Lamartine poetically wondered. By and large, it was a hopeful half-century, with all its perplexities and turbulence— much more hopeful than the latter half. There is an exuberance about its writing that reflects this basic optimism; one sees it in the titanic creative energies of a Dickens or a Balzac, as well as in the explosion of hopeful solutions for all the prob- lems of humanity. "The period was full of evil things, but it was full of hope," Chesterton wrote in his book about Charles Dickens. Its typical giants, like Victor Hugo, dreamed vast dreams of progress and threw themselves furiously into their tasks. So it was not, on the whole, a good time for conservatives, and after a few years of success following the fall of Napoleon, they gave way to more hopeful people who presided over an era culminating in the great liberal-democratic-socialist revolutions of 1848.

Liberalism was a term rather like romanticism, broad and vague, and still is. By general agreement it was strongest in Great Britain, which had an ancestral sort of liberalism (though the word was not used in any systematic way until the 1930s) embracing civil liberty and parliamentary government. The English had not known absolute monarchy and had been living under the mildest of European governments since 1688. Fondly recalling such landmarks as the Magna Carta and the Bill of Rights, the English considered themselves freer than any other people and typically looked with amused contempt on the political broils of the French and other Continental lesser breeds. The storms of the French Revolution caused some curtail- ments of this liberty between 1795 and 1820, producing toward the latter date, at the time of "Peterloo"[3] and the repressive Six Acts, what has been called the ugliest estrangement between English government and people since 1688. But this did not last, and under Whig auspices a series of parliamentary measures between 1825 and 1840 could be called "liberal" in that they extended the range of freedoms: com- mercial (removal of tariffs, monopolies, restrictions on trade), personal (freedom of press, religion), and political (more representative elections to parliament, extension of the suffrage in 1832).

There were other aspects to this "liberalism," for example opposition to facto- ry legislation and to trade unions, which may seem illiberal by modern standards but were in accordance with maximum freedom of individual entrepreneurs from government regulation. Free speech was restored: In 1819 the Habeas Corpus Act had been suspended, journals and pamphlets taxed, publishers imprisoned for criticizing the king—but by 1832 these restrictions had been substantially removed. (On the Continent, Metternich more successfully repressed freedom of the press—a "modern scourge," the great conservative said, inconsistent with organized society— and seven German professors at Göttingen became martyrs to the censorship of ideas

---

[3] A massacre at St. Peter's Fields in Manchester on August 16, 1819 was ironically called Peterloo, recalling the famous British victory over Napoleon at Waterloo. The Manchester Yeo- manry, a police force, attacked or got into a battle with a crowd being addressed by Radical orators.

that was a part of the "metternich system.") In 1829 the Catholic Emancipation Act and repeal of the Test Acts removed political disabilities from non-Anglican Christians, though the Established Church remained and Jews were not similarly relieved for thirty more years.

It cannot be said that the Whigs who supported these last actions were moved by flaming slogans about human rights; they were practical measures. The Reform Bill of 1832, bitterly opposed as it was, left four out of five Englishmen without the vote. At the same time, in the name of "liberal" principles, the most "liberal" of the English supported the harsh Poor Law of 1834 and fought the Ten Hour Bill. Even the most radical of them, like Francis Place, felt that granting any great amount of welfare relief to the laboring poor would "encourage idleness and extinguish enterprise." A courageous band fought to abolish slavery within the British Empire, but a considerable number of these were not "liberals" but Churchmen and Tories. All in all, early nineteenth-century liberalism was a somewhat curious thing as we view it today, and it requires some explanation.

It was associated with two notable intellectual systems of the period: the utilitarians and the political economists. Utilitarianism was the offspring of a strange genius, Jeremy Bentham. Bentham had been writing as early as the 1770s and was

Jeremy Bentham's body, as he requested, still sits in the board room of University College, London. The real head is the one on the floor. (The Bettman Archive/BBC Hulton.)

an old man in 1810 when his school began to become prominent; he belonged to the later Enlightenment and never departed from it in essential spirit. Decidedly no romantic, Bentham was a thoroughgoing rationalist, a scoffer at religion, a man without poetic instincts and almost, it seems, without emotions. John Stuart Mill, son of Bentham's leading disciple, described in his famous autobiography the inhuman regimen under which he was raised, and which finally caused him to have something like a breakdown. His relief came only when he found consolation in poetry and philosophy. After this dramatic and symbolic experience, Mill wrote a series of essays in which he presented Bentham and Coleridge as the two seminal influences of the century. The romantic-conservative and the utilitarian-liberal, rivals and opposites, sent forth two different strains of thought and feeling which even Mill's wise and catholic mind could not quite reconcile, though he strove to do so.

The lineage of utilitarianism can be traced back to various earlier sources. Helvétius, the French *philosophe*, had announced as a momentous discovery the apparently trite idea that good government is that which secures the greatest happiness of the people. He also shared, if somewhat confusedly, the Physiocratic idea that about the best thing government could do to this end was to leave people alone—certainly, to leave trade alone. The recipe for maximum happiness was left somewhat vague in the pages of Helvétius's *Treatise on Man*. In Britain, Francis Hutcheson had used the phrase "greatest happiness of the greatest numbers," and David Hume had arrived at a form of "utilitarianism" when in his criticism of the social contract he had concluded that it was a fiction that might be dispensed with: "It is therefore on opinion only that government is founded." That is to say, there is no sort of sanction for government on rational analysis except the usefulness of that government in the eyes of its citizens. (Hume could scarcely have supported Bentham's view that an objective, rational standard of utility is possible, however.) William Paley, in his influential textbook *Principles of Moral and Political Philosophy* (1785), accepts this and defines utility as the sum of happiness. A law is good or bad accordingly as it increases or lessens this total of well-being.

Based on Enlightenment hedonism, utilitarianism was severely rationalistic, sweeping aside claims of sentiment or habit in government and requiring laws and institutions to justify themselves on the practical grounds of welfare achieved. Utilitarians were the direct opposites, and of course the violent adversaries, of Burkean conservatives in wishing total and immediate reform on theoretical or *a priori* principles. They proposed breathtaking changes: Instead of two houses of parliament there should be just one, aristocracy along with monarchy should go, the common law should be replaced by a codified one; prisons should be reformed, schools should be reformed, everything should be reformed. Most radical of all was the suggestion of democratic, that is, universal suffrage[4] which the utilitarians

---

[4]This included women as well as men, at least at one time. For a tribute to Bentham's feminism, see Miriam Williford, "Bentham on the Rights of Women," *Journal of the History of Ideas,* January–March 1975. But Bentham changed his mind several times, and his final inclination was evidently to restrict suffrage not only to adult males but to literate ones, although "every individual of the human species" should be a part of the "public opinion tribunal."

reached in typical fashion by reasoning that we are the best judges of our own interest and "each should count as one." In behalf of these proposals, the followers of Bentham, including James Mill and many others, wrote pamphlets, edited magazines, tried to elect members of Parliament, and in general crusaded eagerly, inspired by their belief that they had at last found the exact science of government.

They were an interesting and powerful group, reaching their peak in the 1820s as an organized movement but radiating influences down through the whole century. If they were in many ways exceedingly "radical" (a name they proudly adopted), they were in other ways not so much so, according to some standards. They stoutly defended private property, basing their case on the self-interest of free individuals. There was always some tension between the reforming and the individualistic tenets of utilitarianism. In the 1820s they worked closely with other "radicals," including working-class groups, and helped push through the Reform Bill of 1832. After that, they tended to lose their crusading zeal (perhaps the inevitable fate of a movement) and to become more conservative, or more pragmatic, working piecemeal for specific small changes and dropping their demands for total reconstruction of all society. They did not cease to do useful things; to take but one example, though an illustrious one, Edwin Chadwick undertook the sanitary reform of London in the 1840s as a utilitarian disciple. From the total reconstruction of society to sewage systems was a considerable decline, though not necessarily a discreditable one. But later utilitarians tended even more strongly toward *laissez-faire* or the limited state, which respected individual property rights and did not regulate private business. In this respect they adopted the views of the political economists and parted company with socialists. The utilitarian position had always based itself squarely on the enlightened self-interest of individuals.

Bentham and his followers believed they had formulated an exact science of government. They rejected the Natural Rights school, which was one form of liberalism reaching back to John Locke and the Whig revolution. Such alleged rights, apart from and above positive law, are either meaningless or false, they held. "Liberty" is not an absolute right; concrete liberties must be embodied in legislation to be meaningful, and the nature of such legislation should be determined by exact investigation into real circumstances. Bentham shared with Burke this one trait, at least, that he wished to get rid of metaphysical rubbish in politics and law and bring everything back to the touchstone of measurable human happiness. The sum of individual happiness is the social goal, at which legislation should aim. Bentham thought that he could perform the herculean task of providing an objective measuring stick for happiness on which all might agree, a "felicific calculus."

The Benthamite principle of social welfare as the sum total of units of individual happiness, a total which could in principle be measured rather exactly, thus providing the basis for a science of welfare, lasted a long time; as late as 1920, A. C. Pigou, a British economics professor, claimed to have solved the problem of finding this exact science (*The Economics of Welfare*). The effort to make an exact science of welfare economics must nevertheless be regarded as a failure and illusion. Bentham's notion of it certainly was inadequate and received many criticisms and subsequent restatements. But for all his extravagances, Bentham had a genius for practical reform. From his tireless pen flowed a series of projects for the practical reform of everything: schools, prisons, courts, laws. Some of them were fanciful, some ingenious. By sheer energy and perseverance, Bentham and his followers forced upon the public constant consideration of the questions, "What good is it? Can it be improved?"

Utilitarianism spread beyond its native shores to exert an influence in other countries as far afield as Russia, Spain, and Latin America. It offered a simple and rational rule for reform and had the merit of avoiding nebulous sloganizing as well as revolutionary radicalism; it was hardheaded and practical. But its individualistic foundations rendered it less acceptable in France. There the key social theorists of this period, whether conservatives like Maistre, socialists like Saint-Simon, or bourgeois thinkers like August Comte, stressed the social principle and were more statist.

It was this school of utility that Carlyle attacked as piggish and that sent the amiable Coleridge into a rage. Bentham and James Mill cared nothing for the arts, dismissing poetry as nonsense in the best or worst tradition of the Enlightenment; they cared nothing for "society," seeing in it nothing more than a group of individuals. Selfishness and hedonism seemed enshrined in their utterly unheroic ethics. The romantic-conservative, Coleridge-Carlyle temperament could not understand them. Nor, indeed, were they popular anywhere at first; they were radicals, as Lord Brougham remarked in 1827, "in their religion intolerable atheists, in their politics bloody-minded republicans." Bentham's immense body of writing (the best known being *Principles of Morals and Legislation,* 1789) is marked by few if any graces of style. It is rather more prolix and formless than the works of his forerunners in the English tradition, Hobbes and Locke, but it does swarm with ideas for practical reform. Bentham's creed of self-interest has doubtless gone out of style in the twentieth century, but it appealed mightily to the nineteenth-century bourgeoisie and was conceivably a suitable polity for that day—witness the enormous growth of wealth in Great Britain. His method of attacking social reform piecemeal, assailing it with factual research, and avoiding large nebulous slogans, continued in the Fabian Socialists later with the goal being rather different but the method similar. It seemed to suit the English genius—individualistic, empirical, mistrustful of general ideas and metaphysics. And it can be interpreted as a creed for the English bourgeoisie in particular.

But the ethics of utility is not sheer egoism. One sought to do that which makes for the most good for the whole, that is, the sum of units of happiness; perhaps this might indicate one's extinction. In sharp opposition to Kant, utilitarian ethics judged an act by its consequences, not its inherent quality. Critics noted that, strictly followed, utilitarian rules of conduct might lead to euthanasia or genocide: killing an ill-tempered old man whose death would make his amiable sons and daughters very happy or doing away with minorities. (If a law discriminating against blacks makes the white majority very happy, it should presumably be enacted, according to Bentham's principles.) Such odd inferences suggest that Bentham, whose embalmed body, in accordance with one of his eccentric wishes, still sits today in a room at University College, London, had scarcely fully reasoned out his alleged exact science of government. In the last analysis the Hermit of Queen Park Square takes his place in that gallery of ambitious utopists whose prescriptions fail to bridge the gap between theory and practice. But it may at least be said of him that his theories did less harm than others of that ilk.

POLITICAL ECONOMY

Closely related to and allied with utilitarians in the camp of British liberalism were the political economists. In the early nineteenth century the brilliant beginnings in economic thought made by the French Physiocrats and by Adam Smith reached maturity in the writings of such people as Thomas Malthus, David Ricardo, J. B. Say, and Nassau Senior. Say, along with Sismondi, kept up the French contribution, but in the main the British took over this subject. Perhaps this was because its determined individualism suited the British temperament, tradition, and experience. It is significant that Sismondi defected to socialism, while in Germany there were "romantic" economists such as List and Mueller who rejected the individualistic premises of the British "classical" economists. In Britain, too, the great Scottish writer Thomas Carlyle joined Coleridge and other poets and moralists who were dismissed as mere amateurs and sentimentalists by the economists,[5] in deploring the "dismal science." But it flourished and developed influence uniquely in the British Isles. The prestige of the political economists reached a high point with the 1817 publication of Ricardo's *Principles of Political Economy,* followed by Say's *Treatise* in 1821. Popularizations such as those of Mrs. Marcet (1816) and Harriet Martineau's stories in the later 1820s carried the message from on high to the common man in somewhat simplified form. It was the message of the hour, almost bedside reading for modish literates; it became "high fashion with the blue ladies to talk political economy." This ascendancy continued, on the whole, with the assumption being that an exact science had been perfected. In 1856 a distinguished member of Parliament remarked that "Political Economy is not exactly the law of the land but it is the ground of that law." Leaders of government sought the advice of the economists and parliamentary committees turned to them for guidance.

What was the message? The economists were in fact not a completely homogeneous group by any means. They had their heated debates. It is possible to identify a left wing and a right wing, led respectively by James Mill and J. R. McCulloch. Malthus and Ricardo engaged in a memorable debate about effective demand, to which John Maynard Keynes returned a century later in search of new truth and found Malthus righter than Ricardo, though for a century it had been thought

---

[5] John Stuart Mill, in his discriminating and appreciative essay on Coleridge, said that "in political economy he writes like an arrant driveler, and it would have been well for his reputation had he never meddled with the subject." In turn Coleridge regarded political economy as "solemn humbug."

otherwise. As for the greatest of them, David Ricardo, it is hard to know where to put him. Though often associated with the most brutally pessimistic of those who spoke of an "iron law" keeping wages down to the sustenance level ("the natural price of labour is that price which is necessary to enable the labourers, one with another, to subsist and perpetuate their race, without either increase or diminution"), he led to a kind of socialism and was best known for denouncing the landlord as virtually the enemy of society, thus precipitating class war in England. Ricardo evidently believed much less than Adam Smith that there is a natural order of harmony in economic affairs. He saw the landlord and the factory owner as natural foes. Rents raise the price of food, which raises wages, which causes profits in manufacturing to fall. And it was difficult to avoid the conclusion, on Ricardo's premises, that the wage worker is at war with the employer, since the latter must force wages down in order to keep profits up. The long struggle in British politics over repeal of the Corn Laws, or protective tariffs on grain, during which liberal manufacturers like John Bright attacked Tory landlords as parasites, sprang in good part from Ricardo's theory about rents; Owenite socialists took their inspiration from his labour theory of value and Karl Marx built a system on it.

Yet of course the main message, especially in the popularized version of political economy, was that of individualism. Smith and the Physiocrats had claimed that in accordance with a law of nature the "invisible hand" causes individual and social objectives to coincide, the rule of *laissez-faire* generally sufficing, via competition and the profit incentive, to secure the most efficient production and distribution of wealth. "The whole art of government," Smith had thought, "lies in the liberty of men and things." His successors may have moralized less, but they continued to assume that the free competitive system is the best and that state intervention seldom serves a useful purpose. Even if the major political economists never believed in eliminating all government—they assumed a secure infrastructure of authority, in fact—"mercantilism" was well on its way to becoming a synonym for the dark ages of economic thought. Merchants and statesmen began to accept free trade, which had by about 1820 (witness Baring's petition from the London merchants to Parliament in that year) become business orthodoxy. Say's law of the market posited automatic adjustment between production and consumption. The wage fund theory asserted the futility of any "artificial" attempts, such as by trade unions, to alter the sum available for wages. In one of Miss Martineau's little tales, a strike takes place and some wage increases are granted as a result, but the owner then informs the workers that it is necessary to fire some of them. If some workers get more than their share, others will get less.

In another of her stories, it is explained how public expenditure on the poor raises tax rates, which discourages capital and thus intensifies the problem of unemployment. And the Reverend Thomas Malthus had by this time profoundly affected many with his famed tract on population, arguing that population always tends to increase up to the limit of sustenance, thus ensuring perpetual poverty unless something really heroic is done to break the gloomy cycle. The "hard line" Poor Law of 1834, based on an attempt to deter rather than relieve poverty by making welfare relief both hard to get and unpleasant, was actually far from a new medicine. In the eighteenth century Bernard Mandeville, Daniel Defoe, Arthur Young, and a host of others took it for granted that "the poor have nothing to stir them to labour but their wants, which it is wisdom to relieve but folly to cure," that in brief the poor must be kept poor or they will not work, and that too much charity encourages idleness. "It cannot fail to happen," Turgot had written before Adam Smith, "that the wages of the workman are limited to what is necessary to procure him his subsistence." But the prestigious teachings of political economy were thought to have lent credence to this venerable belief.

James Mill observed that capital tends to increase less rapidly than population, and the growth of capital cannot be forced; it must make its own pace. The classical economists would certainly have listened with bewilderment or perhaps amusement to the recent debate about just how to go about "creating economic growth" by the activities of various governmental agencies. Their world was strictly bounded by the limitations of nature; they saw the laws of diminishing returns and increasing population as probable barriers to any great improvement in the overall lot of the human race. They permitted themselves only an occasional hint of a brighter future.

Yet they became the respected arbiters of policy. This was a triumph not only for their obvious intelligence but also for the readiness of the middle classes to receive the message of hard work and austerity. Classical political economy appealed to the Puritan spirit of the industrious small manufacturers and business people who were climbing from poverty to riches in the favorable economic climate of England during and soon after the Napoleonic war. The slogan of the industrial middle class was self-help. The creed which Carlyle thought a monstrous, inhuman "gospel of mammon" seemed to them the law of life and of progress. As Great Britain assumed the leadership in industrialization, it was the presence and the power of this class, more perhaps than any other single factor, that was responsible for its success. They had energy, and the system of competitive capitalism provided them with incentive.

The British economists were both much admired and cordially disliked, and excited a vigorous countermovement. Socialism took its point of departure from the economic inequalitarianism as well as the economic individualism or selfishness of their teachings. Bentham, who had supported political and legal equality, accepted economic inequality. There must be, he wrote, equality in the sense that each of us is entitled to the just fruits of his own labor. But since people have unequal talents and energies, this will mean unequal rewards. Compelling people to share the fruits of their labors with others, the only practical way of securing economic equality, not only violates justice but will prove disastrous. Coleridge reached exactly the same conclusion—a rare example of agreement between the two leaders of rival schools. It is difficult to overstate the importance for the nineteenth century of this apparent truth that one must choose between civil and economic equality, one cannot have both; as students of ethics would put it, it is the problem of personal versus distributive justice.

The great utilitarian admitted that on other grounds equal distribution of wealth was desirable as contributing to the greatest happiness of the greatest number. (The principle of diminishing utility, he pointed out, means that the addition of a unit of wealth to one who already has a good deal of it brings less pleasure than it does to one with less of it.) Thus was posed the dilemma: In the name of social justice and economic efficiency, one sanctioned inequality and hence unhappiness.

Into the making of British middle-class liberalism, expressed in the famed "Manchester School" headed by John Bright and Richard Cobden, went some other ingredients than the intellectual doctrines of utility and political economy. Bright was a Quaker; Manchester was a provincial center. The rising capitalists of the Industrial Revolution were heavily nonconformist in religion, outside the old aristocratic establishment; they were new men. As dissenters they had had to fight discrimination; Bright said he had to be a liberal because of the persecutions his people had endured. Scripture played as much a part in the Manchester creed as political economy. The Bright-Cobden school went into their great crusade against the Corn Laws, symbol of a hated landlord aristocracy, with Bible phrases on their lips and the spirit of a moral crusade in their hearts. Tennyson ridiculed Bright as "This broad-brimmed hawker of holy things," a selfish moneybags hypocritically pretending to be religious. But the close student of Bright knows there was more to it than that. Self-interest was there and political economy contributed its share, but so did a kind of Puritan conscience, which was something more than a mask for self-interest, though it is easy to see why its enemies made this charge. A part of the liberal creed was passionate hatred of militarism and war that led Bright to stand out courageously against the Crimean War. If his Quaker faith dictated pacifism, so did the tenets of economic liberalism: Free trade would do away with war, which was an avocation of the idle aristocracy; nonintervention should be the rule for nations as for individuals. Thus did religion, economics, and interest blend together to make up the faith of liberal England.

Thus, clearly, there were several strains in early modern liberalism, not always in exact agreement with each other, yet they all tended to agree broadly on a negative conception of the state, on something approaching *laissez-faire* as an ideal. The Natural Rights school of Locke stressed resistance to arbitrary and tyrannical government while enshrining private property as one of the basic, inalienable human rights. The utilitarians built their system on the rational self-interest of free individuals. The political economists pointed toward the largely self-regulating economic order. To this must be added the religious nonconformists whose whole history disposed them to be suspicious of establishments and rules imposed by the state.

Of course, the achievements of the French Revolution in general, meaning the liquidation of the old class society (which came more slowly in England, but did come), left a kind of automatic liberalism in effect. The Old Regime having been destroyed, people became equal—equal under the law, that is, of equal rights, opportunities, status. That such an equality might mean, practically, a larger amount of real, economic equality did not occur to people until they saw what happened. Socialism, Harold Laski has written, was based on "the realization that the liberal ideal secured to the middle class its full share of privilege, while it left the proletariat in its chains." With allowance for rhetorical embellishment, the statement comes close to expressing the essence of the matter. Liberty—the liberty of all citizens to prosper or fail in accordance with their energies, abilities, and luck, the law maintaining a scrupulous impartiality and the state refusing to intervene to protect the weaker or less fortunate—meant inequality and even injustice. It meant that those who succeeded had both the protection of the law and the accolades of society, while those who failed, for whatever reason, might expect to hear only that most ancient of cries, *vae victis.*

SOCIALISM

About the same time as conservatism and liberalism were developing, socialism entered vigorously upon the scene. In 1822, Charles Fourier, son of a Besançon merchant, published his *Traité de l'association,* a work not exactly greeted with wild acclaim when it appeared, one among multitudes of strange schemes for the total reconstruction of society, but destined in time to a greater fame than any of these. Between 1814 and 1822 the eccentric Count Saint-Simon, who modestly called himself a combination of Bacon, Newton, and Locke, sent forth a spate of books; the basis of his claim to be the first important socialist has usually been approved. Meanwhile in Britain, Robert Owen, the Scottish factory owner, was popularizing his plan, by example, for a more social organization of industry; thousands came to New Lanark to inspect it. Sismondi had broken with the *laissez-faire* economists, repelled by their selfish atomism and apparently callous disregard of human beings. The word *socialism* does not seem to have come into use until the 1830s, but the idea itself was forming in the 1820s. "Associationalism" was a term then in use.

Naturally, it had earlier roots. Leaving aside the strong tradition of communalism in both Platonism, the Church, and medieval feudalism, and in Christian millenarianism present from medieval times, we can find strands of socialism in the Enlightenment, along with the stronger element of *laissez-faire* individualism. By no means consistently a socialist (indeed, he sometimes called private property "sacred"), Rousseau, in one memorable passage that shocked Voltaire, regretted the origins of private property in an initial act of usurpation. Someone said, "This is mine!" and got away with it, ending the idyll of primitive communism and ushering in greed, civilization, and all their accompaniments. From Rousseau's concept of the General Will—the will of society as a whole, something more than the sum of individual wills—many of his disciples derived a strong statism. Rousseau's *Social Contract* taught that all rights are derived from society, without which they could not exist; the state, therefore, is justified in regulating property; there is no absolute right of property; if property exists, it is at the sufferance of society. Rousseau believed that private property should be permitted to exist but should be approximately equal and represent only what one earned with one's labor. Moreover, he considered the pursuit of wealth an evil, a source of modern society's ills. Though to describe Rousseau as a socialist would be to commit an anachronism, some of his attitudes fed into the nineteenth-century stream of this school. His influence did not encourage the kind of socialism that stressed greater productivity and wealth for he thought the good life was one of Spartan simplicity. Engels once remarked that Rousseau's *Essay on the Origin of Inequality* contained all the seeds of Marxism; it is difficult to exaggerate the influence of this powerful writer on all subsequent social doctrines.

Morelly, called "the only consistent communist among the eighteenth-century thinkers," combined Rousseau's General Will with his attack on private property to arrive at a crude socialist theory. Morelly's *Code de la Nature, ou le veritable Esprit des Lois,* as the title indicates, was a reply to Montesquieu's great book of 1748, *The Spirit of the Laws,* a landmark of Enlightenment thought; as an attack on the famous *philosophe*'s acceptance of private property, it quite failed, being subjected to much ridicule. The socialist element in such writers as Rousseau and more explicitly in Morelly was probably an echo of the mythic Golden Age, embodied in Christianity as the prelapsarian Edenic stage before the apple was bitten. In transferring Original Sin to the invention of private property, Rousseau was not so far from primitive or radical Christianity; and indeed there were to be many Christian Socialists in the nineteenth century.

Equally crude, yet fervently sincere, was the thought of those who backed "Gracchus" Babeuf in his rather pathetic Conspiracy of the Equals in the latter days of the French Revolution (1795). Robespierre, that "child of the ideas of Rousseau," had been willing to use the power of the state ruthlessly in accordance with the General Will concept but had basically been a Jacobin democrat who did not wish to abolish private property. Babeuf, however, advocated a "distributive socialism," a common pool of property to which everyone brings earnings that are then carved up equally. "Nature has given to every man an equal right to the enjoyment of all goods." The same nature that provided the basis for bourgeois property rights might be turned in another direction. A passion for equality and a belief that private property creates inequality moved these people.

Like romanticism, socialism is a large word covering a multitude of rather different things. There have been various sorts of socialism, though one may link them all by certain common denominators. The first half of the century brought forth a profusion of schemes and plans, supplying the basic ideas for all subsequent socialist thought. The eagerness with which people produced and imbibed socialist ideas in this period relates to the general feeling that some new plan of social reorganization was desperately needed, to a discontent with the liberalism of legal equality *cum* free competition, and to the continuing ferment of ideas stemming from the Enlightenment, romanticism, and the French Revolution.

The pioneer socialists were a colorful and interesting lot. Robert Owen, though born a poor boy (as one of thirteen children, he went to work at the age of nine), rose to become a wealthy and successful factory owner in a rags-to-riches story. A man of boundless energy, he went into business for himself at the age of eighteen in Manchester, getting in on the burgeoning cotton textile industry, and later bought the mills at New Lanark in Scotland, destined to become internationally celebrated. But he also found time to read and was clearly influenced by the "philosophic" ideas of Rousseau, Godwin, and other Enlightenment thinkers. At New Lanark he set to work reforming the ignorant, degraded mill hands (largely children) who worked long hours in unsanitary and dismal surroundings. He reduced working hours, improved housing, established schools, banned alcohol, set up communal stores where goods were sold at fair prices, organized pension and sick funds—and found that it paid, for the workers worked better. He was the benevolent dictator of a model community to which visitors began to come from all over the world. Owen's fame as an enlightened employer was such that when he visited the United States in 1825 he was invited to address a special joint session of Congress. He was at this time a respectable example of philanthropy and "benevolence," widely approved qualities, but he soon lost his respectability as he embarked on a variety of schemes for the total reformation of society. He attempted to found a highly unorthodox Rational Religion, a kind of secular-social morality which may be compared with Saint-Simon's New Christianity. But most of Owen's enormous energy went toward attempts to duplicate the New Lanark idea by planting other model socialist communities, sinking the whole of his substantial fortune into such schemes. Though the community at New Harmony, Indiana (which Owen bought from the Rappites[6]), is the best known, there were numerous others of varying sizes in the United States and the British Isles. They invariably failed but attracted thousands of eager experimenters, enchanted by the thought of helping to found what Owen called a New Moral World, to be marked by the spirit of community rather than selfishness.

The Owenite communities, like the later Fourierist ones, seemed, alas, to prove the validity of the liberal-utilitarian claim that people are moved only by their self-interest. The Owenites adopted a simple form of Ricardian socialism in which they attempted to devise a medium of exchange based on labor power to escape capitalistic exploitation of the worker. This proved unworkable. Owenite communities tried to abolish the family, seen as a bastion of private property and egoism, in favor of some form of communal living arrangements—a feature which, along with the religious unorthodoxy, shocked and alienated the neighboring populace. The communities were ill-managed, since Owen could not be everywhere and few of his disciples possessed his organizing genius. They attracted a gorgeous miscellany of unscreened free spirits, cranks, idealists, misfits, and parasites. Often in America the abler members caught the spirit of frontier individualism and went off to become proprietors for themselves. An endless number of such reasons might be given for the almost invariable collapse of these enterprises. Owen was not discouraged; later, in the 1830s, he threw himself into the Grand National Trade Union cause, which also collapsed after a spectacular beginning. Owen never tried to found

[6]The early historian of socialism, J. H. Noyes, called the Shakers and Rappites "the real pioneers of modern socialism." These were religious communitarian sects, the former being an offshoot of Quakerism, while Father Rapp stemmed from the German Pietistic tradition (cf. the earlier Moravians and Mennonites). Essentially this was just a version of Christian monasticism.

a political party, regarding himself as a missionary and educator. In its day the Owenite movement made a tremendous stir. "In the peak years 1839-1841," writes J. F. C. Harrison, author of the best book on Owenism, "two and a half-million tracts were distributed; 1,450 lectures delivered in a year, Sunday lectures attended by up to 50,000 weekly." More than one hundred Owenite journals existed at various times. In the 1820s, when evangelical religion was popular, Owenism took on the qualities of a sectarian religion; later, there were Owenite Halls of Science.

After all this stir, the Owenite movement died away upon the death of its remarkable founder in 1857, leaving little behind except a memory. (The cooperative movement, largely fathered by the Owenites, is an exception.) The same was true of other British socialist tentatives of this period, associated with the so-called Chartist movement among the working classes. They seemed to lack adequate intellectual foundations. Was it the incurable individualism of the English that caused the failure of socialism there?

A Frenchman, Sismondi, in 1819, attacked *laissez-faire* economics, urging that the state intervene to regulate the use of property for the well-being of the community. Political economy based itself on an assumption of human selfishness and took human nature as it is. Adam Smith had posited the "economic man," seeking his own advantage, and made this self-seeking individual the key to his system; so did Ricardo, perhaps even more. That everyone wishes to obtain additional wealth, as efficiently as possible, Senior made his starting point. It should be noted that the supremacy of individual desires was a keystone of the whole structure of liberal economics. Suppose the state directs its citizens to produce something they are not producing. The view of the classical economists was that this must mean a diversion from what is desired to what is not, and this was a sufficient refutation in their eyes. Some romantic economists protested that the nation might wish to elevate itself by choosing a standard of production other than just what people want; it might wish, for example, to create more musical instruments and fewer evening clothes for the wealthy. This cannot be refuted by the classical economists, except that they would simply dismiss it as "uneconomic," that is, going beyond their system. They would add that a directed economy must burden itself with an expensive bureaucratic system, whereas the undirected one is largely self-running. But in large measure they identified efficiency with meeting the desires of individuals.

It was this individualist and egoist principle that critics of liberal economics, including Sismondi and, in Germany, Fichte, resented and assailed. Their moving impulse was an ethical desire to create something nobler than a selfish scramble, a "mere congeries of possessors and pursuers," as Lord Keynes once called it; or, again, a rational impulse to *plan* rather than leave matters to a chaos of contending individual wills. The difficulty was that this led to highly authoritarian structures in which an intellectual elite planned for and governed the entire community.

France gave birth to most of the doctrines of socialism. When, in 1842, young Friedrich Engels, a German then living in industrial England, became interested in socialism, an interest he was soon to communicate to his friend Karl Marx, he began to study the French social thinkers and identified no fewer than eight important ones. Another friend of young Marx, Moses Hess (much later an important pioneer of Zionism), wrote a book in 1840 suggesting that France, Germany, and Great Britain, the three major European countries, ought to combine forces in a social movement. The British had the most practical experience of modern industrialism, the Germans were philosophically gifted, but it was the French who had gone in for actual economic and political schemes. To Engels' big eight, it would in fact be possible to add some other "utopian" socialists, as Marx was later to call them (not entirely in derision). Marx was drawn to Paris in 1843 to meet as many of these French social thinkers as he could, in the hope that he would carry out Hess's idea (which did not succeed). Among them were disciples of Saint-Simon and of Fourier, as well as more recent prophets such as Etienne Cabet, Louis Blanc, and Pierre Proudhon.

Claude Henri de Rouvroy, Comte de Saint-Simon (1760–1825), was a French aristocrat who traced his ancestry back to Charlemagne. He fought in the American Revolution and was wounded at Yorktown. During the French Revolution he made a fortune in financial speculations, narrowly escaped the guillotine, and then, like Owen, poured all his fortune into his schemes for a new moral and social world, dying in dire poverty. Between 1802 and 1825 he exuded a stream of writings and journals and left behind a cult.

Saint-Simon did not suggest equality, but rather a hierarchy. He looked upon society as one great workshop whose efficient organization was the main task of modern times. Science could surely answer this need, Saint-Simon thought, and he proposed an elite of social engineers planning and running society on scientific principles. He added, later, the need for a new public religion, a "new (rationalized) Christianity," also presided over by a priestly elite. One can see why this nobleman appeals to the present Communists of the Soviet Union, who grant him a place with Marx and Lenin among the makers of modern communism. On the other hand, Saint-Simon did not usually suggest class war or the dominance of the "proletariat." The new elite should be drawn from the industrialists and engineers. "Technocracy," a later scheme which enjoyed a brief vogue in the 1920s and 1930s, expressed more nearly what was in Saint-Simon's mind than did Marxism. Perhaps, indeed, this is the way the world is going, whether in the West or in the Communist world today.

Rather like Jeremy Bentham in England, Saint-Simon was an eccentric who succeeded in planting an idea that percolated down through the nineteenth century in his native France. The Emperor Louis Napoleon (1851 to 1870) was one of his influential disciples, even writing a book on *The Extinction of Poverty.* Certain aspects of his thought were carried on by August Comte (Chapter 3). Saint-Simonianism was not necessarily "radical," as noted; its "captains of industry" might be industrialists, and Saint-Simon was quite willing to accept even the Bourbon monarchy if this regime would back his plan. Like the Physiocrats of the preceding century, Saint-Simon preferred enlightened despotism to democracy. He announced a new epoch marked by industrialism and the power of scientific and technological knowledge, and he called for a new aristocracy to replace the defunct orders of church and nobility. He stressed increased productivity to satisfy material wants, agreeing with Bentham that the social goal is "happiness," which he defined largely as the satisfaction of physical wants. All this could be as attractive to a business person as to a proletarian, perhaps, though the element of state compulsion might be repellent. As a matter of fact, Saint-Simon inspired most notably a number of public-spirited administrators who wanted to impose a rational plan on the disorderly economy. One of the leading disciples, Pierre Enfantin, was later prominently associated with the building of the Suez Canal; a passion for huge enterprises of this sort marked the Saint-Simonians. The French down to the present have shown less enthusiasm for the free, unregulated economy and society than have the English. It is possible to see at work here the urge toward order and lucidity of the French mind, always influenced by classicism and rationalism. It might be added in regard to Saint-Simon that he was not a nationalist, but advocated and predicted a European society and economy.

Saint-Simon and Thomas Carlyle, who owed much to him, reiterated their message that Europe had entered the industrial age, the "mechanical age," a new epoch calling for wholly new methods of government and thought; they called attention to the fact that the "social question" (Carlyle) was the burning issue of modern times and would not be solved by *laissez-faire* negativism. They did not have any exact blueprint for this new order but were sure that the "captains of industry" would have to assert leadership rather than content themselves with profits; they were sure that society needed a plan ("That Chaos should sit empire in it, that is the Worst," Carlyle exclaimed). These ideas, vigorously expressed, exerted an incalculable influence in Europe. It is impossible to imagine Marx and the other later socialists without this background.

Charles Fourier, who filled enormous books with his plans, thought in terms of social harmony, cooperation, "association." Like the economists, he presumes a preordained harmony and a perfect plan for society, only unlike them, he does not believe in the separateness of the individual atoms but thinks they must be placed in association according to an exact formula. Everybody has a precise niche in Fourier's carefully constructed plans. Science, speaking through Fourier, has determined the organization of the community down to the last detail. The ideal community must contain between sixteen hundred and eighteen hundred people, with a certain proportion of each occupation and age group and psychological types; they are to be housed in certain types of buildings; they rise at specified hours. There are communal dining halls; no one is to be left, or let, alone. It is rather monastic (Fourier was religious) and rather depressing. It had the attraction of being a precise plan, where others had been vague. It suggested the perhaps enduringly important idea of a balanced society. And Fourier promised the elimination of all vice, crime, unhappiness. The state will become unnecessary. Fourier, writing between about 1803 and 1832, was indeed one of the Socialist pioneers. He declared that his scheme was completely voluntary. He hoped, by setting up model communities, to demonstrate the superiority of his cooperative system to the competitive anarchy of the Economists, against whom he launched violent diatribes. He wished to make labor enjoyable instead of unpleasant. Many experimental communities did indeed come into being, inspired by the pages of the *Treatise on Association;* most of them were not very successful, as we might guess.

In his attitude toward sexual morality and the family, Fourier was far bolder than any other early socialist, a fact responsible for much recent interest in him. A bachelor himself, Fourier identified the monogamous family as the root institution of bourgeois selfishness, and in his utopia there would be instant divorce, total promiscuity, complete sexual "emancipation" in which couplings would take place in all sorts of combinations; man was not meant for one woman alone, or even several, the "harmonian man" clearly believed. Some have seen an anticipation of Freud in his "passional attractions" or of Wilhelm Reich in his connection between sexual and economic oppression.

We can smile at Fourier, but we may be surprised at the number of people who took him seriously enough to try out his scheme. Harriet Martineau, the liberal Englishwoman who may be supposed to have had no special love for socialists (Coleridge regarded her as an incorrigible social atomist), wrote that the principle of cooperation "will now never rest till it has been made a matter of experiment." It was. Numbers of the sturdy individualists of New England founded Brook Farm on Fourierist lines, with predictable results. The fad for socialist communities, to which Robert Owen and his son had contributed, took on fresh life under Fourier's influence. Indeed, Fourierist ideas spread all over the world. The Russian scholar Zilberfarb, a leading Fourier expert, finds traces in eastern Europe, Scandinavia, Latin America, China, as well as other European countries; in Russia, between 1845 and 1849, Petreshevsky spread the ideas of "Sharlia Fure" by connecting them with the Russian peasant village, the *mir*. Perhaps, via eastern Europe, the present Israeli *kibbutz* owes something to Fourier. Though it was (and still is) common to laugh at Fourier's dreams, this retired clerk, who fed his cats and waited each day for the millionaire who would finance his schemes to save the world, was an interesting and important figure. More than Owen or Saint-Simon, Fourier was a keen psychologist who tried to base his social system on an examination of human nature. He did not, like the Owenites, wish to abolish private property, because he thought it too deep a human instinct to eradicate. The trick is to harness this force and make it serve the public interest. The proper collaboration of interests, as well as passions, leads to a happy community. A gentle and nonrevolutionary socialist, hating strife, seeking concord, bucolic and joyful, Fourier's utopia was perhaps not a thing of this world.

Etienne Cabet, author of the 1839 utopian romance *Voyage to Icaria,* was a "communist" in the sense of vesting total ownership and absolute power in the community—a veritable police state, suppressing all freedom of thought, in the name of an ideal society where economic efficiency was joined to perfect social harmony. The "Icarians" joined the Owenites and the Fourierists in establishing social communities in the New World (Illinois, Iowa, Texas), one of which survived until 1898 though, in general, the utopian ideal was not realized in practice. It was Cabet who popularized the term "communism" as a more total and thorough form of socialism, and from whom chiefly Marx and Engels learned this term. It should be repeated that these "utopians" were nonviolent and nonrevolutionary; they hoped to spread socialism or communism by the force of the ideas and the power of example in the voluntary experimental communities. There *was* an insurrectionary tradition, violent and rather mindless, the tradition of the barricades stemming from the French Revolution, carried on by such as Blanqui in the 1830s; it was a different one. Marx and Engels drew them together.

Thus there were various kinds of socialism. Agreeing in their desire for some sort of social control over private property and individual rights, the socialists differed in the degree of control they would exercise, in its manner, and in its institutionalization. In the thought of Saint-Simon, Fourier, and Cabet, socialism is sometimes vague and often foolish, but it was an exciting beginning.

Modern socialism and communism have lain so heavily under the influence of Karl Marx that his predecessors in this field sometimes are forgotten. One book on Marxism does not even mention Saint-Simon, Fourier, and their numerous offshoots; it says that Marx is the "heir of Jan Hus, Thomas Moore [*sic*], Thomas Paine, and Jean-Jacques Rousseau." Doubtless he was, but in a much more meaningful sense he was the heir of the numerous socialists who had filled the press of Europe with their schemes and debates all through the years when Marx and Engels were growing up. Marx had more theoretical and philosophical talent than most of them; he syncretized a great many of their systems, marrying revolutionary Babeuvist communism to Saint-Simonian and Owenite conceptions in a Hegelian ceremony. But he really created few, if any, of the various ideas he strung together so ingeniously. To a large extent this creativity belonged to the half-mad Saint-Simon and the eccentric Fourier, along with their whole generation of (mostly French) messiahs of "social science."

More of them appeared than there is space for: The names of Jones and Harney in Great Britain, of Rodbertus and Weitling in Germany (before Marx), and of the numerous disciples and offspring of Saint-Simon and Fourier in France are among them. Victor Considerant carried on Fourier's work. A remarkable group of Saint-Simonian "apostles" formed a community in Paris where they attempted to live the famous formula of "to each according to his need, from each according to his ability" before dispersing to carry the message into the world. Here was a veritable chaos of socialistic ideas. Socialism before Marx reminds one of Protestantism before Calvin—in danger of perishing from its very profusion and popularity, in need of discipline and unity to save it. Karl Marx would have recourse to the resources of German philosophy in this task, so that it is logical at this point to turn to the thought of the last and perhaps greatest of the German classical philosophers flourishing during these years.

HEGEL

French political and social thought, British economic theory, and German philosophy were the three outstanding areas of new ideas in the period from 1815 to 1830, it was frequently said. In 1831, G. W. F. Hegel, Kant's successor as the leading

German philosopher and much more a system builder than the essentially critical Kant, died. Hegelianism so triumphed in academic circles that by the end of the century, even in Great Britain and the United States (where there was a certain resistance to this kind of thought), the leading philosophers were largely of this school, while in very unacademic circles it also spread widely, especially through the theories of Karl Marx and other socialists who owed much to Hegel.

Hegel's was a vast, labyrinthine, and, according to some, impenetrable system which despite its difficulties exercised this enormous influence. It may be well to ask what message, stripped of all the technicalities, ordinary cultivated men got from Hegel. One of them, the Russian socialist Belinsky who wrote that when he read Hegel he was overcome with emotion and the world took on a new meaning, got the message from Hegel's famous formula, "What is real is reasonable and what is reasonable real." This meant that all of history is the unfolding of reality itself, the idea or mind of the universe; what happens in history is in effect the writing of a book of which God is the ultimate author, but in which humans participate. For those who believed Hegel, history and human affairs no longer were chaotic, jumbled, or meaningless; every great event had its place in an unfolding plot which, when the book was finished, would be seen to have no loose ends, nothing put in without purpose. As Belinsky wrote, "For me there was no longer anything arbitrary or accidental in the course of history."

Undoubtedly Hegel's approach to human history *was* a revelation. He did not invent it; to go no farther back, an interest in history as rational process was taken up by Herder, a pupil of Kant. He wrote an essay on the "Idea for a Universal History from the Cosmopolitan Point of View" in 1784, on which Kant commented, following which Fichte, Schelling, and others made it a leading topic in German philosophical circles. The famous formula of thesis-antithesis-synthesis, the dialectic of history, which Marx took from Hegel, was evidently first suggested by Fichte, not Hegel. (Nor did Hegel consider it the only kind of process.) The original impulse to the new historicism probably came from Vico, writing in the earlier eighteenth century (*The New Science,* 1725, 1744); but that Neapolitan philosopher was not in step with his times. Voltaire was much more typical of the Enlightenment in seeing the past as without any continuity or regular path of development; a record largely of "crimes, follies, and misfortunes" illuminated by occasional and rather inexplicable epochs of reason, most of it without any interest to the philosophical mind. (What point is there in studying the superstitious Middle Ages or the ghastly wars of religion?) Yet at the end of the eighteenth century one of the great paths of discovery for the European mind was that of continuous secular progress, and others besides Hegel saw it. Saint-Simon incorporated into his socialism, before Hegel and Marx, the notion that history has a will of its own: "The supreme law of progress of the human spirit carries along and dominates everything; men are but its instruments." He was at pains to correct those eighteenth-century philosophers who saw only darkness in the medieval period; not only had it played its necessary part in its own day, but from its womb came the next age: "If historians had analyzed and examined the Middle Ages more deeply . . . they would have recorded the gradual preparation of all the great events which developed later and would not have presented the explosions of the 16th and following centuries as sudden and unforeseen." From Rousseau had come what F. C. Lea has called "the romantic myth": progression from alienation to reunion, through civilization to a higher perfection at the end of historic time, when a perfect art, fully realized personality, and an ideal society would exist. Such popular elements of historicism lay about in every direction when Hegel applied his philosophical skills to the task of shaping from them a huge intellectual synthesis.

German philosophy had been searching for the underlying ideal unity of things. Hegel would show that this was a process working itself out in time. Behind the apparently fortuitous jumble of events, the philosopher-historian can discern a great process at work which is nothing else than thought, the Idea, working itself out in reality.

To identify the German philosopher only with his philosophy of history would be incorrect. The self-unfolding of the eternal Idea includes nature as well as humanity. A formidable polymath, Hegel knew a great deal about the sciences and lectured on them as well as on the law, the state, politics, religion. His famous *Phenomenology of the Spirit* is a kind of psychology, seeking to link inner consciousness with the outer pattern of historical evolution while showing how a motive force implicit in the interaction of internal and external leads onward and upward, in an endless dialectic of change. "All the great philosophical ideas had their origin in Hegel," a twentieth-century existentialist, Merleau-Ponty, enthusiastically exclaimed.

In reaction against Kant's critical philosophy, which had seemed to leave the world of thought in pieces, Hegel aspired to a magnificent, if often cloudy, totalism that saw the universe as one great whole. The Absolute (philosophical equivalent of God) is a single totality of all that is; it shows itself in and through the finite human mind developing through history. The Absolute is seeking to complete itself via the evolution of this mind or Spirit (*Geist*). In one of Hegel's formulations the Absolute has three parts: pure idea, the Absolute-in-itself, which Logic studies; Nature, the Absolute-for-itself, studied by philosophy of nature (the empirical sciences are all right in their place and necessary, but not enough, we must grasp their meaning through philosophy); and Spirit, the Absolute-in-and-for-itself. One of Hegel's great, and controversial, inventions was a new *dialectical* Logic, a logic of the concrete, that goes beyond the static, formalistic logic of scientific reason.

Yet the development of human affairs was by far the most important element in Hegel's thought. The self-realization of the Spirit, as it grows to full consciousness, takes place in and through human history; we are the instruments this divine Spirit has chosen with which to realize its cosmic purposes. Those purposes were to realize fully the potentialities of mind, to bring the Spirit to full self-consciousness, to perfect what Hegel called freedom.

Marxists, while recognizing Marx's great debt to Hegel, later charged Hegel with being too "idealistic" in locating the source of change not in material circumstances but in pure intellectual development. "History is mind clothing itself with the form of events." In 1845 and 1846 Marx ridiculed Hegel for preposterously endowing metaphysical categories with physical or human existence. Marx thought Hegel had found the right *method* but had the subject of the process wrong, seeing it as abstract idea or consciousness rather than as real flesh-and-blood people; he had "enveloped it in mysticism." Humans, Marx held, are active creatures realizing themselves in work rather than thought, engendering thought as they work; one must begin with this sentient creature, not with a ghostly spirit. But it is questionable whether this diatribe that occurred as Marx left his native land and denounced "the German Ideology" is an accurate interpretation of Hegel. For Hegel, too—admittedly difficult to understand—seems to see the process as a struggle between Spirit and matter, the former objectifying itself and then trying to recapture its alienation, a process in which humanity at least helps God or the Absolute Spirit achieve its ends. The distance between the two German giants may be less than some have thought. They simply chose to stress different sides of the dialectic. Recent attempts to Hegelianize orthodox Marxism have sought to rescue the latter from a sterile materialistic determinism by introducing more freedom and voluntarism. It is sometimes said that Engels, if not Marx, first construed Hegel as teaching a deterministic idealism and then "stood Hegel on his head" in an equally deterministic materialism, thus repeating the error, which passed into popular Marxism; whereas the true spirit of both Hegel and Marx is a genuine dialectic between idea and matter.[7]

In any case, Hegel's exciting vision of human progress stimulated great interest in history. Later historians, more positivistic by temperament and disillusioned with Hegel's overly rational history, have disparaged him, but all historians probably owe their basic professional debt to Hegel. It was in Germany that the great historical profession of the nineteenth century began, with such contemporaries of Hegel as Leopold von Ranke and B. G. Niebuhr developing the "scientific" historical method (use of archival source materials, careful criticism of the documents). We cannot seriously become interested in history so long as it has only an antiquarian or storytelling value, however amusing it may be; to be elevated to the dignity of a leading professional study, history must be thought of as revealing significant truths about humanity and the universe. Bonald and Maistre saw in it the training school of politics; Hegel saw much more: nothing less than God's Will immanent in the world, the unrolling of a great purpose.

Hegel should be defended against certain criticisms of his history that are frequently encountered. He did not say that all events are logical or that the pattern of history can be determined without reference to the events. The actions of history are the outward expression of thoughts, and these thoughts form a logical, necessary chain of reasoning. We should study the actions, the empirical events, but we should not stop there; we should "think them through" to discover their inner logic. This still seems a sound enough method, whatever mistakes Hegel made in his actual historical reconstructions. The mind of the historian, it is clear, must supply *some* sort of structure for the facts, which by themselves are without meaning. Hegel

---

[7]Lenin once remarked that "intelligent idealism is closer to intelligent materialism than is unintelligent materialism."

seemingly felt that there was a single objective pattern into which all would fit, a faith few historians find relevant to their tasks today.

The three main phases of history, according to Hegel, have been the Asiatic, characterized by absolute monarchy; followed by the classical Graeco-Roman, marked by individual freedom; and finally by the Germanic-European, which fused the two earlier civilizations in a synthesis of freedom in the context of the strong state. Hegel's disciple F. C. Baur applied the dialectic to New Testament studies by finding the thesis in Jewish nationalism, antithesis in Pauline universalism, and synthesis in the mature Church which emerged in the second century. An eagerness to make the facts fit this framework led Baur into some serious mistakes. One may judge from him both how stimulating and how dangerous the Hegelian formula might be.

It is interesting and typical that Hegel defined his historical epochs in political terms. To Comte, the key lay in modes of thought, while Marx found it in the technological-economic sphere. Hegel's preoccupation with the political probably reflected the urgency of that problem in the Germany of his day, disunited and seeking to find its political unity. Hegel has been accused of an excessive nationalism, especially German nationalism, but in his time this was considered liberal and progressive. The key institution of the present age, Hegel felt with some justification, is the nation-state. He bequeathed to most German historians, and indeed to most nineteenth-century historians in all countries, a belief that the proper subject matter of history is politics; "history is past politics," in the definition of E. A. Freeman, the British master. While there was a subsequent rebellion against the narrowness of this definition, it might be defended on the grounds that the political order has usually given the distinctive stamp of epochs and peoples, from the oriental depotisms of earliest times through the Greek city-states, the Roman Empire, feudalism, and down to the age of the territorial state. If tomorrow should bring a world-state or even a federated Europe, this development would surely be so striking and significant that an epoch would be named for it. The "primacy of politics" is often a sound position.

In any case Hegel does not suggest that the process of change has come to an end. Process and organism are Hegelian keynotes. As opposed to the static formulations of Enlightenment thought, he has everything in motion, to be grasped only when its growth and development is understood; no one better reveals the nineteenth century's genetic, evolutionary outlook or contributed more to implanting it. And, though somewhat obscurely, Hegel believed that the universe was not like a machine but like an organism, a view closer to both the older and the newer conceptions than to eighteenth-century mechanism. His logical methodology was based on the organic approach: Nothing can be understood except by reference to the whole of which it is a part. With specific reference to the Kantian categories, Hegel held them to be bound together in a unity; not isolated and separate, but aspects of a single entity, the mind, which itself is a part of all the rest of reality. (That is why the real is rational and the rational real: Our minds and the universe are parts of a single whole, and hence obey the same laws.) We are almost back where we were before Descartes taught men to dissect, to break things down into simple components for purpose of analysis. Hegel was the philosopher of process and of organism.

All this may seem rather difficult. Many found Hegel hopelessly difficult. But the spirit of his philosophy, when one gets hold of it, hangs together and communicates a special vision, an excitingly new one in its day. We asked what some of its implications were and may resume that discussion. Belinsky, our Russian friend, drew from Hegelianism some highly conservative inferences: It seems to teach that whatever is is right, like all systems declaring the universe to be perfectly rational. With particular reference to history, it apparently requires the belief that whatever has happened is for the best: in the Lisbon earthquake controversy, Hegel would assuredly have been on the side of Rousseau and the church against Voltaire's pessimistic protest. He has been accused of teaching that might makes right, and there is a certain truth in this, for "the hour strikes once for every nation" and whoever has the power at a particular moment of history is presumably in the right. Some nations are "world-historical" ones destined to contribute more than others to the pattern of history. And everything, including war, is a necessary part of the pattern. Hegel at times declared that individuals are the unconscious tools of the world-force; they have no wills of their own.

Yet this view of the past greatly encouraged historical research by inculcating a deep respect for each epoch of the past, which made its unique contribution and is therefore worth studying for its own sake. One did not demand that it conform to current prejudices and thus commit the sin of an excessive "present-mindedness," distorting the past by forcing it into a mold of recent construction. One studied each era of the past as if, in Leopold von Ranke's words, it was "equidistant from eternity"—just as much a part of God's plans as our own age. German historians like Ranke, who led a great nineteenth-century renaissance of historical studies, were not Hegelian metaphysicians, but they did broadly share this outlook which saw order and purpose in the events of history and hoped to lay bare the whole mighty plan by their industrious researches.

Politically, Hegel might best be described as a conservative liberal. An ardent Bonapartist in his day, Hegel's chief political work was a product of the reaction (*Philosophy of Right,* 1821). He believed in constitutional government but preferred monarchy to democracy and opposed individualism. He shared some of the presuppositions of the upper bourgeoisie who greatly mistrusted the mob, though in a certain sense they were liberal. Certainly Hegel claimed to believe in progress through orderly government—progress toward freedom. But his version of freedom was the so-called positive one. Freedom, that is, was not to him the negative practice of just letting people alone. The proper definition of freedom is realization of possibilities, Hegel believed. This may be made clearer by the example of the child, whom we compel to go to school, though if given his will, the child would doubtless prefer the freedom of play. We are preparing this child to be truly free by expanding the possibilities of growth. (Rousseau's "forced to be free" will be recalled.) Ignorance is slavery; the savage who is "free" is really far less free than the modern individual who is bound by the rules of a state. No creature is absolutely free, but free only to realize its natural possibilities. A bird is free to fly, but not to swim. We, as creatures of reason, realize our freedom by developing our rational potential, and to do this requires making many sacrifices of our liberty of action. We must live in an organized state, obey its laws, and serve the interests of the community.

Hegel's stress on the state as the highest unit led on to social-welfare protests against extreme individualism (see particularly T. H. Green in England). When Hegel glorifies the state, we should understand that he uses the term in a rather special way. In his system it is the dialectical synthesis of family and civil society, or, in his jargon, the union of universal and particular in the "concrete universal." In more commonplace terminology, this means that the state (as an ideal) is the highest development of the community, the place where a perfect society would find its completest expression. Hegel, in brief, does not conceive of the state as a leviathan standing over against its subjects, ordering them about, and intimidating them; it is more like Rousseau's General Will—the common rational spirit of the whole community—made manifest. This view appealed to moderate liberals because it claimed not to sacrifice the individual completely to the state; nor was it socialistic. According to Hegel, it is only as a citizen that the individual becomes wholly free and possessed of rights. This feeling for association against individualism, though with a conservative cast, made Hegel a significant founder of the more moderate movements of social reform. And if Hegel was a conservative, his disciples do not show it. While some went to the Right and some to the moderate center, the "young Hegelians," including Karl Marx and Ludwig Feuerbach, became materialists and atheists. Belinsky, too, was a socialist or anarchist.

Hegel shared with the socialists, including his sometime disciple Karl Marx, the belief that modern bourgeois economic life is unsatisfactory because it is anarchic; the mere economic realm of competing private interests defeats human solidarity. This realm of "civil society" Hegel did not, however, wish to abolish, but to supplement. As an antidote to selfish individualism, Hegel offered the state, which—properly instructed, of course, by Hegelian philosophers—he thought could provide a real national community. One of Marx's leading criticisms of Hegel, about the first in fact that occurred to him, was a refutation of this view that the state can stand above private interests to represent all of us and temper the imperfections of a society made up only of individual interests. Marx argued that the state can only reflect the economic interests of civil society; hence, at the present time, under private capitalism, it represents only the interests of the dominant economic class and cannot serve that higher purpose Hegel claimed for it. You cannot combine a bourgeois economy with a true social state, Marx declared. Hegel thought you could.

Hegel was apparently a Christian, but Kierkegaard, the Danish pastor who is now considered the chief founder of modern Christian existentialism, accused him of devitalizing Christianity by rationalizing it and making it abstract. There is some truth in this. Hegel's new version of scholasticism made reason and religion coincide, but the highest synthesis is philosophy; Christianity is the symbolic or mythical mode of expression presumably meant for minds incapable of philosophy. Christianity is done the honor of having its representations agree with Hegel's philosophy, though in a slightly inferior manner. If many Christians had their faith confirmed by finding that it agreed with the most advanced philosophy, others like Kierkegaard resented the relegation. One could easily, with Feuerbach and Marx, forget about religion and take the philosophy alone. Hegel was closer to the atheism of Marx than he may have realized. One finds, for example, that in Italy, Hegelianism was adopted by the anticlericals and laicists. The state represents the highest ethical ideal and is above the church, they held. The Roman Catholic Church, when in 1864 it produced its great Syllabus of Errors or list of modern heresies, included Hegelianism as a form of anticlerical liberalism. Actually, Hegel excluded religion from the historic sphere, regarding progress as social and political, not religious; in sharply separating private religion from public, political matters, he was in a traditional Lutheran scheme.

Hegelianism exerted so strong an appeal in good part because it was a complete system, an organic whole, an exceptionally unified, "total" philosophy. It was the first of several such in the nineteenth century—Comte's was another, then Marx's and Spencer's. Of these at least one, Karl Marx's, owed its basic traits to Hegel. It was an evolutionary system, thus incorporating the nineteenth century's most characteristic point of view. By comparison with Kant, the evolutionary or historical element stands out; Kant had failed to see, Hegel thought, that reason is not static.

Hegel's remarkable system of rational metaphysics based on historicism and dialectical evolution was hard to overlook; some have hated it, regarding it more as the scandal than the glory of the century, but like Marxism, its lineal descendant, it demanded attention and commanded allegiance because of the boldness of its stance as a complete reconstruction of human knowledge.

At the end of the century there was a decided reaction against the rigorous monism of Hegel's system. William James thought it a stuffy house with not enough air in it. In our time the "historicism" of Hegel, insofar as it meant a closed and deterministic system, has been assailed.[8] The enormous influence of Hegel is evident as much in his opponents as in his disciples. In protesting against Hegel, two giants of unorthodoxy in his time created movements of future significance: Schopenhauer and Kierkegaard, both of whom reacted against Hegel's cosmic rationalism and optimism to produce ideas of the irrational (Schopenhauer's "Will," a blind striving cosmic force) and of completely undetermined freedom (Kierkegaard's individual existent person). Today Kierkegaard's "existential" religion is more popular than Hegel's rationalized religion. But Hegel's vision of an organic rather than a mechanistic universe was prophetic, and his stress on process, evolution, and development

[8] Karl Popper, in the important but argumentative book *The Open Society and Its Enemies,* Vol. 2, 4th ed. (1962)—the work of a modern philosophical analyst with a bias toward liberalism—attributes practically all the sins of the modern world to Hegel's baleful influence (pp. 25-80). L. T. Hobhouse blamed the First World War on him!

has been basic to the modern mind. His influence can hardly be overestimated. Moreover, there has recently been a significant revival of interest in Hegel, chiefly on the Left.

Another novel and attractive implication of the many-sided Hegelian structure may be mentioned. In effect, very nearly, God is humanity, according to this philosophy—not the individual person, but humanity collectively in its historical evolution. The historic process is "the march of God through the world." The world spirit grows and develops through human history. From this, one may derive a new explanation of the riddle of the human situation, with its lofty aspirations and its frustrations. Each of us possesses something of this universal humanity, whose nature is nothing less than potential perfection, the self-realization of the world. But each of us also is a particular person, bound to one time and place, destined to make only a tiny contribution to the splendid temple of reason that will someday be finished. Hence our soaring aspirations and our limited achievements. We can nevertheless do what our talents permit us to do in the confident knowledge that it does fit somewhere into the great plan. Nineteenth-century optimists who believed in progress found that Hegelianism fitted comfortably into their scheme of things.

Hegel inspired or reinforced a large amount of nineteenth-century nationalism of the messianic sort; perhaps a less appetizing outgrowth than some of the others—we can see what Hobhouse meant when he accused Hegel of encouraging war. As an example, Count August Cieszkowski (1814-1894), Polish nationalist and Hegel disciple, used the Germans (Herder as well as Hegel) to support his vision of a great Slavic state that would adorn the next and perhaps last stage in the evolution of mankind. Hegel's influence in Russia and other parts of eastern Europe was strong for a generation—about 1835 to 1860—and contributed somewhat to the great nationalist myth known as Pan-Slavism. Historicist messianism throve on a simplified version of Hegel, who taught that history has a goal toward which all is tending; and nationalism did too, since the philosopher had seen "historic peoples" and their states as the vehicles of historical destiny. This sort of Hegelian historicism is obviously deeply laid within the popular modern mind. In this study of a twentieth-century American politician, Henry A. Wallace, Dwight MacDonald noted the theme of an "American hour" in world history, prepared for by all previous happenings. God has brought forth the United States in due time to do His bidding in the cosmic drama of historic humanity. Each nation might, gratifyingly, find the god of history on its side.

To a generation confused by many new ideas and by drastic political and social change, Hegel offered an apparently satisfying unity that found a place for everything and discerned the order behind the baffling facade of events. Faced with the question of whether liberals, conservatives, or socialists were right, the Hegelian could answer, all are—each in its place and time, each a part of the final synthesis. Confronted by revolutions and counterrevolutions, wars and political turmoil, the Hegelian could hold that all these occurrences are part of a necessary pattern. Hegel also found a place for both reason and Christianity, which many had seen as locked in mortal conflict: just different ways of stating the same truth. Hegel's synthesis, which seemed to harmonize all things, was almost as impressive as that which Thomas Aquinas had offered at the peak of medieval civilization in the thirteenth century. It proved equally fragile. Some found it distressingly abstract, a mere house of words. Others converted it to materialism and atheism by discovering that there was no need to posit Hegel's spirit underlying the natural world. Still others used the idea of historical destiny to justify all kinds of revolutionary and nationalistic causes.

Hegel influenced practically all schools of thought in Germany, as well as British idealist philosophers of the later nineteenth century such as F. H. Bradley and Bernard Bosanquet who were dominant in the British universities for some time, the Italian philosophers Benedetto Croce and Giovanni Gentile, and many others. Socialists made use of him, historians knelt at his shrine, both the religious and the antireligious seized on pertinent aspects of his thought for their purposes. He lent authority to conservatives and radicals, reformers and foes to reform. His ability to be all things to all people is perhaps an indictment of Hegel as well as tribute to him.

Karl Marx in his youth belonged to a group known as the Young Hegelians, who were all left-wing exponents of a modified Hegelianism. Among these, Bruno Bauer and David Strauss showed a decided interest in Biblical and religious studies— Strauss's critical biography of Jesus being one of the century's most sensational books—while Ludwig Feuerbach treated the theme of religions in a more general way. All the Young Hegelians believed that Hegel's thought represented the most advanced creation of the human mind thus far. But they thought it needed restatement, a very sweeping sort of restatement, in a sense really the abandonment of Hegelianism. For Hegel had been wrong in his idealism. He should be turned over, "set right side up." Reality is actually material, and ideas are only a projection of physical being. The idea of God had been invented as a symbol for human ideals and goals; as such it served a useful purpose, but may now, at a higher stage of self-awareness, be abandoned.

Feuerbach was far from a great philosopher, but this somewhat vulgar materialism, atheism, and (in the specifically modern sense) humanism was extremely significant. August Comte was, even then, pointing out that the nineteenth century had witnessed the birth of the Positive Age, replacing the ages of theology and then metaphysics. The new God was materialistic science, the only goals practical, mundane ones. The Absolute as well as God would have to be relegated to the realm of fairy tales. Hegel himself pointed out that science was relegating art as well as religion to the sidelines in the modern age. Marx was the most celebrated of those who did so, after Feuerbach.

In his early manuscripts, which remained unpublished until recently, Marx does incessant and rather obscure battle with Hegel's *Phenomenology.* Marx remained strongly under the influence of Hegelian concepts even as he struggled to go beyond the master. Hegel, it should be noticed, instilled in his followers a desire to surpass him just because they were his disciples. Had not Hegel taught that the dialectic goes on, and each age has its own statement to make? Hegel had made the ultimate statement for his generation; the next generation must say something else, something beyond this. The Hegelians of the years after the master's death in 1831 tended to think that he had brought pure philosophy, speculative thought, as far as it could go. What remained? To translate this thought into action, to change the world and not just understand it. The age of metaphysics had ended with Hegel, the age of humanism had begun.

The element of political ideology, then, in the seemingly metaphysical system of Hegel, becomes evident. The great object of knowledge is history, and especially political history; at the end, by a slight alteration in Hegel, we decide with Feuerbach that "politics must become our religion." The sole aim and interest of humanity is to discover and create the good society on earth, with the aid of scientific intelligence.

SOCIAL ROMANTICISM AND THE REVOLUTION OF 1848

The ideas of Fourier, Saint-Simon, and Owen, formulated during the 1820s, enjoyed considerable popularity in the 1830s and 1840s and were joined by others. The disciples of Saint-Simon tended to split up, but the movement nevertheless went on. As their 1830 manifesto stated, they rejected the equal division of property and accepted the "natural *in*equality of man," thus favoring a hierarchical society; but "each is placed according to his abilities and rewarded according to his works" by planning and coordination, property being held by the state and not individuals. (The one-time secretary of Saint-Simon, August Comte, who will be dealt with separately, probably cannot be classed as a socialist, though the influence of Saint-Simon remained on his thought in the form of a stress on authority and the subordination of individuals to the state.)

The most popular French political tract of the 1830s was probably the *Paroles d'un croyant* by La Mennais, or as he now called himself (the change is significant of a democratic shift) Lamennais. We may recall him as an enthusiastic disciple of the "reactionaries" a decade earlier. He now became an equally enthusiastic social democrat. The change is not so great as we might imagine, for most French socialists acknowledged some debt to Maistre and Bonald. The "words of a believer" came from one who was a Catholic priest but was not long to be, for the Church would not tolerate his left-wing views. His romantic eloquence made him the individual of the hour, and enthusiastic followers proclaimed Lamennais the new messiah, while Metternich, the statesman in charge of keeping down revolutionary discontent in Europe, grumbled about "this anarchist ... fool ... abject being." No work had more to do with the revolution of 1848. In this and ensuing books, the Breton priest expressed a lyrical, if vague, awareness of a "tremendous revolution going on at the heart of human society," a revolution that was the march of "the peoples" and would produce a "new world." He denounced "wage slavery" and castigated the rulers of society for neglecting their responsibilities to society. "If you reject peaceful reform you will have reform by violence." The obvious British counterpart to Lamennais is Thomas Carlyle, whose electrifying prose called attention to the "social question" in an enduring classic, *Past and Present* (1843).

Lamennais and Carlyle represented a blending of romanticism with social reform in what has been called "social romanticism" or "political Messianism." The late romantic writers, Victor Hugo, Lamartine, and George Sand, were caught up in it. As David O. Evans observes in his little book on *Social Romanticism in France 1830-1848*, "*Les Misérables* was the culmination of a massive literature of social novels and dramas which flourished between 1830 and 1848," including those of Sand and Balzac, from which Friedrich Engels said he had learned more than from all historical and economical treatises put together. The ground was thus prepared for that remarkable revolution of 1848 of which the leaders were a poet, Lamartine, and a social theorist, Blanc. As one might expect from romantic poets and novelists, the spirit was rather more emotional than logical. The mood was messianic or apocalyptic; the "people" were on the march, tyrants trembled on their thrones or in their counting houses. A splendid new world would dawn after brave deeds by popular heroes and heroines had overthrown them. The French Revolution, heretofore unpopular, was rehabilitated by historians like Michelet and Quinet, not to speak of Louis Blanc. Had there not been something splendid, if terribly splendid, about that volcanic upsurge of the people? They had announced their arrival with an explosion that signaled the great revolution of modern times, the democratic revolution.

Lamartine and Hugo were not really socialists, as 1848 was to make clear. Under the impact of that event, a split developed between the republicans or democrats and the working-class socialists which helped doom the revolution. Prior to 1848 these two strains mingled in a chorus of slogans about social justice, popular rights, and the march of the masses. The young romantics made a cause out of Victor Hugo's defiance of formal literary conventions in his 1830 play *Hernani*, defending it against the taunts of traditionalists in a famous theatrical riot of that year. Romantic bourgeois youth was soon firing at broader targets. "Bohemians" with long hair and bizarre clothing created a surrogate society in the 1830s, featuring hard drugs, little magazines, spitting on the flag, unconventional morals, and much cursing of the bourgeoisie from which they sprang (nothing much has changed in a century and a half). In 1835, following an insurrection among the artisans in the silk industry of Lyon, the French government held a "monster trial" of 164 radicals, mostly young, and convicted 121 of them. A land weary of revolutionary bloodshed gave them little sympathy at that time, but the ferment continued.

In England there was something similar, if more restrained, befitting the national temper. There was nothing restrained about the Scotsman Carlyle or such working-class speakers as the Irishman Feargus O'Connor. The novels of Dickens and Mrs. Gaskell contain their share of social protest. The Chartist movement was a more impressive organization of the actual working-class people than anything in France. But Britain already had its liberal reforms and a national Parliament with deep roots in the national tradition. The great debate of the 1840s turned on the relatively concrete issue of free trade versus protection. During this struggle to repeal the tariffs on grains, Richard Cobden and John Bright organized the Anti-Corn Law League and carried political debate down to the grassroots level. Great Britain avoided revolution in 1848 and proceeded toward social democracy at a more moderate pace.

Democracy might now be observed in relatively successful operation in the United States of America. In the mid-1830s Alexis de Tocqueville returned from his visit there to write *Democracy in America,* one of the political classics of the century. Countless others went to America and wrote travel books, but Tocqueville's was a uniquely philosophical mind. He wrote against the background of a considerable discussion of democracy in France at this time. And he brought to the task the new ideas of a social-scientific methodology as proposed by Bonald, Saint-Simon, and Comte. Consequently, *Democracy in America* is a good deal more than a travel book; it is a work of systematic sociology. Highly praised at the time, it has retained a considerable repute ever since. It is a truly objective work, not a partisan one: Tocqueville was amused to find that some thought that he had written against democracy and others that he had written for it. A liberal noble, Tocqueville reminds us a great deal of Montesquieu; he had learned from Burke, too, as well as many others. The integrity, moderation, and wisdom of a book that nevertheless sparkles with ideas has earned high standing in the literature of politics and society.

The question in which Tocqueville was really interested was whether this new thing, democracy, which his historical sense told him was inevitably on the way, could be reconciled with liberty and with traditional European civilization. Was it a triumph of barbarism from within, a revolt of the blind masses certain to destroy culture? Would it lead to a new despotism? These things had been said. The social scientist in Tocqueville wished to test them by a method more fruitful than mere theorizing. So he went to the United States and observed.

Social scientist that he was, Tocqueville was not free from ideological influences. As a moderate, a liberal, he wished, he said, both to "allay the terrors" of the reactionaries and "calm the ardor" of the radicals. Perhaps Tocqueville found in America what he wanted to find—as it has been alleged. The charge is only partly true. He did find a mixture of good and bad. For example, Tocqueville allayed the fears that democracy meant wild instability, dictatorship, destruction of property, and irreligion. Here in the democratic United States, property was safe, religion flourished, and there was no fear of violent revolution. Give power to the people and they will become responsible, Tocqueville implied; democracy has its own safety valves. On the other hand, he found science and literature mediocre in the United States and the uncommon individual intimidated by the mass, and he feared that this was a law of democracies; he was among the first to complain about democratic conformism and the "tyranny of the majority." To some of his contemporaries in Europe he apparently taught that democratic society destroys liberty. But in the main his temperate and sympathetic appraisal helped the republican cause in France. Tocqueville himself, though by no means an egalitarian, served in the short-lived Second Republic born of the revolution in 1848 and never learned to love the despot who ended its life, Louis Napoleon. Liberty was Tocqueville's passion. He loved England, as Montesquieu had, and John Stuart Mill was one of his friends; thus he seems close to British liberalism.

His moderate note was unusual in France in the 1830s and 1840s. Among the new socialist voices of the 1840s was Pierre-Joseph Proudhon, himself a man of the people, whose chief message was to abolish unearned increment and unproductive property: "What is the producer? Nothing. What should he be? Everything." An enemy of statism, Proudhon suggested "mutualism" or farmers' and workers' co-operatives as the answer to economic injustice; he was an ancestor of the anarchist-syndicalists, and perhaps also of the populists and Henry George agrarians. Marx later ridiculed Proudhon for the crudeness of his thought, but he influenced Marx, being in the 1840s and 1850s the best known of the radical socialist theoreticians. Proudhon had no faith in democratic processes as such; "social reform will never come out of political reform, political reform must emerge from social reform." "Universal suffrage is the materialism of the Republic." But Proudhon seldom stayed long in one position; he seemed "determined that none should share his views." Marx was right about the shoddiness of much of Proudhon's thought. But he possessed a style, an aptitude for phrase-making, along with a burning sense of social injustice.

Paris was discontented and bored with the prosaic "bourgeois monarchy" of Louis-Philippe, which had come into existence in 1830. Though liberal enough to permit free speech and encourage education, its constitution denied representation to all but a few and its social philosophy was largely *laissez-faire* liberalism—its motto, "enrich yourself." The dominant class was the *grande bourgeoisie.* In the cafés of Paris, lesser men listened to Proudhon's call to revolution. When the revolution came he disagreed with it; "they have made a revolution without ideas," he declared. He laughed at the panacea of the influential socialist Louis Blanc: state-owned factories. To Proudhon the root of the matter was demand, not production. Leave the working class without adequate purchasing power and the state factories would stagnate quite as much as privately owned ones would for want of a market. Proudhon's was the classical statement of the underconsumption theory of economic depression.

Proudhon's *What Is Property?* (1841) had been preceded by Louis Blanc's *The Organization of Labor* (1840). At this time Etienne Cabet's *Voyage to Icaria* appeared, with its message of utopian communism. Blanc, an indefatigable writer, produced a stream of works in these years, including a laudatory history of the French Revolution and a *History of Ten Years,* in which he cataloged the sins of the capitalistic Orleanist regime. Blanc stood for a blend of Jacobin democracy and socialism that perhaps lacked logical consistency but was proclaimed with great eloquence; it rejected Saint-Simonian authoritarianism in favor of a more democratic political order, yet was socialist in its attacks on private property in the means of production. Blanc did not, like Blanqui, call for violent revolution. He evidently believed that the people would freely vote for socialism if given a chance. The results of the elections of 1848 severely disillusioned him, and he appears then to have discovered for the first time that France was a country of peasants and not of Parisian left-wing journalists. At that time he retreated somewhat from democracy.

Later, however (he lived well into the Third Republic), he continued to support a moderate, democratic, and "gradualist" socialism against Marxists and Anarchists.

Among other rebels and prophets who led the way to 1848, there was the Italian Giuseppe Mazzini, a passionate Genoese who as a youth joined the *Carbonari* and vowed his life to the cause of national liberation for Italy under a popular government. He spent most of his life as an exile in London but returned during the revolutions of 1848 to take part in those tumultuous events, presiding over the short-lived Roman Republic of 1848 to 1849. His prolific and eloquent pen gained him a place as one of the chief writers of this time and a great leader of the Italian *risorgimento,* which in 1860 and 1861 became the most exciting movement in Europe. If the gallant soldier of liberty, Garibaldi, was the most popular figure of the Italian national political revival, Mazzini was its spiritual leader. Belonging as it does to the generation of "social romanticism," the eloquence that so bedazzled his contemporaries may seem bombastic and hollow today, though on the whole it wears better than most of that sort. Mazzini, with Louis Blanc, belonged among the democratic socialists. Hostile to liberalism because it was too negative and selfish, he affirmed the value of both democracy and "association." He was equally against class war and individualism; all people should be brothers and sisters, there should be solidarity, and there should be religion, a religion of humanity. Mazzini quickly quarreled with Marx and Bakunin in the First International; he was too radical for Italian liberals, who fought him for control of the *risorgimento,* but too conservative for the left-wing proletarian rebels. Like Blanc, he called himself a republican and obviously derived from Rousseau and the French Revolutionary tradition; he was an Italian Jacobin. (Northern Italy had been as eager for the French Revolution as France; Mazzini's father had lived under the Ligurian Republic.) But his stress on national liberation and a social-democratic *mystique* put him in the center of nineteenth-century ideology.

Nationalism mingled freely with socialism and democracy in the mixture of progressive or revolutionary ideas that preceded 1848. To liberate oppressed peoples crying for their freedom (supposedly) from foreign rule went along with liberating oppressed classes, seen as much the same thing. A generation of enthusiastic liberationists did not much distinguish between victims; they all came together in that magnificent abstraction "the people." This included the emancipation of women, for, considering Mary Wollstonecraft, George Sand, and others—the Saint-Simonians placed considerable stress on feminism[9]—there was a significant group of women "libbers" in the 1840s. But the cause of national liberation, especially for the Italians and Poles, each groaning under the rule of a foreign tyrant,[10] was

---

[9] The Disciples, after Saint-Simon's death, lived in a commune near Paris in 1831-32 where they formed a religion that included the expectation of a woman messiah to come from the East—or perhaps from the marriage of Prosper Enfantin, leader of the disciples, and George Sand. This never materialized.

[10] The Poles, partitioned among Prussia, Austria, and Russia between 1773 and 1795, were partly restored to independence by Napoleon but were given back to their tormentors in the 1815 Vienna settlement following Napoleon's defeat. Between 1815 and 1830, an autonomous Poland under the Russian tsar existed, but following an unsuccessful revolt in 1830, this Congress Poland was fully absorbed into Russia.

especially prominent as a revolutionary force. The first highly organized, totally dedicated, elitist revolutionary party may well have been Young Italy in the 1830s.

Lamennais, Blanc, Proudhon, and Mazzini supplied a good part of the fuel for the engine of revolution that roared down the track, only to crash in 1848. Broadly speaking, they formed a family of social protest with generous ideals, but they failed to agree, and their thought was often vague. These limitations must probably be held responsible in good part for the failures of 1848. Nevertheless the ferment of social thought in this generation must be recognized as a powerful force in modern Europe. It produced most of the ideas, in embryo, on which social reformers of all sorts have been living ever since.

But the experience of 1848, a year that began with democratic revolutions all over Europe and ended with the confusion and discomfiture of these revolutions, caused a temporary reaction against all forms of "social romanticism." In general, the sad failure of the revolutions of 1848 was like a large bucket of very cold water poured on the slogan-intoxicated men who had begun them so hopefully. All over continental Europe the sobering up was much in evidence; people felt that there had been too many daydreams and vague formulas, too little precise thinking. The reaction was toward realistic means and limited objectives. Like all reactions, it went far in the opposite direction. The feeling spread that power alone counts, and practical methods of politics are alone significant. It was a German (evidently Ludwig von Rochau) who coined the word *Realpolitik*, but the same idea could be found from one end of Europe to the other. Thus 1848 was almost a repetition of 1789 in that the ideals and ideas that inspired it turned out to be too vague and were held to have caused more harm than good because of this flaw: zeal without knowledge. The counterparts of Rousseau and Voltaire were Proudhon and Mazzini; although with more of romantic fire, they had as little of concrete social engineering. If Bonald and Maistre had suggested a more realistic approach, it was swept aside because they were conservatives; if Saint-Simon demanded science, he had in reality supplied only ideology. Evidently much yet remained to do before that ideal human society could become more than a vision or dream. Again there was a reaction away from utopias.

Not until the 1880s did the socialist movement really revive; only in the 1860s did it show any spark of renewed life. "Social romanticism" and indeed romanticism of all sorts went out of fashion among men and women of letters. The success of the Italian national liberation movement in 1861 might seem to be an exception to this, but in actuality this miracle was the work of realists and moderates, not of Garibaldi and Mazzini. During the French Second Empire, when another Bonaparte arose on the grave of the Republic, the reigning intellectual system was the austerely scientific credo of positivism.

But it is also true that bourgeois liberalism of the "classical" type became less harshly dogmatic. It too had had its heyday between 1830 and 1848; the uncompromising features of the *grande bourgeoisie*'s political and social outlook had contributed not a little to that outburst of resentment, the revolutions of 1848. After 1848 the suffrage was less restricted, despite the apparent failure of that revolution. Even Napoleon III was careful to have his mandate affirmed and reaffirmed from time to time by universal suffrage, which has never ceased to exist in France, whatever the regime, since its installation in 1848. Napoleon ran something of a welfare state; the realistic conservative Bismarck installed sweeping welfare measures in Germany. *Realpolitik* turned away from romantic visions of utopia, but it also turned away in some measure from pure competitive capitalism, equally visionary.

Whatever the final verdict, this generation from 1815 to 1848 must be granted primacy in the modern Western world, perhaps repaying close study more than any other one by those who wish to understand present-day problems, dreams, and outlooks. These ideologies—liberal, socialist, nationalist, conservative—are still the basic value structures for most people in Europe and its offshoots.

chapter 3

Classical Ideologies of the Mid-Nineteenth Century

Mill, Comte, Darwin

Nothing exists in nature, is born, grows, multiplies except by struggle. It is necessary to eat and be eaten for the world to survive.

Emile Zola

THE MID-VICTORIAN ERA

After revolution and romanticism receded in 1849, Europe entered upon a period which could well be described as the classical age of the nineteenth century. It was the mid-Victorian era, with all the phrase conveys: middle-class domination, comfortable bourgeois virtues, industrialism and free trade, political stability with an undercurrent of working-class distress. Victoria, the personification of the bourgeois virtues, reigned only in Great Britain, but Great Britain led the way into the Industrial Age, and in other places, notably Germany and the Low Countries, "Victorian" phenomena could be observed.

In Great Britain at midcentury, the classical school of economics reigned, its free enterprise injunctions only slightly modified by the post-Ricardian economists; by 1846 it had converted most statesmen. Along with it flourished the popular ideology of self-help, making perennial best sellers of such books as Samuel Smiles's *Lives of the Engineers,* the stories of poor boys who made their way to wealth and glory: Faraday was a blacksmith's son, Stephenson a collier's, Telford a shepherd's. George Orwell, the modern essayist and novelist, remarked that his father had read only two books in his life, the Bible and Smiles's *Self-Help*—probably a typical Victorian intellectual history. The powerful London *Economist* assumed dogmatically and without any question that the sum of private interests "is always the same as the public interest." Free trade conquered in the struggle concerning repeal of the Corn Laws (grain tariffs) in the 1840s. While the factory laws removed the worst abuses of child and female labor, the country having been stirred by parliamentary investigations into this cruel scandal, there still remained no protection for adult male workers against the law of the market in wages; the trades unions had barely begun their long march to respectability and power in 1850. (They did not receive legal recognition until 1870 and were not a strong factor before the 1880s.) With government as well as wages cheap in this incredible paradise of private enterprise by modern standards (no taxes, no labor unions!), industry and invention flourished, the nation seemed to grow rich, and British power, influence, and prestige were never greater. Victoria came to excel even Queen Bess as a long-lived symbol of greatness.

This was the heyday of the middle classes, whose peculiar ethos permeated the era. Recently arrived through hard work and frugality, the middle classes radiated respectability. This was the "age of improvement," as historian Asa Briggs has named it. Some have spoken of a "mid-Victorian combination of Puritanism and Enlightenment." French morals were frowned upon (witness the reaction to Swinburne), as were those practiced by English romantics and lords in the Regency era just prior to Victoria's accession. Such magisterial organs as the *Edinburgh Review* dispensed the dogmas of "free trade and tight morals," high intellectual seriousness, and a robust common sense, along with a deplorable lack of taste and imagination in the arts. Indeed, the arts were often declared to be a waste of time. The middle class doubtless shared some traits all over Europe, but Puritanism and individualism were not so prominent elsewhere. In Vienna, on the banks of the beautiful blue Danube, the bourgeoisie at this time built a culture marked by music, gaiety, and charm. Nor could the French bourgeoisie ever have displayed that egregious prudery found among the British middle classes, who (so we are told) segregated the male and female authors on library shelves.

The most potent influence in Victorian life came from what was called the Evangelical movement, arising within the Church of England early in the century and gathering strength through succeeding decades. Christian evangelicalism always stresses complete commitment and practical changes in conduct after the conversion experience. Initially, British Evangelicalism was a reaction against the merely nominal Christianity of the lax eighteenth-century Church and accompanied the Romantic movement, a sort of bourgeois equivalent of the poetic and philosophical revolution (a reaction, too, against the godless French Revolution). Theologically simple, stressing will rather than elaborate doctrine, the Evangelicals were austerely moral and full of the work ethic. Their enemies, in the end numerous and vociferous, accused them of narrow-mindedness and philistinism, which was undoubtedly correct; but their achievements were impressive, especially in the area of personal behavior. A founding father of Anglican Evangelicalism, William Wilberforce, upon his retirement from the House of Commons after forty-five years recalled that body's transformation over the years from an assemblage of drunken and brawling rakes to the sober legislative chamber it had become. This discipline and energy of a dominant minority transformed England into an industrial society, with all its great strengths as well as its weaknesses. Evangelical zeal for reform manifested itself in the antislavery movement, in the overseas missionary cause (very strongly), and to a degree in efforts to protect workers from gross abuse; but the Evangelicals did not challenge the existing social order, counseling workers instead to accept subordination, eschew revolt, and pull themselves up by hard work. With their amazing energy and seriousness, dedication to reform in some ways but not others, their narrowness and fanaticism (destined to drive many a Victorian youth to revolt), the Evangelicals are a riddle; but of their influence there is no doubt. The queen herself was of their number. Evangelical Christianity came close to being the ideology of the strongest element among the reigning bourgeoisie.

Victorian prudery must not be misunderstood as an anemic rejection of the sexual impulse. As Walter E. Houghton points out, "The major reason why sex was so frightening to the Victorians was the glaring fact that . . . sexual license in England not only existed on a large scale but seemed to be increasing." The romantic cult of free love (Shelley, Byron) survived, and French socialism and bohemianism threatened from across the channel. The Obscene Publications Bill of 1857 reacted to a large popular literature of pornography. The Victorians knew that sex was a potent force—in need of restraining rather than encouraging, Matthew Arnold observed. There was still a savage underworld of "dangerous classes" in Paris as well as London, respectable citizens thought, which it was best not to stir up. Dickens's Mr. Podsnap, whose standard in the publishable was whether it could bring a blush to the innocent cheeks of a "young person," might secretly sneak off to the company of one of London's scandalously numerous prostitutes. What later critics denounced as hypocrisy, the Victorians thought only common sense. The whole treatment of women, against which much of the twentieth century would rebel, later seemed the ultimate in hypocrisy; it was, in fact, as George Bernard Shaw noted, based on idealism:

> That sort of feeling that you must have something to adore, something to lift you up, gave them the curious notion that if they took the women and denied that they were human beings . . . if they set up a morality and a convention that women were angels, . . . [1]

they would then have a large congregation of angels to adore. And so if Shaw, as he relates, never knew until well into young manhood that women had legs, it was because the "angel in the house" was conceived of as belonging to a higher realm of being—some women, at least. It is well to remember also that the great crusade to

---

[1] G. B. Shaw, "Woman—Man in Petticoats," *New York Times Magazine,* 19 June 1927. Regarding France, Theodore Zeldin in his *France 1848-1945,* Vol. I (1973), Part II, Chap. 13, notes the "simultaneous idealization and repression" of women.

gain equal rights for women—property rights in their own names, the vote, access to education—began in mid-Victorian times, above all with John Stuart Mill's essay on the subjection of women (1869).

The high seriousness and earnest moralism of the Victorians was a bond that stretched broadly from Samuel Smiles to Matthew Arnold, whatever other differences the merchant and the poet-intellectual had. The wish to edify and to improve, to overcome evil and to spread enlightenment, was at the bottom of it—no unworthy spirit, despite the prudery into which it might stray. For all their blind spots, the British middle classes, strong and energetic, led the way to prosperity and success and wished to build a vigorous society in their own image.

On the other side of the picture, callousness, poverty, ugliness, and degradation caused Carlyle, Ruskin, and others to protest against the very foundations of this civilization, alleging it to lie in selfishness and materialism. Hazlitt had written that "the carriage that glitters like a meteor along the streets of the metropolis often deprives the wretched inmate of the distant cottage of the chair he sits on, the table he eats on, the bed he lies on." Shelley had burned with indignation at the factories of England and the suffering they imposed on the hapless creatures who labored incredibly long hours at work that was both body- and soul-destroying. Coleridge had declared that if society disclaimed all responsibility to the poor, as the economists and liberals preached, then the poor would feel no sense of belonging and would eventually rebel in a class war. In 1844 Disraeli wrote in his celebrated novel *Sybil* that there were indeed two nations in England, the rich and the poor, utter strangers to each other.

John Ruskin claimed that the ugliness of the factory towns, and the appalling lack of artistic sensitivity in the country generally, were a part of the social order, knit deeply into the outlook of the middle classes whose ideology was a blend of puritanism and utilitarianism, both absolutely hostile to all the arts. In *Unto This Last* (1860), Ruskin voiced an eloquent protest against the economics of irresponsibility and the social creed of selfish neglect—for which he suffered ostracism.

Dickens in *Hard Times* (1854) flagellated a society that had just finished congratulating itself, upon the occasion of the great Crystal Palace Exhibition, for its infinite progressiveness. It is a world made up of Bounderbys, greedy capitalists unscrupulously pursuing success, and Gradgrinds, who, aided by utilitarianism and political economy, have reduced life to statistics and forgotten its beauty. The city has become a place of loss of identity in the lonely crowd; the factory is a scene of ugliness and inhumanity; the *bourse* and marketplace erase human connections. And this society does not even deliver its one specialty, more and more material goods, for hundreds of thousands are in want and "hard times" may throw the whole economic system into confusion.

The protest voice, thundering indignantly like Carlyle's and Ruskin's and Dickens's, exposing the structure of exploitation as did, for example, Charles Kingsley's famous tract *Cheap Clothes and Nasty,* indicated a considerable Victorian social conscience. Carlyle became unbalanced in his hatred of the liberal orthodoxy and discredited himself by some of his later pronouncements, which have a fascist ring to modern ears. (Such were the abjurations against parliamentary "talking shops" and in favor of strong, silent dictators; the contempt for democracy; the worship of heroes; the scorn for humanitarianism, seen as shabby sentimentalism. The Tory socialist became more and more the Tory.) An incomparably vivid prose stylist, Carlyle was read by the Victorians, but they discounted his views as chronically wrong-headed, just as they thought their one-time favorite art critic, Ruskin, had gone mad when he began assailing the social order.

It would be unfair to suggest that the Victorians did nothing about social problems and evils. Apart from the fact that the great revolt against the negative state and social irresponsibility began in the 1880s in good part as a result of earlier spadework, there were heroic victories much earlier in some areas. In 1858, London confronted a grave crisis of public health threatening the very existence of the city, and surmounted it by purifying the Thames River. The appalling slums gradually receded before the advance of new avenues and street improvement, but this was less spectacular than the rebuilding of Paris in the time of the Second Empire (1851 to 1870), which also saw purification of drinking water and construction of sewerage systems. One cannot accept Ruskin's indictment of Victorian architecture at face value; even London was a bit more than "a ghastly heap of fermenting brickwork," all jerry-built for quick profits by stony-hearted Bounderbys. Today people yearn to preserve and restore many beautiful and solidly built Victorian buildings, whose craftsmanship in woodwork and masonry puts others to shame.

EMINENT VICTORIAN THINKERS

John Ruskin began as a student of architecture, making himself the Victorian oracle on this subject and prophet of the Gothic Revival with *The Seven Lamps of Architecture* and *The Stones of Venice* (1849 to 1853). He believed that all great art comes from a sound society; the Gothic, he thought, stemmed from the free medieval craftsworker not yet a degraded appendage of the machine. Ruskin carried on Carlyle's fierce hatred of modern industrialism and unregulated capitalism. Shaw said that Ruskin's jeremiads made Karl Marx sound like a Sunday School teacher. He increasingly thundered at modern soullessness and destruction of beauty; "we manufacture everything but men." In his later years he tried to create medieval orders dedicated to social service. With a prose that had the power to move people, he stimulated and influenced an incredible number of successors: William Morris and British socialism, Tolstoy, Proust, Gandhi, Frank Lloyd Wright. The historian of the Manchester School (W. D. Grampp) credits Ruskin with doing more than any one else to discredit and destroy the old *laissez-faire* creed. A little mad in his old age, he launched his diatribes like an Old Testament prophet and was increasingly ignored, but he seared the souls of a dedicated few. His stature today is recognized and his reputation as a great Victorian secure. Few have so influenced certain aspects of the modern mind.

Another eminent Victorian critic of society, Matthew Arnold, was a poet and critic who also branched off to political and social thought. Hardly a popular writer, he tremendously affected literate England, and no one better carried on the grand traditions of European culture in an era of bourgeois philistinism. He preached no panacea, but like John Stuart Mill aimed at a "certain temper of mind"—a civilized mind, broad, intelligent, critical, refined. Civilization, he reminded his progress-enchanted Victorian readers, does not consist of material things and mere numbers; it is a development of intellect and taste. In *Culture and Anarchy* (1867), Arnold rejected anarchy in cultural matters and asked for use of the state to promote the arts and letters. Like the French esthetes by whom he was much influenced, Arnold looked largely to literature for salvation: "The best poetry will be found to have a power of forming, sustaining, and delighting us, as nothing else can." The barbarians and philistines of industrial Britain might, he sometimes thought, be converted to sweetness and light. Though savagely critical of their taste and manners, Arnold admired the energy and curiosity of the middle classes and did not entirely despair of their conversion. Arnold essentially upheld an ideal of high culture—the best of the great Western tradition from Homer to Baudelaire—as best he could in a time of cultural decay, as he saw it. No one felt more keenly the decadence of the modern, with its "sick hurry and divided aims," or longed more for some kind of healing faith to cure the disease of modern skepticism. He also besieged the parochialism of the English from his position as connoisseur of world literature, aware of the value of the modern European greats (German as well as French—Goethe and Heine were among his favorites) as well as of the ancient classics.

If Matthew Arnold, perhaps the most civilized of all the Victorians, was a critic of the narrowness of the bourgeoisie, the "philistinism" of the middle classes as well as the crudities of the landed gentry, the fact is that almost all the greater Victorian writers were critics of their society. The charge of complacency will not stick against Tennyson and Browning, the great Victorian poets, though they have been accused of it.

The most celebrated and symbolic thinker of mid-Victorian England was John Stuart Mill. His early career may be familiar to many from his well-known *Autobiography*. Brought up in the strictest Benthamite discipline, he rebelled and turned to Wordsworth and Coleridge for relief. His searching essays on Bentham and Coleridge reveal the patient catholicity of his fine mind, looking for the value in each figure while peeling off the dross. He became interested in Comte, finding in his discipline and social sense a corrective to British individualism, though there was much in that Frenchman he could not stomach. Indeed Mill, who lies buried with his wife at Avignon, always owed much to the French, something to be remembered when one sees comments on his "typically British" philosophy. He read the novels of Dickens; he formed a firm friendship with Carlyle for a time. Tocqueville's great work on democracy attracted him; Kant and Hegel mostly repelled him, being too metaphysical for Mill's essentially positivist mind. In the long run the mark of Bentham prevailed: Mill was essentially the rationalist and liberal. But his thought has been summed up as a series of compromises, and no nineteenth-century thinker read more widely and sympathetically than did Mill.

What compromises did Mill suggest? Empiricist and positivist in his philosophy, he refused to say with the Kantians (as he construed them) that the laws of thought are merely mental categories; he held them to exist objectively, and he prepared a systematic treatise of inductive logic. A classic defender of the liberty of the individual, he showed some sympathy to French socialism up to a point; fearing the element of compulsion that lurks in every socialist scheme, he approved voluntary cooperation. In his famous textbook on the *Principles of Political Economy* (1871), his foundation was individualistic capitalism, yet he was prepared to entertain exceptions to the rule wherever a sound case could be made—and the exceptions, it has been noted, grew with every edition of the *Principles,* so that Mill has been claimed as an ancestor of English socialism (Fabian). Skeptic in religion, near the end of his life he felt the bankruptcy of "scientism" and edged cautiously toward belief in a finite God; at any rate he recognized the human need for religious experience. He had always been willing to temper the narrower individualism of the Benthamites with some of Coleridge's feeling for the community. Doubting sometimes about democracy because of his love for liberty, he believed the strongest argument for it to be that it is a process of education; Mill always remained the optimist, feeling perhaps that all were potentially as rational as himself. British empiricism was deeply engrained in him, and a part of that tradition was an openness, including Locke's doctrine of a malleable human nature (Mill believed this strongly) and Hume's dislike of dogmas. He remained resolutely open-minded all his life, and thus has seemed the classic "liberal."

His strongest hatreds were of censorship, intolerance, conformity—anything that interfered with individual liberty. His best known work, the essay *On Liberty* (1859), to which his wife, Harriet, contributed much, is the classic argument for the maximum of individual liberty. "The only purpose for which power can be rightfully exercised over any member of a civilized community against his will is to prevent harm to others. His own good, either physical or moral, is not a sufficient warrant. He cannot rightfully be compelled to do or forbear . . . because in the opinion of others to do so would be wise or even right." (Mill stressed that this was in a *civilized* community; "barbarians" would do best with an enlightened despot.) The goal and purpose of civilization, the only end worth striving for, was to Mill the complete development of the individual's powers to the highest possible point; he quoted Humboldt and remarked that "few persons, out of Germany" comprehend this, suggesting a Kantian or romantic source of his doctrine of freedom.

The argument of *On Liberty* then majestically unfolds for liberty of thought and discussion. The doctrine we suppress may be true, unless we assert infallibility for received opinion; or, if not true, it may contain *some* truth; or, even if it contains little or no truth, dissent is necessary to prevent intellectual stagnation; if we do not have to defend our creed, we will forget why we hold it.[2] Mill next makes it clear that under certain circumstances speech cannot be free, as when it is "a posi-

---

[2] Mill's fellow Victorian, the great Roman Catholic John Henry Newman, adjusted his religion to liberalism by arguing, similarly, that heresy is necessary to faith. Unless error forces us to clear thinking, we do not perfectly know our creed.

tive instigation to some mischievous act." Justice Oliver Wendell Holmes later observed that there can be no freedom to cry "fire!" in a crowded theater, and this is about what Mill meant. One always wonders when reading Mill how far agreement could ever be reached on the exact or even approximate boundaries of the limits he mentions. Holmes used the foregoing principle to ban free speech in wartime by those who allegedly did not support the war, a ruling that others thought to be an outrageous violation of civil liberties. But Mill seemed to think that these boundaries can be made clear.

He believed at any rate that the liberty necessary to human dignity and growth was all too lacking in the modern world. He stressed the danger from the "tyranny of the majority," which had replaced regal despotism as a threat to liberty. "That so few now dare to be eccentric marks the chief danger of the time." Everything was becoming standardized, from shoes to ideas, and Mill complained, as so many have done since, of the mass culture that was stamping conformity and mediocrity on everyone. Reverting to his effort to defend the individual, Mill sought to meet the objection against his own criteria that, after all, everything we do *does* concern others. After reading this extraordinary essay, one is likely to feel that while Mill has presented an incomparable discussion of the issues and made an eloquent appeal for the free individual, he has not resolved the ancient dilemma of liberty versus authority, the individual against society. He has expressed a preference for the individual; but anyone who prefers to stress society's claims can easily turn most of Mill's formal arguments against him. (One such Victorian answer to Mill was written by James Fitzjames Stephen, *Liberty, Equality, Fraternity.*) But this tract with its magisterial style and high seriousness remains one of the great Victorian period pieces.

Mill's social-economic views, while also fundamentally "liberal," were not complacent. He questioned in a well-known passage whether all the machinery thus far invented had yet lightened the toil of a single person and said that "the restraints of communism would be freedom in comparison with the present condition of a majority of the human race." In *Principles* he defined property as what one has "produced by one's own exertions" (or received by legitimate gifts from one who did so earn it.) But he held that the worker in the factory is not entitled to the whole of his or her produce, because machinery and materials are also involved. He often expressed sympathy for the ideals of socialism while doubting that it could work without compulsion in the present state of human nature. As noted, he was willing to make exceptions to the rule of economic individualism, and the list of these steadily increased.

But as the classic mid-Victorian liberal, Mill fought for such causes as votes for women, admission of Jews as members of Parliament, freedom of the press, and freedom for the orators on soapboxes in Hyde Park, which he once saved by a filibuster when he sat as an independent member of Parliament. Written in 1861, *On the Subjection of Women* thus is rightly situated in that decade that in so many ways marked the crucial turn toward "modernization." It belongs to the same year as the emancipation of the Russian serfs, the beginning of the American Civil War, and Garibaldi's march to Italian unification. Emancipation was one of the great processes involved in modernization; a liberation the results of which were sometimes less exhilarating than expected. The essay was not published until 1869, following unsuccessful, indeed forlorn, efforts to include women in the voting reform of 1867. Mill wrote it in collaboration with his wife, Harriet Taylor, and her daughter by a previous marriage (a marriage that caused John and Harriet to wait many years for the consummation of their relationship, until the death of her husband; divorce was still hardly a feasible alternative). "The legal subordination of one sex to the other," the Mills argued, was simply wrong. Against the almost universally accepted view that women's nature was different from men's and that this essential nature dictated different roles ("separate spheres"), Mill declared that sex differences are rooted in social usage not innate psychology and that women, having the same potential as men, should receive the same education. These were drastic views and Mill was derided for them; they were opposed by other eminent Victorians including John Ruskin. The world was readier for the emancipation of slaves or of nationalities than of women, it seemed. The movement Mr. and Mrs. Mill were instrumental in starting bore little fruit for some years. "The notion that women have minds as cultivable, and as well worth cultivating, as men's minds is still regarded by the ordinary British parent as an offensive, not to say revolutionary paradox," James Bryce observed in 1864. A typical attitude toward women may be seen in Thomas Carlyle, that great and in many ways unorthodox Victorian sage, married to a woman of strong intellect: Her role was to support and care for him, women being by nature "passive" rather than "active."

So Mill in many ways extended the meaning of "liberalism." He may be credited with almost single-handedly giving liberalism the larger meaning it has since conveyed to the minds of Anglo-Americans, of "an attitude rather than a set of dogmas" (Theodore M. Greene)—the attitude of open-mindedness, dispassionate and skeptical consideration of all views, faith in a process, a method, a climate of opinion rather than in any particular creed. Liberalism had previously meant, much more nearly, the doctrines of atmostic individualism, hedonisn, and also *laissez-faire:* the "economic man" of Adam Smith, the calculating pleasure-seeker of Jeremy Benthem. As such, it had been a somewhat narrow and barren ideology, if a potent one. Generous-minded individuals, filled with large visions of hope in human kinship, people such as Mazzini, for example, who despised what he knew as "liberalism," were repelled by it, declaring it to be selfish and materialistic. But Mill imparted to English liberalism his own catholicity and libertarianism, his steadfast faith in the free individual as something spiritually noble. "The saint of rationalism" has occasionally been seen as at heart a kind of narrow-minded fighter for his own particular set of preconceptions; but this view is unusual and the interpretation strained: Mill's typical spirit is quite the reverse. Under his influence even liberalism's deep-seated fear of the state could melt, for no dogma is sacred, only the individual is, and perhaps may be defended and strengthened by some forms of state aid.

Midcentury liberalism was represented in France, where it was weaker than in Great Britain but far from nonexistent, by Prévost-Paradol, whose *France Nouvelle* (1868) is a kind of Gallic *On Liberty*. (Both Mill and Prévost-Paradol, as a matter of fact, were influenced by Alexis de Tocqueville, perhaps the greatest liberal of them all and also French.) Prévost-Paradol regards democracy perhaps a bit more favorably than Mill, seeing in the people a check on Parliament, though he would have the popular will checked by an upper legislative chamber not popularly elected, an independent judiciary, and strong institutions of local government. This decentralization and pluralism carried echoes of the Ancien Regime in a France strongly centralized since Napoleon; antistatist and antisocialist, but libertarian and to a degree democratic (universal suffrage), Paradol's *New France* would indeed have been a new blend of ingredients in the French tradition and was not so far from what soon came into existence in the Third Republic. He wrote it in the last days of the Second Empire, when even Napoleon III was making his way toward the "liberal Empire." After his defeat in war and the subsequent shock to French pride, against all expectations a liberal-democratic republic arose from the ashes and gradually put down roots in France.

This tribute to the spirit of the age was matched by Great Britain's step in liberalizing the suffrage in 1867, after intensive debate and much lamentation from those who feared the death of liberty as well as stability at the hands of a mobocracy. These "Adullamites," as John Bright derisively christened them, led by Robert Lowe, contributed the most brilliant and enthusiastic speeches to the great debate. They had not changed from Macaulay's earlier liberal pronouncement that universal suffrage would be a new despotism "utterly incompatible with the very existence of civilization." So too in France, Benjamin Constant had believed that "unlimited popular sovereignty is an evil no matter in whose hands it is placed." The liberal statesman Thiers, a Voltairean, said that universal education would be like building a fire under a huge empty pot! But these early-century fears of the power of a still ignorant and brutalized plebs receded somewhat after mid-century. A new era of politics came in the wake of the Second Reform Bill, with new leaders and new issues. It was, for Britain, the decisive turning point of the century politically, the First Reform Bill of 1832 having not brought any marked change in the aristocratic tone and tenor of British political life. Whether the delicately balanced British political mechanism could really survive democracy, commentators as wise as Walter Bagehot honestly doubted; it was as much a gamble here as in France. But in both countries the feeling was that there could be no turning back, and for the rest of the century the task was adjustment to this potent force, mass democracy.

Many dynamic processes were at work transforming Europe and the world in this epoch. Italy and Germany attained their national unification (1860 to 1871) in the most exciting developments on the Continent. Russia freed her serfs (1861) and began slowly to advance toward a modern industrial civilization. The 1860s was a crucial decade in modern history. The American Civil War, the Russian serf emancipation, the unification of Germany and Italy as national states, the fall of the Second Empire, and the beginning of the French Third Republic joined the 1867 Reform Bill in Britain as landmarks which shaped, or recorded the shaping, of their people's future.

Between 1858 and 1870 the intellectual landmarks were Darwin's *Origin of Species,* Marx's *Capital,* Bagehot's *English Constitution,* Arnold's *Culture and Anarchy,* Ruskin's *Unto This Last, Sesame and Lillies,* and *The Crown of Wild Olives,* Mill's essays *On Liberty* and *On the Subjection of Women* together with the late edition of *Principles of Political Economy*—to name only the most famous. The "higher criticism" came to England in 1860 with the publication of the jointly authored *Essays and Reviews.* Spencer, Acton, Newman were active; Dickens wrote his splendid last novels, George Eliot had become an oracle. The list could be much extended. These were vital times.

Spiritually, Europe was far from at peace; the surge of mid-Victorian prosperity carried in its wake grimmer phenomena, such as industrialism's bleak landscapes and exploited workers, or a bourgeois vulgarization of culture. It also brought the celebrated Victorian crisis of religious faith. But the classic age of the nineteenth century produced some classic ideologies. Among the most important figures were August Comte, Karl Marx, and Herbert Spencer, as well as Mill, all of whom might be described as synthesizers of social doctrine, creators of systems of secular ideology. Charles Darwin promulgated a scientific ideology for the age of science. Socialism, liberalism, and democratic nationalism assumed the stature of popular creeds by which people lived, with traditional Christianity's hold generally declining. Romanticism received a check, or at least a dilution: Literary realism and naturalism became prominent, bearing strong social themes—one is more likely to meet novels about working people or ordinary burghers than about exquisite souls or North American savages.

The mid-Victorian age has been categorized as an age of equilibrium. Its balance was between aristocracy and democracy, country and city, the old deferential, hierarchical society and a new one based, in a great Victorian's analysis (Henry Maine), on contract rather than status. In terms of ideas, the mid-Victorians were poised between ancestral religious belief and the new secularism of science and skepticism; it was their central preoccupation. Their great novelists—Dickens, Eliot, Trollope—were absorbed in the changing human relations of an industrializing and modernizing society. Their concern was indicated in the title of Thomas Carlyle's famous *Past and Present.* They did not always wish to leave past things behind and looked with some trepidation on an uncertain present, but on the whole they were optimistic. They had yet to look upon some of the more frightening features of the new society.

Standing out among the intellectual achievements of the era were social ideologies. The works of Comte, Marx, and Darwin hold rank as the classic statements of the middle third of the nineteenth century. These are the three giants of that century's noontime.

COMTE AND POSITIVISM

Comte's first writings go back to the early 1820s, when he was working under Saint-Simon; the crux of his positive philosophy appeared in six volumes between 1830 and 1842. Partly overlooked during the romantic revolutionary excitement of the 1830s and 1840s, positivism emerged, somewhat transformed, to become the reigning intellectual orthodoxy of the Second Empire from 1851 to 1870. Through John Stuart Mill principally, Comte's influence spread into England. It is recognized now as one of the leading systematic philosophies of the century. These vast edifices of thought that tried to subsume everything in one system seem incongruous today; they were the work of amateurs who assumed omniscience. But the intellectual energy that went into them cannot be denied, and for the nineteenth century they were the nearest thing there was to a new synthesis of knowledge. Basil Willey has commented that Comte was a nineteenth-century schoolman, basing his *Summa* "not on dogmatic theology, but on dogmatic science."

He did feel acutely the need for a complete reconstruction of ideas to replace the "intellectual anarchy" that was an aftermath of the French Revolution, a feeling he shared with Maistre, Saint-Simon, Hegel. As Saint-Simon's secretary he came to feel that the socialist count was too much in a hurry. He was right in seeking to found a new science of society based on the positive facts and scientific method, wrong in leaping to his conclusion about the shape of the new society. But when Comte branched out on his own, he showed himself quite as doctrinaire as Saint-Simon. Certainly the note of authority was strong in his plan for social reconstruction. Order must be reestablished in Europe, and having found the right foundation Comte proposed to make everybody accept it, by means of a suggested authoritarian social structure of which the high priests of positivism were to be the directors. Comte was as anti-individualist as any socialist, though he preferred to keep private property and the family. He was, if anything, more so. John Stuart Mill, who was attracted to some features of positivism, pronounced Comte's social plan "the completest system of spiritual and temporal despotism which ever yet emanated from a human brain, unless possibly that of Ignatius Loyola." Its hostility to representative government and approval of the Napoleonic dictatorship gave it its standing under the Second Empire. It is also true that in their arguments seeking to justify their "peculiar institution" Southern slaveholders in the United States (George Fitzhugh, Henry Hughes) made use of Comte: the idea of an organic, stable, and authoritarian society.

Comte thought he had laid the foundations for social reorganization in his philosophy. The method appropriate to modern times is the scientific or "positive." Comte put forward his famous "three-stages" theory of human development, according to which society passes from the theological to the metaphysical to the positive stage, based on the dominant mode of thought typical of each period. His history, like Hegel's, was highly speculative; it seems impossible to fit the actual facts into this scheme. For example, anthropologists no longer accept the progression within religion as postulated by Comte, from fetishism to polytheism to monotheism. Historians would have to point out among other things that science appeared as early as the ancient Greeks and metaphysics as late as Comte's contemporary Hegel. If the Comtean formula is reduced to the statement that primitive peoples are not capable of modern thought, it becomes little more than a tautology.

In brief, the same objections to so staggeringly oversimplified a scheme may be raised against Comte's as against other examples of this sort of thing: Marx's five stages, Hegel's three political epochs, and so forth.[3] Nevertheless, these "philosophies of history," if now outmoded, were exciting at this time, and the nature of their appeal may readily be seen. This was already discussed in connection with Hegel. So discriminating a critic as John Stuart Mill thought the three stages an illuminating and reasonably accurate key to the natural evolution of civilization.

Europe was now in the positive stage and needed to reconstruct its civilization on that basis. To Comte this meant a highly organized social order. The existing stage of liberty and *laissez-faire* he regarded as the interlude of anarchy between two eras, an anarchy he proposed to bring to an end as speedily as possible. The new scientific order would not be less organic and hierarchical than the older orders dominated by priests and metaphysicians.

Positivism means the method of observed facts handled with the use of hypothesis but refraining from any conclusions about the substantive nature of reality. Comte agreed with Kant that science studies only the phenomena. In his own words, "The human spirit, recognizing the impossibility of obtaining absolute ideas, renounces the search for origins and goals of the universe and the effort to know the innermost causes of things, in order to concentrate on discovery, by experiment combined with reason and observation, of the effective laws, i.e., their unchanging relations of succession and similarity." This was not exactly new, and Ernest Renan later reproached Comte with having said, "in bad French," what all scientific minds had known for two hundred years. This was not quite fair; it had really only been known widely and clearly since Kant, and Comte undoubtedly revealed some of its practical implications. He was perhaps philosophically more astute than those Marxists and others who assumed a dogmatic materialism which Comte knew was untenable: We are not justified in saying what the essence of reality is. (Marx held a low opinion of Comte, perhaps in part because he was a rival; "this is miserable compared to Hegel," he thought. Lenin would follow Marx in discarding positivism or phenomenalism for a direct-copy theory of sense perception which seems naive but permits a full-blooded materialism. The Marxists have seemingly felt there is something wishy-washy about positivism, inappropriate to revolutionaries.) Comte felt that we are not justified, either, in atheism, only in accepting the impossibility of having certain knowledge about God. Science is descriptive only; we should not even speak of "causes," only of "observable sequences."

---

[3] In Italy the "new science" of G. Vico, dating from the eighteenth century, came into its own at this time. Vico's phases of all civilizations were the religious (theocratic), heroic (aristocratic), and humane (democratic).

In his *Course of Positive Philosophy,* Comte undertook to arrange the sciences in a logical order; his, obviously, was a mind delighting in tidiness. From the most abstract, mathematics, we proceed through astronomy, physics, chemistry, biology, and finally to the most concrete, sociology, a word of Comte's invention that has stuck in our vocabulary. Sociology, at last possible in the positive stage, steps forward to become queen and capstone of all the sciences. Of this last and greatest science Comte, of course, regarded himself as the discoverer.[4] It included what one should now call social psychology, economics, politics, history, and originally ethics. Later Comte put ethics and religion at the top, above even sociology, and gave the world the Religion of Humanity.

Comte seems hopelessly to have confused his multiple roles as social scientist, social reformer, and inventor of a new religion, though he believed he had unified them. As one of his British disciples, Frederic Harrison, observed, "Positivism is at once a scheme of Education, a form of Religion, a school of Philosophy, and a phase of Socialism." Could it be all these things at once, effectively? As a school of philosophy it has survived, though the English would be more apt to think of Hume as its founder. Sociology has survived as a discipline, but many others than Comte have contributed to it, and its scope is much narrower than Comte conceived. The Religion of Humanity for a time showed a surprising vitality. Positivist societies were formed in England and France for the worship of great people; there were Comtean churches as far afield as Brazil. (Positivism had a considerable popularity in Latin America.) This was in George Eliot's mind when she expressed her poetic wish,

> O may I join the choir invisible
> Of those immortal dead who live again
> In minds made better by their presence.

Hero-worship had a considerable Victorian vogue in wider circles than Comte's disciples; quite evidently it "inherited the functions once fulfilled by a living Church" (Walter E. Houghton)—it was a substitute for religion. From Sam Smiles to Ruskin, many a Victorian author held up to admiration, for inspiration, the lives of great individuals. But as such, the Religion of Humanity fell far short of its author's expectations. Positivism served chiefly as a rallying point for the militantly anti-religious.

In regard to positivism as "a phase of socialism," if defined as such, it never had much appeal. Comte's social utopia most closely resembled an iron dictatorship of social scientists, which is perhaps a fate to be avoided. In practice he sanctioned the ill-fated "democratic despotism" of Napoleon III. But it may be conceded that

---

[4] It is to Comte's credit that he recognized that each of the sciences has to have its own methods; you cannot "reduce" social science to biological, or biological to mathematical. Certain sociologists who seem to wish to convert social phenomena into statistics are ignoring the warning of the founder of their science—that this sort of procedure often "disguises, under an imposing verbiage, an inanity of conceptions."

Comte did something to advance the cause of socialism by his criticisms of *laissez-faire* and by his belief that the social instincts evolve with humanity. The path of development is from selfishness to altruism, he taught. A British Comtean, Professor E. S. Beesly, was a friend of Karl Marx's and chaired the first meeting of the First International in 1864.

Louis Napoleon's regime, established in 1851 on the ruins of the Second Republic, was much influenced by Saint-Simonian and Comtean ideas and undertook some interesting if inconclusive experiments in state socialism. Its economic and social policies were not failures, the collapse coming from an ill-advised foreign policy and defeat in war at the hands of Prussia. But its denial of representative government and full liberty caused its demise to be unlamented. Comte and most of his followers rejected individualism and democracy as the equivalent of anarchy.

If many of the details of Comte seem absurd, his central conception may be a valid intuition of modern humanity's problem. It is easy to agree with Comte that modern European civilization is "positivist." Is it possible to have a civilization on this basis, that is, without faith in God, without a metaphysic, with only science and technology, which supply our wants very well but give us no values, except to go on supplying more and more wants? Is modern society condemned to be "fissiparous," with no unity—soulless, with no values?

Many of Comte's successors were absorbed in just such problems. Positivism became extremely fashionable in France between 1850 and 1870. Its disciples included Emil Littré the lexicographer, Claude Bernard the psychologist, Hippolyte Taine, critic and historian, and Ernest Renan, one of the most brilliant and versatile French men of letters of the century. This group tended to reject Comte's dabblings in religion as an eccentricity and accepted only his scientific method. They distinguished themselves from atheists and materialists in the manner indicated: We cannot know ultimate things or essential qualities, only the observed phenomena. They evidently thought, however, that science does give certain knowledge, which a thoroughgoing phenomenalist (*vide* Hume) could hardly believe. They searched for a religion of science. Most of them finally became aware that science itself cannot give us values, ideals, goals. Insofar as we have these, they must come from outside science.

Renan, a passionate seeker, deeply troubled by his skepticism, looked long for a religion he could square with his scientific outlook. He rejected Christianity on the grounds of evidence (his *Life of Jesus*, his best known work, shocked the orthodox all over Europe by its critical handling of the supernatural claims), and he rejected Hegelianism as too metaphysical. He occasionally came close to doing what some disreputable young poets were about to do, make a religion of art. Like Matthew Arnold, his British contemporary and perhaps kindred spirit, Renan felt the need for religious experience and suggested an esthetic equivalent. But a "religion of science" remained his lifelong quest and he failed to find it, ending in skepticism. He came closest to finding it in a positivistic version of Hegelianism, a theme of progress running through history which gives evidence of God.

In France after 1870 positivism suffered a decline. True, there were some eccentric survivors, especially the leader of the reactionary, nationalistic *Action Française* movement of the twentieth century, Charles Maurras, and also so vigorous a literary personality as Julien Benda. But strong forces in French thought rejected "scientism" and returned to metaphysics and religion in flat defiance of the positivists. (Compare Henri Bergson, or the Catholic revival, or more recently existentialism, in literature, symbolism, and surrealism.) Intellectual France has never since felt much attraction for positivism, apparently having received a thorough immunization in the period from 1850 to 1870.

In Italy, positivism reigned as the leading philosophical school in the later part of the century, its chief systematizer being Roberto Ardigo. Comte's influence in nineteenth-century England (and the United States) was far from negligible. A British disciple was Richard Congreve, Oxford don in the 1850s, whose pupils included the leading publicist of English positivism, Frederic Harrison, as well as Beesly. But Comte's influence extended to people who were not in any sense "disciples" but whose own independent thought received definite impulses from positivism: powerful voices such as Herbert Spencer and H. G. Wells. In Germany, Comte's direct influence was not great, but there was a parallel movement in the form of "back to Kant"—the positivist or phenomenalist Kant, in reaction against the romantic and Hegelian metaphysics; one might also include the materialism of the Young Hegelians. By and large, the period from 1850 to 1880 was uniquely "positivist."[5] Anglo-Saxon philosophy since World War I has been invaded by other forms of positivism (logical positivism) which owe less to Comte than to other sources, though there are affinities. This more recent theory in intellectual history will be handled later in Chapter 7.

In the broadest sense it might be said that modern Western civilization is positivistic in that metaphysical or religious modes are not congenial to it. Everyday life is so surrounded with the technological and the scientific, so extensively "rationalized," so conditioned to mechanical models and explanations that conscious mental life runs naturally and normally in grooves that can be called "positivist," that is, scientific, rational, nonmetaphysical, averse to mysticism or any truths not immediately verifiable by experiment or demonstration. For better or worse, that is the kind of culture in which most people live. "What grows upon the world is a certain matter-of-factness," Walter Bagehot wrote. He blamed it on business as well as science. So Comte, though far from inventing this feature or being the only thinker to express it, identified himself with a basic trait of modern civilization. And his belief in a tightly organized, hierarchical society ruled by the scientists may not miss by much the modern forms of totalitarianism.

---

[5] James H. Billington in "The Intelligentsia and the Religion of Humanity," *American Historical Review,* July 1960, discusses the vogue for Comte among Russian intellectuals in the 1870s; the French positivist tended to supplant Hegel and to precede Marx as the leading influence from the West on Russian sociopolitical thought.

LITERARY REALISM

The specific post-1848 atmosphere was, of course, highly conducive to a positivist reaction against the romanticism, idealism, and sentimentality of the previous generation. All over Europe, people in all walks of life felt what Napoleon III's minister, Emile Ollivier, expressed when he said, "We have collected in our hearts enough images, sentiments, aspirations, too many. . . . We must, to make these things useful, fill ourselves with practical facts." This was the generation of Cavour and Bismarck as well as of Pasteur and Darwin: the realistic, fact-minded generation. The reaction extended into literature, which reacted strongly against romanticism by retreating to a realistic, even humdrum description of the ordinary. Romanticism had begun to fade by the 1840s and was almost fully out after 1850, despite lingering vestiges. In France the "art for art's sake" movement accused the romantics of sentimentality and sloppiness, demanded a greater sense of form and discipline, and also rejected romantic subject matter ("Deliver us from the Middle Ages!" cried Theophile Gautier, the leading spirit of this school.) *Art pour l'art* insisted upon more careful craftsmanship as well as less moralizing and philosophizing in literature. These French writers were disgusted with bourgeois society, retreated to a private world, became rebels and "bohemians," and thus began a literary attitude destined to carry on into the later period. Flaubert, the leading novelist of the 1850s and 1860s, practiced a severely objective, "scientific" approach to literature and dealt realistically with far from heroic people.

The book of the hour was *Madame Bovary* (1857), which is among other things a savage satire on romanticism. Poor Emma, a lady of some spirit and intelligence, trapped in marriage with a clod in the provinces, dreams of Prince Charmings and a grand world but is led to destruction by her inability to grasp reality. Yet Flaubert includes a hatred of this stupid society in which Mrs. Bovary, a person of potential creativity, is trapped. She is Jude the Obscure and Tönio Kroeger and all the American "rebels against the village" of a half-century and more later. Flaubert, like the poet Baudelaire, was a bitterly alienated personality. For them art was a retreat from a most unsatisfactory world, an ivory tower: "Give me the highest one possible," cried Flaubert. A fierce hatred of the existing bourgeois society accompanied an extreme disillusionment with politics, associated with visionary romantic schemes and dreams. The thing about *Bovary* that most startled and upset Flaubert's readers was its amoralism. No edifying moral was drawn; it was a sad piece of life ending in tragedy and left at that. Even Sainte-Beuve complained that "the good is too much absent; not a single character represents it," while Ruskin contrasted such "foul" fiction, utterly demoralizing, with "fair."

Something of Romanticism remained in this "realism," especially a sense, now much exaggerated, of alienation and disenchantment. Flaubert read *René* and *Werther* as books of disgust with life, read Byron for the solitude of great-souled people spurning the masses and spurned by them. This post-Romantic generation encountered fully the horrible vulgarity of the upstart bourgeoisie at the same time

John Stuart Mill in 1873, as seen by the famous *Vanity Fair* caricaturist, "Spy." (*Vanity Fair,* March, 1873.)

as Romanticism's high-flown dreams turned sour and its style became repulsive—Flaubert could not endure the "flowing style" of George Sand. The "realism" of this post-romantic generation was a strange one; it was realistic because Romanticism had been idealistic, because it wished to expose the horrors of the bourgeois world, and also because there was a certain thrill in the pose of ironic detachment. The realism of Flaubert was near kin to the dandyism of Baudelaire, blowing his cigar smoke in contempt at the dreary world he watched. It was a realism that concealed a profound estrangement from the real world. The estrangement was so great that the only way of coming to terms with that world was examining it as if it were a strange and unclassified object, making it thus intellectually problematic. And the soaring hopes of the Romantics for a better world toward which the artist could lead humanity now seemed painfully naive, something to be laughed at and satirized.

Flaubert's lean, spare, detached style, using irony, "dry," shaped with fastidious craftsmanship, could be found in the poems of Baudelaire and in the writings of other great "realists" of this era such as Flaubert's friend, the Russian emigré Turgenev. The philosopher for this disenchanted post-1848 antiromanticism was, in its gloomier moods, the brilliant misanthrope, Arthur Schopenhauer. In his younger years Schopenhauer had challenged the great Hegel but failed to win adherents; in his old age, after 1848, he became fashionable. Philosophically, Schopenhauer asserted that the universe is not Hegel's Reason but is Will, a blind amoral striving expressed in us as wanting, desire, appetite. In seeing the world as an arena of power without meaning or purpose and in seeing reason as a tool of instinct, Schopenhauer's vision came close to Darwin's, though expressed in quite different terms. He recommended art as the only antidote to an intolerable existence—other than that extinction of the will to which Oriental philosophy aspired as the ultimate wisdom. In esthetic contemplation we can achieve a degree of disinterestedness and thus escape from the tyranny of the will. An interesting and highly readable philosopher, Schopenhauer appealed to this generation both in his elegant pessimism and in his estheticism.

The French writers shocked the English; but in Britain too there was an anti-romantic reaction. The great Victorian novelists—Thackeray, Trollope, George Eliot—followed what might be called the cult of the commonplace; "the setting of tragedy moves to the abodes of the humble," observes Mario Praz, whose book on the Victorian novel is titled *The Hero in Eclipse*. A democratic art, celebrating the simple virtues of ordinary people, may be found here. The great poet Robert Browning examined humanity as it is. This Victorian literature differed as far as possible from the French in that it observed the Victorian reticence about sex and was highly edifying and morally earnest, as well as basically optimistic (though George Eliot was as aware of a crisis of faith as was Matthew Arnold). The exceptions, like the Francophile Swinburne, were scandals. But the same theme of realism may be seen in both, and it is in good part a reaction to the excesses of romanticism.

THE DARWINIAN REVOLUTION

The progress of science had continued at the end of the eighteenth century and into the nineteenth. More precise calculations on the moon, planets, and comets perfected the Newtonian system. The discovery of the planet Uranus and the satellites of Saturn owed most to the German-born English astronomer, Herschel. Having measured accurately the distance to sun and moon and arriving at a notion of the fantastic distances of the stars, astronomers by the end of the century came upon the stunning fact of the existence of other *galaxies*. Herschel and Laplace formulated hypotheses concerning the origin of the stars and planets. The latter in 1796 summed up the *System of the World,* presenting it almost rhapsodically as a triumph of scientific method and a proof of the orderliness of nature.

There was also the breakthrough in chemistry. It is interesting that Coleridge, speculating about the influence of scientific ideas on other branches of knowledge, thought that the discoveries of Scheele, Priestley, and Lavoisier, "reducing the infinite variety of chemical phenomena to the actions, reactions, and interchanges of a few elementary substances," would affect philosophy and other fields of

Darwin and Evolution: A Contemporary View. (Washington, D.C., Library of Congress.)

thought no less than Newtonianism had done in the eighteenth century. It did not quite prove so, but the influence was hardly negligible. It may be significant that Friedrich Engels, when illustrating the laws of dialectical materialism in the physical sciences, tended to use examples from chemistry.

The path of progress in electrical phenomena, from Volta and Galvani at the end of the eighteenth century to Michael Faraday's discovery of the generator in the 1830s, prepared for that mighty invasion of the life of individuals by electricity later in the century. Another landmark of the 1860s was the mathematic formulation of the laws of electromagnetism by the remarkable Scottish genius, James Clark Maxwell (1864). From the distant vantage point of the twentieth-century Einsteinian revolution, this scientific event seemed as momentous as the freeing of the Russian serfs or American slaves, the unification of Germany, or the enfranchisement of the working class; for the seeds of a total revision of Newton's presumably sacrosanct laws lay hidden here. But the practical immediate consequence was to open the way for all sorts of miracles to emerge within a few decades, not only electrical power to light cities, run trains, and power factories but radio waves, X rays, and other kinds of radiant energy.

But with all due regard for these celebrated achievements, destined to alter the lives of millions and contribute to their welfare, the most significant developments in the sciences in the nineteenth century, at least from the standpoint of thought in general, lay in the realm of biology, of life, especially its evolution. The Frenchman Pasteur has been called "the Galileo of Biology" because of his contributions to bacteriology and medicine; but in the history of ideas, by far the largest figure is Charles Darwin.

The road to Darwin's theory of biological evolution actually led through another science. The science of geology came into its own in the closing years of the eighteenth century. The Geneva geologist, de Saussure, seems to have been the first to use the term in 1779. It may be said to have attained full status in 1788 when the Scotsman, James Hutton, presented his "uniformitarian" theory. All during the eighteenth century there had been speculation about the meaning of fossils and about the earth, but it was often fanciful. The German mineralogist, A. G. Werner, proposed a hypothesis in 1780 that the earth was originally engulfed in ocean, which subsided, leaving behind the various formations, minerals, and fossils. This was the "catastrophist" or "neptunist" school, which had many followers, in part because it squared well with biblical stories. Hutton then caused a sensation by proposing to account for the phenomena by the steady operation of the same natural forces over what then seemed immensely long periods of time. This was "uniformitarianism," and it stirred the wrath of some religious critics because it could hardly be adjusted to a literal reading of the Old Testament. Between the catastrophists and the uniformitarians a lively competition ensued—which is always good for the progress of a science. One would say today that both were partly right; but concerning the matter of the time element, Hutton was right, and this revolution in time constitutes on any reckoning one of the great changes in our conception of this world. Coming between 1788 and 1830, this revolution is comparable in some ways to the seventeenth- and eighteenth-century revolution in astronomy: To the immensity of space, it has been well said, was added the immensity of time. "Oh, how great is the antiquity of the terrestrial globe," Lamarck, the French paleontologist, exclaimed. "And how little the ideas of those who attribute to the globe an existence of six thousand and a few hundred years duration from its origin to the present!"

There were those, during the period of conservative domination in England from 1794 to 1820, who attacked Hutton and his followers as dangerous subversives; so also Lamarck in France. But as data were collected, especially in the area of paleontology, rigid conservatism had to give way. The Reverend William Buckland, an Anglican clergyman, became a leading geologist and devised a sort of compromise between scriptural and geological views; he seemed to uphold the Deluge, yet the Bishop of Chichester noted his ambivalence in a witty paraphrase of Pope on Newton:

Some doubts were once expressed about the Flood:
Buckland arose, and all was clear as mud.

In the 1820s Buckland claimed to have established beyond doubt that there had been a flood about six thousand years ago, surely the biblical one. But his modified catastrophism accommodated the accumulating paleontological evidence (being collected by such masters of fossil analysis as William Smith and the French scientist Cuvier) by proposing a series of floods, perhaps four, each of which had wiped out existing life and had been followed by a fresh Divine creation. Thus God had done several times before, for lower forms of life, what according to Genesis happened some fifty-nine hundred years ago. Why the deity should have chosen to achieve His work in several stages, punctuated by dramatic catastrophes, rather than all at once was a mystery; but the catastrophists saved the biblical account at the cost of admitting a kind of creationist evolution.

Geology had become the favorite outdoor sport of the English upper class, and to it amateurs like the Reverend Buckland made contributions; but scientific activity was increasingly organized in private societies such as the Lunar Society of Birmingham and the Royal Societies of London and Edinburgh (generally outside the traditional universities of Oxford and Cambridge). And, of course, science was international, the French in particular making brilliant contributions. It remained for an Englishman, Charles Lyell, from 1830 to 1833, to write the definitive geological synthesis.

Lyell was a thoroughgoing uniformitarian, and he brushed aside religious objections as irrelevant. His geology formed an important part of the background for the biological discoveries of Darwin; "I feel as if my books came half out of Sir Charles Lyell's brain," Darwin once wrote. The time revolution disposed of one obvious objection to an evolutionary theory, while increasing knowledge about fossils suggested its possibility. But Lyell was not an evolutionist. He could not find in the fossils sufficient evidence for the transformation or progression of species, that is, one actually growing out of another. Indeed for many centuries this had been the invincible obstacle; it was a stumbling block to evolution comparable to that which the problem of motion had presented to the Copernican theory. As in the case of the slow acceptance of the Copernican hypothesis, one finds here that biblical prejudices played a smaller part in delaying the evolutionary theory than is often suggested. The real difficulty lay in overcoming the dogma of constancy of species, which the biological evidence seemed to support. No examples of such change of species seemed to be found in nature; the evidence, notably the sterility of animal hybrids, showed the opposite.

Since the time of Aristotle, European thought had speculated about a "great chain of being," a logically complete range of life forms arranged in a hierarchy from lowest to highest. The chain ascending upward may suggest evolutionism to us, but it was always then conceived as a *static* hierarchy, a plan emanating from God's mind that was pleasing in its order and that was given for all time. Forms stayed as they were and did not change. The chain of being might be conceived as organically related, like a single great body or like an electrical circuit, and it could evolve into an evolutionary theory. But the traditional doctrine did not entertain any notion of evolution through time, of the transformation of species by gradual and natural means. Aristotle held that the world was created from all eternity and had no beginning—a most profoundly unevolutionary outlook. This is not to say that no one had ever proposed the idea of evolution. Among the ancient Greeks, who canvassed all ideas, Anaximander and Empedocles suggested it. As in the case of astronomy, Aristotle prevailed over their view.

The eighteenth century had shown an enormous interest in biology. Buffon was one of the most popular writers of the age, and other distinguished *philosophes,* including Maupertuis and Diderot, speculated on the origins of life and the nature of species, speculations quite natural in any curious age released from conventional explanations. Biology was somewhat of a factor in romanticism and German philosophy, suggesting organic to replace mechanistic images. Diderot and Maupertuis may readily be seen as anticipating Darwinism, but again, there seemed no convincing evidence for transformation of species, and the great authority of Buffon was, on the whole, it would seem, thrown against it. These stimulating writings did serve to arouse great interest in the question. It can be said that this period between about 1750 and 1850 was like the century that elapsed between Copernicus and Newton: The question had been raised, there was much interest in it and growing knowledge; eventually a master jigsaw puzzle worker would fit all the pieces together.

Curiously enough an early proposer of the evolutionary theory was Charles Darwin's own grandfather, Erasmus Darwin, a poetic physician.

> First forms minute, unseen by spheric glass
> Move on the mud, pierce the watery mass,

Erasmus theorized (1798),

> These, as successive generations bloom
> New powers acquire and larger limbs assume;
> Whence countless groups of vegetation spring
> And breathing realms of fin, and feet, and wing.

A different sort of eighteenth-century amateur anthropologist was the eccentric and prolific Scottish jurist Lord Monboddo, who believed that some of his friends had tails and that orangutans could be taught to play the harp.[6] (Of the widely ridiculed Monboddo Dr. Johnson remarked, "Other people have strange notions but they conceal them.") The lively eighteenth-century curiosity about Noble Savages and alleged new forms of life from the New World thus contributed to the discussion. But such ruminations and speculations were far from offering a reasoned and persuasive notion of evolution.

[6]See recent studies of Monboddo by E. L. Cloyd (1972) and Antonio Verri (1977). Professor Verri concludes that Monboddo was not really a precursor of Darwin, for he did not conceive of the transformation of species by natural processes. Again, note that development might mean God's separate, progressive creation, as with the Buckland catastrophists and also the romantic Nature philosophy.

The pieces to be fitted together came, in a fascinating manner, from many different areas of thought. Darwinism constitutes one of the most interesting of all studies in intellectual history because it shows how much science is a part of the "climate of opinion" of its day. The idea of "survival of the fittest," which Darwin was to turn to such good account as an explanation of biological evolution, was suggested to him by Thomas Malthus and Herbert Spencer. Reading Malthus's *Essays on Population,* which expounded the tendency of population to increase faster than food supply, Darwin saw that this must lead to a struggle for survival in which the less durable organisms would die and fail to reproduce themselves. As for Herbert Spencer, this Victorian oracle preceded Darwin in setting forth a ruthlessly competitive natural order. The idea of natural selection through competition in a world where some must go under because there is not enough sustenance for all came first from the economists. It was "in the air" by the 1830s, and Darwin, a naturalist, picked up and applied it to his field of study. He had his hypothesis many years before presenting his proofs in 1858.

From 1800, Europe seemed to be grasping for the concept of evolution, though not until 1858 did Darwin (and, almost simultaneously, Alfred Wallace) cage the elusive idea. The romantic approach to science known as *Naturphilosophie,* an interest of some German philosophers, thought in evolutionary terms and sometimes believed in transmutation, but, not strictly scientific, its explanation was closer to what later became known as vitalism, that is, a life force immanent in nature that strives to fulfill itself. Schopenhauer, the interesting German philosophical pessimist, strongly believed that this life force appears as an instinct to live, which nature uses to trick us into striving, so that the species may be reproduced; an outlook some of which may have worked its way into Darwinism. We hardly need to remind the reader how historical and evolutionary the popular systems of Hegel and Comte were; this undoubtedly conditioned men to think in terms of the genetic, developmental explanation of things.[7] So it seems that the century conspired to bring about the theory of evolution.

Already, before Darwin, the French paleontologist Lamarck had proposed a theory to account for the evolution of species. He believed that developed characteristics could be inherited. There are (to choose an example) Polynesian swimmers who have developed in the course of generations an unusual lung capacity, enabling them to stay under water (so we are told) as long as six to eight minutes. Lamarck would have explained this as, perhaps, many people today might do unthinkingly: Each generation stretched its lungs by long practice and then handed on this lung power to the offspring. This is wrong, according to modern biologists, who follow Darwin; what happened was that people with unusually large lungs became divers

---

[7]But Hegel, an evolutionist in his philosophy of history, was not so in his philosophy of nature. There is no temporal, only a logical relationship between humans and the lower organisms. "Nature and history are different things," and "Nature has no history" were Hegelian axioms. The cycle of nature is endless repetition from which nothing new evolves, contrary to the situation in human history.

and the others did not, or perhaps drowned. Darwin usually disparaged and ridiculed Lamarck, whom he accused of intruding desire or purpose into the picture, as if the bird's *wish* to fly gradually succeeded in stretching an organ into a wing. Evolution is simply the mechanical result of survival value, on Darwin's more "scientific" explanation. Some birds happened to have more nearly wing-like organs and these survived, the process being repeated for many generations. Lamarck's theory, of course, rested on the vulnerable hypothesis of the inheritability of acquired traits.

In 1844, the Scottish encyclopedist Robert Chambers published, anonymously, *The Vestiges of the Natural History of Creation,* a work that substantially set forth the Darwinian hypothesis although without Darwin's careful accumulation of scientific evidence. It caused a considerable stir of controversy. Thus the state of the question when Darwin arrived was about as follows: The hypothesis of evolution, in the sense of the transformation of one species into another, all descending from one original form of life, was already familiar, but the evidence for it did not seem sufficient to overcome long-standing and apparently strong objections—chiefly, the seeming fixity of species, as attested by the sterility of hybrids, but also certain moral and theological prejudices. Geology and paleontology, however, had strongly suggested its possibility. The "climate of opinion" was favorable to the evolutionary outlook, and some economic writers had called attention to the struggle for existence. It was urgent, it seemed, to either prove or disprove the assertions of Chambers, which had aroused controversy. The Lamarckian theory was not convincing.

Rapidly developing scientific knowledge in a number of fields and far-ranging scientific expeditions over the whole face of the globe had produced much new data about life on earth. Darwin himself had sailed on the famous *Beagle* voyage from 1831 to 1836, studying and collecting zoological evidence. As a sickly youth, marked by few signs of genius, Charles Darwin had tried and failed to follow his father's profession of physician but had his life changed by a teacher at Cambridge who got him to apply for the *Beagle* post. He had no notions of overturning long-held and deeply cherished views when he set out; but as he gathered and observed specimens of flora and fauna, he found questions forming in his mind. As he observed the unusual forms of life on isolated islands, such as the giant turtles on Galapagos, he became convinced that species are not immutable; if so, why should different environmental conditions give rise to different plants and animals? Darwin had his hypothesis by 1835 and his theory, from Malthus, by 1838; he spent the next twenty years patiently assembling every possible strand of evidence with which to tie it all together. As early as Chambers, that is, 1844, Darwin had a manuscript, but he would not publish it until he had made it entirely convincing. By 1858 it had grown to one thousand pages, which he considerably abridged for publication.

That many more are born than survive, then, Darwin learned from Malthus. "It at once struck me that under these circumstances favorable variations would tend to be preserved and unfavorable circumstances would be destroyed. The result of this would be the formation of a new species." The famous book Darwin brought out in 1859, following an article in 1858—both elicited by his discovery that Alfred

R. Wallace was working toward the same theory[8] —is a masterpiece of scientific persuasion designed to make us see that the notion of transformation of species, so long regarded as unthinkable, is really quite plausible. (1) Variations do exist in every species—some people, for example, are taller, stronger, smarter, fairer than others. (2) More offspring by far are produced than survive: Darwin provides striking examples, such as the fact that if all elephants even survived (the slowest animal to reproduce), the earth would in no great time be overrun by elephants. (3) Therefore, there must be competition for survival: What determines why a relative few survive, while most are condemned to perish without reproducing? (4) Variations with survival value must live and reproduce, others not. (5) Given the vast length of time we now know that the earth existed, these factors might very well produce change from one species to another. Darwin did not prove his case, but he made it plausible. The argument unfolds in these logical steps with a wealth of pertinent examples and with a skillful style. The tradition of classical rhetoric informed Darwin's lucid essay in persuasion.

Darwin assembled all the pieces and gave an answer that convinced most of the independent minds of his day. In so doing he wrote the most important book of the century, by rather general agreement, and took his place along with Galileo and Newton among the greatest of scientists, those who have altered the entire mentality of civilization. A poll of distinguished people taken at the end of the century to determine the ten most influential books of the century showed that *The Origin of Species* was the only book on every list. Today the story would hardly be different, though one or two others might also gain unanimous support. A.D.—after Darwin— all was changed utterly.

Darwin's achievement has occasionally been disparaged, because so many other people *almost* hit upon his idea, but while scientific discovery like technological invention is always a social product, no credit may justly be taken away from the person who has the genius to make that discovery. Darwin was a very plain and straightforward professional scientist without philosophical pretensions. His last work was on *The Formation of Vegetable Mould Through the Action of Worms*! Subsequently, he was drawn into some philosophical issues that were perhaps beyond him. But the combination of scientific research and clear thinking found in *The Origin of Species* is very nearly up to Newtonian standards.

Darwin's views, even among scientists, did not prevail without considerable difficulty. His supporters alleged "a conspiracy of silence." Twelve years after the publication of *The Origin of Species,* a conference of French anthropologists found "no proof or even presumption" in favor of natural selection as a cause of transformation. The pace of acceptance varied in different countries; many French saw Darwinism as a kind of ideology of Anglo-Saxon imperialism—it was notoriously difficult to separate scientific from ideological elements in the consideration of

[8] There are still those who think Wallace deserves the credit Darwin was to get. The case is overstated by Arnold C. Brackman in *A Delicate Arrangement: The Strange Case of Charles Darwin and Alfred Russel Wallace* (1980). See also H. Lewis McKinney, *Wallace and Natural Selection* (1972); John Langdon Brooks, *Just Before the Origin* (1984).

Darwinism. Darwin himself noted "it is curious how nationality influences opinion." In the end Darwinism prevailed among scientists, as by and large it has continued to do since, so one must be sure one knows just what it was that Darwin alleged. It is important to note that he did *not* originate the theory of evolution. What he did do was (1) provide a wealth of evidence for it, that is, for the mutability of species and (2) propose the theory of natural selection to account for it. Darwin convinced most people that evolution had occurred. Assembling data from paleontology, anatomy, experimental breeding, and other fields, the new view represented a triumph for thoroughness and collation of scientific research, a victory that rightly enhanced the prestige of science as a social institution. That is to say, it became clear with Darwin that scientific discovery is less the fitful inspiration of genius than the certain result of steady accumulation of data and the patient collation of it. Darwin had genius, but his warmest admirers confessed it was the genius of infinite pains rather than superhuman intelligence.

Darwin was persuasive not only because of the empirical evidence he drew together but because of the striking hypothesis he put forth to explain how evolution takes place. It is noteworthy that the two things were intimately connected: Darwin began his great twenty-year campaign of fact collecting *after* he hit upon the theory of natural selection, from which we may infer that a good theory both stimulates and directs research. But it could be that the hypothesis was wrong as explanation, that evolution indeed has occurred but not in the way that Darwin imagined. The theory of natural selection has been modified since Darwin, principally by an understanding of the mechanism of heredity, which was not generally known until 1900. (The Austrian monk Gregor Mendel published his pioneer findings in 1866, but they were ignored by scientists until 1900.) Today few biologists deny natural selection's importance, but the function of mutation, including macromutation or the accidental production of extreme variants, has brought in an additional factor. The majority of scientists think that variations in heredity *plus* natural selection account for evolution. There are a few who question whether natural selection is really a *major* cause of evolution. (No one can deny that it occurs and plays *some* part.) It should be noted that Darwin was wrong insofar as he proposed slow and gradual evolutionary change, declaring that "nature makes no leaps." Modern mutation theory stresses the sudden leaps. The giraffe did not get his long neck inch by inch, as Darwin thought, but by monsters of long-neckedness that sporadically appeared and proved to have survival value—so runs the current view, roughly, as against original Darwinism. Darwin's view that offspring blend the characteristics of their parents rested on ignorance of the mechanism of heredity (as he knew) and entailed difficulties he could not solve. If a slightly longer-necked giraffe did appear, by mating with an ordinary one, the effect of the mutation would be partly lost, on Darwin's supposition. Modern genetics has established that heredity does not work by simply blending the parental traits; in the genes all traits are preserved and may appear unimpaired in some later individual.

Not only the persisting "creationists" but professional scientists quite recently have thought that Darwin needs revision. His gradualism has come under even heavier fire; the evidence indicates that species remain unchanged for eons and then a new species will appear quite suddenly. The Darwinian model of slow, step-by-step change through constant small adaptions seems faulty. Evolution occurs, but in a different manner, described in recent literature as "punctuational." Thus, our own *homo sapiens* species arrived on the scene rather suddenly about forty thousand years ago, without much preparation, and took over comparatively quickly from *homo neanderthalis*. Some leading biologists are persuaded that this is the chief model for all evolution. This is perhaps the equivalent of quantum leaps in twentieth-century physics. Evolution has continued to evolve; but this does not diminish Darwin's role in having started the realm of life moving, just as Galileo had put the earth in motion.

REACTIONS TO DARWIN

All this may be studied in textbooks of biology or zoology. Clearly Darwin was the founder of large and important areas of modern biological science, whatever modifications of his original theory new knowledge has made necessary. Our main interest is in his impact on wider areas of thought and in the sharp moral and religious controversies that ensued.

"With the one exception of Newton's *Principia,* no single book of empirical science has ever been of more importance to philosophy," Josiah Royce wrote. Equally important to social and religious thought, and soon brought into the hustings of popular debate, Darwinism eventually affected just about everything in the modern world. It was immediately controversial, as Darwin had foreseen. Most epoch-making books have been greeted in total silence and had to wait years to be accepted as important: Marx, Freud, and Nietzsche, for example, all took about twenty years to gain recognition. *The Origin of Species* sold out on its first day of publication and made its author immediately famous. Many were dismayed, a feeling not confined to the clergy, shocked at the refutation of Genesis. Some of the keenest minds of the age, and some of the least orthodox, joined in the dismay. George Bernard Shaw wrote, "If it could be proved that the whole universe had been produced by such selection (Darwin's "survival of the fittest"), only fools and rascals could bear to live." Von Baer, the distinguished German scientist, refused to believe in a theory that made humanity "a product of matter" and debased it to the level of animals, while the professor of geology at Cambridge, Adam Sedgwick, declared that acceptance of Darwinism would "sink the human race into a lower grade of degradation than any into which it has fallen since its written records tell of its history." Was not Darwin another Schopenhauer, his science teaching that only accident and blind will rule the universe, or, if gods, "gods careless of our doom," as Matthew Arnold put it? Apart from the fate that might overtake orthodox Christianity, were *any* moral values possible in a Darwinian world? The implication that we are not unique children of God endowed with souls, but rather offspring of the amoeba by way of other animals, was disturbing; so was the apparent view of life as an amoral struggle, "nature red in tooth and claw," filled with pain and death, the sacrifice of countless individuals to the species. Still more so was the indication that the universe is nothing but chance and luck.

Though Darwin made some gestures of appeasement in his book to the religious, he was not a religious person and steadily grew less so. In his *Autobiography*—the undeleted version—he explains how he first rejected Christianity about 1840 and later also dropped the "theism" that appears in the last two pages of the *Origin*. He undoubtedly shared the position popularized by his vigorous proponent, Thomas Huxley, as "agnosticism." The acrimony with which the war between science and religion soon began to be waged owed much to the belligerence and even arrogance of Huxley, as well as to the blindness of his most famous adversary, "Soapy Sam" Wilberforce. Huxley and Bishop Wilberforce met in a debate in 1860 on which occasion a famous exchange of insults took place—the clergyman observing that he would rather not claim a monkey for an ancestor and Huxley retorting that he would rather be descended from an honest ape than from one who, though endowed with brains, refused to use them! Huxley was driven by a rage against the clergy that led him to write privately of an urge to "get my heel into their mouths and sc-r-unch it around"; he made the wholly inaccurate statement that "extinguished theologians lie about the cradle of every science as the strangled snakes beside that of Hercules"! Not all clergymen rejected Darwinism—some soon began to find it agreeable to theism—while its foes included many nonclergy, scientists among them. Roman Catholics were more inclined to accept, or at least to tolerate, Darwinism because they were freer from biblical literalism.

But Darwin undeniably moved away from religion. His life story reveals one who earlier was quite pious but whom Lyell's geology led away from biblical Christianity; then the hypothesis of natural selection destroyed in his mind the classical arguments for natural religion, drawn from the evidences of design and purpose in organisms.[9] His concluding paragraphs in *Origin* point to a theism that was in fact quite widely adopted: It is not less wonderful, but *more* so, that God chose to plant the seeds of all life in a few simple forms rather than create each species separately. But Darwin abandoned this position, as a study of his letters and subsequent published writings reveals. There was too much chance and too much evil in the biological world he saw to permit him to believe in a benevolent plan. "I cannot persuade myself that a beneficent and omnipotent God would have designedly created the Ichneumonidae with the express intention of their feeding within the living bodies of caterpillars, or that cats should play with mice." It was the old problem of evil that destroyed Darwin's faith, along with the muddle and untidiness of the evolutionary picture that went so far to discredit the notion of an orderly plan. Darwin

[9] The textbook long used and widely influential in early nineteenth-century England, affecting the young Darwin himself, was William Paley's *Natural Theology* (1802), a work that argued with a wealth of carefully observed detail that the marvelous adaptation of organisms to their environment proves deliberate contrivance by an "intelligent Creator"—the "argument from design" spelled out carefully. But with a change in perspective, many of Paley's examples could be seen as adaptation via natural selection rather than providential design.

was certainly not, like Huxley, a naturally irreligious man. He simply was driven by the evident facts to lose his faith in a "beneficent and omnipotent God." If reproached for destroying religion, he could only answer that he did not invent these harsh facts; they existed.

The thought also struck him, later, that the mind of humanity itself is a product of the evolutionary order, thus merely a tool of survival. This same idea was to jolt others. The result was evidently to dethrone intelligence or soul as a separate principle, making it merely a factor in evolutionary adaptation. Oddly enough, this would seem to destroy science along with theology as having any higher validity; everything would have to become just a weapon in the struggle for survival. At any rate, Darwin's somewhat confused speculations mirror those of many others; all had been thrown into disorder by this amazing new knowledge. Unwilling to be dogmatic, Darwin called himself an "agnostic" though a careful study of his religious views concludes that it would not be too unjust to equate them with atheism. Darwin found absolutely no evidence for a divine creation and providence; that he was not an atheist was owing only to his reluctance to be dogmatic about anything. Perhaps—who knows?—such evidence might appear in the future. Darwin did not find it.

The disciples of Darwin have continued to be militantly antitheist. Thus wrote Julian Huxley, grandson of Thomas Huxley and distinguished twentieth-century biologist: "Newton's great generalization of gravitational attraction made it possible and indeed necessary to dispense with the idea of God guiding the stars in their courses; Darwin's equally great generalization of natural selection made it possible and necessary to dispense with the idea of God guiding the evolutionary courses of life" (*On Living in a Revolution,* 1944) (Huxley's comment on Newton is inaccurate in that eighteenth-century thinkers did not so construe Newtonianism.)

> I find no hint throughout the Universe
> Of good or ill, of blessing or of curse;
> I find alone Necessity Supreme;
> With infinite Mystery, abysmal, dark,
> Unlighted by the faintest spark
> For us the flitting shadows of a dream.

So wrote James Thomson in "The City of Dreadful Night." Thomson was by nature a pessimist, but he was not alone in drawing gloomy conclusions from Darwin and science. At a time when belief in the divine inspiration of every line of Scripture was still regarded as the sole foundation of Christianity (Gladstone, the great Oxford-educated liberal statesman, so argued in 1865), and Christianity was regarded as the foundation of the social order, the discrediting of Genesis was no small matter, and the blows that came from Lyell and Darwin fell on a body already bruised by those of the positivist historians and the schools of biblical criticism. The theological-biblical debate has somewhat lost its importance, for most Christians no longer construe the Scriptures so literally; but as late as 1925 in the United States (the Scopes trial) it retained considerable power to arouse emotions.

Wider than this was the moral debate, concerned with the question of whether Darwinism did not destroy all values by eliminating purpose and design from the universe; many who were not at all orthodox Christians joined in disapproving a creed apparently consistent with no sort of belief in rational order in the world. In one of his books, the Victorian author Winwood Reade told of a young man's suicide, under the impact of Malthus and Darwin, whose books he placed, bound in somber colors, on the table in his room, the *Essay on Population* labeled "the Book of Doubt" and *The Origin of Species* labeled "The Book of Despair." Yet others were able to accept Darwinism as meaning progress.

The great debate went on with endless ramifications. A classic story is that of P. H. Gosse, lay minister and naturalist (father of Edmund Gosse, whose *Father and Son* is a Victorian classic), who, struggling to reconcile his Christian faith with his science, hit upon what he regarded as a brilliant answer: God had created the world "prochronically," at a particular and arbitrary moment in its life, *as if* its past history had existed (*Omphalos: An Attempt to Untie the Geologic Knot*). He was laughed out of court. By 1872, Darwin could write that "almost every scientist admits the principle of evolution" and also the theory of natural selection as its means of operation. Yet Louis Agassiz, the famous American (Harvard) naturalist, would not accept Darwin and spent the rest of his life laboring to prove this "monstrous" theory false. Samuel Butler, Victorian freethinker and critic of religious orthodoxy, began by admiring Darwin but came to think that the Cambridge scientist was a deceiver who supplied the wrong explanation; Butler accepted evolution but not natural selection and was led back to Lamarck via St. George Mivart, the Roman Catholic biologist, author of *The Genesis of Species* (1871). In *Evolution Old and New* (1879) Butler attacked the scientific establishment as more bigoted than the religious. Bernard Shaw also became a neo-Lamarckian, but moralists found this more appealing than scientists. It is easy to see why. Butler worked out an attractive evolutionary religion in which each person makes his or her contribution to the development of human knowledge and consciousness, passed on to the next generation that can go on to other higher achievements; we may all feel that what we have learned and created is not in vain but a link in the chain of human growth. This, however, is only true on Lamarckian terms, that is, the inheritance of acquired characteristics. Few scientists have thought this true. What we learn is not passed in the genes to our children.

There were harmonizers and accommodators who sought to show that even Darwinian evolution is consistent with divine purpose. Was there not something sublime in the ascent of humanity through the eons from primeval slime to intelligent and spiritual being (Henry Drummond)? Admitting the cruelty and suffering, one still had as an undeniable fact the grand result.[10] Asa Gray, the American naturalist, complimented Darwin for having *restored* teleology to nature. There was design, if "on the installment plan": Darwin himself had once been reduced to awe

---

[10]"Red in tooth and claw" was somewhat overstated; survival depends more on the struggle against nature than between organisms, and cooperation may be a help to survival. "Strength," indeed, may be less important than efficiency, energy, intelligence.

at the greater wonder of God contriving to draw all life from a single simple beginning. In any event, as Mr. and Mrs. Carlyle had observed, whether we are or are not derived from the amoeba is irrelevant to our spiritual life. Josiah Royce, the distinguished American philosopher, held to an evolutionary idealism and pointed out that the human mind does seek values, is not animal-like: These are facts as incontrovertible as Darwin's, if puzzlingly different from them. Darwin had not and could not make us brutes. He had given us new and puzzling knowledge, but so long as human consciousness exists it will rise above matter to seek understanding and the good. A recent study has pointed out that some of the most conservative theologians, the old-fashioned Calvinists, had the least trouble accepting Darwin; had not suffering and conflict, the result of Original Sin, always been a part of basic Protestant doctrine? Only liberals who wanted to believe in a good progressive world were disconcerted by this repeating of the thought that the world is (as Coleridge put it) not a goddess in petticoats but the devil in a straitjacket.

It needs to be added that Darwin's godless and chaotic world has encountered resistance down to very recent times; night riders bombed schoolhouses where Darwinism was taught in West Virginia in the 1970s, while creationists lobbied to get laws passed banning the teaching of evolution. Although a spate of scientists rushed to deplore this belated obscurantism, and creationism had no professional standing, its reappearance suggests a kind of timeless quality about the Darwinian debate, still alive and kicking after nearly a century and a half.

There were also vitalist approaches to evolution that pointed out that Darwin had not addressed himself at all to the important question of what really (in a final sense) causes the evolutionary process. Granted that natural selection does take place and with an apparent blindness and cruelty (millions of individuals, whole species even, may perish because of some accidental change in their environment), it would seem that other factors are present, too, including an intelligence that runs through all life. The behavior of organisms is often so remarkably purposive that one has difficulty in attributing everything to a mechanistic process. At any rate, can natural selection account for the emergence of life itself? There is also running through life a will to live, as Schopenhauer and Bergson noted. Can this inextinguishable vitality be the result of a mechanical process? It must have been there to begin with, though strengthened by natural selection. Perhaps this life force is really the "cause" of evolution, natural selection only one means it uses. If we see a large group of people running a long race and notice that some of them fall or drop out while a few run strongly and forge to the front, it would seem odd to say that the cause of the winning of the race (evolution) is the fact that some drop out from unfitness (natural selection), without raising the really interesting question, why are they running? Why do they bother with this rigorous competition at all? Why do they not all sit under a tree and rest? Darwin pointed out that there is competition in nature and refrained from speculating about the reason. This is good; but was he justified in implying that the question has no importance and need not be raised? If natural selection is made into a dogma, it may divert our eyes from other questions of great moment and distort our outlook on nature. So, at least, Henri Bergson was to argue.[11]

The outcome of all these efforts at accommodation with evolution was perhaps uncertain, but in general people learned to live with it, sometimes by making a separation between animal world and human world, nature and value. On this view a great change had taken place in "nature." "Nature" to the eighteenth century had suggested order, harmony, benevolence, indeed something to be imitated, an agreeable model for humanity. After Darwin nature might be thought of as fascinating, but it was in part terrible and it was not a proper model for human beings. But on the other hand, there were those who embraced the new "naturalism" that placed humanity in the setting of the natural order and did not separate us so sharply from it as had, for example, the Cartesian or Kantian dualism. Darwinians were "monists" (their foes said materialists) who could not accept any mind-body dualism, and separation between the physical world and the mental. The human animal is an organism like any other, responding to its environment and in part shaping it while responding. Humanity became a part of the biological natural order as it had not been before.

If some of the more thoughtful drew pessimistic or tragic conclusions from evolution, most people probably integrated it casually with the reigning belief in progress. Constant and inevitable progress does take place on Darwinian terms, progress of the species or race if often at the expense of individuals. Organisms adapt to their environment and grow steadily more efficient; if the unfit perish, the fit live, and life evolves from lower organisms to higher. It was one version of the "idea of progress" for which Victorian stability and economic prosperity provided a favorable atmosphere.

Philosophically, Darwinism helped discredit idealism or intellectualism. Young philosophers like John Dewey abandoned Hegel for some more naturalistic outlook. Mind, it seemed, must be a product of evolution, ideas of natural selection. Mind could hardly be detached from the organism and erected into a separate principle. If we even believe that the universe makes sense, as Nietzsche was fond of saying, is this not just because those of our ancestors who could not make sense of it failed to survive, and natural selection bred those who did? Reason is a survival trait. A character in a Shaw play remarked that the modern view is not "I think therefore I am," but "I am therefore I think." A new reason for distrusting reason had appeared: Reason is a product of the nature it purports to understand. If I believe in God, or say that the universe is orderly, I may be doing so because of traits bred into the intellect by the struggle for survival, and if I am tempted to assume the absolute truth of these beliefs, I am caught up by remembering that my mind itself is an evolutionary product, hence essentially a survival tool, like the monkey's tail or the giraffe's neck! This "irrationalism" might take various forms: Pessimistically,

---

[11] There were other French vitalists—Vandel, Mercier, Varagnac, and more recently the celebrated Jesuit father, Teilhard de Chardin.

it could be presented as grounds for despair with blind will and instinct ruling the universe; optimistically, it might be said that human intelligence is no less a creative tool for being a part of the natural order. But there remained a fundamental difference between all the new thought and the old, in that for many it was no longer possible to set the human mind *outside* nature. Being a part of nature, the mind had to give up its proud claim to be able to understand it as one understands something from which one is detached. The mind is just that part of our organism that participates in a certain way in the great game of life. Humanity was no longer Pascal's "thinking reed," its intelligence set against the world.

The implications of Darwinism are too numerous to be recorded. "Evolutionary views have deeply penetrated our present thinking in almost every conceivable field. . . . It has become regular procedure to study phenomena in terms of their development. . . . Interest in evolution has moved out of academic circles even into the field of commerce and industry."[12] Perhaps this judgment attributes too much to Darwinism as such, for the bent of the nineteenth century toward historical explanations and the idea of progress was rather more general; Darwinism may be seen as only a part of this larger pattern, which included such independent forces as Hegelian philosophy, Burkean political thought, aspects of Comteanism, and the maturing profession of historiography. But it is interesting to note that John Dewey, in his famous assessment of Darwin's impact on philosophy (*The Influence of Darwin on Philosophy,* 1909), attributed to him the enthronement of "the principle of transition," or seeing things as involved in processes of change rather than as Platonic "eternals." Clearly Darwin did exert the greatest force in this direction. Unlike Hegel and Comte he seemed truly scientific. Dewey added that Darwin had shattered the closed metaphysical system of Hegel in favor of a pluralism and experimentalism. Thus to many living in the later nineteenth century a whole new vision of things opened up, and evolutionism seemed a refreshing breeze blowing over the somewhat desiccated landscape of idealism.

The rise of science as the prevailing mode of thought, predicted by Comte, owed more to Darwin than to any other one figure. Many noted this change at mid century. Mark Pattison dated it between 1845 and 1850. Oliver Wendell Holmes, Jr., the great American jurist, reminiscing many years later, thought that of all the intellectual gaps between generations, that between his own and his parents' (about 1865) was the greatest: "It was the influence of the scientific way of looking at the world." He mentioned, in addition to *The Origin of Species,* Herbert Spencer and Henry T. Buckle.[13] Buckle was an amateur historian, author of a multivolume *History of Civilization in England* (1857-61), the Toynbee of his day, whose volumes lined the shelves of many a Victorian library and who sought to reduce history to an exact science. More famous yet was the apparently omniscient Herbert Spencer, who did not confine himself merely to human history but claimed to have reduced the whole of the cosmos to an exact and evolutionary science.

---

[12] Walter J. Ong, in *Darwin's Vision and Christian Perspectives* (1960), pp. 1-2.

[13] Leonora C. Rosenfield, *Portrait of a Philosopher: Morris R. Cohen* (1962), p. 321.

Spencer, the most celebrated of mid-Victorian philosophers, was a sort of combination of Comte and Darwin. Like the former, he was a tremendous synthesizer of every field of knowledge under the general rubric of a scientific or positivistic method—a synthesis that greatly impressed his contemporaries, eager for an integration of thought, but which has since considerably depreciated in value. Someone has called him "the Marx of the middle class"; he could equally well be called the British Comte. A distinctive feature of his philosophy was its stress on evolution, a stress indeed not lacking in Comte, Hegel, and Marx, but which in Spencer is even more pronounced. Influenced by Lyell and von Baer, he popularized "survival of the fittest" before Darwin. Unlike the Cambridge scientist, Spencer proceeded to set about creating a full-scale philosophy of evolution. While Darwin was largely content to nail down the lid on evolution with a large supply of experimental facts, Spencer assumed the case closed and set off on cosmic speculative adventures with it.

The entire universe obeys the same laws of evolution, Spencer affirmed. He wished to show that the evolution not only of life but of the physical cosmos and human society could be reduced to the same laws—an exciting idea, indeed. Spencer found that things invariably evolve from (1) the homogeneous to the heterogeneous, (2) the undifferentiated to the differentiated, and (3) the unintegrated to the integrated. "From a relatively diffused, uniform, and indeterminate arrangement to a relatively concentrated, multiform, and determinate arrangement," so ran his formula. The cosmos began with separate, simple atoms uniformly dispersed through space and will end, presumably, with highly organized structures working together in a single complex system (rather the reverse of the "primeval atom" theory later popular). Human society began with isolated individuals performing simple tasks without specialization and proceeded toward an order at once more diverse, specialized, and interdependent. Writing voluminously with an encyclopedic knowledge few could match, Spencer tended to bowl over opposition by the sheer weight of this formidable erudition. Darwin called him "about a dozen times my superior" and said Spencer would go down as the greatest thinker of the century. He was certainly the most popular of all serious thinkers, to judge by the sale of his books. "Probably no philosopher ever had such a vogue as Spencer had from about 1870 to 1890," wrote the American publisher, Henry Holt, who had the enviable privilege of selling Spencer's books in the United States. (Between 1860 and 1903, some 368,000 copies of Spencer's various works were sold in authorized editions in the United States, countless others in unauthorized ones.)

Spencer combined with his evolutionary outlook a Comtean positivism (it came to him from more native sources) that insisted that scientific laws are descriptive statements only, telling nothing about essential natures or origins. The latter doubtless exist but are "unknowable." Like Kant, Spencer invites a certain sense of awe before this realm, but one can have no real knowledge about it. Positivists have generally been divided between those who say that there is no point in even talking or thinking about what we cannot know and those who would not rule out our speculations and intuitive insights into it provided we do not confuse these with knowledge of a scientific order. Spencer belonged to the latter group; he does not forbid us from speculating about the unknowable. Still, faithful Christians classed him among the "agnostics" who did so much to undermine religious faith. At the same time, it is obvious that (like Marx) he really offered a sort of religion in the trappings of science.

But in time many of his generalizations came to seem rash, founded on inadequate evidence, made by one who was determined that the facts prove his theory. A Victorian giant, Spencer's reputation has fallen perhaps faster than he deserved. But he was certainly guilty of letting his speculations outrun the facts on which they were supposedly based. Little if anything now remains standing of his vast intellectual edifice. The exception is his sociology, which exercised considerable influence on later theorists, in its stress on social change via unstable equilibria in a single social organism. Unlike Marx's, Spencer's social change is steady and gradual rather than sudden and revolutionary. Perhaps we may see echoes here of the old debate between uniformitarians and catastrophists. Doubtless Spencer's, and Darwin's, gradualism reflected the society of Victorian England and the values of its dominant class. But Spencer's abortive world system, which William James called "the most ambitious attempt at synthesis of all knowledge since St. Thomas or Descartes," stemmed from the intellect's protest at an increasingly complex and fragmented world of knowledge.

SOCIAL DARWINISM

By far the most notable feature of Spencer's exuberant thought was its application of evolutionary ideas to human society; and of all the speakers for what was termed "social Darwinism," he was the most renowned. There is some irony in Spencer being known as *the* "social Darwinist" since his conception of biological evolution (which he formulated before Darwin's was published) was more Lamarckian than Darwinian: He believed in the inheritability of acquired characteristics. On the other hand, he fully accepted the Darwinian notion of a struggle for existence as the key to evolution. "Survival of the fittest" was his term. An editor of the *Economist* at one time, Spencer knew the tradition of economic liberalism before he turned to evolution and shows us the intimate connection between the two. John Maynard Keynes, the modern economist, wrote that "the principle of the Survival of the Fittest could be regarded as a vast generalization of the Ricardian economics." Typically British, the principle of individualism remained powerful in his evolutionary synthesis. While society grows more complex with progress, it also grows freer and more diverse. The evolution of the individual is toward greater freedom and less constraint. Competition is the key to progress. Spencer's complacent identification of the poor with the unfit who may safely be left to die out is in good part responsible for the later dislike of his whole philosophy. The oft-quoted passage in *Social Statics* (first published in 1851, revised in later editions but not changed in any significant way) argued that "to prevent present misery would entail a greater misery on future generations"; "When regarded not separately but in connection with the interests of universal humanity," individual suffering is seen to be for the best. Spencer was sure that "as civilization advances, government decays"; in this opinion, he was as far as possible at odds with Comte, whom in some other ways he resembles. He takes us back to the Godwinian anarchists at the beginning of the century. He was the principal source of a revival of radical antistatism in Victorian England, against which however there was to be a strong reaction after 1880.

"Social Darwinism" has been a loosely used term. There are in fact several different ways of applying the formula of evolution via natural selection or "survival of the fittest" to human social development. Spencer sometimes mixed them up. One could postulate a competition, first, between whole *societies,* perhaps between nations or states, which compete against each other peacefully and sometimes go to war against each other. Applied here, a social Darwinian might hold that such competition is healthy, even that war tests the character of a people (Hegel as well as Spencer occasionally said this), that out of this struggle for survival between social units we get increasingly efficient societies. Spencer presented this sort of social Darwinism at times, declaring that societies are organisms akin to individual bodies, being functionally organized and experiencing growth; they are tested by their environment and evolve from small and simple to large and complex types.

Or, again, evolution via competition might be said to occur among specific social *institutions* such as the family. As E. B. Tylor, another social evolutionist, put it, "the institutions which can best hold their own in the world gradually supersede the less fit ones, and . . . this incessant conflict determines the general resultant course of culture." Finally, competition with resultant progress could be applied to *individuals*—the form of social Darwinism most often associated with Spencer. Here, there is perhaps a logical distinction to be made (Spencer sometimes confused them) between *biological* competition—the sickly dying off, the healthy surviving—and *economic* competition. In any case, the competition between individuals *within* a society is clearly a different thing from the competition *between* societies, and some have thought Spencer guilty of inconsistency in holding both ideas. But he thought, more or less consistently, that free competition makes for the best society and the best humanity as well as the best individuals ("best" meaning most efficient, best adapted to the challenge of the environment).

Beyond any doubt, Spencer freely mixed ideological elements into his alleged science of society. He owed much to the tradition of liberalism, reaching back through the Manchester School to Locke and Hobbes, and he perhaps owed something too to the school of Burke, which had tended to see society as an organism too complicated to tamper with safely. Spencer's world view betrayed his own time and place, just as Comte smuggled his Saint-Simonian predilections into a system supposedly scientific. Yet Spencer gave a great boost to the supposed sciences of sociology and anthropology. The latter rather clearly dates from Darwin and Spencer; it was born under evolutionary auspices. It was assumed that "primitive" peoples represent the first stage in a ladder of development, comparable to the biological ladder; they are our ancestors in the same way that simple forms of life are the ancestors of the human race. There are universal stages and laws of development. For example, in religion animism always comes first, monotheism last, in a single straight-line path of evolution. Today these views have been discarded or enormously qualified, but the study of different societies gained its initial impetus from an expectation that research would uncover simple laws of development. Thus E. B. Tylor, less dogmatic and more empirical than Spencer, nevertheless expected that in time the laws of development would be revealed; "human institutions like stratified rocks succeed each other in series substantially uniform over the globe." Skepticism about such grand laws of evolutionary succession appeared by the end of the century, when anthropologists tended to find that each primitive society is unique and can be fitted into no schematic pattern. But for the English-speaking peoples, Spencer was the fountainhead of both anthropological and sociological science. And the fact that sociology failed to become an important academic discipline in England until the 1950s, suffering a severe setback in the first half of the twentieth century, is due in part to the discrediting of Spencer about 1900.

Spencer's brand of "social Darwinism," with its sanctioning of a ruthlessly competitive social order ("root, hog, or die" is the law of life, the American social Darwinian William Graham Sumner bluntly put it), created something of a dilemma for other Darwinians, less inclined to grant indulgent smiles to a capitalistic society. In 1893, Thomas Huxley, the aggressive champion of Darwinism, argued in a well-known series of lectures that in human affairs natural selection is *not* the rule to follow. Progress, he said, consists in working *against* nature and evolution, "checking the cosmic process at every step." He could agree with Matthew Arnold that

Man must begin, know this, where Nature ends;
Nature and man can never be fast friends.

"It is an error to imagine that evolution signifies a constant tendency to increased perfection," Huxley wrote. What survives, because it is the best adapted, is not necessarily or usually the best in an ethical sense. Unguided evolution may well lead to moral regression and social failure. Thus did Huxley in part withdraw his faith in evolution.

Clearly this must be so. Victorian social Darwinians usually wished to approve a fairly civilized process of competitive economics against any sort of state socialism. But if one applied Darwinism to human society literally and thoroughly, one would evidently revert to the prehistoric jungle. The biographer of Adolf Hitler (Alan Bullock) tells us that the only idea the infamous Nazi dictator held to was "a crude Darwinism." To Hitler this meant that only power counts, individuals may be ruthlessly sacrificed, the ill and injured put to death, whole races wiped out because allegedly less biologically fit. Anyone stupid or evil enough to take this sort of social Darwinism at its full value would seem to find in it sanctions for the law of the jungle applied *à outrance*. Though nature might be "red in tooth and claw" in the animal world, no sane person could wish to reduce human society to such a condition.

There were those who pointed out that even in the subhuman biological realm conflict is not the only rule. Cooperation also exists as a means of biological survival, as numerous examples of symbiosis and social organization in the animal world testify. Moreover the will to power, the life force, the instinct to survive that pulses through all living things, can be "sublimated" so that it works for good rather than evil. Humanity, in particular, evolves by inventing new modes of social cooperation; it has passed to a higher phase of evolution, *rational* evolution, involving the use of brain power rather than brawn. Animals do this to some extent; humanity has made it supreme. Why should "natural selection" mean physical strife and bloodshed? There is more survival value in the intelligence that organizes peace and social welfare. It was possible in this way to turn the argument against Spencer's cult of dog-eat-dog competition. And, in fact, after 1880 Western Europe turned rapidly toward social welfare modifications of the competitive economic order.

In "Why Darwin Pleased the Socialists," G. B. Shaw made the point, half-seriously as usual, that it took the capitalists down a peg to be told that they were rich not because of their virtue or the design of providence, but simply by accident. Darwinism's hostility to religion, along with its reinforcement of a naturalism that looked squarely at harsh social facts, rendered it pleasing to the Left. The most notable literary offshoot, the naturalist school of Emile Zola, Jack London, and others of the sort, was daring, brutally frank, and much interested in the lives of the lower classes. Zola was not really a socialist since he thought, consistently enough with a naturalist outlook, that no one was to blame and everyone was a victim of circumstances, the capitalists no less than the workers. But no one is likely to read *Germinal* without acquiring a good deal of sympathy for the coal miners. So "social Darwinism" did not always mean rugged individualism of the sort most pleasing to expectant capitalists. Careful research has revealed that Darwinism was much less frequently employed by businesspeople to justify their acquisitive instincts than used to be thought. Marx and Engels admired Darwin, though it is now known that Marx did not, as once was claimed, try to dedicate *Das Kapital* to the author of *The Origin of Species.* Socialists sometimes tried to appropriate Darwinism. In his preface to an 1894 book on socialism and science, the British socialist Ramsay MacDonald asserted that "Darwinism is not only not in intellectual opposition to socialism, but is its scientific foundation." That struggle is the law of life; the conditions change and institutions must change too were principles easily bent to radical usages.[14] It may be relevant to add that Darwin, Huxley, and Spencer were all compassionate people shocked at human suffering and hopeful of alleviating it and that they all believed progress possible. Spencer was a vigorous anti-imperialist

---

[14] Alfred Kelly, *The Descent of Darwin: The Popularization of Darwin in Germany, 1860-1914* (1981), notes a strong association between Darwinism and socialism in Germany. Marx's 1861 verdict, in a letter to Lassalle, was that "Darwin's book is very important and suits me well as giving a scientific basis to the historical class struggle. One has to accept, of course, the crude English way in which the theme is developed."

who also believed that war was obsolete in the modern world. He deeply influenced radicals as well as conservatives and, in fact, was by nature much more a rebel and an outsider than a member of the British intellectual establishment. So one would be wrong to think of "social Darwinism" only as a creed congenial to the successful. It revealed what Nietzsche called "that Janus-face possessed by all great ideas."

Darwin himself was largely content to leave the question of human social evolution to such as Spencer; "I think I shall avoid that subject altogether, it is so surrounded with prejudice, though I fully admit it is the highest and most interesting problem," he wrote to Alfred Wallace in 1857. Nevertheless in his later book, *The Descent of Man* (1871), Darwin, who expressed great admiration for Spencer, wrote that it must be injurious to the human race to keep alive "the weak of mind or body" rather than eliminate them as he says "savage" tribes do and also that "an endless number of the lower races will be eliminated by the higher civilized races throughout the world." Darwin himself obviously shared some of the applications of his theory that many were to find obnoxious. (Believing firmly in the separate nature of women, he was also a Victorian sexist in the view of some recent women.[15]) Darwin's cousin Francis Galton, in his *Hereditary Genius* (1869), coined the term "eugenics" and began the attempt to find and perpetuate the more intelligent genetic strains—planned selection for human improvement. The sinister possibilities of such a project, needless to say, are something that, after Hitler, we are all too aware of. But it would be unjust to project these misuses back onto Darwin, as unjust as it would be to blame the crimes of Stalin on Karl Marx.

Little in the ensuing generation was unmarked by the impact of evolutionary thought, whether Darwinian or (as some still preferred, not least in France) Lamarckian. Among these influences we have mentioned "naturalism" in literature. Emile Zola was born in the same year as Thomas Hardy; both the French and the English novelist were 19 when *The Origin of Species* appeared and thus belonged to the generation that felt most the power of the new scientific thought. These writers of the last quarter of the century are discussed further in Chapter 5. Here we may simply note that to the specific influence of Darwin and of the theory of evolution via natural selection was added that of science in general, now attaining its acme of prestige and success; of positivism, especially in France, applying the scientific method to philosophy and literature; of rapid change in society, accompanying the spread of technological and industrial progress. For Zola, a further stimulus was the shocking defeat of France in the 1870 war with Prussia—evidence, it seemed, that a nation must adapt or perish, in a competitive and rapidly changing world. Thus everything conspired to drive home the lesson that stability was no longer the norm; the new god was Change, and one failed to accept this fact at one's peril.

---

[15] See Lorna Duffin, "Women and Evolution," in Sara Delamont and L. Duffin, eds., *The Nineteenth-Century Woman: Her Cultural and Physical World* (1978); Flavia Aloya, "Victorian Science and the 'Genius' of Women," *Journal of the History of Ideas,* April-June 1977.

THE IDEA OF PROGRESS

At least one substantial common denominator in all these nineteenth-century ide-ologies was progress, that idea the nineteenth century so generally bowed to. "The history of the human race is the history of growth," the English Comtean historian Frederic Harrison proclaimed as "the meaning of history." The Hegelian, holding that the spirit of God dwells within the historical process and guides it to ultimate completion, and the positivist, refusing to acknowledge such a metaphysical hy-pothesis as God or Absolute, were equal sharers of the optimistic world view that found in history a steady advance from one beginning to one end, and that a glori-ous one. One thought that progress worked through the Absolute without man even being aware of it; the other believed that only in rejecting the Absolute and becom-ing conscious of his human powers did humanity learn to advance; neither doubted the existence of progress. Marx, next to be considered, inherited the Hegelian spirit; Comte's lived on in many bourgeois versions, liberal or conservative, of the idea of progress. (J. B. Bury, in his classic study of this idea, wrote that Comte did more than any other thinker to establish it as a permanent fixture on the mental land-scape.) Mill agreed with Comte on this, and Darwin taught most people that inces-sant advance is the law of life, though doubtless they mistook him if they thought he believed in a purposeful progress. Spencer's incredibly popular evolutionary ide-ology proclaimed a steady advance, onward *and* upward. A disillusioned post-1919 critic, Emil Brunner, called the idea of progress "an axiomatic belief which needed no proof nor could be disproved . . . a pseudoreligious creed, which to negate was a kind of blasphemy." One can round up some doubters, but there were not many at the high tide of Victorian optimism, and as late as 1908 the distinguished statesman-philosopher of Great Britain, Lord Balfour, proclaimed that "there are no symp-toms either of pause or regression in the onward movement which for more than a millennium has been characteristic of Western civilization." What seems remarkable is that these beliefs in progress assumed not only a steady onward and upward move-ment, but a movement of the entire society. One would be inclined to say today that some things doubtless "progress," if the term is defined in certain ways—technology becomes more efficient, scientific knowledge accumulates—but other phases of life remain much the same and some deteriorate. It would be a rash person who would claim that art, morality, even political wisdom have advanced. The nine-teenth-century optimists supposed that society is a unit which progresses as a whole, so that every part of it is engaged in constant improvement.

What Georges Sorel later called "the illusions of progress" did not escape some nineteenth-century criticism. Writing in the bitter disillusionment that followed the failure of the 1848 revolution, the Russian emigré Alexander Herzen asked,

> If progress is the end, for whom are we working? Who is this Moloch who, as the toilers approach him, instead of rewarding them, only recedes, and as a consolation to the exhausted, doomed multitudes, can give back only the mocking answer that after their death all will be beautiful on earth?

Poets and artists had occasion to comment that in these really important areas there is no "progress"—or, Theophile Gautier added, in lovemaking! Such voices were a distinct minority, often a fleeting one, before the last quarter or so of the century. Those thrown into despair by Darwin have been mentioned, but the general temper of the first half of the century, filled as it was with the excitement of meaningful change for perhaps the first time in human history, was generally optimistic. In his book on Charles Dickens, G. K. Chesterton wrote that "the first period [of the nineteenth century] was full of evil things, but it was full of hope," while the last part, full of good things, lacked hope.

This optimism, fed by a steady procession of technological gains, in Britain a newfound political stability, a general prosperity, and the conquest of some social evils, survived the Darwin-induced crisis of faith. It is a tribute to it that even the greatest critic of Victorian society, Karl Marx, embraced the creed of optimism too, in his way. It was a significant point of contact between high thought and low, philosophers and common people.

chapter 4

Nineteenth-Century Ideologies

Marxism

If previously the gods dwelt above the earth, now they have become the center of it.

   Karl Marx

The fundamental problem of social science is to find the law of motion according to which any state of society produces the state which succeeds it and takes its place.

   Karl Marx

MARX'S LIFE AND CAREER

Karl Marx, prophet of the proletarian revolution, was by no means of working-class stock himself, but the son of a (we would say) district attorney, a moderately well-off lawyer and public servant of the Rhineland town of Trier. Marx's lineage was Jewish on both sides, and heavily rabbinical. Those who like to probe the psychological origins of great persons find much matter in Marx's early years. His father, in order to keep his post, had to renounce his Judaism and become a nominal Christian when the Rhineland reverted to Prussia following Napoleon's defeat in 1815. This evidently caused Herschel (Heinrich) Marx little pain, for his outlook was that of Enlightenment rationalism; he was in effect partly a willing and partly a constrained defector from his ancestral faith. So was his son, who, baptized as a Christian and educated at the local Jesuit-run gymnasium, later showed considerable scorn for Jews: describing them, for example, as "a collection of parasites, a gang of money lenders" and "a repellent example of the social malaise of our time." Yet many think that Marx not only sublimated his rage against the established order to which his father was forced to conform, but transferred his Jewish heritage into secular terms, retaining strong elements of its chiliastic, millenarian basic structure in his revolutionary ideology.

However that may be, Marx was a confident and pampered eldest and only male child who received a good education, was sent to the university at a time when only a tiny minority had this privilege, and for a bonus won the rich girl of the neighborhood (daughter of Baron von Westphalen, a local grandee who liked and befriended Karl). He was handsome, to boot.

The question may arise why so favored a young man turned into the leading revolutionary theorist of modern times. Born in 1818, Karl was exposed first to Romanticism, in its flower during his youth; he certainly had both a love of literature and a romantic temperament, and he tried his hand without much success at poetry and drama in his salad days. At Bonn University, his first higher-educational stop, he was exposed to the Romantic thought of the philosopher Schlegel, but spent more time in the taverns than in the classroom, to the despair of his father who had him transferred to Berlin in 1836. Like his Jewishness, Marx's Romanticism was only overtly abandoned; romantic themes of rebellion, alienation, Promethean defiance of the gods remained implanted in his thought. The whole structure of his later socioeconomic analysis can be seen as a case of romantic irony in which the capitalist unconsciously undoes himself and raises up the forlorn creature he oppressed.

At Berlin Marx encountered the influence of Hegel; the great philosopher who had died a few years before Marx came to Berlin had left behind a powerful legacy and a number of competing heirs. More serious at Berlin, Marx took up philosophy and joined a Hegel discussion group. He became one of the so-called Young Hegelians who took Hegel in a leftward direction. Many ideas associated with Marx were products of others in this group. The Pole, Ciezskowski, first said that since Hegel had carried philosophy as far as it could go, the next step was action, to change the world not merely understand it. Marx's teacher, the fiery Bruno Bauer, declared that religion was the opiate of the people. Idol of the young Marx, Ludwig Feuerbach, explained that we now realize God is but a projection of human needs and desires. The Young Hegelians, among whom one might count the notable biblical critic David Strauss, focused much attention on religion and, to the detriment of their academic career prospects, planned an Archives of Atheism. We will recall that Moses Hess, whom Marx once criticized as the "Communist rabbi," was the one most interested in socialist ideas and introduced these to the Berlin circle.

A new monarch mounted the Prussian throne in 1840 and proved to be a reactionary; Bauer was dismissed, and Marx lost his chance for a professorship though he completed his doctorate with a dissertation, taken at Jena rather than Berlin, on the ancient Greek materialists, Democritus and Epicurus (drawing a comparison between the state of philosophy then, after Plato and Aristotle, and now after Kant and Hegel). Karl's father died, as did his friend, Baron Westphalen. He was estranged from his pious and practical mother. Matters were not working out so well for the brilliant and fiery young philosopher. But he got a job as a writer and then editor of the *Rheinische Zeitung* (the *Rhineland Times*), a newspaper in Cologne; he married

Karl Marx (Washington, D.C., Library of Congress.)

Jenny Westphalen and found new friends, among them Friedrich Engels, the self-educated son of a wealthy Rhineland industrialist.

Although Marx predictably lost his job with the newspaper for being too radical, the years 1843 to 1845 were stimulating and crucial for him. He encountered socialist ideas, went to Paris, and undertook a systematic critique of Hegel. In an article published in the first and only issue of an abortive French-German magazine Marx tried to establish in Paris 1843–44, the proletariat makes its appearance as the destined emancipator of the human race, in alliance with philosophy.

The young Marx thought in Hegelian concepts, though by 1844 he had rejected Hegel and German idealism as an inversion of reality, putting spirit before nature rather than vice versa. Left-wing Hegelianism led him to see God as really only the alienated (externalized) essence of human nature. He continued to struggle with Hegel through much of his early, formerly unpublished writings, especially the 1844 "Paris Manuscripts." Practically unknown for more than half a century after his death, these writings reveal a rather different Marx from the tough-minded "social scientist" on which his disciples had long drawn. They make extensive use of the "alienation" idea, almost missing in the later works, and are more concerned with the individual personality in a complex society than the later treatises; for that reason, along with their less dogmatic tone, they have attracted more interest in recent years than the "classical" Marx-Engels texts that had seemingly led to totalitarian dictatorship. Changing Hegel's "alienation," which was Spirit externalizing itself in nature, Marx used it to analyze what happens to the worker when excessive division of labor, along with ownership by others of what is produced, deprives the individual of the satisfactions of creative labor. Under capitalism, the workers are alienated not only from the product of their labor, but also from themselves and their fellow workers. Later Marx talks of labor as a commodity and of the "fetishism" of money, an alien power objectifying and masking a human relationship; this is a link with the "alienation" theme.

Marx left Germany in disgust in 1843 after battling censorship for a time as a journalist. In Paris he breathed the intoxicating air of that intellectual capital in the giddy forties, when the socialist ideas of Fourier, Saint-Simon, and especially Proudhon were being discussed. Here also came colorful Russian revolutionaries such as Michael Bakunin. The meeting with Engels resulted in a friendship for life, bringing to Marx support, both financial and intellectual, on which he was often to lean. The two men seldom disagreed, an unusual partnership and one of considerable moment, for without Engels, a man of some means, Marx could surely never have spent his life writing books that few bought. Engels, who was managing a branch of his father's textile factory in Manchester, England, had just written a report on *The Condition of the Working Class in England* in 1844 using materials from the parliamentary investigation that scandalized the British public at that time.

Upon the suggestion of the French government, prodded by the Prussian, Marx moved to Belgium in 1845 where he spent the next three years writing and studying. In his theses on Feuerbach and in two books co-authored with Engels, *The German Ideology* and *The Holy Family*, Marx further refined his position

Marx's fellow socialist and sometime rival, Pierre-Joseph Proudhon, as seen by the great French caricaturist Honoré Daumier. (National Gallery of Art, Washington, Rosenwald collection.)

through critiques of his former mentors, and with an increasing interest in economics. Guided by his theoretical position, that thought must enter into a dynamic relationship with the real world of work and struggle, Marx ventured into politics, becoming associated with what was finally called the Communist League. (With a growing family, Marx like so many other Germans at this time thought about migrating to the United States; it is tempting to speculate on Marx in Milwaukee as a successful capitalist. A colleague and rival among these German left-wing refugees, Willich, did end as a Civil War hero whose statue graces an Ohio town.) Marx had known no actual proletarians, only theoretical ones; he now encountered some artisans among the Communists and was not very comfortable with them, often inveighing against their stupidity while they accused him of intellectual arrogance. Prominent among these was the moralistic tailor, Wilhelm Weitling. A "more scientific understanding" was needed, thought Marx, than this "unrealistic humanism."

Marx further defined his thought in polemics with the popular French socialist-anarchist, Proudhon, hurling at poor Proudhon also the charge of being "utopian." Capitalism is not wrong or bad or "unjust"—how should we judge? It will perish when historical necessity overtakes it and its social relations come into conflict with powers of production, that is, when capitalism no longer means an expansion of material plenty but is an obstacle to its further development. This is a matter of scientific economic analysis.

A considerably simplified version of Marx and Engels, modified by the views of the artisans they spoke for, appeared in the famous *Communist Manifesto* of 1847. History as class struggle, the sharpening of the conflict today as capitalism reaches its crisis, criticism of other socialisms as unrealistic in putting their abstract ideas ahead of social realities—these Marxian propositions accompanied a rousing call to welcome the coming inevitable triumph of the proletariat. It was an apt statement, for the long-awaited revolution was about to erupt.

It turned out to be rather different from Marx's own dreams. Marx returned to Germany in 1848 to edit the new *Rheinische Zeitung*. During the revolutionary year he generally argued that Germany must go through her liberal bourgeois revolution first; thus, the immediate goal should be not socialism, but universal suffrage and abolishing the remnants of feudalism. He also supported war against Russia to unify Germany and defend the revolution. During this amazing year, Germany tried to unite her many small pieces into one nation as well as liberalize and democratize, overthrow the monarchs of Prussia, Saxony, and so on, and avoid conflicts with other peoples undergoing the same revolutionary turmoil.

Marx's modest role came to an end at the same time that the revolution sputtered to a close; he was expelled from Germany in March 1849. He arrived in Paris in time to witness the fizzling out of the revolution there, too, although Marx had predicted "a colossal eruption of the revolutionary crater." Suppression of a rather feeble workers' demonstration in June crushed the hopes of the revolutionists and doomed the Second Republic.

Marx was invited to leave Paris in July. He sailed for England in August, with his wife and three small children, as Jenny pawned the family jewels. He would live the rest of his life in London, long amid poverty and isolation. The 1848 fiasco was the last significant revolution in Western Europe; the era of revolutions was over. Marx never accepted this, but he did realize that a new era had begun, in which the inevitable proletarian liquidation of capitalism was a long way off—"ten, twenty, perhaps fifty years." By 1851 Marx had withdrawn from politics, as the affairs of the Communist League trickled to a dismal halt. Many refugees headed for England in 1849, not only a band of Germans, but Russians, Italians, Hungarians, and others—Mikhail Bakunin, Louis Kossuth, Giuseppe Mazzini, Louis Blanc, and Victor Hugo among them. (Others like Richard Wagner, who had taken part in an uprising in Dresden, found temporary asylum in Switzerland.) The refugees squabbled among themselves and had little contact with other national groups. So, for the time being, Marx's affairs hit rock bottom.

Sustained by the loyal Engels, and undeterred by problems that included the deaths of two of his children and the birth of an illegitimate one—an event that, we now know, cast a considerable cloud over a marriage once depicted as idyllic—Marx threw himself into research and writing, laying the British Museum library under heavy contribution. For many years Marx earned some income from the New York *Tribune* newspaper (Horace Greeley's organ) whose European correspondent he was.[1] Receiving gifts and some money from his inheritance, the Marx family was able by 1856 to move from the miserable Dean Street lodgings to a comfortable house in Hampstead; though for years Marx's improvidence and lack of steady income made for occasionally difficult finances. At length, Engels inherited his father's fortune, moved to the London area, and supported Marx more generously. There were many visitors, friends, and a lively family life as the Marx daughters—Jennie, Laura, and Eleanor—were given good educations. Marx's serious intellectual work concentrated on the vast project—from which he was often distracted by journalism and other enthusiasms—of which Volume I of *Das Kapital* (1867) was the only completed part. The 1857 *Grundrisse* (or *Outlines of a Critique of Political Economy*) was a draft of enormous proportions. What Marx later published in the one completed volume of *Das Kapital,* as David McLellan points out, covered only a portion of the ground that had been staked out in the *Grundrisse.* Marx's predilection for extruding vast and formless manuscripts had not ended with the 1844 Paris manuscripts and, indeed, would never end. Yet he could pause to throw out gems of pamphleteering such as *The Eighteenth Brumaire of Louis Bonaparte* (1869).

Interrupting this literary effort was Marx's return to politics to become for many years the dominant figure in the First International (International Working Men's Association). The 1860s brought him back to politics, as well it might. He attended a great rally of London workers on behalf of the North in the American Civil War, in October of 1863. The Polish revolt of 1863 was the event directly re-

---

[1] Altogether between 1851 and 1862, the *Tribune* published 487 articles from Marx; Engels however wrote 125 of these for him and collaborated in several others. Some 350 were by Marx written in a vigorous and interesting style; some found their way into *Kapital.*

sponsible for the creation of the International. Garibaldi had just had his enormous reception, said to have been the largest turnout for a foreign visitor in the history of the city. Whereas hopes of revolutionary activity had slumbered for a decade in the stunned post-1848 coma, they now revived. Marx labored for many years on behalf of the International, yet it cannot be said that this exercise in *praxis* was any more successful than his earlier experience with the Communist League. For a time in the late 1860s, there were well-attended International conferences, but fierce feuds between different socialist factions damaged the organization. Marx fought Proudhonists and also followers of the fabled Russian anarchist/revolutionary Bakunin, with whom Marx had many memorable battles over the years. Even within German socialism, Marx was challenged by his friend, the flamboyant Ferdinand Lassalle, until the latter's death in a duel in 1864. In his struggles with these factions, Marx resorted to some fairly slippery practices. The coup de grace to the First International came from the war between France and Prussia, which in 1870-71 just as in 1914-18 divided the supposedly internationalist Left. Not until 1889, six years after Marx's death, was the International revived.

By this time publication of *Das Kapital,* Vol. I, at long last (1867) had given Marx a measure of recognition as did his pamphlet on the Paris Commune of 1871, a brilliant piece of polemical literature that wrongly hailed the attempted secession of Paris as the beginning of the proletarian world revolution. But he never finished another volume of his magnum opus though in time three additional volumes of *Das Kapital* were pieced together from his fragments. In his later years, beset by illness, Marx lost none of his intellectual curiosity but inevitably some of his creative energy. Some see him as discouraged by the failure of revolutionism. He filled his countless notebooks with detailed information on all manner of things, creating employment and enjoyment for scores of scholars in recent years. He was a great letter writer; the total output of Marx and Engels in the complete edition of their works laboriously assembled in our times (never yet fully translated into English) fills more than sixty fat volumes. The informed student of Marx is likely to be struck by the contrast between a Marx of legend and of the disciples, author of a rather simple dogmatic system, and this real Marx who started everything and seldom finished anything, a person of gargantuan curiosity who was always revising his views, and who once burst forth upon reading something from the disciples "Thank God I am not a Marxist!" ("He laughs at the fools who parrot his proletarian catechism," an acquaintance testified.)

Marx was financially more comfortable in his later years, but he had not received much recognition outside the little world of German (and to some extent French and Russian) socialism at the time of his death, at age 65, in 1883. Had he lived only a few years longer, he would have been gratified at his growing fame; the major reception of Marxism came in the 1890s.

We have sketched Marx's not uninteresting life, which included some attempts—not very successful—to apply theory to life. Many have commented on Marx's personality or character: arrogant to some, cocksure, certain of his rightness (a "right" man, in one categorization of temperaments);[2] a hard-hitting, sometimes sarcastic polemicist, a fierce hater guilty at times of unscrupulousness in debate; capable of sudden enthusiasms in an almost trendy way—a man, however, who respected competent opponents and could change his mind. A lover of life, given to pub-crawling with Fred Engels and other German cronies in his earlier years (there is one account of a drunken brawl with police in London), Marx evidently collected pornography and, as we know, fathered at least one illegitimate offspring. Yet he was a good family man, too, delighting in his children and adored by them, enjoying picnics on Hampstead Heath and often reading aloud at home in the Victorian manner. Not much interested in the other arts, Marx was steeped in literature: "he needed the words of great writers to confirm and sanction his own" is the judgment of a splendid study by S. S. Prawer, *Karl Marx and World Literature* (1976). His daughter Eleanor recalled evenings with Homer, Don Quixote, the *Niebelungen Lied,* but especially Shakespeare, read almost every day, "the Bible of our house." And many others. Marx was a special admirer of Balzac and Dickens as well as the great nineteenth-century Germans, Goethe and particularly Heine, with whom he had a close friendship. He had a superb acquaintance with European literature.

Like many alienated bourgeoisie since, Marx was a plebeian much more in theory than in practice, living when he could a comfortable life. His excessive consumption of cigars, as well as alcohol, may have cost him some years of his life. His "passionate and earnest dedication to the cause of the proletariat" not even Bakunin questioned though he found it "mixed with personal vanity," as did numerous others: Karl Marx, clearly, was far from the most modest of men. No one doubted his superb intellectual gifts. He gave abundantly of his energies to the organizations he served. His conception of *praxis,* however inadequately realized, may be his richest single legacy: theory and reality must meet and work together, the arm-chair theorist is inadequate, but so is the activist unguided by ideas; the thinker must enter the real world, test his theories, let them be modified by actuality, and attempt, "dialectically," to modify actuality in turn. Marx honestly struggled to do this; it is a rare achievement. The notion itself was hardly unusual in Romanticism; thus the American sage, Emerson, in his 1837 "American Scholar" address (delivered in the year Marx began his serious intellectual quest) opined that "A great soul will be strong to live, as well as strong to think."

SOURCES OF MARX'S THOUGHT

Marx can best be viewed as a remarkably synthetic thinker, that is, one who drew together a great many strains in a unified structure. Some of these strains we have mentioned, and are obvious. He found socialism and communism, as we know, in

---

[2]Often quoted is the reaction of Carl Schurz, celebrated German-American statesman: "I have never seen a man whose bearing was so provoking and intolerable . . .. Everyone who contradicted him he treated with abject contempt . . . ." For the full quote see Schurz's *Reminiscences* (1909). And of Mikhail Bakunin, his Russian rival: "He called me a sentimental idealist; and he was right. I called him vain, treacherous, and morose; and I too was right."

the many ideologists of the generation before his. They emerged during the turbulent years when he was growing up. Born just as the great French Revolutionary and Napoleonic era ended, Marx arrived at maturity in time to inherit the first harvest of social ideas produced by the need to reconstruct society after this convulsion. He was familiar with and admired the great pioneer socialists, especially Saint-Simon, Owen, and Fourier; he bestowed on them the epithet "utopian" because he felt they were naive about means of attaining socialism; naive in supposing evangelical exhortation aimed at a moral regeneration would serve to install the new order. Against their inadequacies Marx reacted with typical vehemence, sometimes ridiculing these simple souls. He seemed to reject the moralistic criticism of capitalism, as "unjust" or "wrong." He did not think socialism would be established by a violent revolution stirred up by emotionalism; that was Blanquism or adventurism. One had to understand the historical process and the actual workings of economics. The later Marx was more realistic than the younger, because he shared the sobering disillusion that followed 1848. But it is important to note that he always assumed the validity of socialism or communism as a higher social order, marked by an overcoming of "capitalism's" weakness, which would mark the next advance of humanity and would lead to a virtually perfect condition. There is no way of getting around Marx's own occasional "utopianism." "Communism is the solution to the riddle of existence."

We know that Marx drew on Hegel, too; he found there the sense of a single great unity in the cosmos, linking history, humanity, and nature, and he found the principle of dialectical interaction of matter and mind, reality and spirit, in an ongoing cycle of continuous contradiction and resolution—thesis, antithesis, synthesis. Of course, he rejected what he saw as Hegel's idealism, putting the cart before the horse, making the son beget the father: not Absolute Spirit but flesh-and-blood creatures make history and evolve ideas. But he kept Hegel's totalism and his dialectical method—which is the source of Marx's great principle of *praxis.* This holism is the root of some of Marx's problems, for he wanted to put the entirety of human history into a single work, which was of course impossible. It is also the source of his greatest appeal, offering to bewildered modern man a coherent vision of reality. Vulgarized, it became the Historical Necessity that directs all humanity down a single predetermined road.

Marx further, and increasingly, drew on the political economists, the school of David Ricardo, which he criticized but extensively used in the analysis of capitalism presented in his greatest single book. With the aid of economic analysis he sought to show in concrete detail how the dialectical contradictions of capitalism were encompassing its death while at the same time bringing to birth, within its dying body, the new socialist order that was to supplant it.

Thus socialism, Hegelianism, and political economy merged into a more or less harmonious system in Marx's thought. He drew on the best knowledge of the three major nations of Europe—German speculative philosophy, French social thought, and British economic theory—encountering these directly in the course of a life that had taken him from Germany to France and to England. To this trinity, merging the major intellectual achievements of three peoples, one should add some other influences on Marx that came from his era. We have referred to the persistence of Romanticism as a deep structure of this thought—coloring it with drama, the irony, the verve, the literary qualities that made him an exciting thinker and, often, a great writer. (Marx could be as tedious as social theory, German philosophy, and technical economics suggest; much of what he wrote was abstruse and hard to understand. That he sometimes overcame this is owing to his sense of style.) Marx then passed into a more scientific phase in the Darwinian 1850s and 1860s, looking for exact "laws" of human evolution, seeking the "science of society." Some have thought this scientism of the *Das Kapital* phase a mistake, but it then lent strength and prestige to his work, endowing it with the mana of the new god, Science. So we can see Marx bringing fruitfully together the "two cultures" of science and literature (as another great Jewish thinker, Sigmund Freud, was later to do.)

KEY IDEAS OF MARXISM

What was Marx's legacy of ideas? If he sometimes scoffed at his simpler-minded disciples, we must indicate this "proletarian catechism" that was to form the basis of a powerful political movement. On his death, Marx left a movement organized as the Social Democratic Party, which soon was the most vigorous and successful socialist group in the world. The Communist party was a subsequent offshoot of this movement. The success of these parties, as well as their failures perhaps, could be traced to the vigor and clarity of Marx's thought. Yet it is somewhat problematical whether their leaders really spoke for Marx. One need only instance the Russian party's conversion of Marxism into an iron dictatorship, based on very slender foundations in Marx himself and, according to experts, foreign to his spirit.

Marx's disciples in the organized socialist movement—a common fault of disciples—drastically simplified and dogmatized his thought, converting it into a kind of secular church-militant marked by the trappings of religion, including a scholastic theology. In part this was Marx's own fault, for he had insisted that his thought was not merely speculative but practical. Philosophy had heretofore only understood the world, now it must change it, he proclaimed. Hegel had brought speculative philosophy as far as it could go; the next step, taken by Hegel's successor, was to convert this knowledge into actuality. "It is not the consciousness of men that determines their being, but, on the contrary, their social being that determines their consciousness." The individual working, struggling, acting comes first, ideas are a product of this activity; history is nothing but the actions of real, sentient people in pursuit of their ends. Ideas are engendered from this process and, in turn, exert an influence; Marx was no crude "economic determinist." But in the end it is "the economic structure of society" that determines thought, not vice versa, according to Marx and Engels.

It therefore seemed necessary that Marxism be understood by the masses, and leaders of the Social Democratic parties produced simplified catechisms: The workers are exploited, they must break the mental as well as physical chains of capitalism, the great revolution is inevitable and will usher in a classless society, the last millennial state of humanity completing its long journey through successive stages from slavery to freedom. It was a thinly disguised version of the Judeo-Christian eschatology, but it rested also on the allegedly scientific economics of Marx. These disciples knew little or nothing of the early writings, but rested their faith chiefly on the analysis of capitalism contained in *Das Kapital.*

Deliberately presenting a simplified Marxism for popular consumption, the German and Austrian Social Democrats stressed these points: (1) The economic mode of production determines social, political, and cultural forms (meaning, as a practical matter, that existing bourgeois values are not eternal and sacred but only a smokescreen or apology for their class rule). (2) History is a record of class struggle; this element of conflict has given human affairs their dynamic since the dawn of history, proceeding through the domination, first, of the slaveholder, then, the feudal lord, semifinally, the capitalistic bourgeoisie, now challenged by the last exploited class, the proletariat, destined to triumph and end the historic cycle by introducing a classless society. (3) In bourgeois society, exploitation of the workers is disguised by the market and money system; the feudal lord simply made his serfs work for him half their time, the factory owner pays his "free" workers a wage, but this masks exploitation. The value of a commodity is determined by the amount of labor socially necessary to produce it. But in receiving wages amounting to less than this value, the workers do not get the full value of what they produce. Thus (4) the wealth of the propertied classes is derived from the surplus value produced by their employees. (5) This rate of exploitation is steadily increasing, as the capitalists face declining profits; thus the plight of the proletariat grows steadily worse. (6) Small business is also being destroyed. (7) Monopoly capitalism is a fetter on production; only after the expropriation of the expropriators will it be possible to produce enough for all to live in abundance. (8) The final hour of capitalism is approaching; declining profits, growing worker misery, and swelling numbers of the exploited proletariat herald the end. Capitalism will fall virtually of its own weight, but the Great Day of the Revolution nevertheless will come suddenly. (9) After this, humanity will enter into a bright age marked not only by material abundance but the elimination of greed, crime, war, and all manner of evil. The State will also cease to exist, there no longer being any need of coercion because a ruling class no longer exists.

Such a list of items in the Marxist decalogue might be modified or extended but everyone will recognize the familiar elements. Some of these propositions were derived from general philosophical or quasi-religious considerations, for example, a seemingly preestablished, necessary course of events, and a dialectical pattern (no gradual change or steady-state situation, but the buildup to a sudden change—contradictions implanted in every society compelling it to transform itself into something higher). Some came from a theory of history, tracing several broad stages defined by technological-economic factors on the basis of which relationships of "class" emerged and finding the motive force of history in class conflict. Others, perhaps the most striking, grew out of the economic analysis Marx had given in his *Das Kapital,* purporting to prove that the seeds of its destruction lay in the very workings of the capitalist system of wage labor and market production. And some were sociological theories of culture: Religion, art, and politics grow out of the economic basis to form a derivative (or partially derivative) "superstructure." Marx raised a host of issues in this seemingly simple catechism; they were all to prove controversial, and they began an endless debate stretching over many areas of thought and knowledge—touching, in terms of our modern "departments" of knowledge, philosophy, history, economics, sociology, and others as well.

To chase down all these innumerable hares started by Marx is of course impossible to do here; and indeed the hunt still goes on. Hundreds of books and articles about aspects of Marx and Marxism have appeared in recent years and continue to appear; modern scholarship has managed to make almost every line of Marxism problematic, whereas unlettered people once thought they understood him perfectly. (Recent schools of Marxist interpretation are discussed later in this book, in Chapter 8.)

Criticism of Marx came early, right after he became famous or notorious. Economists were in general not much impressed with the arguments found in the (unfinished) *Das Kapital.* Let us take up this point first, for after all, this was Marx's major work. He thought that he had made a momentous discovery in unveiling the true laws of economics, and it was primarily owing to the evident cogency of this analysis that Marxism came to dominate the socialist movement. Marx based himself on the great bourgeois economists, especially David Ricardo, for whom he had enormous respect; he thought he had corrected their errors and perfected their science. In doing so, he made use of the labor theory of value and produced an account of capitalism's inevitable and fatal contradictions.

MARX'S ANALYSIS OF CAPITALISM

Prior to Marx many less weighty socialist theoreticians had charged that the factory owners exploited, in other words, cheated, their employees. The revelation of brutally long hours and pitifully low wages, frequently using child labor, while the owners drew large profits, had projected the "social question" (in Carlyle's phrase) onto the conscience of Europe when Marx was still a juvenile. The notion quickly grew that the wage system was a method of exploitation. A workers' jingle current before the *Communist Manifesto* was written (in 1847) made the point:

> Wages should form the price of goods
> Yes, wages should be all,
> Then we who work to make the goods,
> Should justly have them all.

This was a crude statement of the labor theory of value on which Marx erected his economic analysis.

The labor theory of value may be traced a long way back; it was forcefully stated by Adam Smith and adopted by Ricardo, where Marx found it. Later economic theory was to discard it, but Marx seized upon it and attempted to work out all its implications. It was still partly economic orthodoxy in Marx's time, though the "bourgeois" economists did not put it to the uses Marx did, needless to say. Value to them was "cost of production," which included materials and the natural reward of capital (the result of "abstinence" from present consumption) as well as labor. Remnants of the Ricardian labor theory of value existed in classical economics as represented most popularly by J. S. Mill at this time. The clean break with it was not to be made until Alfred Marshall and W. J. Jevons, about 1870.

The labor theory of value, plus the subsistence theory of wages, suggested to socialists that labor does not get its full and just price because wages are determined in the market, by the principle of supply and demand, whereas the products are sold for their "true" price, based on the amount of labor put into them. The difference was said to represent a surplus of value appropriated by the capitalist. Robert Owen had tried to change this pernicious system by using a currency reflecting units of labor, so that the price of a product would be exactly the amount of labor put into it. This naive idea proved entirely unworkable. Agreement could never be reached on just how many labor units commodities are worth, a major objection to the labor theory of value being that labor values submit to no accurate quantitative measurement. One carpenter might make a table in half the time another took; and how could one compare highly skilled labor to unskilled—how many hours of carpenter labor is one hour of an expert surgeon's time worth? Marx attempted to meet this objection by postulating a "socially necessary" amount of labor for every commodity.

Marx ridiculed the labor-exchange idea. He believed that only the abolition of capitalism—of private property in the means of production—would solve the problem, and he used the labor theory of value not to support labor-exchange or social credit schemes but rather to demonstrate, as he thought, the dynamics of capitalism as it worked toward its self-destruction.

Among the features of capitalism that seemed alarming were the periodic panics or depressions that afflicted it, tendencies toward monopoly, and of course the low wages and deplorable working conditions that frequently were the lot of the factory hands, to which one might add the demoralizing separation of workers from their tools and products, as they worked with machinery owned by others to produce goods that were not theirs to sell. For all these observable features of the nineteenth-century economic order in Western Europe, Marx tried to supply explanations. The whole of his argument was designed to show that capitalism is a doomed system because it is unavoidably digging its own grave. The labor theory of value is the foundation stone for Marx's concept of the *falling rate of profit,* which is chiefly how he explained crises, consolidation, and the increasing misery of the working class.

Profits must come out of labor. Therefore, the increasing use of machinery forces the capitalists to exploit their workers ever more mercilessly. They are forced to adopt machinery because of technological advances and competition; but as they increase the proportion of this "constant capital," as Marx called it, they have less and less of labor power or "variable capital" from which to make profits. Today it seems odd that Marx should have supposed that mechanization destroys profits by displacing human labor. One should assume that it would be more likely to *increase* profits, by cutting down the wage bill or stepping up efficiency of production. But he had his eye fixed on the labor theory of value, from which his conclusion seems to follow logically. This is the chief of the "contradictions" of capitalism according to Marx: that as it progresses, measured by the use of advanced machinery, it must intensify the misery of the working class, for profits must be squeezed out of human labor power. The more machinery used, the lower the wage of the worker has to be.

Strive as they will, the capitalists cannot, however, prevent their profits from declining. Of this unhappy fact another result is that some manufacturers are driven to the wall and fewer and fewer capitalists exist, holding bigger and bigger enterprises. This, too, unwittingly prepares for socialism; the huge industrial concern is already socialized, and at the last there are scarcely more than a handful of capitalists left to be taken over by society.

"In proportion as capital accumulates, the lot of the labourer . . . must grow worse." Marx evidently abandoned his early theory that wages must fall to the level of bare subsistence and in other writings spoke of spiritual rather than economic impoverishment, or a relative impoverishment: Workers may be better off but the employers are even more so. The fact is that absolute impoverishment of the working class was not happening; the evidence clearly indicated rising real wages through the later nineteenth century, not falling. So Marx often stressed the moral degradation of workers, through being made "appendages of a machine" and subjected to humiliating conditions of toil. He continued to insist that in some sense the workers became ever more miserable under capitalism, but this was not necessarily, one gathers, from material impoverishment. Marx is rather slippery on this vital point.

The labor theory of value on which Marx leaned so heavily was soon to be abandoned by economists, and today most of them think that it will bear little or none of the weight he put on it. His explanation of depressions, then, along with his theory of profits and wages, seem invalid. As for his predictions that small business would succumb entirely to big, and that with the advance of machinery people under capitalism would be worse off and not better—the doctrine of the declining rate of profit and the increasing misery of the working class—these things have not come about, though at times they may have looked plausible. By the end of the century workers were better off in material terms, not worse; the long-term effects of technology were to increase the whole national income greatly, though unevenly; and (it has been persuasively argued) the belief that the proletariat was growing ever more miserable was an illusion fostered partly by novelists, partly by that familiar phenomenon known as "relative deprivation"—we can think we are worse even when in absolute terms we are better off, because we perceive more things we want and do not have. The capital that Marx saw (under capitalism) as pushing the workers under was actually elevating them, gradually, unevenly, unequally, it is true, but in the long run steadily. In his formula of exploitation, Marx had not sufficiently allowed for the enormous extent to which machinery raises the productivity of labor.

Many of Marx's own followers finally came to feel that a wholesale revision of his economic theories was needed. The main stream of economic analysis traveled away from Marx, and in later times John Maynard Keynes spoke for most professional economists in calling *Das Kapital* "an obsolete economic textbook." But Marx's doctrines have of course exerted an enormous influence on the Soviet Union since its revolutionary birth in 1917. Still, economic practice, even the Soviets, does not owe much directly to Marx, who failed to describe in detail the economics of socialism. He thought he had charted with scientific accuracy the last fatal illness of capitalism, and all Marxists continue to believe that "capitalism is doomed."

Perhaps it is, but apparently not for the reasons Marx gave. Sometimes it is suggested that Marx was a good prophet in a general sort of way, though he missed many details; for has not the economic order, even in the West, traveled a long way from the unregulated individualism of the nineteenth century toward a "welfare state" system which is in the broadest sense socialistic? It has indeed, but it should be noted that Marx has not really proved a good prophet here. The welfare state or "interventionist" economy was not really what he had in mind. Marx believed that the state would die; his vision of the future was essentially anarchist, or perhaps utopian. Social ownership of the means of production did not mean to him statism.

Classical Marxism expected the middle class to be ground to bits, the class struggle to become more acute, the factory workers to grow ever unhappier until they rebelled, and the capitalist order to end in revolution, with private property in the sector of production disappearing. In all these respects he proved a poor prophet. It took a disastrous war to bring socialist revolution to Europe, and then it came to a backward, almost precapitalist society, quite contrary to the expectations of most Marxists.

Even as Marx was writing *Das Kapital,* economists such as Stanley Jevons were criticizing the labor theory, doing away with the mystical idea of a true or inherent "value" of a commodity that is not the same as its market price. They substituted a sophisticated version of supply and demand, the marginal utility theory.[3] Others pointed out that Marx's surplus value would not do; why should competition not cause it to disappear? It was argued that capital is more productive than Marx thought. But if in the eyes of experts not much was left of Marx's elaborate theorizing in his *magnum opus,* which he left unfinished, it remained a

[3] Developed almost simultaneously by Carl Menger in Austria and M. E. L. Walras in Switzerland along with Jevons in England, marginal utility analysis represented on charts the curve of diminishing utility as an individual—or, by extension, a nation—acquires successive units of a commodity. To a hungry person the first loaf of bread is extremely valuable, but each successive one decreases in its value to that person. The final increment, the marginal one, determines exchange value. "Commodities exchange at ratios such that their marginal utilities are equal." The student may consult textbooks of economics for full understanding of the principle. Employed by the influential economists Alfred Marshall in Britain and J. B. Clark in the United States, marginal theory tended to dominate academic economics in this "neo-classical" phase. Marshall's *Principles of Economics* supplanted Mill's as the standard textbook.

compelling document. In many portions of the book Marx abandoned the pretense of scientific objectivity to emit thunderous indictments of working conditions in the factories and the iniquity of capitalism. And the whole seemed an impressive vindication of the larger dialectical philosophy. Apparently Marx had shown in detail how capitalism destroys itself and in the process creates socialism, its "negation" that had always been included in itself. Socialism emerges out of the very womb of capitalism, as the dialectic predicts. Capitalism brought into existence the working class, forced it into the factories, and reduced the number of capitalists, thus inadvertently "socializing" the economic order and the technological system; it created advanced machinery, broke down parochial social units to create the national and even international economy, and also accustomed individuals to a rational, materialistic outlook. According to Marxists, capitalism had an indispensable historical role to play, and until Lenin they practically all felt that every society must work its way through capitalism before it is ready for socialism. There was an ambiguity here, to be sure, revealed in the later history of the Marxist movement. One might choose to dwell on the horrors of capitalism, the misery it caused the workers, the need to destroy it; or one might point to its inevitability and the things it achieved to prepare the way for socialism. But it is the latter that is most characteristic of Marx as opposed to the mere moralists whose outlook he despised because it was not "scientific."

MARX'S IDEA OF HISTORY

Marx was more than a mere economist, of course; he embedded his economics in a conception of the whole of historic development. One might indeed be a Marxist yet reject the economics as trivially in error owing to the state of the art at the time (much as some Christians excuse the Bible for not being scientifically accurate, regarding this as no barrier to accepting its larger truth). Of an interest second only to the theories about surplus value and capitalistic profits were Marx's views about the nature of the historic process, and the relationship between components of human culture. Along with Comte and Darwin or Spencer, he is one of the founding fathers of sociology; and as historian he was in the middle of a flourishing nineteenth-century activity.

Both Marx's historicism and his "sociology of knowledge" contributed to his political goal of revolution; they were not purely scientific. To believe that "history is on our side" is a powerful stimulus to any movement, and most of the nineteenth-century ideologies whether liberal, socialist, nationalist, or other made use of it. A liberal like Benjamin Constant or John Bright, the Saint-Simonian socialists as well as the Marxists, preachers of national mission like the Russian Slavophiles, all claimed that successive ages of the past pointed toward their cause as the denouement of a long unfolding story; history has a plan, it is a journey with a goal—and that *telos* or meaningful end they found, of course, to be represented by their party or nation or idea. Time is a redeeming river; "in the fullness of time" comes the revelation of God's purpose, or Nature's, a revelation that He or It chose to deliver not all at once but in slow stages. This was a very general nineteenth-century faith that can be regarded as a naturalization of Christian Providence. So Marxists believed that human historical evolution led to the triumph of socialism and communism. The tactical value of Marx's historical materialism must also again be noted. Marx borrowed the term "ideology" (from the late Enlightenment ideologies, who used it in quite a different way) to mean the falsity or incompleteness of those ideas which, excreted by a class-dominated order, betray the bad faith of their origin by distorting the truth. Such a view was a weapon against the existing social order. Its values and knowledge are not the eternal truths they claim to be, but merely the propaganda of the ruling class. Whether religious teachings or economic theories, the proletariat will eye them with suspicion, knowing that they are only "ideology."

The "materialist interpretation of history" which, as Engels asserted in his speech at Marx's funeral, Marx was the first to grasp, held that "the production of the immediate material means of subsistence and consequently the degree of economic development attained by a given people or during a given epoch form the foundation upon which the state institutions, the legal conceptions, the ideas on art and even on religion . . . have been evolved, and in the light of which they must, therefore, be explained." (Did this include scientific knowledge, mathematics, logic? works of literature?) We understand, then, that what the capitalists or their intellectual lackeys tell us is the law, or the nature of the social order, or the moral values we should cherish, is not the truth but a class-conditioned distortion, perhaps negation of the truth. We learn, as workers, to mistrust what we read in their books and papers, or hear from their pulpits. This material has to be decoded. Its underlying purpose is not disinterested knowledge but defense of the bourgeois state. Such, in crude form, was the practical import of the historical materialism that placed knowledge in the "superstructure" of class society.

At the end, presumably, truth will emerge in all its objectivity. Or will knowledge still be relative to the social order? Although the disciples accepted Marxism as true with all the fervency of true believers, Marx's influence in the end joined Darwin's in undermining belief in timeless truths. Truth is socially conditioned; it is relative to time and place and cannot be divorced from the practical interests with which it is involved. Even the most austere sage or scientist finds it impossible to divest himself of those biases of time, place, and culture that insinuate themselves into his language and thought, his unconscious mental habits. Marx said that the bourgeois truth and the proletarian truth can never be the same; others would say that the French and the German truths must be different. Nietzsche will soon say that "There are many kinds of eyes, and hence there are many kinds of truths, and consequently there is no Truth." Marx would have said that there are many classes, many interest groups, hence many truths and no Truths—unless maybe it is my own. (Among the Young Hegelians of Marx's early days, one, Max Stirner, went so far as to argue that truth is purely private; Feuerbach's Humanity, he said, is as unreal an abstraction as Hegel's Spirit, all that really exists is Me. But Marx and Engels in *The*

German Ideology ridiculed this anarchist individualism of "Saint Max." Marx agreed that Feuerbach's Humanity was a fetish, but he saw reality in social class, with its basis in the economic relations of production.)

A simplified economic determinism proved to be something of a mare's nest for Marxists. A hard or strong version, which would deny any autonomy or causal effect to ideas, culture, or noneconomic elements such as the political, is impossible for anyone with the slightest knowledge of history to maintain. Marx himself, who changed history by the force of his ideas (which derived from no sort of proletarian economic foundation) is a refutation. Ideas often seem more important than material things.[4] Marx himself knew that literature escapes class determinism, his beloved Homer and Aeschylus were not just apologists for slave owning. (He tried to account for the superiority of Greek literature by saying that since it came first it had the freshness and charm of childhood.) To deny the autonomy of politics and of culture is to be blind to essential data of human experience. Engels, in his later years, expressed extreme annoyance with stupid Marxists whose "fatuous notions" had "twisted" his and Marx's views; they had meant nothing so absurd, he declared, as that economic factors determine every last, petty detail, such as the boundaries of the various German states. He tried to save the primacy of economic factors "ultimately" and "in the long run."[5] But if you weaken the determinism in this way, admitting that the "superstructure" is not a product *only* of the economic basis, and admitting that elements of the superstructure can exert a significant causal influence on human affairs, the theory tends to decay into one too vague to have any explanatory value.[6] A crude economic determinism fails to explain many of the more important and interesting facts of history, such as the differences between various national cultures. And its weakness may account for the failures of Marxist prophecy: Marxists expected the socialist revolution in Great Britain first because capitalism was most advanced there, but this overlooked a host of obvious reasons for the English being the least revolutionary of peoples—reasons rooted not in economic factors but in political and social. Again, Marxian interpretation proves inadequate in explaining medieval feudalism, which was not an economic but a political phenomenon, and had little to do with class struggle.

There are countless such debates in historical interpretation exposing the problems in any monocausality, which tries to reduce everything to a single "basic" factor, whether economic, geographic, or other; the truth seems to be that in the seamless web of human affairs one cannot privilege any one factor, they all work together. One can credit Marx with being among the first to call attention to the

---

[4]Karl Popper suggested that if all the existing physical plant and scientific apparatus were destroyed but the knowledge behind it, in books and human brains, were left in existence, it would be possible to rebuild the apparatus; but if the physical plant remained while the knowledge was lost, the machinery would fall into disuse and perish. See *The Open Society and Its Enemies,* Vol. 2, 4th ed. (1962), pp. 107–08.

[5]See the letters on historical materialism to Joseph Bloch, Conrad Schmidt, and Franz Mehring, 1890–93.

[6]For illumination on this point see the article by James P. Scanlan in *Studies in Soviet Thought,* June 1973.

overlooked economic side of historical processes, or one can reproach him with making exaggerated claims for it. The fact is that Marx wrote surprisingly little about these questions in any detail. For example, he is widely credited with calling attention to the role of social class; but Marx never got around to writing that part of *Das Kapital* which would have treated this subject in depth.[7] Many historians and sociologists doubt that "class" is a useful term at all prior to modern times, or even that it has played much of a role in modern history except in a few instances. Which has not prevented others from enthusiastically adopting it as a key that hopefully will unlock the secrets of history.

Marx was scarcely the only thinker to note the importance of class; in *On Liberty* (1859), John Stuart Mill observed that "wherever there is an ascendant class, a large portion of the morality of the country emanates from its class interests and its feelings of class superiority." Herbert Spencer remarked that ideas are largely a product of "surrounding conditions," including "the social state," and went on to discuss (without much clarity) the extent to which ideas "govern and overthrow the world," concluding that they are not effective unless society is ready to receive them. Marx never claimed to have discovered the concept of social class, mentioning the historians Guizot and Thierry as well as the economist Ricardo as predecessors. Ricardo, it will be recalled, so important an influence on Marx, in an important part of his work had found the interests of landlords and manufacturers to be in conflict. Marx thought he was original in explaining the *origins* of classes, in the contradiction between the forces of production and the relations of production—between, in effect, technology and social organization.

Some Marxologists stress the need to separate Marx himself not only from the disciples but from Engels. The shrewd and jovial Engels was much less a profound thinker than Marx, though an energetic and facile writer. His writings, or those that he and Karl wrote jointly, are among the ones often selected by superficial students of Marxism because they are the least demanding. There has been a tendency to assume that the two men were so harmonious that they can be lumped together, but this is not true. Marx had to put up with much from Friedrich because he relied upon him financially, but privately Marx could ridicule his partner's ideas as he so often did those of lesser mortals. Some would put the blame for "vulgar Marxism" onto Engels's broad shoulders.

This is especially true of "the dialectics of nature," a book by Engels that gave rise to the "dialectical materialism" long considered to be the heart of Marxism. It was eventually noticed that Marx himself rarely if ever used this term. Prominent Marxists of the next generation took it over from Engels: Plekhanov in Russia, Karl Kautsky in Germany, Jules Guesde in France, whose associate was Marx's son-in-law, Paul LaFargue. Lenin and especially Stalin then made it Marxist orthodoxy in the Soviet Union. Engels installed the dialectical process as an attribute of

---

[7]When Marx did write a specific work of history, such as the analysis of the collapse of the 1848 Second Republic in France, in *The Class Struggles in France 1848-50* and *the Eighteenth Brumaire of Louis Bonaparte,* he recognized more complicated patterns than his theories would indicate; thus not two classes in France but about six!

matter itself—giving its laws as the transformation of quantity into quality (e.g., when water suddenly freezes after absorbing successive degrees of coldness), the interpenetration of opposites, and the negation of the negation. Everything in nature contains its opposite, as the seed contains the plant. Thus Engels, rather like Spencer vis-à-vis Darwin, attempted to formulate cosmic principles of social evolution; human society allegedly is governed by the same laws as physical matter and biological life. But this dialectics of nature has not fared any better than Spencer's evolutionary cosmology. It led to disasters for Soviet science in the Stalinist era when it was held that socialist, Marxian science had different and superior methods than "bourgeois" science. Categories such as Engels tries to impose on matter are not there, but in the conceptual framework of the scientist. The true dialectical method is between mind and nature. In postulating a mechanism within matter, Engels repeated in reverse the error that Marx attributed to Hegel, of endowing Mind with the power to create everything from its own operations. There is little support today, even among Marxists, for the dialectics of nature, which is ranked along with a simple economic determinism among the mistakes of a "vulgar Marxism."

THE INFLUENCE OF MARX

Marx's daring if doubtfully successful attempt to unite thought and action was reflected in the legacy of influence he passed on to the next generation (c. 1885–1914). In the academic, professional world of thought, Marx at first made little impact. The economists, who in the later nineteenth century were engaged in absorbing neoclassical theory (Jevons, Marshall, et al., as we previously noted), found Marx largely wrong-headed and irrelevant. One of his severest and most persistent critics was the Austrian economist Boehm-Bawerk, who concentrated on the weaknesses of the labor theory of value alleging that Marx failed to finish his book because he could not plug up its leaks.

Philosophy continued to be Hegelian; and the German universities did not readily accept socialists, to put it mildly. There were a few Marxist professors in Russia (the "legal Marxists") who found Marx by Russian standards to be a mild and reasonable revolutionary. In Italy, Antonio Labriola lectured at the University of Rome in the 1890s on the materialist conception of history, while the great Neopolitan philosopher and editor Benedetto Croce was much interested in Marxism; but Croce's *Historical Materialism and the Economics of Karl Marx* (1900), still a very useful critique, rejected dogmatic Marxism. The problem of Marxism was indicated in Croce's experience; it was one thing to acknowledge Marx's genius and many insights, but seemingly one had to swallow Marxism as a whole system excluding any other approach. This intolerance or exclusivism was built into Marx's thought in a curious way: The theory of class cultures relegated all existing "bourgeois" thought, it seemed, to the status of ideology or false consciousness, and claimed a monopoly of truth for the proletarian thought (Marxism) that replaced it. It was evidently all or nothing. Marxism was not just an idea that entered the bourgeois house to mingle with all the many other guests; it was another building entirely, and one had to choose which to live in. This was in some ways a strength but in others a weakness.

Discussion of Marx was abundant in circles outside the universities or establishment organs, often in reviews or journals that sprang up in this era of the little magazine. These were in general the disciples; most of them were more interested in Marxism as a social movement, a political cause, than as pure thought. Marx's continuing intellectual influence was not least evident in sociology, not then yet an accepted University subject, but soon to be developed by such giants as Max Weber, who was indebted to Marx (see further pp. 211-13). But let us discuss that lively phase of the socialist movement which institutionalized Marxism in the two or three decades prior to 1914, first however, putting Marxism in the context of the broader socialist movement.

OTHER FORMS OF SOCIALISM

Not well known in Europe until the 1880s, Karl Marx's formidable theories thereafter tended to mold and dominate continental socialism but never had that kind of success in Britain and never monopolized the field anywhere. Socialism was far broader than Marxism. It ranged, taking the term in its largest dimensions, from a fairly conservative bourgeois right wing, including Christian socialism and moderate welfare-state reformism, to a revolutionary far left that by the 1880s had come to be designated "anarchism." In between lay many species in rich variety. Marx's contemporaries included Mikhail Bakunin, the Russian revolutionary, with whom he did many a battle; Louis Blanc, in exile in England after 1848 but tough enough to outlive the Bonapartist regime and return to France in 1871; Mazzini and Garibaldi, the Italians who became internationally famous in 1861; and the American, Henry George, whose book *Progress and Poverty* exerted a remarkable influence in Britain and parts of the Continent. Then there was William Morris, Ruskin's as well as Marx's disciple, poet, and craftsman, who popularized "guild socialism," a return to the spirit of medieval artisans. Proudhon, the French "mutualist," long retained a strong following in France, and the First International of 1864 produced quarrels between the Marxists and Proudhonists. In Germany, Ferdinand Lassalle, a romantic figure who disagreed with Marx on some matters, was a more important leader in the 1870s than the latter. In Russia, "populist" revolutionaries arose in the 1870s.

Then, within a few years after the major reception of Marxism and its success in the 1890s in capturing the strongest socialist groups on the Continent, came a major effort to "revise" Marx in the light of new developments; while in Great Britain the important Fabian movement rejected Marxian theory to build a more eclectic brand of reformist socialism. All this and more is part of the rich history of socialism and social reform in these latter decades of the nineteenth century, when

Europe moved rapidly toward an order more urban, industrial, and democratic. A brief review of this long story follows.

Revolutionary socialism, or working-class socialism of any sort, sank almost out of sight after 1848 for some time, suffering from repression and disunity. The Second Empire in France jailed Proudhon, exiled Blanc, and stifled press freedom while "buying off" the workers with its great public works projects. With the softening of Louis Napoleon's regime in 1860, socialism revived somewhat, only to be crushed again in the gripping episode of the Commune of Paris, 1871. Working-class socialists were accused of fomenting class war in Paris and the reaction again brought severe repression. This phase of French socialism was Proudhonist. Under the banner of "mutualism" these followers of the Besançon-born working man, who died in Paris in 1865, manifested a hatred of the state and centralized power that marked them off sharply from other socialists. They thought proletarian revolution should lead to a decentralized, "federal" political structure, for Proudhon could see no purpose to the existing state except militarism and the repressive defense of property, both of which would vanish with the bourgeoisie.[8] The economic order would be one of cooperatives, the workers in each factory, farm, or store jointly managing it. Somewhat fuzzy and inane, Proudhon's utopia had the merit of upholding liberty; he accused Marx of fomenting a new tyranny while Marx sneered at the simplicity of the Frenchman's economic ideas. In this respect Proudhon repeated the charge brought by the celebrated Russian revolutionary, Mikhail Bakunin, against Marx: His ideas would lead to a new state tyranny. For though Marx and Engels expected the state to "wither away" (Engels's term) after the socialist revolution, they advocated seizing it and using it in the interlude between this revolution and the final achievement of communism. With considerable accuracy the anarchists predicted that the Marxists would be corrupted by the state power as they used it. The revolution, in the anarchist view, must be made outside the state and must immediately destroy the hateful monster.

In 1871, when the Parisians decided to secede from the rest of France after the abdication of the Emperor Louis Napoleon (defeated by the Germans in war), they were acting in large part on Proudhon's ideas. (Communes were proclaimed in several other French cities.) There were to be sure, other kinds of socialists, including the extremely romantic revolutionary followers of Blanqui, the legendary insurrectionist. Blanquists, Proudhonians, and other socialists and radicals formed a decidedly inharmonious group among the Communards, whose defeat might be

---

[8]Proudhon's colorful prose as well as his hatred of the state is contained in his assertion that

> To be governed is to be kept under surveillance, inspected, spied upon, bossed, law-ridden, regulated, penned-in, indoctrinated, preached at, registered, evaluated, appraised, censured, ordered about by creatures who have neither the right nor the virtue to do so . . . . It is, under the pretense of public benefit . . . to be requisitioned, drilled, fleeced, exploited, monopolized, extorted, squeezed, hoaxed, robbed . . . then at the slightest resistance to be squelched, corrected, vilified, bullied, hounded, tormented, bludgeoned, disarmed, strangled, imprisoned, shot down, judged, condemned, deported, sacrificed, sold, betrayed . . .

These were some of the better things Proudhon had to say about government.

blamed in part on this dissension. The defeat of this revolt, and the brutal reprisals, caused the death or banishment of some twenty thousand Communards and crushed French working-class radicalism to earth for another generation. One of the casualties, as we know, was the First International.

From the shattering defeat and civil strife in 1870 to 1871, France headed slowly toward the Third Republic, under which freedom would revive and a new socialist movement gradually reappear. In Germany laws against the socialists were enforced in the 1870s and 1880s, while at the same time Bismarck tried to alleviate the lot of the workers with Europe's first state-administered social welfare system, including old-age pensions and insurance against sickness. But the German Social Democratic party, now firmly Marxist, survived the persecution, developed able leaders and a magnificent organization, and after being legalized in 1890 following Bismarck's removal from power, went on to become one of Germany's largest political parties (*the* largest by 1912) and the dominant force in the Second International. The latter world organization dates from 1889 to 1890 and enjoyed considerable success until 1914, with its international congresses and its annual May Day demonstrations being impressive. It counted twelve million members by 1914; the war destroyed it.

The 1880s and particularly the 1890s saw a widespread interest in social legislation on all fronts; it is the watershed for the change of direction from *laissez-faire* economic liberalism to a more socially conscious, state-interventionist order. There were many signs of this change and many versions of it.

In Britain, the prosperity and stability of the period from 1850 to 1870 washed away Chartism and Owenism, marking the high tide of liberalism in its individualist, antistate phase. But the 1880s brought a significant change. In 1881 the philosopher T. H. Green began at Oxford University a school of social thought influenced by Hegel and stressing the social origin of rights, the social responsibilities of property. The rapidity of change in outlook may be judged from a comment of Lord Milner: "When I went up to Oxford [in the early 1870s] the *laissez-faire* theory still held the field. . . . But within ten years the few men who held the old doctrines in their extreme rigidity had come to be regarded as curiosities." This was a respectable revolution. Green borrowed from Hegel a feeling for the claims of society and the positive role of the state, without any admixture of revolution or violence. At University College, London, economist Stanley Jevons undermined dogmatic *laissez-faire* by simply asking for scientific, empirical investigation in particular areas to determine "where we want greater freedom and where less," a solution of problems piecemeal, rather than in accordance with some general formula. This was the path taken by the Fabian socialists. It was a reaction against the dogmatic individualism often proclaimed by Victorian liberals (for example, Auberon Herbert and the Non-Interference Union), as much as against dogmatic socialism.

In 1887 the young Irish critic, essayist, orator, novelist, and playwright George Bernard Shaw introduced Marx (as he was soon to introduce Nietzsche) to the British public. But the sharp-witted youths with whom Shaw joined to form the Fabian Society at about this time soon rejected Marx's labor theory of value and with it the rest of his economics: They retained only his moral indignation at the alleged stupidities and wrongs of a capitalistic, acquisitive society, and this they got from others besides Marx—from Carlyle, Ruskin, Mill, and Morris. The Fabians emerged from the chrysalis of something called the Fellowship of the New Life, founded by a remarkable Scotsman, Thomas Davidson, in 1882. The Fabian Society broke away from Davidson's group in 1884. Shaw joined it in 1885. He had turned socialist after listening to Henry George. Fabianism was eclectic in its origins, not imprisoned by a dogma, and permeated with the spirit of British empiricism. Initially, after Jevons and Alfred Marshall had discredited the Marxian labor theory of value in favor of a marginal utility theory, the Fabians tried to elaborate a general theory of exploitation on this basis, using the Ricardian theory of rent. But before long they decided that "abstract economics" was not of much value.

A mentor of Fabian founder Beatrice Webb was Charles Booth, author of an exhaustive pioneer social study of *Life and Labour of the People of London* (9 volumes, 1892 to 1897). "The *a priori* reasoning of political economy, orthodox and unorthodox alike, fails from want of reality," Booth wrote. Booth had been influenced by Comte and by the German historical school of economics (Schmoller). The result was an economics mainly historical and descriptive; the chief works of the Webbs were massive historical studies of local government, trade unions, and poor relief. Problems should be tackled piecemeal with the aid of thorough factual documentation, they believed. Fabian pamphleteering was often hard-hitting and bitterly critical of bourgeois society. But the movement's enduring importance lay in the patient accumulation of facts and ideas directed at particular abuses, under the guidance of the industrious Sidney and Beatrice Webb.

Clearly a faith was at work here: The Fabians did not doubt that socialism was a higher form of human society, the next rung on the ladder of social evolution, and they worked for it with a missionary spirit. The following statement by C. E. M. Joad may suggest something of the mood, as he recalled it in later years:

> England before 1914 was a land of gross social and economic inequality, in which the poverty and misery of the many were outraged by the luxury and the ostentation of the few. Under Socialism we believed the poverty and misery would disappear and the inequality be rectified. This was the first, fresh springtime of the Fabian Socialism, and we saw ourselves marching in irresistible procession with Shaw, Webb and Wells—slightly out of step—in the vanguard, to the promised land of State ownership of the means of production, distribution and exchange which we believed lay just around the corner.[9]

Socialism functioned as a substitute religion for the young intellectuals of England; they had lost their Christian faith to Darwin, Marx, and the Higher Criticism. Links may be found also to Victorian radicalism reaching back to Chartists, Owenists, and Utilitarians. A revival of Christian Socialism, after a generation of relapse, occurs too at the end of the century.

[9] "What I Still Believe," *The New Statesman and Nation,* May 19, 1951.

In their early days at least, the Fabians were not too scholarly to take part in demonstrations and harangue working-class audiences. On November 13, 1887, Shaw, William Morris, Annie Besant, and other intellectual socialists were roughed up by the police at a demonstration in Trafalgar Square. After this they chose the path of gradual change by parliamentary means, their duty being to furnish the politicians with the facts of industrial life so fully and plainly that even a politician could not do otherwise than recognize the necessity of social legislation. In this they were remarkably successful. If, prior to World War I, there was in Britain no very large Labour or Socialist party (there was a small Labour party, not Socialist until 1918, with less than 10 percent of the seats in the House of Commons),[10] this was largely because the older parties, especially the Liberal party, had been quietly infiltrated by a good deal of social welfare doctrine.

If they rejected Marx's economic theory, the Fabians agreed with his faith in the future of socialism. It was, they thought, evident that socialism was the wave of the future. But it would come gradually, was coming everyday, rather than all at once in one great revolution. Parliamentary democracy and other institutions of self-government would ensure its peaceful adoption. The Fabians placed great stress on local government; contrary to a common opinion, they did not propose the nationalization of all industry, but at this time (pre-1914) hoped that the county and borough councils, recently established in Great Britain, would own and operate a great deal of it. They did believe in public ownership as a panacea that, by driving the landlords and capitalists out of business, would increase the workers' share and lead to an era of plenty for all. In this they were often quite naive.

But Fabian tactics helped ease the way to acceptance of social-welfare principles by moderate men in Great Britain. Under conservative auspices, paternalistic perhaps and including such things as municipal ownership of utilities ("gas and water socialism") and state-run health insurance or old-age pension plans, it could attract broad support; in 1889 a British peer remarked that "we are all socialists now." The sheer facts of life in a complex, interdependent industrial society forced people to modify *laissez-faire* capitalism. Bismarck declared in his great speech to the German Reichstag on social insurance legislation that the modern state could not disclaim all responsibility for the welfare of its working-class citizens; if it did, it would invite revolution. More modestly, Birmingham industrialist Joseph Chamberlain found that the upper classes could not ignore sanitary conditions among the lower classes in a modern city, because cholera germs were no respecters of class lines.

Also, trade unions became accepted and respectable and gave the workers a modest voice in the affairs of industry and the state. They were at least a force with which to be reckoned, backed by the weapon of the strike. In the 1900s, British trade unions overcame the Taff Vale decision, making them responsible for damages

[10]The parliamentary Labour party was born in 1900. On its doctrinal side it owed something to the rather eccentric Marxist H. M. Hyndman and rather more to William Morris's Socialist League, as well as a little to the Fabians, but it was much more motivated by practical trade union goals prior to World War I.

in a strike. Bitter strikes swept France and Italy as well as Britain in this decade. While in France "syndicalists" dreamed of accomplishing the revolution by a great general strike, trade union leaders were apt to scorn the socialist intellectuals who preferred theoretical argument to "practical work inside the labor movement." Orthodox Marxism deplored the "opportunism" of trade unionism that aimed at nothing more than getting some workers a bigger slice of the rewards without "changing the system." But in Germany the unions and the Marxist Social Democrats struck a close alliance. (The French unionists, by contrast, rejected such a relationship.) By 1906 it was the unionists who had the stronger position, but they accepted the Social Democrats as their political arm. In all the countries of Western Europe, the unions, growing rapidly in the 1890s, were strong in the 1900s.

"Socialism" in this sense, as a pragmatic modification of *laissez-faire* capitalism in trade unionist and state welfare directions, became an accepted part of the late Victorian political landscape, though not without its bitter controversies: As late as 1910 in Britain the Lloyd George budget, including an income tax for social insurance financing, inspired an opposition that ended only in the "swamping" of the House of Lords and the passing of a Parliament act sharply reducing the power of the peers to block legislation. There followed what an English newspaper called "the greatest scheme of social reconstruction ever attempted"—the National Insurance Bill of 1911.

MARXIST REVISIONISM

Quite different was the situation in Germany, where a strong Marxist party developed, by far the strongest and best organized one in Europe. The German Social Democrats won great prestige by their success against Bismarck's efforts to destroy them. After 1891, save for one brief period, this party thrived on legality, having shown that it could survive illegality. It was a well-disciplined mass organization, publishing its own newspapers, and led by educated Germans of the caliber of August Bebel, Wilhelm Liebknecht, Eduard Bernstein, and Karl Kautsky. Entering into close association with the trade unions, in 1912 it was the largest single political party with one-third of the electorate. The Social Democratic leaders accepted the possibility of overthrowing capitalism by peaceful, democratic means. In the meetings of the Second International they opposed the radicalism of the anarchists and preached the inevitability of socialism on the basis of Marx's theory of the self-destruction of capitalism, the dialectically necessary triumph of socialism. Unlike the Fabians they did not view socialism as a piecemeal program but awaited the day when the entire capitalistic system would crumble, meanwhile generally refusing to collaborate in government with the "bourgeoisie."

Bernstein went further in the direction of reformism. His efforts to "revise" Marx touched off a battle of words within the SPD in which revisionism was finally rejected. Bernstein believed that Marx's prophecies about the decline of capitalism and the increasing misery of the working class had proved false. Small and medium properties had not disappeared but were even increasing; the working class was getting better off, not worse off; the class struggle had become less acute, not more so. Drawing conclusions from this, he suggested a reformism not far in spirit from British Fabianism. He held that political democracy, having arrived in Western Europe, made it possible to establish socialism by parliamentary means. "In all advanced countries," he urged, "we see the privileges of the capitalist bourgeoisie yielding step by step to democratic organizations." The party refused to accept this gradualism in theory, remaining officially committed to the winning of the proletarian revolution by means of the class struggle. It would not participate in governments in collaboration with the "bourgeois" parties. It almost read Bernstein out of the party, though he was an old and dedicated servant. But while rejecting gradualism, the large majority of the party accepted legalism. Engels himself, living on into the 1890s, announced that "the time of revolution carried through by small minorities at the head of unconscious masses is past." The path to the revolution would be a democratic and parliamentary one.

Similar issues agitated the French Socialist party which, rent by schism, managed to achieve unity in the 1900s but not unanimity. In 1899, after the socialist Millerand had accepted a post in the government headed by the leftist republican Waldeck-Rousseau, the French socialists earnestly debated this action, and it was the occasion for exchanges between their two outstanding leaders, Jules Guesde and Jean Jaurès. Jaurès argued that it was good to penetrate bourgeois positions in this way, for would not the capitalist regime fall little by little, and how could it fall if its outposts were never occupied? But Guesde carried the day, by a narrow margin, with an eloquent exposition of socialist orthodoxy—the doctrine of the class struggle, of the solidarity of the working classes, of the utter incompatibility of socialism and capitalism: There could be no "mixture" or in-betweens, it was a matter of either-or. In the 1914 elections the party won about one-sixth of the seats; like its German counterpart it refused to take ministerial posts in any government in which it would share power. Right-wing–left-wing tension still existed, with unity maintained only at the cost of a rather imprecise program. French socialism was complicated by the presence of strong traditions other than Marxism. If Guesde, "Torquemada in lorgnettes," was a rigid Marxian dialectician, Jaurès, the greatest individual in the party and one of the great Frenchmen of his generation, was a deeply civilized humanist who drew from many other sources than Marx. For Jaurès, Leon Blum later wrote, socialism was "the summation, the point of convergence, the heritage of all that humanity had created since the dawn of civilization." Proudhonist and other elements still lingered on in France despite a strong Marxian incursion.

Similarly in Italy there were reformist, revisionist leaders (for example, Filippo Turati) arguing that democracy had rendered revolution obsolete but finding bitter opponents on the left to whom this was dangerous illusion. There was a lively Marxist discussion in Italy, including Professor Labriola's distinctions that were somewhat too subtle for popular consumption and, by contrast, Achille Loria's crudely positivistic determinism.

In Russia the Marxist debate took a not dissimilar turn. Marxism entered Russia via the remarkable intellect of G. V. Plekhanov, a self-educated man who, exiled like so many other politically conscious Russians, lived and wrote for many years in Switzerland. In the 1870s the political faith of revolutionary Russians was populism, a courageous, self-sacrificing but intellectually not very clear movement, based on a belief in the uniqueness of Russia and especially of her communal peasant population. The "big three" of earlier Russian socialism had been Belinsky, already mentioned as a Hegelian; Bakunin, the fabulous revolutionary who, influenced in Paris by Proudhon, became an anarchist and attacked Marx for his statism; and Alexander Herzen, the powerful publicist who came to Paris in 1848 to receive a shattering blow from the "June Days" when the workers' insurrection against the Republic was savagely repressed. With the aid of a German historian, they discovered in the *mir* or Russian peasant village an allegedly natural foundation for Proudhonian mutualism. Subsequently somewhat discredited, Bakunin and Herzen nevertheless deeply influenced the populist movement of which the Social Revolutionary party was the political offshoot. In the 1860s the *mir* socialists, though not a violent group, were repressed by the tsar's government; Chernyshevsky and Pisarev were imprisoned, Moscow University closed in 1868. The result was the famous "To the People" pilgrimage of young idealists in the 1870s, which suffered rude disenchantment and brought about the arrest of hundreds; and then, in desperation, a wave of revolutionary terrorism. This too led nowhere; and in opposition to the romantic excesses of populism, which resorted to assassination, climaxed in the killing of Tsar Alexander II in 1881, the cool, analytical approach of Marxism was welcome. Marxism in Russia in the 1890s had the effect of turning minds from illegal revolutionary pamphlets to the systematic study of economics, sociology, and history; the stress was on a well-grounded intellectual outlook, careful planning, no childish adventurism. Marxism even allowed some to accept the progressiveness of capitalism. It was a weapon against both agrarian populism and revolutionary terrorism.

A civilized, even fastidiously esthetic intellectual, Plekhanov believed in the Marxist laws of historical evolution and counseled waiting for a democratic revolution which would come about spontaneously after Russia went through a capitalist phase. Instilling Marxist precepts into a generation of Russian revolutionaries, Plekhanov found some of these disinclined to wait. In 1903, Lenin proposed the creation of an elite of professional revolutionaries, trained to seize power. To Plekhanov's orthodox Marxism this was little less than Bonapartism or Blanquism. The majority of the Russian Social Democratic party followed him and a split occurred. Lenin's "bolshevik" group was in fact in a small minority most of the time, the "mensheviks" a more numerous and prestigious group. Victory and fame would come to the stubbornly independent Lenin in 1917: prior to that he was thought to have departed widely from Marxian orthodoxy and was isolated at the far left of the socialist spectrum. (On Lenin, see further pp. 215-16.)

To sum up the Marxist debate: On the Continent, though not in England, Marxism prevailed as the reigning orthodoxy in the socialist or social democratic parties, which were well organized and gaining adherents, on the eve of 1914. But within the parties sharp debate took place centering on the issue of whether class struggle, revolution, and the complete destruction of capitalism at one stroke had not become an obsolete program in the era of democratic politics, trade unionism, and welfare capitalism. The usual answer was to refuse to abandon Marxism for Fabian gradualism (Bernstein) but also to reject stress on violent revolution through illegal or conspiratorial means (Lenin). The majority of socialists held to their faith in an apocalyptic revolution that would change the entire system but thought this could come peacefully as soon as their political party won a majority of the electorate, and they refused meanwhile to take any share of power. Their rate of growth between 1890 and 1914 held out some hope that this might happen. But this compromise was an uneasy one and gave rise to a degree of internal tension. Between Albert Thomas and Jules Guesde in France, Eduard Bernstein and Rosa Luxemburg in Germany, or Plekhanov and Lenin in Russia, one found a considerable ideological and psychological distance. This ambivalence can be directly related to unresolved dilemmas at the heart of Marxian doctrine; particularly between voluntarism and determinism, elitism and democracy, revolution and evolution. On one side there was the call to action, to an uprising of the downtrodden led by revolutionary leaders; and on the other there was the belief that the objective laws of historical development were fast preparing the way for the inevitable triumph of democratic socialism.

ANARCHISM

Viewed more broadly, Marxism itself was a kind of center between a right and left wing of the entire "social" movement. To its left lay the anarchists, who seldom could be contained in the same party with the socialists though the congresses of the International provided a place for a less than friendly exchange of views. (The socialists passed resolutions against the anarchists at the International and told them they were not welcome, but, as trade union delegates, some anarchists always got in.) Anarchism was weak in Germany (though sometimes spectacular), stronger (as "anarcho-syndicalism" or direct action through the trade unions) in France, still stronger in Italy and Spain, where the condition of the lower classes was more desperate and industrialism was less advanced. An "anarchist" might be a peace-loving enemy of centralization, a Proudhonian friend of liberty and cooperation; but in the 1880s and 1890s a much more familiar type resorted to assassination and other violent actions. They all disbelieved in the value of political action through elections and parliaments. Some of them were Marxists or partial Marxists: What they had learned from the master was that economics determines all, that representative legislatures are a sham to cover the dictatorship of the bourgeoisie (this from Proudhon, too), and that capitalism owns the state and always will until smashed in the proletarian social revolution. After the revolution there would be no more parliaments or states anyway, anarchists held; there would be the pure freedom of the classless society—no government at all. Most anarchists were inclined to be far out on the voluntarist wing of Marxism, so far as to be beyond the pale of party orthodoxy. They stressed the freedom of individuals to change their situation by acting; nothing is predetermined. They might go as far as George Sorel in deciding that socialism is simply a myth, a religion, not a science at all. Sorel found Marx most unimaginative and the social democrats exceedingly dull—even bourgeois! A good example of such trends within socialism is Arturo Labriola, the Italian anarchist; a little later, Henri de Man, the Belgian.

The rapid growth of trade unions as an indigenous, spontaneous process encouraged some social thinkers to believe—as the Russians had believed about the *mir*—that here were "the units upon which the future society will be built" and others to theorize that the revolution would come about not through parliaments but by means of the general strike, when all the workers simultaneously would put down their tools and bring the economy to a halt. Sorel was identified with this position for a time, until he became disillusioned with the trade unions as agents of revolution.

Many varieties of anarchism existed, and indeed by their very nature these individualistic radicals could not be regimented into any one creed. But significant numbers of them tried to foment revolution, preparing the workers for it by sermons or, better, by action. Ultra-anarchists engaged in a wave of assassinations in the 1890s that shocked not only the bourgeoisie but also the social democrats, who denounced them furiously. Terrorists assassinated a tsar of Russia, a president of the United States, the empress of Austria, the king of Italy, and a president of the French Republic between 1880 and 1901; they continued in the 1900s, killing the enlightened Russian prime minister Stolypin, among others. On July 4, 1914, three anarchists were killed in New York when a homemade bomb intended for John D. Rockefeller, Jr., blew up. Just a month before, if we agree to call young Gavrilo Princip and his friends anarchists, they had touched off World War I. But it was not merely the great who were targets of assassination; the famous French terrorist Ravachol, who bombed the Chamber of Deputies, had several politically motiveless murders attributed to him. In 1894 a 22-year-old French anarchist named Emile Henry tossed a bomb into a railroad station café in Paris, killing two persons and wounding twenty in an assemblage of workers, small shopkeepers, civil servants, none of any political prominence; reproached at his trial for killing innocent people, he proudly replied, "Everyone is guilty!" Another French militant in 1881 set out to assassinate the political leader (moderately left) Leon Gambetta; not finding him, he shot the first bourgeois he met as a reasonable equivalent. These believers in the "propaganda of the deed" simply wanted to get the public's attention, dramatizing what they held to be monstrous injustice perpetuated by public authority.

It is depressing to record so much hate, but the anarchists were idealists; many of them had known the suffering of the most deprived classes in the community. Their intellectual antecedents were vague but plentiful: all the denouncers of injustice and leaders of revolt from Spartacus to Marx, all the haters of ruling-class sham from Lucretius to Baudelaire. If they were educated they knew these; most were not, except for scraps of secondhand learning. They were the extremists of a revolution, the Black Panthers of the nineteenth-century proletariat. Much of their spirit got into the Russian Revolution that, nominally Marxist, was led by those who shared a good deal of the anarchist *ésprit*. But during the Revolution the anarchists were to be ruthlessly destroyed by the victorious Bolsheviks.

If the anarchists stood to the left of the Socialists or Social Democrats, there were many on the Right, among them the Fabians, simple trade unionists, and bourgeois upholders of the welfare state. British "Lib-Labs" or trade unionists often seemed highly out of place at International meetings taken up with debates between German Marxists and Italian anarchists. Lord Harcourt, needless to say, who had said "we are all socialists," would hardly have been welcome there at all. Conservative upholders of the *status quo,* pillars of society, might show an interest in mild socialism. Bismarck, as well as England's Disraeli and Joseph Chamberlain, and Italy's Giolitti,[11] held that some concessions to the workers would keep them from following lunatics into violent revolution; if to conserve is to preserve, preservation demanded an end to the irresponsibility of *laissez-faire.* In 1890 the emperor of Germany, Kaiser Wilhelm II, having just fired Bismarck and repealed the antisocialist laws, called an international conference to consider "international labor legislation." In France, following the turmoil of the famous Dreyfus Case, the bourgeois left wing (Radicals, and soon Radical Socialists) flirted with socialism: Basically Jacobin democratic, people like Aristide Briand and Georges Clemenceau were prepared to tax big property for the benefit of small, and the government budget of expenditures on welfare rose sharply. The *Solidarisme* of politician-intellectual Leon Bourgeois found nature as well as society filled with cooperation and interdependence rather than dog-eat-dog competition. At the same time these Radicals showed no sympathy toward anarchist violence and used troops to break strikes.

Of these varieties of socialism, one more at least needs to be mentioned: Christian socialism. The great papal encyclical *Rerum Novarum,* 1891, was the most famous pronouncement here, though there were Protestant versions also. It was not difficult for the Church to approve a kind of socialism. Christian dislike of materialism and selfishness, the doctrine of stewardship by which the rich should aid the poor, the deeply implanted Christian concern for the meek and disinherited, all might be turned in this direction. Catholic social doctrine gained prominence earlier in the century from the writings of Lamennais, but the Breton firebrand had run afoul of orthodoxy. Albert de Mun and La Tour du Pin subsequently brought to Catholic social doctrine an interest in the corporate economics of the Middle Ages; politically, they were conservatives. W. E. Ketteler was a pioneer of social Christianity in Germany; the Mainz priest tried to bring the working-class issue to the attention of the Frankfurt Assembly in 1848. The trouble with this by no means insignificant tradition of *caritas* was that it shunned class conflict and hoped to convert the wealthy rather than organize the poor.

---

[11] Giolitti, according to Denis Mack Smith "had studied *Das Kapital* with application and profit." He was the almost perennial Italian prime minister between 1900 and 1914.

Pope Leo XIII was deeply interested in the cause of regaining the working class for Christianity. *Rerum Novarum* opposed modern capitalism and, while rejecting "materialistic socialism," called for a fundamental reorganization of economic life to correspond with Christian principles. In France, Germany, and Italy Catholic trade unions were organized, many priests devotedly dedicated service to working-class education, and there were individual examples of capitalists (like Leon Hormel) moved to experiment with "the Christian factory," but it is doubtful if the Catholic social movement achieved very much. In England, an unusual group of Christian socialists had emerged in the 1850s, including notably Charles Kingsley, F. D. Maurice, and John Ludlow; this died out for a time but there was a revival toward the end of the century, which tended to merge into the broader movement of social reform (T. H. Green, the Fabians, and so forth) without achieving much identity. Christianity had lost most of the proletariat to the secular religion of socialism. Karl Marx was its new prophet.

By the 1900s, there were those who thought this secular socialism was dying of dogmatism and an obsolete, simplistic set of *idées fixés*. (See the remarks of Benedetto Croce, in *Cultura e vita morale,* 1911; or the view of Charles Péguy, leading French writer of the 1900s who broke with the Marxists to become a kind of Christian socialist.) In Western Europe, considering the subsequent history of social democracy of all sorts, this was probably true. One need not be reminded that there were other parts of the world where it had quite a role to play. For Western Europe, the later nineteenth century was the great age of this secular religion or ideology: the Age of Marx.

THE RISE OF HISTORICAL STUDIES

As a footnote to Marx's exciting if controversial historical scheme, we note that history was of serious interest to many in the nineteenth century. Despised in the seventeenth and developed only in rudimentary ways in the eighteenth, it received its philosophical certificate of legitimacy from Burke, Herder, and Hegel and became a respectable academic citizen in the mid-nineteenth century. For example, a chair of modern history was first established at Cambridge University only in the eighteenth century and for long after that amounted to little but leaped to the front in the era of Lord Acton. The great historians—Voltaire, Gibbon, and on to Macaulay and Michelet in the earlier nineteenth century—had been amateur *literati*, more noted for their literary gifts than any professional competence, though often they did do capable research; now, beginning in Germany (especially at the University of Göttingen), history came of age as a specialized profession marked by the "scientific" use of materials and careful research in the primary sources, with thorough criticism and collation of knowledge. Making possible this advance was the collection and organization of historical materials in the great libraries, archives, and museums of Europe, something that was accomplished only toward the end of the eighteenth century.

The romantics stimulated imaginative interest in the past; German philosophers saw it as the unfolding of Truth, Burkeans as the school of political wisdom. It became possible to widen the range of historical studies to include social and economic history; this was partly a matter of having access to the sources of such knowledge, such as the records of medieval manors, but also partly the perspective of an age acutely aware of economic and social issues. In general, with the retreat of confidence in religion or metaphysics to answer the big questions about the meaning and conduct of life, people turned to history. There one found a repository of wisdom and experience, a treasure house of knowledge throwing light on the present human situation. Darwin and other evolutionary thinkers popularized explanation of a genetic sort. With the arrival of professional methods and the organization of materials, history seemed to be passing from the realm of conjecture and opinion to the status of a genuine science. Quite a few others in addition to Karl Marx had the idea that a real science of history was now possible. Henry Buckle was dogmatic about it in England, Mill thought so more cautiously; the German scholars, doing their arduous detailed research, felt that some day, somehow, the fruits of painstakingly accurate spadework would be gathered in the form of a universal synthesis. Leopold von Ranke, dean of the German school of academic historians, who had brought exacting source criticism and the seminar method to the study of history and had written scores of volumes in medieval and early modern history, embarked at last upon his "universal history" at the age of 90!

The belief in a science of history in this sense—the sense indicated by historian J. B. Bury when he declared in his inaugural lecture as Regius Professor at Cambridge in 1902 (succeeding Acton) that "there will no longer be divers schools of history," only one, true history, since history is "simply a science, no less and no more"—has almost died since then. But the nineteenth was, beyond question, an historical century; Bury was not wrong in asserting that "in the story of the nineteenth century, which has witnessed such far-reaching changes in the geography of thought and in the apparatus of research, no small or isolated place belongs to the transformation and expansion of history." The leading ideologies, as noted, were historical—Hegel's, Comte's, and Spencer's as well as Marx's. Among the great intellectual figures of the century whose interest in history was much more than incidental one could list in addition Tocqueville, Renan, Mill, Arnold, Newman, and many others.[12]

And the reason for this "historical revolution" was that investigation of the past had become not just the indulgence of idle curiosity or trivial antiquarianism but something charged with the deepest meaning because it could explain the fate

---

[12] Acton, together with his German friend the Munich professor I. Döllinger, dedicated historians as they were, formulated an historical theology of Catholicism according to which the Christian truth gradually revealed itself in history through the medium of the Church. Unfortunately the Vatican could not accept this because of its implications that individual popes might have erred (did not have the full truth in the past). It remains an interesting example of the impact of history on the age. "Metaphysics could not be relied upon to promote religion— that could be done only by history," as Acton reported the view of Döllinger.

and future of humankind. It could reveal the great laws of development, the cycles of growth of the human race from earliest times to today—and tomorrow. All the great nineteenth-century theories of history posited an ascent from lower to higher, in one way or another. Bitter critic of capitalist society that he was, Marx was as optimistic as any Victorian in the long run: One more turn of the wheel of history and the millennium would be reached.

chapter 5

The Crisis of European Thought 1880-1914

Our intellect—what a very small thing on the surface of ourselves!

Maurice Barrès

NATIONALISM

Popularly, one obvious feature of post-1871 Europe was the upsurge of nationalist feeling, led by the newly united Germany, which leaped to the forefront of European power and developed an overweening sense of pride. If Germany's was a nationalism of success, France experienced a kind of nationalism of failure; dethroned from her long supremacy in Europe, declining relatively in population, watching both Germany and Great Britain outdo her in industrial development, the French underwent a paroxysm of national soul-searching while seeking compensation in acquiring colonies and holding "expositions" (1889 providing of course the most obvious of pretexts).

This was the time of Western civilization's spectacular conquest of the outer world, when the continents of Asia and Africa were forced to submit to the domination of the aggressive Europeans. This vast process was in the widest sense a tribute to the amazing success of Europe, its higher technical skills, and also its organizing genius. But it brought evil with it, and to many thoughtful Europeans it was a dismaying moral lapse, perhaps a symbol of decline and fall. The average person certainly found it gratifying; but eventually it would produce revolutions against Western domination on the part of Asiatic and African peoples. For the time being what it most notably produced was an inordinate pride and boastfulness, the jingoism that helped fan the flames of war in 1914.

Nationalism was not absolutely new, but it had really only appeared as a major force in the early nineteenth century which as we know articulated its ideology. It now became much more popular. Nationalism accompanied the modernizing and urbanizing of society. If "the outstanding feature of European history in the nineteenth century is the growth of nationalities," as has been aptly claimed, this growth accelerated after the decisive modernizing decisions of the 1860s (see pp. 100-101.

The creation of national societies and cultures was a long-term social process, begun long ago—historians delighted in tracing the origins back to the early Middle Ages—and scarcely completed even well into the nineteenth century. A recent study of "the nationalization of rural France" (by Eugen Weber) finds the traditional village culture still immersed in customs and beliefs primordially old, even toward the end of the nineteenth century—just then beginning to yield to the assault of roads, railroads, urban influences, capitalism, modern communications, mass education. The village, Weber notes, ignored the Dreyfus Affair which, one reads in the textbooks, was tearing apart "all of France." Another study of a medium-sized German city around the turn of the century discovers little departure from old habits of following one's ancestral line of work in an essentially static society.[1] "Modernization" in some ways was just beginning its sweeping of traditional communities into the urban megalopolis, dissolving the small local units into one "great society."

Dangerous though it might be, nationalism in the nineteenth century offered a wider sense of community, along with material advantages, to the masses of people. In the exhortations of such prophets as Mazzini, nationalism took on the attributes of a religion, in the same way socialism did, equipped with regeneration, rebirth, and salvation symbols. Born of a spiritual revolution, the national people achieve a sacred bond, which is their destiny and their salvation, and then they go forth to redeem the world. "Nationality is the role assigned by God to each people in the work of humanity; the mission and task which it ought to fulfill on earth so that the divine purpose may be attained in the world." Nationalists talked of universal unity ("He who wants humanity wants a fatherland"); but typically they saw their own country as just a bit more privileged. The Germans were the central people, the keystone of the West. In different accents but with a similar message, Mazzini reminded his country's people of their ancient Roman heritage of ruling and civilizing Europe. So did the Pan-Slav mystagogues.

The rise of popular nationalism in the nineteenth century can be illustrated by the creation of the Joan of Arc cult in France. The "virgin, heroine, and martyr to the State, chosen by Providence to reestablish the French monarchy" (to quote

---

[1] David Crew, "Social Mobility in a German Town, 1880-1901," *Journal of Social History,* Fall 1973; *Town on the Rhine: A Social History of Bochum 1860-1914* (1979).

the subtitle of a 1753 book) had of course lived in the early fifteenth century; but her deeds excited little interest at that time and for several hundred years after. Bishop Bossuet's history of France granted her but a few lines, and Voltaire, singularly enough from a later point of view, treated her as rather a ridiculous figure in his play *La Pucelle.* A few always kept alive the story of the Maid's bravery and devotion, but until the nineteenth century she remained fairly obscure. Napoleon, in 1803, referred to Joan as a symbol of French unity against English invaders. The romantics of course were interested in the Middle Ages, and one finds the British poet Robert Southey as well as the German dramatist Schiller using Joan as a literary theme. Schiller's *Maid of Orleans* (also 1803) was indeed a key document: A German helped give the French their national heroine.

But it remained for the great nationalist historians of the nineteenth century to project the Maid as an image of French patriotism. Of these, Jules Michelet was the foremost, and Michelet depicted Joan in eloquent prose as the mother of the French nation. The legend of Joan grew. Finally she was canonized in 1920 as a saint of the Church. Her canonization in French nationalist hagiography had occurred earlier. A notable worshipper at her shrine was the distinguished writer Charles Péguy (who died in 1914 at the Marne). Charles Maurras and the conservative *Action Française* made much of her; but so did socialists and liberals, anticlericals as well as clericals: Joan was the symbol of national unity. Conceivably it was because the French lacked a monarch that they settled their common loyalty on an almost mythical figure from the past. For the British public, of course, the figure of Queen Victoria functioned as a living mother-image and symbol of unity through much of her long reign (1837-1901).

The poet and the historian both participated in this shaping of national consciousness. "A nation," wrote Ernest Renan in a famous definition, "is the common memory of great things done jointly by our ancestors, along with the desire to remain united in order to do yet more of them." The nation, in brief, is a literary creation. The Italian nationalist movement began with Alfieri (1749 to 1803), who reminded Italians in romantic writings of their past glories. Koraïs performed a similar service to Greece, and an American named Smith is credited with beginning the "Arab Awakening"—so says the distinguished scholar George Antonius—when he revived the study of the Arabic language and literature midway in the nineteenth century. The Irish, who had almost lost their ancestral tongue, tried to revive it, or at least some of the literary and Irish nationalists did; the Gaelic revival accompanied the Irish nationalist movement. A revival of Catalonian nationalism in Spain dates from the 1880s; so does Ukrainian separatism in Russia, while in southeastern Europe an upthrust of nationalism threatened to blow up ancient multinational empires and destroy Europe's shaky balance of power.

In 1896, Theodor Herzl's book, *Der Judenstaat,* laid the foundations of the Jewish revival and focused on the establishment of a modern Jewish state in the ancestral land of Palestine; the Zionist congresses began in 1897. The Dreyfus Case in France and the ferocious persecution of the Jews in Russia, as well as anti-Semitic stirrings in Germany, had brought home to the Jews the fact that Europe was again in the grip of intolerance. Medieval anti-Semitism, the result in good part of religious emotions, had all but disappeared in the tolerant eighteenth century, Now toward the end of the nineteenth, intolerance reappeared in the guise of nationalism. (It also had economic, anticapitalist overtones; the myth of the Jew as the sinister international banker made its appearance. But the main charge against the Jews in the Dreyfus Affair was that they lacked loyalty to France.) In Vienna, cultural and intellectual center of Europe, anti-Semitism loomed as a significant political movement in the 1890s. From its leading figure, Georg von Schoenerer, Adolf Hitler as a stripling learned his hatred of Jews; Schoenerer, son of an industrialist, became an agrarian populist lamenting as much the cultural corruption of the cities as their exploitation of the honest farmer. To this anticapitalist agrarianism, which William Jennings Bryan was articulating at the same time in the United States, Schoenerer added anti-Semitism, for he blamed this predatory modern capitalism on the Jews (a blast against the Rothschilds struck also by E. Drumont and other antiDreyfusards in France).

There had been a little anti-Semitism in Marx and a lot of it in Proudhon. But Schoenerer saw capitalism less as the enemy of the working class than as a destroyer of the sound, soil-rooted culture of the *Volk,* threatened by forces of dissolution. Schoenerer also favored the Pan-Germanism of those who wanted to join Austria to Germany and get away from the Slavs. Denouncing the "vampire that knocks at the narrow-windowed house of the German farmer and craftsman," he appealed to the little man and the traditionalist, threatened by all kinds of modernisms. His chief ally in *fin de siècle* Vienna, elected mayor in 1897 for a brief time, was Karl Lueger, like Lenin the son of a school superintendent who earned a law degree before turning to politics. Lueger's Christian Social Party was, as the name indicated, influenced by the clerical social gospel of Leo XIII; it became anti-Semitic in pushing for restriction of Jewish immigration, coming from the Russian empire. His model was the Chinese Exclusion Act of 1882 in the United States! So nationalism with xenophobic overtones could flourish in the confusion of the big cities where an uprooted populace became victims of what Emile Durkheim called *anomie,* losing their values and bearings and ready to believe bizarre stories about Jewish conspiracies.

Nationalism reached its apogee or nadir in the fateful epidemic of jingoism that accompanied the imperialist movement of the 1890s and preceded the great war of 1914 to 1918. A powerful social process involving all aspects of history, it cannot be left out of intellectual history, for many writers contributed to it. Of these, historians and novelists, thrusting into consciousness the past traditions of the people, were the most prominent. In addition to Michelet, the German historian Heinrich Treitschke, the American George Bancroft, the English Thomas Macaulay come to mind, by modern critical standards rather lacking in strict accuracy, but eloquent and inspired in their evocation of the national story of their respective lands in whatever guise they saw it. Never was history so popular as in this period when it dwelt on the rise of the nation and the destiny of its people.

Social Darwinism contributed its bit to the nationalist mixture. It is interesting that Herbert Spencer was a staunch anti-imperialist, a relic perhaps of his Cobdenite days; but the view that peoples and cultures are in competition, with the strongest or more efficient rightly surviving, was hard to dissociate from popular social Darwinism. H. G. Wells provides an example of a highly intelligent man and influential writer, moreover, a leftist socialist and rationalist who nevertheless believed that Darwinian science had "destroyed, quietly but entirely, the belief in human equality." Some peoples, and some races, are inferior to others; the inferior peoples, "these swarms of black, and brown, and dirty-white, and yellow people, who do not come into the new needs of efficiency," will have to go; "it is their portion to die out and disappear." That international life is a struggle, that those nations not prepared to compete in the arena of power will go down to extinction and will deserve to do so was a widely shared article of faith around the turn of the century; it swept even the United States in the Teddy Roosevelt era and was entertained by quite sophisticated minds. For example, John Davidson, the British poet, influenced by Nietzsche toward the view that "the universe is immoral," enthusiastically supported British imperialism, which he regarded, *à la* Rudyard Kipling, as having a sanction to rule and rule vigorously over the lesser breeds. The British scientist and mathematician, Karl Pearson, was taught by social Darwinism that races and nations, as well as individuals, are in a ruthless competition for survival from which progress results.

Nationalism rose to an almost frenzied peak in the years just before 1914. Gabriele D'Annunzio, flamboyant Italian writer, a weathervane who had adopted almost all possible positions just for the fun of it, became a fierce nationalist about 1909, calling on Italians to sharpen their sword on Africa and then advance on the world, phrases which found an all too frenzied response. The *Alldeutscher Verband,* or Pan-German League, entertained fantasies of German domination of all Europe. In France, Charles Maurras's significant *Action Française* popular among students, was anti-Semitic and anti-German, militantly patriotic, and militaristic. In Russia, and throughout the east of Europe, there were various versions of Pan-Slavism. In the 1870s, Danilevski had argued that the next turn of the wheel of history would put the Slavs on top, the Latins and Germans having had their turn. Russia, the Pan-Slavist Fadeyev declared, must either advance to the Adriatic or retire behind the Urals; it was Russia's destiny to unify all the Slavic peoples of Europe. The personification of nations as having "destinies" was common; no doubt this was what the British philosopher Hobhouse had in mind when he blamed the war on Hegel, this sort of thinking being obviously related to a vulgarized Hegelian historicism. Seeley told the British about their imperial destiny, and according to Esmé Wingfield-Stratford, "The Press reeked with blood and reverberated with thunder" (*The Victorian Tragedy*). "Every important nation had become acutely and aggressively race-conscious," the English historian adds. It was one of the most apparent causes of the first world war.

DEMOCRACY

The accompaniment of nationalism was democracy. Here again the preliminaries reach far back, but no previous European age had felt the impact of the ideology and the practice of democracy as the one from 1880 to 1914. Most liberals of the earlier nineteenth century stoutly opposed universal suffrage. "Because I am a Liberal," wrote a member of Parliament and editorialist of the *London Times* in 1867, "I regard as one of the greatest dangers with which the country can be threatened a proposal to . . . transfer power from the hands of property and intelligence, and to place it in the hands of men whose whole life is necessarily occupied in daily struggles for existence." Tocqueville and Mill mistrusted democracy because they feared the degradation of intelligence and quality by the imposition of vulgar standards. Comte, as well as Bonald, equated democracy with anarchy, the absence of social order. Spencer wrote that the divine right of popularly elected parliaments would have to be resisted as firmly as the divine right of royalty if it should threaten liberty. Many of the socialists scorned political democracy as a fraud, designed to deceive the working classes, who could only win their freedom by a social revolution.

Yet throughout the century there was a democratic thrust, which the generation of Tocqueville and Chateaubriand had felt and which became irresistible after midcentury. It was associated with the economic revolution; it followed necessarily from the bourgeois revolution. Political rights could not be withheld from the masses once political authority became a matter of convenience, not sanctity, and when wealth became more widely diffused. Throughout the century illiteracy declined—in France declining from 39 percent to 18 percent by 1878 as measured by conscript soldiers—while the press became increasingly free and increasingly cheap. In 1870 the Education Act established free primary schools in Great Britain, compulsory within a few years after that. The "penny daily" made its debut about the same time. These are landmarks without equal in popular intellectual history.

In 1867 and 1884, Great Britain took steps toward full manhood suffrage, and by 1910 women were agitating for it. France never actually lost universal suffrage after 1848, but under the Second Empire it was managed and manipulated in a way that deprived it of much meaning; after 1874, however, the Republic came back. Imperial Germany had a Reichstag elected by universal suffrage though it lacked responsible powers. "An assembly of 350 members cannot in the last instance direct the policy of a great power today," Bismarck held. Perhaps it could not, but in Britain, at least, the system of government by a cabinet drawn from and responsible to the House of Commons found success in these years. All governments had to pay more attention to public opinion—which might or might not be a good thing, critics noted, depending on how enlightened public opinion was. In the realm of foreign affairs, it was all too likely to be xenophobic, shrilly nationalistic, disdainful of the rights of foreigners. At home, those unconverted to democracy complained of unseemly and undignified electioneering methods, of political machines and bosses, of cheaper politicians driving out finer in a kind of political Gresham's law. But very few discerning people thought that the rule of the few in politics and society was any longer possible. For better or for worse the rule of the many had come to stay.

Intellectuals were inclined to worry about this, perhaps, more than to hail it. In his essay on *Democracy,* first published in 1861, and reissued in 1879, Matthew

Arnold wrote, "Our society is probably destined to become much more democratic; who or what will give a high tone to the nation then? That is the grave question." A society is of real value not because large numbers of people are free and active, nor because of the creation of wealth; it is valuable insofar as it produces things that are noble and of good repute. When Arnold lectured in the United States of America on the need to "elevate" society, he seems utterly to have failed to make contact with the minds of Chicagoans. But America's sage, Walt Whitman, addressed similar warnings to his country's people in his old age.

Democracy in itself, considered simply as the principle of mass or numbers, is no ideal, can easily become moral anarchy or mammonism; the old criticism made by Plato was repeated often in the later nineteenth century. Nineteenth-century European thought is filled with outcries against certain aspects or consequences of "democracy." "The crowd is the lie," wrote Kierkegaard. Democracy is "a form of decadence," declared the well-known French writer Emile Faguet, who had been influenced by Nietzsche. "If I am a democrat, it is without enthusiasm," observed the great French political leader Clemenceau, who had once led the popular party in 1908. A notably hostile Victorian witness was Henry Maine (*Popular Government,* 1886). Nietzsche, treated later in this chapter, expressed hostility to democracy in aspects of his thought. The rule of inferiors, the herd spirit, the debasement of culture to the mass level, were to him among the chief diseases of modern civilization, to be cured only by the most drastic elevation of supermen-heroes to the helm of state, men strong and ruthless enough to whip and drive the masses toward some worthy goals. Like Dr. Stockmann in Ibsen's play *An Enemy of the People,* Nietzsche believed that "the minority is always right." The leveling of the human personality into the conforming mass-man appalled him, and he thought democracy was responsible for this.

"It is a question," Edmund Scherer cried, "of knowing whether in traversing this crisis humanity will not lose everything of genius, beauty, grandeur; it is a question of knowing whether, in this tragedy of mediocrity, in this sullen and terrible adventure of the peoples, there is one which will not disappear from history." This esthetic antidemocracy, or at least antimass, permeated the *fin de siècle* with its damned poets, its decadent esthetes, its hatred of the vulgar crowd.

A further discovery of this era was that, paradoxically, the effort to implement democracy only leads to a new kind of elite rule. "Everywhere, whether within or outside democracies, politics is made *by the few,*" Max Weber put it. His friend, Robert Michels, discovered the "iron law of oligarchy" in accordance with which democratic institutions, especially the mass political party, fall into the hands of a small group of insiders. An "invisible government" of political bosses controlled the parties, which were the instrument of allegedly democratic government, in the United States. In the last analysis, all societies are governed by elites, and a so-called democracy is really only one way of selecting this ruling class—and not necessarily the best way. Those who make their way to the top in a democratic society may be those who, as U.S. President Theodore Roosevelt said, have a gift for office-mongering as others have a knack for picking pockets. They may be demagogues, or manipulators, or bureaucrats. Practical experience with mass democratic politics from 1870 on resulted in much disenchantment with the high hopes of democratic idealists. The best known theories of elitism came from the Italians, Vilfredo Pareto and Gaetano Mosca, perhaps because the *delusione* with soaring *Risorgimento* expectations was so severe in Italy from about 1880 on.

IRRATIONALISM: THE CASE OF FRIEDRICH NIETZSCHE

In part because of mass society, precipitate change, and technological revolutions, the thought of this end-of-the-century era was marked by a growing "irrationalism." The names of Nietzsche, Freud, Weber, Bergson, and Sorel are enough to suggest it. Objective social reality and subjective cultural consciousness split apart. The "intellectuals" made their appearance as a group whose sensitivity involved them in an intolerable conflict with "bourgeois" society. The "masses" were losing their traditional folk culture in an urban environment which gradually eroded forms of community long basic to human living. Capitalism, urbanization (into megalopolis and beyond, which Lewis Mumford was to name necropolis), deracination, atomization, anomie, contract replacing status (Henry Maine's terms),[2] cash-nexus instead of human, an overly rationalized set of norms, *Gesellschaft* (society) rather than *Gemeinschaft* (community) in the famous words of Friedrich Tönnies—a bevy of social theorists gave different names to what at bottom was much the same thing. One might describe it as basically a conflict of the emancipated individual ego with mass, industrial society.

On the level of ideas, irrationalist strains gradually penetrated the European consciousness. Late in his life (1837) the philosopher Schlegel startled his listeners by suggesting that the truest thought is not rational-conceptual at all but intuitive-mythic—not so far removed, after all, from some romantic strains. The most famous exponent of irrationalism, however, was another and less reputable German philosopher. "Almost without exception, philosophers have placed the essence of mind in thought and consciousness; this ancient and universal radical error must be set aside. Consciousness is the mere surface of our minds, which, as of the surface of the earth, we do not know the inside but only the crust. Under the conscious intellect is the conscious or unconscious will, a striving, persistent, vital force, a spontaneous activity, a will of imperious desire." Thus wrote the eccentric essayist and philosopher Arthur Schopenhauer, an offshoot of the romantic and idealist German philosophers (see Chapter 1). Schopenhauer's distinction between Will and Reason, the former being fundamental, could be seen also in Darwin's scheme of nature in which the intellect is only a tool of survival, a part of the whole organism that struggles to adapt to its environment. Schopenhauer, the pessimist, thought the world spirit tricks people into making the struggle; the enlightened philosopher outwits the

---

[2] In 1875, Maine pointed out, the law of masters and servants was replaced by the law of employers and employees as the basis of British economic society.

world spirit by suppressing desire, renouncing the game of life. He had been influenced not a little by the Hindu Upanishads, which became known to the West near the end of the eighteenth century and attracted some of the romantic and idealist philosophers.

The Oriental pessimism of Schopenhauer did not make much of an impression, but the belief that the will is a deeper force than the conceptualizing reason left its stamp on the European mind. One whose mind was awakened by reading Schopenhauer was the brilliant German, Friedrich Nietzsche. Confronted with what seemed to him a decadent civilization, Nietzsche thought that he had found one cause of its enfeeblement in an excessive development of the rational faculty at the cost of a creativeness that comes only with the spontaneity of instinct or will. The brilliant young philologist and classicist, whose first book was a study of Greek drama (*The Birth of Tragedy*, 1872), traced this disease far back into Western civilization. It had begun with Socrates and Plato, the triumph of logic over literature, reason over will. Another antirationalist of this era, the Frenchman Georges Sorel, independently made this same discovery that Socrates had been the root of all evil rather than of all good as conventionally taught. Excessive development of the rational faculty enfeebles; the habit of conceptual thought paralyzes the will. Europe had intellectualized too long; the result was the weary mediocrity Nietzsche thought he saw about him in this age of bourgeois materialism. In perhaps his greatest work. Nietzsche has Zarathustra say, "I saw a great sadness come over men. The best were weary of their work. . . . All is empty, all is indifferent, all was." Western humanity had lost the capacity for believing in anything, intellectualizing had led to skepticism. The only solution lay in a new primitivism that would lead back to heroism.

The Birth of Tragedy revealed both his deep insights into Greek civilization and his almost frightening originality. Among other things, Nietzsche saw the genius of Hellas as stemming not primarily from joyous optimism (as so often suggested by the romantics) but from tragic suffering and consisting not in scientific and philosophical rationalism so much as in primitive emotionalism tempered by reason. Dionysus, whose cult engaged in ecstatic and orgiastic ritual dances, became for Nietzsche a symbol of this primitive force, without which men cannot be truly creative. The Greeks had been great because they had Dionysus as well as Apollo. They had not been merely rationalists, but were infused with the will to live. Their greatest age was the time of the early philosophers and dramatists, of Heraclitus and Aeschylus. Plato and Euripides already mark their decadence, which Western civilization unfortunately inherited more than their grandeur.

The electrifying reversal of previous perspectives was typical of Nietzsche's sharply iconoclastic thought, his "transvaluation" of values. A lyrical poet as well as a philosopher and deeply learned man, Nietzsche's challenging, radical books were to wake up intellectual Europe in the 1890s. He wrote most of these books in a frenzy of creativity in the 1880s against the threat of oncoming madness which was evidently the result of syphilis contracted in youth. Among his rejections were Christianity (a religion for slaves, denying life) and traditional morality ("morality is the most pernicious species of ignorance"). The supermen needed to rescue a decadent civilization must be beyond morality, for they must be "without pity for the degenerate." Democracy and nationalism, the vulgar superstitions of modern dwarf-men, also were targets for his sneers. More remarkable and celebrated was his atheism: "God is dead"; European man had killed him; one could no longer believe in any principle of cosmic order. Nietzsche did find something to believe in, escaping from his terrible skepticism to a "joyful wisdom" which to most others must seem scarcely less pessimistic: the love of life, as it is, in all its disorder, ugliness, cruelty, just because it is life (*amor fati:* love of fate). We are part of the cosmos, which is a blind incessant striving (it goes around in huge circles, coming back eventually to repeat itself), and we can affirm our own life force by living and striving. We can accept Dionysus and reject Christ. "You have understood me? Dionysus versus the Crucified"—these were the last words.

There are some interesting parallels in the lives of Marx and Nietzsche, the two great nineteenth-century German prophet-philosophers, born just a generation apart. Both came from religious families, Nietzsche's father, who died when Friedrich was very young, having been a Protestant clergyman. Nietzsche attended the best prep school in Saxony and then went to Bonn University where Marx had started, transferring subsequently to Leipzig where he was a classical scholar of prodigious brilliance. Marx, it will be recalled, was denied his professorship because of his atheism; Nietzsche, too, lost his faith, at the hands of David Strauss, the Young Hegelian of Marx's circle. Nietzsche took a professorship, at an unprecedented youthful age, at the Swiss University of Basel; but he was not happy in the academic world and subsequently directed many of his verbal barbs at the "mole-like" activities of sterile academics. They severely criticized his first book, *The Birth of Tragedy,* which, filled as it was with brilliant insights, was factually erratic and hardly the sort of exercise a career-minded young academic was supposed to produce. At Basel, Nietzsche encountered Jacob Burckhardt the great historian; more important, he visited Richard Wagner and his wife Cosima living at this time near Lucerne in Switzerland. What Hegel was to Marx, the philosopher Schopenhauer was to Nietzsche, the master from whom he learned but later criticized; Wagner was the other major influence, also subsequently rejected. The stupefying genius and domineering personality of the musician who hoped to create a new art for modern man worked a spell on Nietzsche for some time. Nietzsche was a far lonelier figure than Marx. He never married, and probably never found a really close friend; nor did Nietzsche attach himself to a political party or movement. Nietzsche was much more the artist and much more, in a sense just beginning to be used, the "intellectual." In this he reflected the movement of history, carrying the political order and the individual consciousness ever farther apart.

Resigning his professorship because of ill health and his unhappiness in academia, Nietzsche experienced a deep personal crisis that accompanied his most skeptical book, *Human, All Too Human* (1878), published in the centenary of Voltaire's death. The post-Darwin Nietzsche is even more skeptical than the great Enlightenment scoffer; reason itself, science and logic, turn out to be myths, erected on the basis of some unprovable assumption, and surviving only because of their value in the struggle for life. But then as he took up the life of a wanderer and had an (ultimately unsuccessful) romance with the remarkable Russian Jewess Lou Salome, Nietzsche recovered his confidence and, in a short period of inspiration in 1883, wrote his most famous book, in the form of the ancient Grecian hymn to Dionysus or Bacchus. Most of Nietzsche is written in a hard, terse, lucid prose, aphoristic and epigrammatic. But in *Also Sprach Zarathustra* he created a kind of philosophical poem, joining a select group in the Western tradition that includes Lucretius, Dante, and Goethe. Always deeply musical, Nietzsche had tried his hand without much success at musical composition; now he found his genre in this musical poem and projected onto the figure of the Persian sage Zoroaster or Zarathustra his philosophical idea. It was here, in the often difficult, often delightful, stories of the prophet and his disciples, that Nietzsche best expressed his theses of the death of God, the invention of new values for a valueless world, the falsity of anything except utter faithfulness to one's own inspiration, and the need to do this in the knowledge of the terrible truth that the same things will recur over and over again in a universe infinitely vast in time and space. Such is the final test for the "higher men" who must surpass the existing degenerate mass of humanity.

The universe is irrational, it simply *is*. One can reject it, choosing with Schopenhauer to renounce life by suppressing all desire like the Indian *fakir*; or one can accept it, fully realizing its irrationality, pain, and horror. Not easy to understand, and perhaps tending in his later works toward the madness that approached him, Nietzsche at his worst suggests a shocking hatred of civilization and a desire for barbarism; at his best, he reminds us that man can create values by his own nobility though the universe be hostile. The supermen he called for to reshape the human race should not be thought of as brutalized Hitlers, rather as enlightened poet-philosopher leaders. It must be said in his defense, and has been said by recent students concerned with rescuing him from wild misinterpretation, that he despised all nationalism and militarism, including German, and also was no racist or anti-Semite, though the Nazis later made use of him. His wilder ejaculations of rage against the human race can charitably be excused as products of the sufferings of a morbidly sensitive and physically sick man; of enduring value in Nietzsche is the hatred of falsehood and sham, of mediocrity and vulgarity, along with deep insights into human creativity and a fierce sincerity: one should live one's philosophy. His fantastic sensitivity to ideas makes Nietzsche a barometer registering virtually every variation of the modern mind.

Chief among these insights was an awareness of the role of the darker, submerged, unconscious, "Dionysian" elements in human nature, which by being "sublimated" enter into creativity. Nietzsche, like Schopenhauer, anticipated Freud. This force is partly sexual, and Nietzsche suggests that Christianity and conventional morality have grievously damaged Western civilization by surrounding sex with taboos. It is, more basically, just the joyous spontaneity of the animal. It is the dithyrambic dance of primitive man. Civilize it, smother it with morality and reason, and you destroy something necessary to humanity and to culture. The highest culture requires something of the intellectual element but too much of it means decadence.

Nietzsche combined and held in suspension an amazing number of modern attitudes. There is something in him of the alienated artist, saying with Baudelaire, "The world has taken on a thickness of vulgarity that raises a spiritual man's contempt to a violent passion." He is an important precursor of twentieth-century existentialism, in question here being his call for humanity to create its own values by sheer willpower, as well as his rejection of all merely theoretical philosophy. "I have written my works with my whole body and life," Nietzsche could say proudly. He is the gloomy prophet of the totalitarian state and modern mass-man. But most of all he is the philosopher of the will-to-power or life force—the irrationalist, prober of drives deeper than reason, anticipator of Freud and Jung, psychologist of the unconscious.

In all his moods and guises, Nietzsche is clearly something quite new and different, compared to Victorian orthodoxy. He has the flavor of the *fin de siècle,* over which indeed his influence was spread widely, André Gide, the French novelist, remarked that "The influence of Nietzsche preceded with us the appearance of his work; it fell on soil already prepared . . .; it did not surprise but confirm."[3] As so often happens, an idea's hour seemed to have arrived and a number of people felt it independently at about the same time. One of the ideas this period seemed destined to discover and probe was the unconscious irrational within the human psyche. Almost contemporary with the great writings of Nietzsche in the 1880s came the first work of the Viennese physician, Sigmund Freud. Nietzsche also greatly influenced Carl Jung.

It would be difficult to overstate the influence of Nietzsche. As a recent writer (Werner Pelz) has commented, "It is not a matter of agreeing or disagreeing with his philosophical conclusions, but of having passed through his corrosives of metaphysical, moral, and psychological doubts. They leave a man scarred and purified; certainly changed." Through this fire the mind of modern Europe has passed. Nietzsche's influence spread widely over Europe, reaching England by 1904, after sweeping through France in the 1890s; the young Yeats felt the fire of Zarathustra as keenly in Ireland as Franz Kafka did in Prague or Merezhkovsky in Russia. The influence was strongest on artistic and poetic temperaments, but affected all manner of people. Gustav Mahler and Richard Strauss set its spirit to music.

Nietzsche's political impact was in more than one direction, like Darwin's. Atheist, radical critic of conventional religion and morality, destroyer of all manner of orthodoxies, this most dramatic of thinkers held a natural appeal to the Left, and one finds many socialists and anarchists responding to his message, associating it with revolutionary activism. It seemed to suggest an apocalyptic ending to the whole Western past and the inauguration of a completely new age. He was the

---

[3] In his article on "Nietzsche and John Davidson," *Journal of the History of Ideas,* June 1957, John A. Lester, Jr., notes another case of one who "may have been a Nietzschean before he ever heard the name of Nietzsche," but whose native inclinations were stimulated by contact with the German. There were many such instances.

darling of the *avant-garde,* the bible of the defiantly alienated artist-intellectual. In his name one could throw off traditional religion, defy the conventional moral rules, scorn the bourgeoisie, and predict a day of doom. Yet Nietzsche also scorned democracy and socialism, which he linked to the slave morality of the Judeo-Christian world view. He preached the inequality of man and could be used to sanction imperialism, despotism, and war. Benito Mussolini was deflected from left-wing socialism toward the new cult of fascism in part by Nietzsche; Hitler and the Nazis subsequently glorified him, even if, as his defenders insist, they distorted him. During the war of 1914 to 1918, people in the Allied countries fighting Germany quite commonly linked Nietzsche to the ruthless war-making of the Hohenzollern legions, who were depicted advancing on their barbarous mission armed with Nietzschean admonitions to be brutal. If this was an hysterical caricature, the fact remains that German youth just before the war were strongly affected by the cult of adventure and heroism, derived in no small part from the aphorisms of *The Will to Power* (rather tendentiously edited by Nietzsche's reactionary sister) and other Nietzschean writings. "I am dynamite," the sage of Sils St. Maria had said; there was indeed an explosive quality in the rhetoric of this great writer. He could act as an energizing agent on all kinds of different people.

For Germans of this generation, Richard Wagner, the great musical composer and ideologist, sometime idol, later object of Nietzsche's anger—too Christian, too *Reichsdeutsch* also—functioned as a symbol of the new culture. Wagner's *Bayreuther Blätter* began in 1880 to proclaim the vital connections between religion and art, as one of the century's greatest geniuses turned from sublime music to dubious evangelism. In standing for totally committed art, Wagner played a role somewhat similar to Ruskin's in England or Charles Baudelaire's (one of his early champions) in France, except that he became a national institution through his organizing abilities. Filled with a vague discontent at the whole of modern life, young poets and artists revered both Nietzsche and Wagner, overlooking their quarrel; a curiously significant work of 1890, Jules Langbehn's *Rembrandt as Educator,* the "Greening of Germany" of its day, preached a popularized mixture of the two giants.

HENRI BERGSON

A milder and more respectable figure than Nietzsche, the French[4] philosopher Henri Bergson contributed no less to the revolt against reason or against scientific positivism which characterized the *Zeitgeist* of the years from about 1885 to 1914, an "Age of Unreason." Bergson, whose first notable work appeared in 1889 when he was 30, exerted so strong an influence that by the 1900s he was easily the most important force in French thought, being frequently compared to Descartes, Rousseau, and Comte among earlier sages of an epoch. His lectures at the University

[4] Bergson was actually Jewish, the son of a Polish father and an English mother, educated in Switzerland as a boy. But, receiving his university education in Paris, Bergson went on to teach at the Sorbonne and was an ardently patriotic French citizen.

of Paris were likened to those of Abelard in the Middle Ages for the sensation they created, and his repute spread widely abroad too. His considerable role in twentieth-century thought is generally conceded. Bergson's gift of style assured him an audience. Like Nietzsche, he used metaphor and poetic imagery because he believed that conceptual thought does not best communicate the nature of reality. Also like the German, he appeared to his contemporaries as a liberator, opening up fresh horizons, calling for creativity, and expressing it in his richly gifted prose.

In a romantic manner, Bergson sharply distinguished between the rational, conceptualizing intellect and the intuitive understanding. The former, the scientific, analyzing function, is a practical tool, concerned with useful knowledge, but not truth-giving because reality may not be so divided up and conceptualized. (The student may here be reminded of Kant.) Reality is a continuum, to be grasped by the intuition. It flows through immediate experience as the "life force" that is in all things. Intuition (meaning instinct become self-conscious and reflective) takes us to "the very inwardness of life," while the intellect is not in this sense in touch with reality. Bergson said that he began his philosophical speculations by considering what is meant by *time* and found himself led to conclude that the clock time of everyday life or of the physicist is a convention very different from the real time of experience. The intelligence that analyzes and divides things has given us the former conception which is useful but not true to experience. When we grasp immediate experience by intuitive means, what we find there is an indivisible continuum, a "duration" that we can scarcely describe save in poetic imagery; this represents a fundamental reality. So it is in other things. Science tells us that the sound of a bell is a series of vibrations, but we experience it as a whole. A melody is not a series of notes; it cannot be described; we intuit it. Science, as Wordsworth had written, "murders to dissect." Reality is indivisible and hence unanalyzable; insofar as we do analyze it, as for convenience's sake we must do, we falsify it.

This is no attack on science within its limits, but it *is* rather sharp deflation of the pretensions of science to provide complete knowledge, pretensions which at that time existed. "Science consists only of conventions, and to this circumstance solely does it owe its apparent certitude; the facts of science and, *a fortiori,* its laws are the artificial work of the scientist; science therefore can teach us nothing of the truth; it can serve only as a rule of action."[5] (Nietzsche also had viewed scientific systems as basically myths.) Critics of pragmatist and Bergsonian indictments of the "conceptualizing" process, as conventional only, were not lacking, as might be expected, and often pointed out that these philosophers themselves could not escape the use of conceptual or intellectual language. To do without it would be to abolish thought. To follow Bergson all the way in his intuitionism would be to destroy all analysis and lapse into chaos. It was generally agreed that concepts and reality are not the same thing, also that conceptual knowledge does not exhaust reality or constitute the only mode of dealing with it; but the implication that the two realms are completely divorced, that science tells nothing at all about reality but only about

[5] R. B. Perry, *Present Philosophical Tendencies* (1912), pp. 230-231.

its own arbitrary signs and symbols was frequently rejected. Still, the persuasively conducted Bergsonian offensive against science made its impact felt; the chief result was to vindicate and rehabilitate forms of "immediate experience" such as literature, religion, and various mystic or nonrational experiences.

Bergson proposed a vitalistic evolutionary theory, arguing against Darwinian mechanism that life has within it some purposive forces, without which evolution cannot be explained (*Creative Evolution,* 1908). Doctrines of "emergent evolution" received the support of a number of philosophers at this time, the most prominent advocate after Bergson being the British philosopher Samuel Alexander. Reality creates itself gradually, rather than existing from all eternity; life evolves ever new and unpredictable forms. We participate in a universe that is not finished and help in the making of it. A striking idea, and as Bergson noted, a radically new one in the Western tradition, "creative evolution" turned the rather somber mechanistic atheism of the Darwinists into a feeling for the wondrous freedom of a world in growth.

In general, Bergson's persuasively presented philosophy urged the importance of spontaneity, of intuition, and of immediate experience, as over against those "tentacles of cold, prying thought" (Nietzsche) which gives us useful knowledge at the cost of cutting us off from reality. Getting away from cold science and bathing in the refreshing waters of intuition clearly seems to have value for Bergson. To him as to the American pragmatists, the world properly seen is rich, inexhaustible, vital. Though his stress on spontaneity and immediate experience influenced the existentialists, Bergson was on the whole not a tragic philosopher but a joyous one. The anti-intellectualism or anti-rationalism of which he may be accused was rather gentle, and to tie this deeply religious man to the subsequent movements of fascism or Nazism appears perverse. Few philosophers have attached such basic importance to liberty. Among his leading disciples in prewar France was the editor and writer Charles Péguy, who so far as he can be classified might best be described as a Christian democrat and socialist. He was, in fact, quite an individualist. Bergson, like the pragmatists, encouraged freedom unbounded by dogma and tended not to set up any "school." One French critic detected in the disciples of Bergson a sort of lyrical insanity, celebrating the chaos of things in "orgies of subjectivism"; he cited Albert Bazailles and Alphonse Chide. The same could be said of Péguy in some of his moods.

So the subjectivism which Kant and romanticism had begun was deepening; people became ever more aware that (1) truth is created by the free human mind, not found, as something objectively existing just as it is taken into the mind; and (2) myth, intuition, is the best means to this creation, rather than reason, conceptual thought. Bergson more than Freud or anyone else gave novelists the idea of presenting an unedited "stream of consciousness." His "life force" philosophy may be found prominently in that avid consumer and popularizer of ideas, George Bernard Shaw, who also introduced Marx and Nietzsche to a somewhat amazed British public. Colin Wilson has observed that Shaw's plays "are all about the same theme: the obscure creative drive of the 'Life Force' and the way it makes people do things they find difficult to understand in terms of everyday logic." "Our intellect—what a very small thing on the surface of ourselves!" Maurice Barrès, the important French writer and politician of this era, exclaimed. It was the theme of the hour.

The pragmatists and Bergson broadly agreed in their attack on intellectual or conceptual knowledge. Immediate experience is deeper and forms the matrix within which intellectual knowledge takes place. As John Dewey put it, there is an "experience in which knowledge-and-its-object is sustained, and whose schematized, or structural, portion it is." We encounter "reality" only in immediate, intuitive experience, as distinct from intellectual ratiocination. We must reject, as Nietzsche cleverly put it, the dogma of immaculate perception. If we want to know the music, we do not analyze it into notes or vibrations, we simply hear it. We can perform, and usefully perform, the former function, but we should recognize it for what it is, a secondary and derivative one. In this respect Bergson and the pragmatists coincided with the aims of Edmund Husserl, today considered the founder of phenomenology, who was also philosophizing at about the turn of the century, though at that time much more obscure than Bergson. Husserl used the term "phenomenology" in 1900 to mean the systematic study of how things and concepts are given to the mind directly, at the deeper, more "real" level, exactly as it happens and not as it is formalized in conceptual thought.

The Englishman F. C. S. Schiller and the Italians Papini and Prezzolini represented pragmatism in Europe, where it was much less important than in the United States. The vigorous American William James was a man of international reputation who knew Bergson as well as Schiller and Papini. Pragmatism had affinities with the message of revolt and liberation; it denied the existence of final, abstract truth, asserting that we make the truth as we act. Life is an open experiment in which we constantly test our hypotheses against reality and use our intellects as tools. Pragmatism was popular for a time in Italy about 1900 but dissolved because of a certain vagueness; it stood for "freedom, creativeness, and originality" and appealed mostly to poetic writers. Papini subsequently became a fascist, indicative perhaps of pragmatism's tendency to take on the color of its surroundings and embrace any active creed that seemed to have vitality—something also alleged of Bergsonism.

In other ways, too, Bergsonism reflected broader currents of the day which may be seen mirrored in other minds. The stress on the value of religious experience, *qua* experience, found in William James's famous lectures on *Varieties of Religious Experience,* could be found also in the serious interest in supernormal psychical phenomena (to which C. D. Broad, Cambridge philosophy professor, among others, lent his name); in George Santayana's interest in the "splendid error" of the Catholic faith, a great myth: While religions are not of course literally true, it is a shallow person who thinks them disposed of when this is pointed out. It could be found in the Catholic Revival among men and women of letters, not only in France but in England and in many other places. There was unquestionably some weakness in treating religion as not true but useful, or nice to believe. Simone Weil later complained that Bergson presented religious faith "like a pink pill of a superior kind, which imparts a prodigious amount of vitality." But the turning to religion in a self-conscious way, treating it as poetry or a pleasing myth, was very typical of the *fin de siècle* vanguard. Carl Jung came to regard religion as good psychotherapy.

In Germany people spoke of the revival of metaphysics, citing Hartmann, Lotze, Eucken; Max Scheler is a good counterpart of Bergson or Santayana—a sensitive, esthetic, introspective, nondogmatic philosopher. In Britain Hegelian idealism was modified in the direction of a greater personalism, and an awareness of the multistructured nature of reality (Bradley, McTaggart). If Bergson contributed to the revival of both religion and metaphysics and to a nondoctrinaire subjectivism which stressed experience for its own sake—participating in the great stream of life—his most notable influence was on literature. He was very much a philosopher for poets and novelists. He directly inspired the imagist poets as well as the "stream of consciousness" novelists and had a good deal to do with others of the many literary movements that proliferated—symbolism, expressionism. For Bergson encouraged the artistic imagination to plumb its deepest levels, cutting loose from rational thought in search of spontaneous experience—finding there, he supposed, the utmost reality.

The Bergsonian message, like that of Nietzsche and William James, must be set against the background of science's virtual monopoly of knowledge; he broke through the ban on religious or metaphysical speculations decreed by the positivist regimen. "For the first time since Comte and Kant metaphysics had waged war against scientific determinism on its own ground and won it," Etienne Gilson has written in his recollections of what Bergson meant to his generation. Charles de Gaulle spoke of Bergson as one who "renewed French spirituality." Later events revealed some of the limitations of this cheerfully affirmative philosophy; it could lead to approval of almost anything that was active and dynamic, like war and fascism.

But Bergson lived on to add to his reputation with the book some think is his greatest, *The Two Sources of Morality and Religion,* published in 1932, a work of rich texture, interwoven with insights, whose general theme conforms to his guiding vision of humanity as needing to surmount its practical scientific reason with the creative insights of religion and poetry. Standing somewhere between Freud and Nietzsche, Bergson like them was essentially a gifted student of the human interior mind, the subjective dimension, the undiscovered self.

SIGMUND FREUD

It was an "age of the spirit," reacting against an excess of positivism. "The important thing was to 'have soul,' " Jean Guehenno remarks of this ambience from 1890 to 1914. "I have always considered myself a voice of what I believe to be a greater renaissance," wrote the great Irish poet W. B. Yeats in 1892, "the revolt of the soul against the intellect—now beginning in the world." Symbolist poets (discussed later in this chapter) experimented with a kind of expression that would convey inexpressible emotional moods—saying the unsayable. Many saw art as the only way of bridging the gulf between consciousness and society.

Nevertheless science was far from dead. This revolt was a movement of a small minority of disaffected rebels, whose great significance is now seen but who were then far from the mainstream. As it continued to parent a host of technological marvels—this was the age of electricity, the first automobiles, radio, X rays—science never stood higher in popular esteem. And among the acknowledged intellectual giants of this period, the Viennese physician Sigmund Freud was not a poet or prophet, but—apparently—a hardheaded empirical scientist. The Austrian doctor brought strange knowledge from the underworld of the human psyche but summed it up in perfectly rational concepts and offered a systematic clinical approach to it.

If no greater influence on modern thought exists than that of Sigmund (born Sigismund) Freud, the answer lies partly in this unusual amalgamation of science and humanism that marked the Viennese physician-author. Having received his medical degree from the University of Vienna in 1881, Freud practiced as a clinical psychiatrist all his life. Freud's general spirit was averse to metaphysics, mysticism, religion, or anything except the empirically verifiable hypotheses of scientific method. In this respect he shared in the vogue for scientific positivism that characterized the last decades of the nineteenth century. At the same time, Freud was steeped in the classics and made use of concepts drawn from literature (which he influenced enormously): He was in many ways an obviously imaginative writer. Few major intellectual figures have so successfully straddled the two cultures which are both essential to modern man but which have so often been antagonistic.

Freud's influence stems also from the vigor and clarity of his prose, but it was chiefly the daring originality of his thought which captured the imagination. Freud worked out his key ideas between 1885 and 1905, then co-founded the International Psychoanalytical Association, which disseminated his views widely and survived the notable schisms besetting the movement. He added significantly to his corpus of writing after 1920 despite a painful cancer that afflicted him through the last fifteen years of his life. The 1920s saw a worldwide reception of his ideas; Freudian terms such as *unconscious, repression, Oedipus complex, id,* and *ego* became household words. Freud's theories, along with those of Albert Einstein, seemed the most exciting and radical of the ideas changing the world in that iconoclastic period. Psychoanalysis developed into a major profession, especially in America. (Its vogue in the United States as a gadget to fix people's "hangups" did not please Freud, whose aristocratic Old World temperament strongly disliked American culture.)

Essential Freudian concepts, in the formulation of which he was highly original, even when transforming older ideas, included the *Unconscious,* which Freud thought played a large part in human life; the idea of mental illness as traceable to traumatic events which are repressed and buried in the Unconscious; the sexual nature of most of these traumatic events involving infantile experiences (Freud, it is said, slew the Victorian myth of innocent childhood); the therapy for neurosis in a dialogue between patient and physician which aims at uncovering the buried and repressed memory; the interpretation and therapeutic use of dreams, which offer clues to the Unconscious; and the application of theories of the Unconscious to everyday life, in explaining jokes, dreams, and "Freudian slips" of the tongue.

Freud sketched theories of early sexual development, wrote up his most interesting cases and applied his theories to the explanation of works of art (*Hamlet*, Leonardo's "Mona Lisa"). After World War I he added aggression to sex as a basic drive and wrote of the death instinct as well as the erotic force. *Id, Ego, and Superego* presented a dramatic picture of conflict between antisocial and authoritarian pressures bearing on the divided self; the later Freud, more speculative and philosophical, visualized man as tragically torn between these irreconcilable claims of society and the individual. In *Totem and Taboo*, Freud attempted to relate his theory of individual behavior to human history, postulating a primeval rebellion of the sons against the father on grounds of sexual jealousy—the social counterpart of the Oedipal complex, a racial memory presumably imprinted in all humans.

Freud like Marx drew freely on the ideas of others but made of them an original mixture. The idea of the Unconscious had a long prehistory. Freud claimed no originality for the idea, saying that he found it in poets and novelists (Shakespeare, Goethe, and Dostoyevsky "had come closer to the fundamental truths of psychoanalysis than had the physicians,") but applied it scientifically. One significant source, which Freud acknowledged, was Schopenhauer, who indeed anticipated Freud in mentioning the significance of sex, repression, and the importance of childhood sexual experience.[6] The philosopher Eduard von Hartmann, a Schopenhauerian, wrote a book on the philosophy of the unconscious which was popular in the 1880s. Indeed the unconscious was almost as old a subject of speculation as dreams, which Freud was to write his most impressive book about, or the sexual drive. What Freud sought to do was weave these primeval but dimly understood phenomena into a system of scientific thought and experiment. A careful examination of the sources shaping Freud's thought can yield, as in the cases of Darwin and Marx, a host of influences from a number of different directions that this synthesizing mind absorbed and assembled. Freud even had his Wallace: The French psychologist Pierre Janet always claimed that he did first what Freud got most of the credit for (Janet published a number of case histories between 1886 and 1893). Nor should Nietzsche's powerful influence be ignored: the Id, *Das Es*, was borrowed from the philosopher who had blamed Christianity for repressing sexual impulses at the price of creativity and had used the term "sublimation." Schopenhauer, of course, was a common influence on both Freud and Nietzsche.

The Freudian movement was part of a larger evolution of human consciousness, which included individual liberation from social controls, accompanied by a greater self-awareness and enrichment of consciousness—at the price, sometimes, of painful conflicts with society and of psychic tensions. Freud was not the only one working toward the franker discussion of previously taboo sexual matters. Apart

---

[6] See R. K. Gupta, "Schopenhauer and Freud," *Journal of the History of Ideas*, October–December 1975. For the influences of another philosopher, see P. A. Y. Gunter, "Bergson and Jung," *Journal of the History of Ideas*, October–December 1982.

from the novelists, Freud's fellow Viennese physician Richard Krafft-Ebing published his much discussed *Psychopathia Sexualis* in 1886. The pioneer sexologist, the Englishman Havelock Ellis, can be mentioned in this context. In 1910, Lou Salome—whom Nietzsche had courted, who knew Freud, and who became the mistress of the poet Rilke—wrote a book on eroticism (*Die Erotik*). D. H. Lawrence was beginning his literary explorations of eroticism, as was James Joyce. In the 1900s, Edwardian England said goodbye to Victorian "prudery" with the amorous adventures of King Edward, the plays of Shaw, and novels of H. G. Wells such as *Ann Veronica* (1911), in which a liberated woman practices free love. More popularly, a typical piece of Edwardian fiction was Elinor Glyn's *Three Weeks,* portraying sophisticated adultery. In all sorts of ways a freer, more "emancipated" attitude toward sexual morality, a greater openness in discussing physical sex, was beginning to spread, though largely confined to literary elites such as England's Bloomsbury set; it would continue into the 1920s. In bringing into the open what had long lain under restraints, Freud shared in the spirit of his age among the intelligentsia.

His energy and imagination, combined with some of the trappings of empirical science, assured Freud's great reputation. It did not come quickly. Apart from the reactions of scandalized moralists, orthodox medical practitioners rejected and to a degree ostracized Freud as being far too speculative. He started his own movement and gathered about him a few disciples, who gradually grew in numbers. In the 1900s, Freud was only just beginning to be known. It is said that *The Interpretation of Dreams* (1900) took eight years to sell its initial printing of six hundred copies in English. Finding an able and congenial partner in the brilliant Carl Jung, he founded the International Psychoanalytic Association in 1910. The Freud-Jung partnership, destined to break up three years later, was then in full swing; the two founders of psychoanalysis sensed that "the ferment is at work," though at times Freud feared that they were trying to move too fast. They lectured in the United States during 1909 and 1910, a landmark in the dissemination of their doctrine.

Freud is one of the seminal minds of the modern age, by almost universal consent; he ranks with Newton and Darwin as one of those scientists who altered the fundamental conditions of thought and changed Western civilization's view of itself in basic ways. He ranks also with Marx and Darwin, it is frequently said, among the big three of the nineteenth century. This is despite the fact that, like those other two giants, his theories may prove to have been wrong in many details. Freud himself was convinced he had made epochal discoveries: "I have the distinct feeling that I have touched on one of the great secrets of nature," he wrote, and on occasion compared himself to Copernicus and Darwin. Freud was hardly an arrogant man, though inclined to be somewhat dogmatic, and in pointing to the importance of his ideas he was stating only a generally acknowledged truth. His place in modern thought seems secure, though there is increasingly a tendency to doubt that Freud founded an exact science or that his imposing structure of thought will prove any more lasting than other speculative ideas. The verdict on Freud may come to resemble that on Marx, in that he will be viewed less as a scientist than as a pioneer who opened up new horizons for others to explore. His name has become a household word, and his influence extends over the whole of contemporary culture.

Since the largest impact of the Freudians came in the 1920s and 1930s, it will be appropriate to continue the discussion of Freud in the next chapter. But his greatest creative phase came in the 1890-1914 period. His richest, most fulfilling book was the *Traumdeutung* (1900); it followed a crisis in Freud's life during which he undertook a self-analysis and thought he found in himself evidence of the celebrated complex by which the boy child experienced erotic attachment to his mother and sexual jealousy of his father, this at a very early age. The stimulating collaboration with Jung precipitated an organized psychoanalysis movement; the break with Jung just before World War I caused a clarification, rather dogmatically, of Freud's position about the primacy of the sexual drive. During these years, Freud was working every day as a practicing therapist and writing up those fascinating cases—Dora, the Wolf Man, Little Hans—which provided the alleged basis for his theories. He was attracting a remarkable, often bizarre, collection of disciples, many of whom, like Jung, would later go their own psychoanalytical way amid a swirl of controversy. In 1915 Freud was just getting to be famous; in the United States in that year, Walter Lippmann, a young American intellectual of a notable generation, remarked that the Vienna doctor had "set up a reverberation in human thought and conduct of which few dare yet to predict the consequences."

CARL JUNG

Nineteen years younger than Freud, who was born in 1856 (the same year as George Bernard Shaw and Woodrow Wilson, three years before Emile Durkheim and Henri Bergson), Carl Jung was the son of a Swiss parson and attended the University of Basel, where Nietzsche once taught. He was in fact powerfully influenced by Nietzsche, but turned to psychiatry because it seemed to combine religion and philosophy with science. It is commonly said that Jung always was less scientific, more drawn to philosophy, religion, even mysticism than the hardheaded Freud, who had rejected his ancestral Judaism and believed religion to be a neurotic manifestation drawn from the Oedipus complex. Yet Jung in some ways had more empirical experience in psychiatry than did Freud, for upon finishing his studies at Basel in 1900, he began work at the famed Berghoelzi hospital in Zurich where he encountered a wide variety of mental patients. He met Freud in 1907 after having read and admired his works; at their first meeting they talked for thirteen hours without stopping. Eager to show that psychoanalysis was not confined to a circle of Vienna Jews, Freud put Jung forward as the first president of the International Psychoanalytic Association, and the two worked well and hard together to advance the new cause. Jung was a man of immense energy and great ability, though never the master of writing style that Sigmund was. He was to live until 1961 and become a world-famed seer, a true master of the modern mind along with the man with whom, in 1912-13 he engaged in one of intellectual history's best known quarrels. The breach between the two giants of psychoanalysis left them shouting insults at each other in a way that casts doubts on their own psychological maturity—not the last time the affairs of the IPA were marked by fervent emotionalism. (Freud fainted when he first heard that Jung criticized the theory of infantile sexual fixation.)[7]

Freud, convinced that his erstwhile colleague and heir-apparent (or adopted son) was not only "brutal and sanctimonious" but "crazy," retained control of the IPA as the Swiss withdrew, Jung going his own way thereafter. Their differences were indeed substantial, though they shared a belief in the unconscious as a psychic determinant, and in dreams as a key to the content of the unconscious. Jung attached less importance to sexual repression and infantile experience as a source of mental disturbance; dissociation, the divided self, was more a problem to Jung than was repression, and the unconscious was a much more favorable domain to Carl than to Sigmund—a source not of savagely antisocial impulses but of nourishing myths or "archetypes." What we need to do is harmonize the collective part of the unconscious, on which Jung laid great stress, with our personality. Freud saw the unconscious, at least the id part of it, as something to be abolished or negated: "Where Id was, there shall Ego be." But to Jung the unconscious is a potential source of creativity. One may see here an echo of Nietzsche's "Dionysian" energy that lies behind great art.

Jung incurred the contempt of the scientific psychologists but the admiration of others by wandering into the fields of religion, art, literature, and history. Shocked by what he termed Freud's "materialistic prejudice" and "shallow positivism," Jung might have agreed with D. H. Lawrence who scolded Freud for creating a "technology of the heart." The "collective unconscious," which Jung thought he observed to exist in remarkable ways, appears in mythological motifs, in fairy tales, in art and poetry, as well as in dreams and in conscious behavior. Its archetypes are found in all the great religions and in literature. A fabulous scholar and polyhistor himself, Jung cast his net widely over civilizations past and present in his search for the archetypes of the collective unconscious. His disciples have tended more toward comparative mythology and toward the analysis of art and poetry than anything else. He manifested some deeply mystical and religious tendencies.

To Jung, religion and art are essential to the healthy human psyche. The great "myths," expressing as they do the language of the mind at its deepest level, with roots in the collective life of humanity, satisfy fundamental instincts. Without them, human nature shrivels. Here Jung touches Nietzsche's conviction that the modern individual is overly rationalized and needs to regain contact with some healthy primitivisms. While Jung, too, always claimed to be an empirical investigator, his critics think that he often lost himself in fanciful speculations. But no other pioneer

---

[7]In rebelling against the father figure, Freud's disciples seemed to be carrying out one of the teachings of Freud, reenacting the primal scene described in *Totem and Taboo*. One may speculate about the need for genius to find a mentor and then cast him aside, the pattern of Marx with Hegel and Nietzsche with Wagner.

of what Jung called "the undiscovered self" except Freud himself has so drawn attention to this strange, fascinating realm that lies within each person, or so contributed to its elucidation.

Probably Jung's best known contribution to psychology was his classification of personality types, into "extraverts" and "introverts" with subdivisions. He invented other striking concepts, such as "persona" and "shadow," which roughly correspond to Freud's superego and id. The *shadow* is a figure of the unconscious containing evil, antisocial impulses but also other nonconscious elements. The *persona* is our social role, the part society expects us to play, a mask of artificial personality. This seems to bear some relationship to what the existentialists later called the "unauthentic" or "other-directed" self. The fully mature or "individuated" personality must dissolve the persona and integrate the unconscious into the self. This is close to Freud's "sublimation" or to Nietzsche's fusion of "Dionysian" and "Apollonian" elements. The basic idea is that elements of the unconscious mind must be used in the interest of a higher creativity.

"The dynamism and imagery of the instincts together form an *a priori* which no man can overlook without the gravest risk to himself," Jung wrote in *The Undiscovered Self* (1957). Overlooking them, he believed, could be held responsible not only for individual mental illness but also for such social horrors as German Nazism; for the forces latent in the unconscious will break forth in wildly irrational ways if they are not understood and administered to properly. Modern man still lives, he thought, in a make-believe world made up of rational concepts, ignoring the underlying emotional determinants. "The psychiatrist is one of those who know most about the conditions of the soul's welfare, upon which so infinitely much depends in the social sum." The popularity of psychiatry today, growing from nothing to the status of a great profession in this century, offers some evidence that what Jung wrote is true, though we still stand at the mere threshold of real understanding of the self. The popularity of mysticism, Eastern religions, meditation and other such fads in recent years also shows that Jung was right in seeing the problem as less a scientific than a spiritual one. Rejected largely by the professional psychoanalysts, who much preferred the more rational and systematic Freud, Jung made a comeback in recent years among the bewildered youngsters in an overly technological society. World War I moved Jung deeply and pushed him further toward a mysticism always congenial to his temperament. He shared with Freud a belief that "the great gains made by the evolution of civilized society . . . are made at the price of enormous losses." Where Freud saw the cost as chiefly due to sexual repression, Jung stressed loss of contact with the realm of myth and symbol. He strongly believed that objective reason, the intellectual mode of our rationalized society, is a far poorer way of thinking than what he called "analogical" thinking: "archaic, unconscious, not put into words and hardly formulable in words." It is somewhat surprising, in view of this, that Jung wrote so much. But his writing though often awkward does have a strangely compelling power to arouse interest in myths, symbols, and mystic experiences. In this respect he has been a child of the twentieth century.

THE CRISIS IN SCIENCE

The twentieth century opened momentously. In 1901, as Freud published his *Interpretation of Dreams* and Jung began his work in Zurich, another young Jewish scientist, just graduated from the Swiss Polytechnic Institute in Zurich, published his first scientific paper; this of course was Albert Einstein. At about the same time Max Planck, walking in the woods in Berlin, told his son "Today I have made a discovery as important as that of Newton." (Posterity has agreed.)

The popular prestige of science stood of course very high in this period when almost every year brought some fresh technical miracle, whether electric light, phonograph, or automobile. For the more thoughtful, science offered its exciting theories, of which Darwin's natural selection was but the most sensational. (In 1900, several scientists rediscovered Mendel's laws of heredity.) The periodic table of the elements, worked out by the Russian Mendeleyeff; the atomic structure of matter, developed by Dalton and others; the law of the conservation of energy, associated with Helmholtz and Kelvin, a striking tribute to the regularity and constancy of natural phenomena; and other great discoveries aroused awe, but not dismay, since they testified to the orderliness of nature and the ability of science to disclose cosmic principles. "The men of science had become the prophets of progressive minds," to an extent that may be measured by a statement in the British *Annual Register* for 1884 that few other subjects except scientific ones received any attention from the intellectual world. Lonely prophets and offbeat poets, despite the attention properly given them, did not at this time seriously compete with the scientists either in the popular or the intellectual world.

The widespread confidence in science rested on the belief that it was unfolding an accurate picture of reality, that it was solidly based and could not err, that other modes of knowledge such as metaphysics and religion were obsolete. This popular and slightly vulgar scientific materialism was purveyed in the works of such pundits as T. H. Huxley, John Tyndall, the Germans Emil Du Bois-Reymond and Ernst Haeckel (*The Riddle of the Universe*). But at the turn of the century science was about to lose its confident common sense air and to confront shattering paradoxes at the frontiers of physics.

The popular, common sense view of science included opinions such as that reality consists of material bodies, the atoms being thought of as little billiard balls; that these material objects act in a spatial field and temporal world of the sort familiar to human experience, with an objectively existing space and time; that all bodies obey the same scientific "laws," like Newton's laws of motion and the law of the conservation of energy. The universe was pictured as a large machine, consisting of physical bodies in dynamic relationships. Before long, an astounded public was forced to hear from the mouths of the scientists themselves the refutation of all this. Matter, it seemed, consisted of invisible and perhaps merely hypothetical units called "electrons," which within the atom refused to obey Newton's laws, an example of insubordination without precedent.

Even more surprisingly, time and space as they appear to human experience had to be abandoned, since these are relative to some arbitrary standard and no objective standard exists for the universe as a whole. Newton's law of gravitation, foundation of physical science for two hundred years, was evidently not accurate. It became impossible to picture the behavior of "matter" as corresponding to any-thing within the realm of human sensory experience, either at the subatomic or the cosmic level. The universe was not like a machine, nor was there anything in it that one could readily call "matter"; it was even possible for scientists to hold that reali-ty fades into an idea when traced as far as possible. Matter, remarked Bertrand Russell, became a formula for describing what happens when it is not. Space, time, and matter all turned out to be fictions of the human mind, perhaps not so far from the convenient but unreal abstractions of scientific knowledge according to Bergson.

A starting point for these complex developments was the Michelson-Morley experiment, performed in 1887 by two Americans wholly unaware that they were about to stumble onto a new era in science. They were trying to measure the speed of the earth by measuring the time it takes light to travel with, as compared to against, the direction of the earth's motion. The extraordinary result, after repeated experiments, was to disclose the remarkable fact that no "ether" or other substance exists for earth and other bodies to move through. It was found that the velocity of light does not change regardless of whether it is moving with the earth or at right angles to it, or in the other direction, something that seemed to defy common sense, as if a person walking on a moving conveyor belt (such as you find in airports) was found to be moving at exactly the same speed as a person walking at the same pace on the floor. The Dutch physicist H. A. Lorentz soon produced mathematical formulas which allowed for this anomaly by, in effect, contracting the earth, but this was regarded as merely fudging. What this experiment unexpectedly discovered was that the speed of light, the ultimate speed of anything in the universe, is differ-ent from anything else in not being affected by the speed of its source. It also seem-ingly did away with "ether." There is, in effect, no surrounding atmosphere. All through the nineteenth century, scientists had posited such an "ether" substance because of the discovery that light and electricity acted like waves, hence needed a medium through which to pass; this in addition to its uses as a measuring rod for space and time. The ether had become something of a scandal; necessary as a postu-late if the behavior of all sorts of "waves" was to be visualized, it was something no one had ever seen or otherwise established directly as existent. The Michelson-Morley results brought matters to a head. It forced abandonment of the ether or any conception of a "something" space.

If there is no space, as a backdrop to the universe, there is no absolute stand-ard of motion. All speed is relative to something else. The speed on the earth is measured by reference to the earth itself, postulating that it is stable; but of course the earth is in motion around the sun, the planetary system is in motion, too, rela-tive to other systems and galaxies, and so on until the limits of the universe are reached. Then what can be found to measure by? The speed of light, as the Michel-son experiment revealed, being the ultimate speed of things in the universe, is a constant that does not vary relative to other motion and cannot be used to measure them by. If there is nothing in the universe that constitutes an ultimate yardstick of measurement, there can be no absolute speed. The same thing is true for distance as for speed. Space and time viewed from a universal and not an earth-bound angle must disappear as absolutes. From this, many odd conclusions emerged, for instance, that at the same moment it is a different time to observers in motion in different parts of the cosmos.

It took the genius of Albert Einstein to draw forth the conclusions from this. It is questionable whether Michelson-Morley was actually what precipitated Einstein's first theory of relativity, for the young patent clerk had been thinking about such questions in other contexts, especially Clerk Maxwell's mathematical formulas for electricity. Einstein, an unusual personality, who was considered backward and a dreamer as a child and arrogant and rude as a student at Zurich's technical college, could not find an academic position and took a job in 1902 in the Swiss patent office at Berne. In 1905 he published, actually, three papers in an issue of the German journal *Annalen des Physik,* which is now priceless; the most famous of these was on the relativity of time and is known as Einstein's First or Special Theory of Relativity. It has frequently been said that "nothing but the extraordinary power and concentration of Einstein would have been enough" to perform this act of scientific analysis; in other words, no one else was capable of it. Einstein slew the concept of absolute time. The idea of the world as having a basic space-time structure was given up,[8] replaced by what Einstein called four-dimensional space-time. Einstein clarified the principle of the equivalence of inertial systems; that is, each system has its own time, there is no universal clock. (We might compare it with a situation in which each classroom in the university had its own time and there was no clock that kept time for the whole school; what time it was would depend on where you were.) Add to this the fact that the speed of light is not affected by the speed of that which emits it, and the paradoxes of relativity appeared: if an astronaut traveled at an extraordinarily high rate of speed through space for, say, ten years, when he returned he would find that perhaps twenty to thirty years had elapsed on earth. His friends of his own age would now be much older than he.

In this paper too, almost incidentally, as a deduction from relativity, Einstein showed that mass and energy are intimately associated, matter being highly concentrated energy: the beginning of the nuclear power age. (Lasers were also a byproduct of his seeing light as a form of radiant energy.) This stunningly revolutionary theory was far from receiving immediate acclaim. Einstein did not even receive an academic appointment for several years; Berne University turned him down in 1907! There was considerable skepticism. The great laboratory scientist Ernest Rutherford, pioneer in research on the atom then going on at the Cavendish Laboratory in Cambridge, agreed with a colleague who declared that "no Anglo-Saxon can understand relativity" because "they have too much sense": Einstein's theory

---

[8] Einstein's own simplified explanation of relativity, given in later years to inquisitive journalists, was "It was formerly believed that if all material things disappeared from the universe, time and space would be left. According to relativity theory, time and space would also disappear."

Albert Einstein. (Yerkes Observatory
Photograph, University of Chicago,
Williams Bay, Wisconsin.)

seemed to lean heavily on sheer mathematical deduction rather than empirical proof. (Skepticism about Einstein was not unlike skepticism about Freud in this respect.) As Einstein pushed on toward General Relativity,[9] talking about the curved geometry of space-time as a better explanation for gravity than Newton's force, many eminent physicists obviously thought it was "bloody nonsense," as one of them said after listening to Einstein in 1914. The headline of a Vienna newspaper in 1912, just catching on to the 1905 theory, was THE MINUTE IN DANGER: A SENSATION OF MATHEMATICAL SCIENCE. Five years later, the observation during a total eclipse of the sun that seemingly confirmed Einstein's General Theory was immediate world news: SPACE CAUGHT BENDING!

Euclid's solid axioms of geometry were seen to be true only so long as kept to the boundaries of the earth; for outer space, there are other geometries, based on different physical postulates, which turn out to be equally rigorous logical systems. Thus, it seemed, the quality of objective certainty that had always attached to pure mathematics vanished in relativity too.

In regard to Newtonian gravity, the difficulty of conceiving a "force" of some sort acting at a distance had bothered Newton himself a little and had bothered others since. In the eighteenth century Berkeley and Leibniz had explored this

[9] The Special Theory led on to the General Theory because the former forced abandonment of Newton's law which assumed that gravity is a force operating simultaneously over any distance. But now, "at the same time" had lost its meaning; there is no "same time" throughout the universe but many local times.

weakness in a speculative manner. According to Einstein, gravity is not a "force." One should not think of a pull exerted by objects on each other. Einstein's second theory asked a stunned public to believe that bodies move through the curvatures of space-time which, not being independent of each other, become merged in a single continuum.

Whatever else this was, it was not common sense; the scientists were becoming more wildly paradoxical than the artists and poets. At the subatomic level, where in 1897, J. J. Thomson arrived at the concept of the electron or unit of negative electricity as the least unit of "matter," the belief that the atoms could be thought of as miniature planetary systems, with the nucleus as the sun and the electrons circling around it, soon had to be abandoned. Niels Bohr, the Danish physicist who lived until 1962 and became one of the leading theoretical pioneers of the age of nuclear energy, explained that the laws of motion holding for the solar systems do not apply at all within atoms. Thus the laws of Newton, always heretofore assumed to be universal, broke down on both the smallest and largest fields and remained valid only within a zone of fairly gross sense experience. They were crude approximations that worked well enough only when the demand for precision was not too great.

The world within the atom soon became most puzzling, the behavior of electrons breaking all sorts of laws heretofore regarded as sacrosanct. At the turn of the century, Max Planck's quantum theory asserted that energy is omitted discretely and not continuously, in little packages, as it were, and not in a continuous stream. Heat causes electrons to make sudden jumps from one energy level to another. Planck found a "constant," a number which represents the relationship between energy and frequency of radiation, a number which turned up again in wave mechanics in connection with the behavior of electrons. It is a discoverable regularity, the meaning of which lay hidden for the time being. Planck's quantum principle, it has been said, was more revolutionary than Einstein's relativity—though to be sure the great Einstein also made contributions to quantum theory, as the two physicists now worked together at Berlin to which university Planck brought Einstein in 1913.

It remained for the 1920s to bring the puzzlements of subatomic, quantum mechanics nature to the attention of the general public in a brilliant debate among scientists about the ultimate secrets of an increasingly bizarre universe. We can postpone further consideration of this until the next chapter. Einstein's general theory received spectacular confirmation at the end of World War I, indeed at the very time the Treaty of Versailles was being signed in May 1919. Gravity, Einstein postulated in his theory, is not a mysterious instantaneous attraction as had been believed ever since the great Newton revealed its formula in 1687; it consists of waves like electromagnetic waves, moving at the speed of light along the geodesics of space-time. These gravitational waves should be affected by fields of matter. Einstein's theory predicted that light from a distant star would be bent as it passed through the sun's gravitational field on its way to earth. The eclipse offered a rare opportunity to test Einstein's theory. It was an accident of history that the total eclipse occurred so soon after Einstein's statement of his theory, 1914–16, though other evidence has since confirmed the theory, indeed confirmed both theories. The bending observations of 1919, taken from sites all over the world and directed by British scientist Arthur Eddington, caught the public imagination and made Einstein overnight a celebrity. Suddenly the impossible seemed to be verified—a good way to begin the bewildered twenties.

THE CRISIS IN RELIGION

Religion too was in crisis. Nietzsche had announced that "God is dead"; Freud was an atheist; Darwinism had dealt blows to orthodoxy. (Einstein too like so many others lost his faith as an adolescent, from reading the Higher Criticism, discovering however a kind of deistic belief in a rational, orderly, scientist's world.)

The most severe blow to traditional Christianity probably came from the "higher criticism." In his careful study of *The Victorian Church* Owen Chadwick finds the higher criticism and comparative religious perspectives far more a cause of Christian crisis than Darwinism. J. Wellhausen's *History of Israel,* first published in 1878, was a landmark of scholarship. For a number of years before this there had been uneasiness. In 1860 a turmoil in the Anglican Church over the book *Essays and Reviews* had followed immediately upon the *Origin of Species* uproar and seemed like the second of a one-two punch directed at the body of Christian orthodoxy. In this volume, a group of leading churchmen and theological scholars declared in effect that the time had come to accept, reluctantly, that educated men can no longer believe in the literal truth of the Bible. They hoped to show, what Coleridge and Romantic theology had held for some time, that this abandonment of literal truth need not be destructive of Christianity, which rests on other grounds; but to Anglican faithful, the book was shocking and led to a trial for heresy within the Church of England. The 1860s brought other popularizations of the Higher Criticism such as Ernst Renan's *Life of Jesus* and J. R. Seeley's *Ecce Homo* (1865)—the long quest for the "historical Jesus" was underway. It had been inaugurated by the Hegelian David Strauss's 1835 work, we will recall. The Germans in fact were leaders in this kind of careful examination of the Old and New Testaments—a scholarly industry of vast complexity, begun in elementary ways long ago (by Spinoza and Father Richard Simon in the seventeenth century) but now much more developed with the aid of critical methods for which nineteenth-century German historical scholarship was famous.

Wellhausen offered persuasive support to a theory already advanced, that a substantial portion of the earlier books of the Bible (the Pentateuch) was not written until much later than the events they describe and, indeed, not put in its final form until about 400 B.C. (the time of Ezra), nearly a millennium after Moses. Wellhausen carried the day among the scholars, especially the younger ones. The second edition of his *History* appeared in 1883 and was translated into English in 1885, giving rise to a considerable controversy. A French scholar wrote in 1894 that "whoever is not totally prejudiced, whoever has not decided in advance that any kind of criticism is false, must accept the idea that the Priestly Code was not formed until after the Babylonian exile."

To some of the pious, this was a shocking conclusion, for it seemed to cast doubt on the Bible as revealed truth, infallible because divinely inspired. The arguments of liberal theologians, that the history of Israel and Judea in the broader sense justified the claim of a unique religious mission vouchsafed to the Jewish nation, carried little conviction to those brought up to believe (as did, for example, William E. Gladstone, the famous British statesman) that the literal truth of every line of Scripture was the impregnable rock upon which Christianity stood.

In 1872, George Smith called attention to a Babylonian version of the story of the Flood—a significant and shattering discovery. The leading feature of the "higher" as distinct from the "lower" criticism was its awareness of an immense literary tradition among the other peoples of the ancient world, which bore on the Bible at many points. No longer was the Bible seen in isolation, as a totally unique and marvelous book. The Old Testament fitted into an historical context that began to be recovered and understood; thus seen, it perhaps lost none of its wonder nor even its veracity, but it did inevitably become different—a part of human history, not simply the record of a continuous divine miracle. A good deal of the Old Testament has close parallels in the sacred and wisdom literature of the Babylonians and other ancient peoples with whom the Jewish people were in close contact. The uniqueness of the Hebraic outlook—monotheistic, ethical, messianic—remained, but in innumerable details the biblical story lost its ability to pass as something quite outside the experience of the rest of the ancient world. The Jews could never again be quite the "peculiar people" in the old sense. (This was not displeasing to Hegelian philosophers, who declared the entire "world spirit" of an age to be more significant than single nations or individuals.)

Into this same pattern fitted that immense growth in knowledge about other peoples which was the fruit of anthropological research. Popularized in such books as James Frazer's widely read end-of-the-century success, *The Golden Bough,* these data compelled the conclusion that even primitive religions make use of archetypal beliefs similar to those of Christianity and Judaism. Awareness of Indic thought—a whole world of higher religions—advanced steadily in the nineteenth century. All this worked further toward eroding the uniqueness of Christianity. Comparative religion disclosed that the god who comes down to earth, is killed, rises again and redeems humanity, is found in many traditions other than the Christian one—these are virtually Jungian archetypes. Myths of the martyr, the victim, the miracleworker, the Man of the People, the Wanderer, and others found in the Christ saga belong to the storehouse of stories told by every people.

By the end of the nineteenth century, also, critical research into the New Testament had arrived at conclusions concerning the Gospels, which included the view that the authors of Matthew and Luke leaned chiefly on the Gospel of Mark as a source, and even the latter contains theological interpolations not taken from Jesus himself. Again, the net result of intensive historical analysis was, roughly, to cast some doubt on the accuracy of the Gospels as accounts of the life of Jesus and on certain sayings and ideas attributed by them to Jesus. Opening up the problem of the historical Jesus by no means meant destroying Christianity, but simple folk among the pious might understandably think so. A quarrel between "modernists" and "fundamentalists" soon divided most Christian churches. Popularizers of the higher criticism, with an antitheological ax to grind, sometimes exaggerated it and declared that, for example, Jesus never existed and the Bible was a tissue of fables.[10] Scandalized Christians reacted by denouncing the whole critical movement, and it took some time before balanced judgment was restored. In the Roman Catholic Church, "modernism" received a cautious green light from Pope Leo XIII, but Pius X, his successor in 1903, checked this move toward liberalism as he did others, as for example, the Catholic democratic movement.

In 1864, Piux IX, embittered by the Italian liberal-nationalist movement which assailed the papacy's temporal power, had issued his celebrated Syllabus of Errors and in so doing placed the Roman Church in a state of war with much of the nineteenth century. Liberalism and democracy, as well as modern science, were declared to be irreconcilable with Christianity and the Church. In 1870, Pius IX had summoned the great Ecumenical Council, first since the Council of Trent in 1563, chiefly to solemnize the doctrine of papal infallibility. The goal was not achieved without a severe struggle, in which many of the German, French, and English bishops opposed the papal party, and after the decrees some liberal Catholics left the Church. Leo XIII, the great Pope who succeeded Pius IX, did not really retreat much from Pio Nono's position. Though anxious to encourage learning and a friend of the Catholic social movement, he continued to assert that the modern state, based on secular individualism, is fundamentally anti-Christian. In Italy, Catholics continued to boycott national politics on papal orders, though in France there was finally an adjustment to the Republic. In the 1900s, Catholics who embraced liberal and democratic principles were rebuked. They were reminded that political society must be based on Christian principles, not on liberal skepticism and indifference; in regard to democracy, they were told that the Church cannot attach primary importance to the form of government; it can get along with democracy but also with other forms, and what matters is that society be Christian, not that it adopt any particular political ideology. Marc Sangnier and the great Charles Péguy were perhaps the leading French Catholic Democrats who finally (1910) received this rebuke.

By that time, the Dreyfus Affair had caused a sharp conflict between conservative and liberal France with the clergy ranged for the most part on the former side. The victorious partisans of Captain Dreyfus took their revenge by passing legislation to separate church from state in 1901, the occasion of further bitter exchanges between anti-clericals and churchmen. All in all, the Church found itself at

---

[10] Bertrand Russell, the eminent philosopher, held that "historically, it is quite doubtful whether Christ ever existed at all, or, if he did, we do not know anything about him." Russell's *A Free Man's Worship* (1910) was a skeptic's manifesto.

war with basic trends in the modern world at this time and subject to some divisive conflicts. As in the case of the Roman Catholic Church, the same thing might be said in lesser degree of major Protestant denominations. There were liberals who sought to turn the church's major interest to social reform, abandoning traditional theology and accepting the higher criticism; there were conservatives who feared the extinction of Christianity if it thus merged itself into secular liberalism.

In this era, spiritual impulses tended to be diverted to nonorthodox, even non-Christian varieties of faith. The reaction against scientism, especially powerful in France, led to that interest in moral and interior experience already seen in the philosophies of Nietzsche, Bergson, and William James. There was indeed something of a Catholic revival, aided by the conversion of important men and women of literature. But this religion-seeking spirit more often ignored dogmatic orthodoxy. William James developed the viewpoint in his famous Gifford lectures on "The Varieties of Religious Experience" that the various myths or conceptualizations in which religions are objectively embodied are not fundamental; they are the mere husks of religion. What is basic is the instinct to believe, the need for the human spirit to express itself. One could, presumably, just as well believe in any myth. One might, like the great Irish poet W. B. Yeats, invent a private mythology; one might, like Annie Besant or Mme. Blavatsky, embrace esoteric Oriental religions. The former's "theosophy" became a fashionable creed. The "truth" of a religion became somewhat irrelevant; one could never know that anyway. What mattered was the fact of belief itself.

The point was driven home by a later remark of Emmanuel Mounier, who declared that a century ago almost everyone was either a Christian or else a rationalist opposed to all religion, whereas today there are not too many of either sort. One had faith, but not necessarily a Christian faith, or if so only very loosely.

The greatest prophet of the pre–World War I era was doubtless Leo Tolstoy. The Russian novelist was a personality of such gigantic proportions that he captured the world's imagination and became a living legend to whose estate at Yassnaya Polyana visitors came from all over the Western world to do homage. The brilliant novels *War and Peace* and *Anna Karenina* made him famous; but more striking was the spiritual odyssey of the later Tolstoy. Experiencing a deep crisis in which he saw life as absurd and meaningless, this man of passionate "commitment" (to use a modern phrase) was driven to reconsider the most fundamental questions of existence, and after finding neither the abstractions of the philosophers nor the facts and theories of the scientists to be of any help, he ended in a sort of primitive Christianity. There is much in the Russian's agony and redemption to suggest the later movements of existentialism and crisis theology. He found that Christ's true meaning had been falsified by formal religion and by rationalistic conceptualizing. Tolstoy found in the simple message of Christ deep truths which no mere formula could express. His religious writings (for example, *The Kingdom of God Is Within You*) have tremendous force. He felt, also, the influence of the Oriental religions and tried to find the elemental truths that underlie all the great religions.

Tolstoy advocated and in some measure practiced a return to primitive Christian communism. Powerful denunciations of war and of all forms of coercion made him a hero of the pacifist movement and in political principles an anarchist. The principle of nonresistance to evil, which Tolstoy could not always obey himself, was the cornerstone of his religious belief. In suggesting a return to a simple life pared of all artificialities, he was reminiscent of Rousseau or of the American sage Henry Thoreau. Tolstoy, a member of the Russian upper class, ferociously denounced the corruption of this class and its European counterpart. Believing passionately in art and literature, he condemned the decadence of European literature and insisted that only the peasant masses were culturally sound, however ignorant of books. In later years he wrote the simplest of parables for the people, though it is unfortunately doubtful that the Russian peasant responded. But a variety of others all over the world did respond, and Tolstoy became a figure almost unique in Western intellectual history. The Russian government, most despotic in the world, dared not touch him though he advocated anarchism, pacifism, and noncooperation with government. The affair of the Dukhobors was perhaps the most astonishing example of Tolstoy's power. He set out to save this sect of Christian communalists from brutal persecution by the tsarist government, and succeeded in gaining his end and in raising a worldwide fund for the transportation of the Dukhobors *en masse* to Canada.

Tolstoy gave away the money from his literary works and eventually before his death renounced all his wealth. A modern saint, he was formally excommunicated from the Orthodox Church in 1891, which only added to his popularity within and outside of Russia. Tolstoy was a hero of the vigorous antiwar movement of this period. William Jennings Bryan from the American prairies made his pilgrimage to Yassnaya Polyana. Tolstoy's most prominent disciple in the realm of practical affairs was to be the great Mahatma Gandhi, leader of the Indian independence movement, legendary saint and father of the modern Indian nation. Tolstoy cried out against materialism, capitalism, the corruptions of bourgeois society, and demanded a spiritual rebirth. How unorthodox he was may be judged from his reply to the edict of excommunication. He denied the Trinity, Original Sin, the divinity of Christ, and all the church sacraments, which he called "coarse, degrading sorcery." He accused the clergy of ignorance and deceptiveness.

Tolstoy's equally great countryman, Fyodor Dostoyevsky, shared with Nietzsche a preoccupation with the idea of God's extinction and what follows from this. In his striking parable of the Grand Inquisitor (in *The Brothers Karamazov*), Christ returns to earth to be arrested and condemned by the wise old Inquisitor, who sees that Christian freedom is impossible for humanity, enslaved as it is and must be by superstititions. Existing organized religion is a fraud, but perhaps a necessary fraud. We could not endure pure spiritual Christianity; it is possible for only a few, now. Into this parable, so often reprinted, is packed much of our modern religious agony and tension. Modern civilization is depraved, we need but cannot find God, orthodox old-fashioned Christianity is bankrupt, the truly religious today may be the atheist or anti-Christ. Dostoyevsky adopted a belief in the potential mission of the Slavic peoples to redeem decadent Europe because still capable of religion—a kind of spiritual Pan-Slavism. Nietzsche himself learned from this Russian genius, who spent some terrible years in Siberian prison camps for the crime of talking against the tsar's government then came to reject the revolutionary movement as spiritually shallow. No more significant figure exists for contemporary civilization.

Nicolas Berdyaev mentioned Tolstoy and Dostoyevsky among those he called the "forerunners of the era of the spirit," the predecessors of the post-1914 Christian revival. Others in this generation referred to by the Russian existentialist were Solovyëv and Cieszkowski (a Pole) from the Slavic world and two Frenchmen, Leon Bloy and Charles Péguy. The latter, initially a Dreyfusard and a democrat, a moderate socialist, and a fine literary craftsman, edited prewar France's most important intellectual journal, the *Cahiers de la Quinzaine,* opening its pages to all kinds of expression. Though a Catholic, Péguy was essentially a free spirit, on whom the influence of Bergson could be seen prominently. Like Tolstoy, Peguy was in revolt against all that was false in a timid and shoddy civilization and sought to affirm the value of the human soul by preaching integrity, devotion to the spiritual and intellectual life, social justice, dedication to art.

So religion was abroad, but the winds of doctrine were various and confusing. The British scholar J. N. Figgis, writing just before 1914 of *Civilization at the Crossroads,* expressed his dismay at the babel of voices: Nietzsche, Bergson, James, Tolstoy, and Bertrand Russell—atheism, skepticism, intuitionism, the life force, the will to believe, the will-to-power. Had the European tradition dissolved into a thousand fragments? Did civilization evolve from unity to multiplicity, from the Virgin to the Dynamo, as the American writer Henry Adams suggested? Some of the manifestations of diversity in the 1900s were wild indeed. In Russia, where the composer Scriabin upheld the artist's role as messiah and announced himself the chosen one, while the poet Ivanov preached the mystical union of Christ and Dionysus in "ecstasy for ecstasy's sake," there was a mood in which "every kind of new religion and superstition proliferated" (Martin Cooper). At the other end of Europe, James Joyce in Dublin encountered the Hermetic Order and the Theosophical Society, where Madame Blavatsky, Annie Besant (who had passed through Fabianism en route to Theosophy), and other modern mystics and would-be prophets were read. Another magician was the Greek Gurdiyev, who offered occult spiritual forces taken from prerational cultures and associated with artistic creation. In Italy, D'Annunzio was a fabulous personality, tremendously popular, expressing much of the *malaise* of the times.

The serious interest in abnormal psychical phenomena (spirit messages, telepathy, clairvoyance, poltergeists, and so forth) might be added. The turn-of-the-century era produced some interesting occultist fringe figures, such as Frederick Rolfe ("Baron Corvo") and Aleister Crowley (magician and diabolist) who crossed over into the artistic bohemia. But real giants such as Yeats and Jung, who was keenly interested in alchemy, touched occultism in their search for a spiritual cure for the decaying West. Mingling with Freudian themes, Crowley practiced sexual magic. Science itself was becoming occult, was it not? The inner order of the

Hermetic Order of the Golden Dawn was called the Rose of Ruby and the Cross of Gold. Some decades later, in 1960, the first laser experiment used a rod of synthetic ruby with a mirror at its end, which was made to emit a violent flash of crimson. Crowley, who ended life as a drug-ridden degenerate, would doubtless have been delighted.

ESTHETES AND LITERARY REBELS

One of the great adventures of the last half of the nineteenth century lay in the realm of pure literature. It is impossible to avoid the conclusion that, with the decline of the traditional Church and of any agreed-upon orthodoxy in either religion or philosophy, the great imaginative writers have supplied many of the values of the modern world. Further, it is equally true that art became something of a religion for many in this generation. While criticism from Voltaire and Darwin had eroded Christianity's power to compel unquestioned adherence, there was also disillusionment in this period with scientific rationalism, as has been seen. The philosophers of the era, among whom Nietzsche, Bergson, and William James stand out, tended toward intuitionism or naturalism rather than rationalism in the sense of formal, conceptual thought, and expressed their views more in poetic metaphor than logical analysis. Perhaps the greatest single advance in knowledge of the era was being made by Freud, who charted the mysterious, nonrational side of the human psyche. Nietzsche's insights, too, haunted all the writers of this era. Thus most of the major currents of the age combined to focus attention on the poetic, myth-making capacities of humanity.

This was a time when Europe discovered, for better or worse, the depths of the mind that lie beneath rational thought, where myth and symbol reign and strange, formidable powers lurk in hiding. Neither philosopher nor scientist can guide one here, but the poet or novelist perhaps can. In addition to probing the unconscious, these writers gave voice to much of the social criticism that filled the age, criticism of one or another feature of a bourgeois, industrial, democratic society repellent to sensitive souls. But their alienation pushed them toward pure art and toward purely subjective "private worlds" of imagination, for they were disgusted with the public world. Estheticism, art for art's sake, the poet's elevation to preeminence, these attitudes naturally accompanied rejection of the social and moral order by which a hated civilization lived.

The beginnings of this literature of revolt may be found at midcentury or even earlier, when reaction against the older romanticism and disillusionment with a commercial and bourgeois civilization appeared together, a rock flung at Victorian orthodoxy, the esthetic counterpart of revolutionary socialism. The "art for art's sake" writers, offspring of Gautier and Baudelaire, were from the beginning a rebellious, less respectable lot, whose works sometimes had a *succès de scandale* as well as a genuine success of art. In 1857 both Baudelaire and Flaubert faced criminal prosecution, the former for his *Flowers of Evil* and the latter for the celebrated novel *Madame Bovary.* In England the Pre-Raphaelites were criticized as immoral, but this was nothing compared to the storm stirred up by the deliberately provocative poet Algernon Swinburne in the 1860s. These writers, as their slogan implied, tended to make of art and beauty a religion, often with results that shocked the moralists. They were aggressively hostile to Christianity and conventional morality. In Swinburne's unpublished novel *Lesbia Brandon* the theme of homosexual love (handled also by Gautier in his seminal novel *Mademoiselle de Maupin*) accompanies an estheticism in which people cultivate their senses and live saturated in beauty. Baudelaire's "satanism," which seemed to ask the poet to seek out morbid and abnormal themes, was as famous as his theory that poetry should strive for a purity corresponding to color and music. Swinburne, John Morley wrote indignantly in 1866, was "the libidinous laureate of a pack of satyrs." And indeed Swinburne, whose alliterative verses enchanted a generation of esthetes (before he lost his creativity and settled into a placid old age), recommended trading the "lilies and languors of virtue" for "the roses and raptures of vice." His early enthusiasms also embraced revolutionary figures like Orsini who tried to assassinate Napoleon III.

"Every twenty years theories change," a Zola character observes; the modern era in literature and the arts has indeed been marked by a restless generation revolt every few years. In the 1870s the new word was naturalism, and the French writer Emile Zola was its leading representative. Naturalism was an extension of the "realism" of the Flaubert era, realism of a more brutal sort. The naturalists made a career of literary slumming, going into "the living, swarming streets" (Huysmans) to discover criminals, prostitutes, gin-soaked wretches (but Zola did not forget the country where in *La Terre* he found brutality and depravity too). The purpose here was obviously in part to "disturb the bourgeoisie" by revealing the horrors of society as well as presenting shocking material. Naturalism drew intellectually on Darwinism and other scientific ideas, fashionable at this hour, of course. Zola's huge multivolume chronicle, generously peopled with the vicious and the depraved, was designed both as a kind of social history of contemporary France—the novel become documentary, factual—and as a demonstration that people are the determinate products of their heredity and their environment. Zola strove to make a science of the novel.

Grim pessimism, people the helpless victims of blind chance or a malignant deity ("The President of the Immortals had finished his sport with Tess," Hardy remarks at the end of a famous novel), may be found also in Zola's contemporary and fellow novelist, Thomas Hardy. These were the themes of pessimistic Darwinism, and alienated writers made the most of them. In principle naturalism upheld no ideals and found no values; it only exhibited the harsh realities of a world where chance and accident rule. In practice it was likely to stir sympathy for the poor wretches it described; but Zola's novel of industrial strife, *Germinal,* does not really condemn the mine owners for the misery and the tragedy that comes of it, because everyone is trapped on the wheel of fate.

No serious writers were more popular than the naturalists Zola, Hardy, George Moore, and, in the United States a little later, figures such as Jack London, Stephen

Crane, Frank Norris, Theodore Dreiser. They exposed the nastiness of industrial society while luxuriating in the fashionable atheism. Naturalism's vogue lasted a good while with some, but for the *avant-garde* it soon lost its ability to provide the necessary thrills (*frissons*). New literary and artistic movements arose; they were soon to arise in profusion. In sharp reaction against the rather heavyhanded social realism of the Zola school, the 1880s brought symbolism and the decadents. The latter attained notoriety chiefly through the famous novel by Joris Huysmans, *A Rebours (Against the Grain)*, whose hero, Des Esseintes, was the prototype of all dandies, those "super-esthetical young men" whom Oscar Wilde and the *Yellow Book* were soon to introduce to an amazed Victorian public. Emaciated, depraved, and sophisticated, the decadent or dandy behaved as the last pale but exquisite flower of a fading civilization, and found amusement in art, vice, and crime. A carefully cultivated exoticism, an extreme artificiality marked this mode of writing. Picking up a copy of the notorious *A Rebours*, Oscar Wilde's hero in *The Portrait of Dorian Gray* felt that "the heavy odor of incense seemed to cling about its pages and to trouble the brain." "The first duty of life is to be as artificial as possible," Wilde wrote, adding that "what the second duty is no one has yet discovered." Cold, cruel, green-eyed *femmes fatales* filled decadent poetry and novels. Homosexual perhaps like Wilde, the dandy might shade into more sinister types representing what Mario Praz has written about as "the romantic agony." An exciting suspicion of nameless sins hung over this literary assault on respectability, around which grouped those who were weary of Victorian primness.

Less obviously designed to shock the bourgeoisie, symbolism, born about 1886, represented the ultimate in Baudelairean estheticism and produced some great poetry; its goal was to express the inexpressible by an experimental verse that followed the logic of the interior mind, revealing the reality behind the appearances of things by the use of archetypal images or symbols. Much of modern poetry lies under its influence. Verlaine and Mallarmé, later the brilliant young poets Laforgue and Valéry, were its prophets.

This sounds like a more sophisticated version of romanticism, and this is not far from the truth, insofar as the idealist and poet-as-seer elements are concerned. For the poet was indeed a seer, *a voyant*, to the symbolists. But the mood of symbolism was deeply tinged with the related currents of estheticism and decadence. Turning their backs on a disgusting social and material world, many of the symbolists were distinctly otherworldly. Their most celebrated literary character, the hero of Villiers de l'Isle Adam's *Axel's Castle* (which is the title Edmund Wilson gave to his classical study of this movement), lived alone in a Wagnerian castle studying occult philosophy; when he and a girl who had come to murder him fell immediately and sublimely in love, they decided on suicide because reality could not possibly measure up to the perfection of their love as they felt and experienced it at that moment. Living, Count Axel and Sara thought, is too vulgar; "our servants can do that for us." In the same spirit, Oscar Wilde once said that "any fool can make history, but it takes a genius to write it"! Art is superior to life. The earlier, "classic" romanticists had not so distinguished and separated art from life. Symbolism

Caricature of Oscar Wilde. (Ashmolean Museum, Oxford. Caricature by Max Beerbohm.)

was the rebellion of those disillusioned with political revolt, who "could neither accept nor transform" social reality.

About the turn of the century, the more alert young writers of Europe were all smitten with the symbolist message. The young James Joyce, his brother tells us, liked poems that "sought to capture moods and impressions, often tenuous moods and elusive impressions, by means of a verbal witchery that magnetizes the mind like a spell, and imparts a wonder and grace." Poetry must not be rhymed prose; if it is, there is little point in writing it as verse. Poetry is *sui generis,* its purpose being to convey, not ideas, not conceptual knowledge, but "moods and impressions," the subtle inner world of the mind with its emotional states. This is an appeal to immediate experience—the *données* of consciousness, as the philosopher Bergson called it—which lay very close to the heart of the matter in this period. The French poet Rimbaud, who believed that the poet's vision has power to penetrate a deeper reality and show how to live (a romantic idea), also believed that the poet can bypass conceptual thought to express reality, somehow, in an immediate, symbolic sense—a conception that may bear comparison to traditional religious mysticism but was here presented by a man whose life was that of an alienated rebel. This strange genius has been made the object of a veritable religious cult by some moderns. Like

Paul Gauguin the painter, Rimbaud fled Europe, to be followed by many others; "Europe bores me," André Gide exclaimed. A premodern, *sauvage* world was more attractive.

The French symbolists felt an intense indignation against a social order that was destructive of all beauty and integrity—the rule of plutocracy, of capitalism, of the bourgeoisie, "a hideous society," as Des Esseintes exclaims. The achievements of the symbolist school are beyond question; they set the tone for modern poetry, especially in France but with a heavy influence abroad, too. T. S. Eliot brought symbolism's manner and mood into English poetry a few years later. Just prior to 1914 the American Ezra Pound, along with T. E. Hulme and others, founded the "imagist" movement in England, influenced by Bergson and related to French symbolism, with some debts also to Japanese poetry.[11] The object was to get at reality in a moment of flashing insight embodied in a single image:

> The apparition of these faces in the crowd;
> Petals on a wet, black bough.

Symbolism came to Russia too—always an eager importer of European fashions in ideas and expression; Russian symbolism was more mystical and more activist than its Western counterparts, on the whole. Seer and prophet, the artist penetrates arcane mysteries not available to the scientific reason; then, according to the "mystical anarchism" of symbolist poet Vyacheslav Ivanov, this wisdom should be used to transform life and build a new world.

The impulse to create a "pure" poetry, purged of the traditional narrative or argument, was found earlier in Baudelaire and Verlaine and the French school known as "Parnassian" in the 1860s; it is one important ingredient in the modern movement. Its goal was to distinguish poetry from prose by its content as well as its form, a revolt against all previous literary doctrine and against the highly popular Victorian narrative or descriptive poem, such as Tennyson and Browning wrote. Poetry should not be an alternate mode of discourse. In the making of modern poetry the Parnassian strain joins the irrationalist (the mysticism of the Word, Rimbaud's "reasoned disordering of the senses") and the symbolist (allusion, indirect statement, subtle symbolisms) as the leading operative features.

Into this artistic *mélange,* of course, went ingredients from the philosophers who stressed art as the foremost kind of communication and chief avenue to truth— Schopenhauer, Nietzsche, Wagner, known all over Europe. A *Revue Wagnérienne* was founded in Paris in 1885, the sage of Bayreuth became a French rage—not merely his music but his philosophy of total art. Wagner and Nietzsche, with their doctrines of art and individual integrity, also influenced the Scandinavians Ibsen and

---

[11] A minor chapter in intellectual history in this period relates to the discovery of Japan, so recently and dramatically drawn into communication with the West, by European writers and American ones (Lafcadio Hearn) too—discovery especially of the estheticism that runs through Japanese life. Impressionist painting also owed something to Japanese art. "The orient was in the air" in France in the 1900s.

Strindberg, the former possibly the most stimulating and controversial writer of the epoch. Upon the performance of Ibsen's *Ghosts* in London in 1891, a shocked respectability demanded its prohibition. George Bernard Shaw was impelled to write a book, *The Quintessence of Ibsenism,* in defense of the Norwegian, a book that stands as one of the major critical works of the era as well as a tribute to the vitality of Shaw and of his age. For once, England vibrated to a theatrical controversy as France had often done; *Ghosts* was the modern *Hernani.* In his book on Ibsen, Shaw asked how it was that some hailed the Norwegian as the greatest living dramatist, the modern Shakespeare, a genius beyond compare, while others requested his suppression in the name of common decency and public order. (This occurred all over Europe, not just in England, the alleged home of Victorian prudery.) The answer to the latter question lay in Ibsen's shattering attacks on conventional morality. By later standards Ibsen was hardly daring, but in the 1880s and 1890s his brilliant plays were a brand of defiance hurled in the face of the dominant European bourgeoisie. In *Ghosts* (1881), an apparently model wife and mother is shown to be living amid lies, unfaithfulness, and corruption, much as Nora Helmer is in the famous *Doll's House* (1879). In *The Enemy of the People* (1882), respectable society persecutes the honest person who would interfere with its material prosperity by telling the truth about the evil source of that prosperity. Hating *Pillars of Society* (the name of one of his plays), Ibsen had no use either for romantic, idealistic reformers. His *Peer Gynt* is a modern Don Quixote who makes himself ridiculous by blindly living as if dreams were reality.

Ibsen was a hero of the feminists because of *Doll's House;* yet at a banquet in his honor given by the Norwegian Society for Women's Rights in 1898, he disconcerted his hostesses by disclaiming any connection with their cause: "My task has been the portrayal of human beings."

Shaw's own plays reflect a considerable Ibsenian influence, with a special flair for the drama of ideas and a flashing, Voltairean wit lacking in the Norwegian. A peculiar sensitivity to ideas marked this versatile Irishman, along with the ability to present these ideas in dramatic form. Some of his plays expose social evil or hypocrisy, in the Fabian spirit; others reflect his fascination with Nietzschean and vitalist ideas then so much in the air. Most of them slightly shocked the public but amused them so much that they tolerated the unconventional element. Shaw, like Voltaire, became a licensed iconoclast, privileged to criticize the idols of respectability because he did it in such a scintillating manner. Bold, free spirits stride through Shaw's plays, knocking down the proprieties and teaching people to assert their individuality. Following a suggestion of Nietzsche's, Shaw had his Don Juan find that the really best people are in hell, not heaven. The common rules are always reversed: Women drink brandy and smoke cigars, while men are cringing and cowardly; honorable professions are dishonorable, and vice versa, Mrs. Warren's profession (the oldest) is really no worse than any other. Shaw's Caesar is a Nietzschean superman, action controlled by reason, beyond good and evil. *Back to Methuselah* popularized the theory of creative or emergent evolution, and indeed the "life force" became a persistent Shavian theme. Shaw lived to a ripe and creative

George Bernard Shaw. (Washington, D.C., Library of Congress.)

old age in the postwar years, another trait he shared with Voltaire being an amazingly long literary career. His noonday was between 1900 and 1917, his mission to force novel ideas on bourgeois England.

One of the more notable denunciations of the new literature appeared in Max Nordau's book *Degeneration* (1895). Nordau, a rationalistic socialist, saw nothing but "degeneration" in the new literature and philosophy. Nietzsche, Walt Whitman, Wagner, Tolstoy,[12] Ibsen, as well as the French decadents, symbolists, and realists, all he declared to be so many morbid diseases. They were mad, they were antisocial, they were sex-obsessed (sexual overstimulation ruins civilization, Nordau believed). Nordau, one suspects, was almost prepared with Plato to banish the artist from society altogether in the interest of social stability, though he did declare his respect for the "healthy art" of Dante, Shakespeare, and Goethe. Few of the moderns—Hauptmann's *Weavers* was an exception—passed his critical inspection. He rejoiced that the average person remained immune to these siren calls, continuing to prefer music hall melodies to Wagner, farces to Ibsen.

[12]Who, in *What Is Art?* (1897), condemned the new literature and art as elitist, antisocial, and incomprehensible.

Nordau's outburst was characteristic more of popular reaction than of *avant-garde* thought, though he himself was a highly literate person. Nevertheless quite a few scholars and critics reared in the older literature bridled at the new mode of expression, and the mob persecuted it. Oscar Wilde, the chief prophet of the new literature in England in the 1890s, brilliant playwright and epigrammist, ended a broken man after being arrested and jailed for homosexuality. His illness neglected by the prison authorities, Wilde died at 46, a martyr to the popular dislike of the estheticism he flaunted.

The next decade, the years from 1900 on to the war, brought even more startling literary and especially artistic novelties which might have shocked Oscar. The "modernist" revolution in painting spawned a whole series of new schools and spilled over into architecture and music. A compilation of esthetic "manifestos" printed in Europe from 1890 to 1910 turned up no fewer than 730 of them.[13] This era's "fanaticism for art," Stefan Zweig recalled in his memoirs, was such as could hardly be imagined or reconstructed. There were fauvists, acmeists, cubists, supremacists, vorticists, expressionists, futurists—the last two movements stood out from the rest and to some extent were terms subsuming most of the others. "Little magazines," experimental reviews, secessionist salons were a feature of this artistic revolution, which stemmed from a crowd of young rebels breathing defiance of the established forms. "Burn down the museums!" was a futurist battle cry. The artistic revolutionaries broke drastically with tradition. The total breach between the culture of the bourgeoisie and that of the intellectual *avant-garde* occurs at this time.

Faced with the startling novelties of cubists, postimpressionists, expressionists, the general public responded with cries of outrage. A riot greeted the performance of Igor Stravinsky's *Rites of Spring* in Paris in 1913, more famous than a similar one in Vienna accorded the musical offerings of Arnold Schoenberg and Alban Berg. The young British novelists, D. H. Lawrence and James Joyce, could not find printers for their epoch-making novels at this time. Journals called *The Storm, Blast, Action, The Torch,* painters dubbing themselves Wild Beasts and Blue Riders made known by their very names the revolutionary intent of this painting, poetry, music, and sculpture, which was found everywhere in Europe, from Ireland to Russia.

The expressionist credo characteristic of this generation of art rejected realism in the vulgar sense to experiment in abstract forms or inner visions, a parallel to the subjectivism of literature and philosophy. "There is an inherent truth which must be disengaged from the outward appearance of the object," Henri Matisse explained. "Exactitude is not truth." Cubism used formalized geometric patterns to try to get at this "inherent reality." "Objects hinder my meaning," declared another great painter, Kandinsky, whose first abstract painting belongs to the year 1910. "Away from the Thing, away from Matter, back to Spirit" was the motto. This intense antirealism was a feature of the new art that contributed to its unpopularity, of

---

[13] D. Bänsch and E. Ruprecht, ed., *Literarische Manifeste der Jahrhundertwende, 1890-1910* (Stuttgart, 1970).

course; the man in the street could not "recognize" anything in the painting or sculpture. He suspected these artists of poking fun at him, in which there was a grain of truth. Behind expressionist retreat from the "real world" lay an abhorrence of that world, the social world of bourgeois mediocrity, mechanization, bureaucratization, triviality. At the same time there was a genuine metaphysical quest for deeper truths, dredged up from the subconscious mind or found, perhaps, in the designs of geometry. Certainly this era produced a superb abundance of genius, today acknowledged as such, in painters such as Kandinsky, Paul Klee, Pablo Picasso, Matisse, Mondrian, and many others. These were the pioneer "modernists." They broke through the older confines of visual art to create a brilliant feast of colors and shapes for the eye.

If all these new art forms represented anything more than a protest and a probing for novelty, that something was the intuition of Bergson or the unconscious mind of Freud. There was also a scattering of Einstein influence: "Time and space died yesterday!" the Futurist manifesto cried, and this emancipation from conventional perspectives aided the trend toward experimentation. Beneath and beyond merely conceptual or intellectual thought, art as pure expression might get in touch with a reality denied to logic. Its symbols might be the language of the human soul at a level deeper than formal thought. These exciting and disturbing paintings, poems, and musical compositions did certainly bespeak an atmosphere of revolt and novelty. They were created largely by "bohemian" artists, who inhabited the little cafés of the artist colonies from Munich to Paris.

THE RISE OF SOCIOLOGICAL THOUGHT

It was "the time of human consciousness," Anatole France said (in his tribute to Zola and Tolstoy). A new self-consciousness about human relations in society appeared not only among the psychologists and the artists but in the development of the new science of sociology. The years from about 1890 to 1914 marked the brilliant coming of age of sociology. It was the generation that followed the trailblazing during which Comte, Marx, and Spencer had hewed a rough trail. Now came people such as Emile Durkheim, Max Weber, and a host of only slightly lesser lights to refine the crude generalizations of the pioneers, while retaining much of their scope and dramatic power. Durkheim carried on Comte, Weber largely began where Marx left off; though British sociology failed to keep up with French and German, the evolutionary hypotheses of Spencer and the social Darwinists formed a significant backdrop to all social theory.

The leading social stimulus to the development of sociology was the rapid alteration of environment from rural to urban, traditional to modern society. It should be observed that in the hands of a Weber or Durkheim or Robert Michels (who indeed referred to "political sociology") the boundary between sociological and political studies was not sharp. "Sociology," as the "scientific" study of social phenomena, can be applied to all manner of things; the sociologists of this period were much inclined to apply it to politics. Weber studied the forms of political authority and the origins of the Western economic order; Michels examined the structure of political parties. And the interest Durkheim showed in the relationship between individuals and the community had behind it an urgent feeling about the problems of contemporary European society as it proceeded rapidly into an urban industrial setting. Graham Wallas's *Human Nature in Politics* (1908), a landmark in the history of British political thought, declared that political science had heretofore dealt with abstractions rather than considered real people in the real world. When one turns to this reality, Wallas thought, one sees the fallacy of assuming that people act rationally. "Most of the political opinions of most men are the result, not of reasoning tested by experience, but of unconscious or half-conscious inference tested by habit." There had been an actual decline of rationality, Wallas suggested, owing to the "de-localizing" of people, uprooted from the village to be thrust into the mass anonymity of the huge city. In such passages the British Fabian socialist repeated some of the characteristic interests of this generation of sociologists and political scientists.

If one wonders why something called sociology rose to importance at this time, having not existed before (at least under this name), the best answer is that it was precipitated by the disintegration of traditional society, with the emergence of urbanism and what Maurice Barrès, the French novelist, called *uprootedness.* When society is stable, the questions which lead one to study it do not arise, it is simply taken for granted. The prominence of sociology in Germany was due to the unusually sudden industrialization of that country in the later nineteenth century, passing from traditional society, marked by the village community, quite rapidly into advanced modern technology with large cities, factories, and the alienation of the individual from society. The leading pioneer of German sociology in the 1880s, Friedrich Tönnies, was preoccupied with the distinction between what he called community and society (*Gemeinschaft* and *Gesellschaft*)—the tightly integrated community, small and cohesive, such as people had generally lived in since primitive times, and the "great society" of the modern state, vast and complex, in which the individual might feel freer yet lost. George Simmel, too, one of the early German sociologists, tried to examine the impact of the city, this new environment, on human lives: "The deepest problems of modern life derive from the claim of the individual to preserve the autonomy and individuality of his existence in the face of overwhelming social forces." The urban situation was one of more freedom, greater stimulation, more opportunity for expansion of the mind, but also one of rootlessness, loss of social ties, and consequent disorientation.

The great French sociologist, Emile Durkheim, also made this his theme. He was preoccupied with the loss of social solidarity, as he called it, and thought of sociology as a study that could help modern humanity find its way to some higher form of it, having lost its primitive type. The term associated with Durkheim, and surely one of the most significant terms of modern times, is *anomie,* which was his name for the uneasiness which afflicts the individual when there is no accepted social authority to use as a guide. The individual, Durkheim argued, needs such an authority; without it, limits cannot be imposed on the ego and happiness cannot be achieved. The individual who feels bewildered and alone in a huge, impersonal world, who has lost the guidance of tradition and religion (which Durkheim felt were very closely connected) and can find no source of values outside of self, who has lost contact with the community—such a person is surely all too typical of modern urbanized and industrialized society, and the pioneer sociologists directed their attention to this problem. Their own personal lives often pointed directly to this interest. They came from the village to the city and experienced cultural shock. The Jewishness of Durkheim and Simmel added to the sense of being outsiders, perhaps. The brilliant Durkheim felt isolated as a student at the Sorbonne, to which he later returned as professor. These men would seem to have experienced the crisis of the individual thrown into the vastness and confusion of modern urban life.

The greatest in this golden age of sociology was undoubtedly Max Weber. A scholar whose tremendous range and productivity is reminiscent of Freud and Jung, Weber, a professor at Heidelberg, suffered intermittently from illness and died in 1920 at the age of 56. A good part of Weber's inspiration stemmed from Marx, whose crudities he wished to refine, but whose central conception of a scientific approach to social, economic, and political phenomena he shared. Perhaps best described as a liberal, Weber longed to play an active part in public affairs but, in Imperial Germany, of which he was often a keen critic, found this path largely blocked. (He did perform some public functions in World War I, which he supported as a patriotic German, though he sharply criticized German policies.) He was a friend of the Social Democrat, Robert Michels, and when the latter was refused a university post because of his left-wing politics, Weber bitterly denounced the vaunted German academic freedom as a fraud. All in all, Weber's combination of brilliance, erudition, and courageous political activism stamped him as an intellectual and moral leader of his generation in Germany; and his fame has endured through such writings as the stimulating *The Protestant Ethic and the Spirit of Capitalism,* his lectures in *General Economic History,* and his unfinished *Economy and Society.*

As a social scientist, Weber was aware of the irrational side of politics and made this one of his chief fields. He was fascinated by the forms of political leadership and by the path of historical development in society and state. One of Weber's leading interests was the principle of rationalization. He meant by this in general the tendency of things to get organized and subjected to rules and orderly processes. What Michels saw happening to the German Social Democrats, in their parth toward bureaucracy, Weber saw as a universal principle in human history. Beginning in romance or magic, institutions or forms settle down into a stable routine. Music, for example, becomes a science. Government becomes bureaucracy. In this process spontaneity is lost, there is "disenchantment," the pedantic expert takes over from the free spirit; Weber sometimes with Nietzsche accuses the modern world of having lost its greatness of soul, producing petty time-servers rather than champions. At the same time efficiency gains. There is, however, Weber adds, a limitation to the institutionalized or bureaucratic form of authority; it cannot cope with emergencies, being attuned only to times of stability. In times of crisis there is still a reversion to the type of leadership Weber called "charismatic." The great individual arises, commanding allegiance by the peculiar force of personality or genius. Napoleon in the nineteenth century revealed charisma as much as Caesar two thousand years earlier, while on a lesser scale religious leaders and leaders of other sorts continued to appear. (Certainly there was no lack of prophetic figures in the late nineteenth century, from Tolstoy and Stefan George to Mary Baker Eddy and Mme. Blavatsky, exercising leadership in mysterious ways.) Charismatic creations are then institutionalized and reduced to routine, in tradition or bureaucracy. What is done or believed today from custom or because it is enshrined in the routine of law was yesterday the inspiration of some charismatic personality.

Weber shared with his friend Robert Michels, and with Pareto and also Georges Sorel, this interest in the forms and modes of authority—legal, traditional, charismatic, and combinations of these. An historical sociologist, his chief interest was in understanding just how this Western society, with its capitalism, its economic rationality, its powerful political state, came to be. Unlike Marx, he saw it not as one inevitable phase of all societies but as a unique thing, created through the centuries, owing something to ancient Judaism. What one may call the sociology of religion fascinated Weber as much as it did Marx and Nietzsche. In *The Protestant Ethic and the Spirit of Capitalism,* he presented the famous thesis (often misunderstood) that religious ideas interact with worldly activities to produce a characteristic "style of life," and that Protestantism and capitalism had something to do with each other. The analysis of modern capitalism also interested Werner Sombart, who more clearly exposed his dislike of its bureaucratic and depersonalizing features.

It is here that Weber turns into a kind of foe of the Marxists, at least the simpler kind. For against the socialists he argued that collective ownership does nothing to liberate humanity; it "would only mark a further stage on the road to bureaucratization." The industrial society is essentially the same whether "capitalist" or "socialist." Division of labor, professionalization, bureaucracy, "rationalization," discipline, efficiency—the essential features and the essential problems of a modernized society relate to aspects of social organization not touched by the question of whether ownership is vested in the state or a large business corporation. Durkheim's location of the trouble in a loss of social solidarity, Tönnies's diagnosis of the disease of urban uprootedness—the other great sociologists joined Weber here in finding that *any* sort of advanced technological society will experience much the same difficulties. It remained for the future to demonstrate the essential rightness of this view, as opposed to any kind of utopian expectations.

Fritz Ringer has recently seen sociology as based on an attitude of pessimistic resignation in the face of modernization—"a heroic ideal of rational clarification in the face of tragedy." The Italian Vilfredo Pareto, brilliant and versatile thinker, said of his *Trattato di Sociologica Generale* (1915) that if he thought it would have many readers he would not have written it! In criticism of Marx, whom he accused of utopianism, Pareto saw a constant struggle for power between groups and classes, but one that never ends. If Marx's "proletariat" did win, it would become a new ruling class against which others would soon rebel—a quite accurate prediction of what did happen in communist Russia and other communist states. In his disabused or cynical reduction of all ideals to selfish power struggles Pareto reminds us of Hobbes, or his famous Italian forebear Machiavelli. Liberty, he would say, is best served when we are aware of the delusions lurking in ideals, aware of the realities of power and thus able to establish realistic checks on it as far as possible. We should aim at a circulating elite, one which draws the potential revolutionaries into the circle of power. But in general Pareto did not prescribe, he only described, and he was not optimistic about the chances of the existing European ruling class. An interesting feature of his sociology was the attempt to classify the basic emotional determinants of ideas, the "residues," in his terminology, which underlie intellectual systems.[14] Few more ruthless exposers of ideals and ideologies have ever written. This was the essential irrationalism of this brilliant generation of psychologists and sociologists: They were in revolt against formalism, they discovered the deeper, more obscure processes of the mind in which rational thought is embedded and of which it is sometimes a kind of protective screen.

Though enormously learned and often possessed by a disinterested quest for knowledge, these sociologists were far from uninvolved or value-free. They all tended to see a crisis. Raymond Aron says that Durkheim "spoke of sociology with the moral fervor of a prophet" and thought it could save the modern individual by explaining how to achieve solidarity and avoid anomie. Weber, at times hauntingly eloquent, is a kind of ancestor of existentialism: Karl Jaspers was his student. Pareto, apparently the most objective, was the most embittered, and it is plain that what forced him into detachment was his disenchantment. If you have really given up all belief in fairies, to endure life you must stand off and laugh at it all, adopting an Olympian stance. To many sociologists, their science is patently a strategy for rejecting or satirizing their society. The device of pretending to be a stranger, in order to say, "See what odd customs these queer people have! And what absurd things they do!" was an old stratagem of satire, used by Swift and Montesquieu. Certain sociologists do something similar. Someone defined sociology as the village atheist studying the village idiot; one recognizes the genre. The point is that sociology itself may be subject to sociological interpretation; it too was a philosophy, a set of ideas arising at a certain time and related to the social conditions of its time as well as to its intellectual antecedents. The main incentive, to repeat, was the dissolving of ancestral customs and institutions during the "modernization" of Western civilization from about 1800 on, the effects of which were keenly felt after about 1870.

---

[14] Pareto named six "residues," but practically these seem to boil down to two main ones: the "instinct for combinations" and "persistence of aggregates." By these Pareto appears to mean something close to the modernized and the integral, organic society, or *Gesellschaft* and *Gemeinschaft*. The foxes who like combinations are capitalists and wily politicians; the aggregative lions are feudal, heroic, perhaps in Weber's sense charismatic. One can have fun comparing the vocabularies of the great sociological and psychological system-makers, to see how far they mean the same thing.

NEW SOCIAL THEORIES

Weber, Durkheim, Pareto, Simmel were *universitaires,* a group for whom such vigorous amateurs and lay prophets of social thought as Gustave LeBon and Georges Sorel entertained much disdain. A varied array of intellectual and political journals testified to the liveliness of European thought in these years. The organized socialist movement carried on its controversies, often reaching a large audience. Serious social thought was by no means a monopoly of the professors.

While orthodox Marxists continued to preach the word as they understood it from the master, there was novelty in the 1900s and an increasingly strident, extremist, often irrationalist note. A few of the leading examples may be singled out. The two most notable French voices were the protofascist ones of Charles Maurras and Georges Sorel.

The intrepid monarchist Maurras, founder of the *Action Française,* was in the tradition of French classicism and rationalism, of Voltaire and Comte. He admired order and stressed the French national tradition, which he saw as classical and rational. He inherited Comte's dislike of modern society as too anarchic and scorned democracy as lacking a principle of order. A prominent theme of Maurras's thought was the need for leadership by an intelligent minority. "The mob always follows determined minorities." The *Action Francaise* organized the *Camelots du Roi* to engage in agitation and street fighting, an idea subsequently adopted by Fascists and Nazis. Among other ideas it bequeathed to the postwar Fascist movement was that of the "corporate state," a favorite idea of Maurras's that came to him from the Catholic Social Movement in France. Though hardly any threat to the state, the *Action* exercised a considerable influence on French university students just before the war. Violently hostile to the Republic in the 1900s, it tended to rally to its support after 1912 with war clouds on the horizon, for it was militantly patriotic and fiercely anti-German. It put out a well-known newspaper, and from Maurras's tireless pen flowed a stream of books and pamphlets. Nationalist, traditionalist, antidemocratic and anti-Semite, Maurras carried on a war against the liberal, parliamentary state, and he looms ominously as forerunner of the "revolutionary conservatism" of the postwar period.

Georges Sorel ranks with Charles Maurras among the outstanding French political theorists in the years before 1914. A Marxian socialist originally, Sorel adopted the irrationalism of the hour and married a Nietzschean and Bergsonian spirit to his revolutionary radicalism. He charged the orthodox socialists with having become bureaucratized and respectable. Their rationalism and materialism, Sorel felt, were quite inappropriate for revolutionaries. Doubtless he was right in recognizing that Marxism is really an apocalyptical religion. He was quite willing to accept it frankly as such. Do not all persons live by "myths"? Socialism he compared to the church, the modern strikers being the equivalent of Christian saints and martyrs. He spoke of the social "myth of the revolution," or of the general strike. Sorel, a brilliant political theorist, had lost faith in reason and in society; in combining the twin spirits of Nietzsche and Marx, he suggested something like what later appeared in

Mussolini's fascism or Lenin's bolshevism, for both of whom he expressed admiration. Essentially an anarchist, a hater of the state and coercion, Sorel disapproved of the element of statism and nationalism in Italian fascism, as he would have rejected Lenin's ruthless state dictatorship. But he did father the idea of a revolutionary elite violently sweeping aside bourgeois civilization in the name of a new myth or religion, that of proletarian socialism. In this "myth" the working class appears as clean, unspoiled, heroic, but brutal enough to dash to pieces the old corrupt order. Without difficulty one can recognize Nietzsche's "blond beasts" clothed in overalls. A civilization must believe in something; modern European civilization under bourgeois leadership had lost the life-giving capacity for such belief. Only the unspoiled proletarians had it: They at least believed in revolution.

At first placing his faith in the trade unions (*syndicats*) to become the agencies of proletarian revolution, Sorel by about 1910 grew disillusioned with them—they were much too materialistic and bourgeois—and turned to a flirtation with nationalism as the revitalizing myth, drawing close to Maurras. This was an ominous precursor of the postwar Fascist mixture of revolutionary *élan* and nationalist solidarity; and in fact Benito Mussolini owed a great deal to *Sorelismo*. Thus Sorel drifted even farther away from democracy, in which course he unquestionably went with a significant stream of thought in France from about 1905 to 1914.

On the far left as well as the far right, the theory of leadership by an elite appeared. Lenin, destined during the war of 1914 to 1918 to become a successful revolutionary leader "conceived a proletarian revolution as the product of great minds, who, conscious of inexorable trends, would create order and progress out of chaotic elements by organizing the raw material of history in a rational fashion" (Adolf G. Meyer). In this he differed from Marx, who had favored widening the franchise and other democratic political reforms, believing that these would facilitate the triumph of the proletariat. The socialists of Western Europe placed their faith in democratic processes which made it possible to gain power by legal means. If Marx was right, the laws of social development were working relentlessly to destroy capitalism; the number of proletarians along with their class consciousness was supposedly growing so that soon they would be in the great majority. Revolutionary conspiracies were out of date in Western Europe, precisely because Marx had revealed the inevitability of the transformation to socialism. But in Russia, where revolutionary conspiracy seemed the only possible recourse against a reactionary absolutism, Lenin sought to reconcile it with Marxism.

He agreed with Sorel that trade unionism had turned out to be nothing more than "the capitalism of the proletariat" and that the working class, by itself, is capable of nothing more than a trade union consciousness. Ridiculing the "requiem socialism" of the Second International, the man born as Vladimir Ulyanov, a well-educated son of a district school supervisor, had been nourished in his youth on the full-blooded revolutionary writings of the populist movement, especially Nikolai Chernyshevsky's *What Is to Be Done?* (1863). Embittered by the execution of his brother as a revolutionary by the tsar's despotic government, young Ulyanov would adopt the name of Nikolai Lenin and later write his own *What Is to Be Done?* He became a Marxist in the 1890s, when this was fashionable in Russian intellectual circles, but his imperious temperament was restive under its passive interpretation, and his restless intellect sought a justification for quick revolution. To a quick mind and a powerful will, Lenin added an utter dedication to the revolutionary cause which he had derived from Chernyshevsky, and a ruthlessness which occasionally amazed his best friends. (Lenin has no pity for the masses, Maxim Gorki said, they are to him "what minerals are to the mineralogist.")

Lenin and Leon Trotsky showed dialectical ingenuity in arguing not that Russia could pass directly from agrarian backwardness to socialism, which was utterly un-Marxian, but that as the weakest link in the global chain of capitalism, the world revolution might *start* in Russia, spreading then to the more advanced capitalist areas. Precisely because she was so backward, Russia might undergo revolution first; then she would be caught up in the international movement and become a part of the future world socialist society. To train a small, disciplined party for seizure of power illegally in Russia might then make Marxist sense in the long run. Few Marxists were convinced, but in 1917 Lenin was to have a chance to test his theory. Spending most of the years between 1900 and 1917 in exile abroad, chiefly in Switzerland, Lenin theorized and drew around him a small number of loyal disciples, but did not then seem an important figure on the Marxist scene, dominated by Western Europeans. It is worth noting, though, that in his last years, Marx himself, replying to queries from Russian socialists (who had translated *Das Kapital* quite early), cautiously conceded the possibility that Russia might be able to skip or condense the capitalist stage.

To Lenin the proletariat represented the will of history, but only potentially so; it must be organized and shaped by the "vanguard" of trained Marxists. The laws of social development exist, but they must be understood and exploited by this alert leadership. History does not make itself; it is made by individuals. When the decisive moment has arrived, one must strike in a sudden act of revolution. The organized vanguard of the proletariat, disciplined, ruthless, and intelligent, must lead this revolution and install the socialist epoch. A Marxist, Lenin dissociated himself from mere revolutionary adventurism or terrorism but was equally scornful of the passive, legalistic social democrats of western Europe. They had been corrupted by bourgeois democracy, in his view. Not by parliamentary means, but by well-planned and prepared-for revolution would the proletariat succeed in its great mission, and this task called for the leadership of the vanguard elite.

At the Second Congress of the Russian Socialists in 1903 the party split on the issue of democracy; Lenin boldly opted for a tightly organized, highly disciplined elite party prepared to seize power and hold it by violent means. Not the working class but the "revolutionary socialist intelligentsia" is equipped to lead and guide the revolution—a position that seemed almost totally un-Marxist. Most of the time Lenin was in a distinct minority within the Russian Social Democratic party. The 1914 war and the subsequent collapse of Russia gave him his chance to rise from obscurity to a grand place on the stage of history.

THE THEME OF ALIENATION

For the most part the story of this most exciting and formative period of European thought, just preceding the enormous explosion of 1914, has seemed a study in irrationalism. "Human reason was tired," Romain Rolland's hero Jean-Christophe reflects, in the last book of this pre-1914 epic novel, a sensation in the year 1913. "It had just accomplished a mighty effort. It surrendered to sleep . . . Even philosophy wavered. . . . Even science manifested signs of this fatigue of reason." One may object that a violent excitability, rather than weariness, characterized the era's thought, which was immensely creative. But none of its students can miss the note of unreason. Just as obvious is the gulf that opened between *les intellectuels* and the mainstream of society.

Most of the serious thinkers and writers did not travel with the crowd. Indeed, their hallmark is very nearly a rejection of the crowd, of mass civilization, of the breakdown of values, the enthronement of mediocrity. They will use the word *bourgeois* as an epithet; likewise, often, the word *mass* or *popular*. By no means true of all, this is true of those who are the most striking and original: of Nietzsche, the symbolists and decadents, and the major political theorists. They did not find the nationalistic and democratic society of their time satisfactory, and they reacted against it as rebels, "outsiders," deniers and defiers of its conventions.

This is a remarkable feature of modern European thought, whatever one may think about it. The "alienation" of the artist and intellectual from society, these people retreating to a private world, inventing esoteric symbols, or even joining some nihilistic revolutionary movement in their hatred of the everyday world, mechanized, philistine, and commercial as it is, is a peculiarly modern theme. This is not to say that giants of thought were ever particularly popular with the majority. It is rather to say that the majority previously did not enter into intellectual society to any marked degree, while now they did. That which constituted the cultural community had been a restricted circle of the upper class, whether clergy, universities, or *salons*. Now this community was immeasurably broadened, and inevitably at first coarsened. At the same time the texture of thought and expression available to the educated or unusual person became more complex; individual sensitivity was sharpened and refined. So—one may hope temporarily—the gulf between writer and general public widened to a chasm, across which each looked at the other balefully and with bewilderment.

It does not appear to be correct to regard the divorce between popular and good literature as peculiarly modern. There has long been a trash literature. The average person in the eighteenth century was not reading Fielding and Smollett any more than the average nineteenth-century reader was absorbed in Eliot and Hardy; they were reading very much the equivalent of James Bond and Zane Grey. Nevertheless in its intensity estrangement was a new phenomenon. Of the early Victorian writers, Walter Allen remarks in his *English Novel* that they "were at one with their public. . . . They accepted the society in which they lived. . . . The assumptions of their age they fully shared." They might and did criticize, but they did so as those who operate within the family, not as alienated outsiders; they strove to improve the common culture, not throw bricks at it from a distance. Granted that the romantics in some measure began the myth of the alienated, lonely, superior artist, the Victorian age resembled the eighteenth-century society more than it differed from it in its integration, and the Victorian sage was no bohemian. But when arriving at Thomas Hardy near the end of the century, another world is entered; a threshold is crossed about the 1880s, whether looking at poetry, painting, drama, philosophy, or the novel. There is a real bitterness at the world's blind amorality, its utter lack of plan and purpose, its cruelty and its essential barbarity: Hardy's *Tess* does not live in the same moral world as the heroines of Trollope, Thackeray, Dickens, or even George Eliot. Something has happened. In part it was Darwinism, in part capitalism, in part mass culture, in part no doubt other things; the result is clear.

chapter 6

The West in Trouble

World War I and Its Aftermath

My house is a decayed house. . . . .
I am an old man. A dull head among windy spaces.

T. S. Eliot

INTELLECTUAL ORIGINS OF THE WAR

Few need to be reminded that a good part of the twentieth century was to be dominated by the breakdown of international order in 1914, leading to four horrible
years of mass slaughter, out of which came red revolution in Russia, black revolution in Italy, and subsequently nazism in Germany—the forms of modern "totalitarian" dictatorship. The war proved scarcely less demoralizing to the victor states
than to the defeated. It hurled much of Europe toward bankruptcy and internal
collapse. During the war, propaganda took over and truth suffered as never before,
and out of the war there emerged a new kind of cynicism, a loss of faith in humanity and values, such as Europe had perhaps never before experienced in modern
history.

It is tempting to find some parallels between this crisis of the political order
and the crisis of thought and culture that seemed to exist as of 1914. Historians
customarily describe the origins of the World War in terms of diplomatic and politi-

Displayed quotation from "Gerontion" in COLLECTED POEMS 1909-1962 by T. S.
Eliot, copyright 1936 by Harcourt Brace Jovanovich, Inc.; copyright © 1963, 1964 by T. S.
Eliot. Reprinted by permission of the publisher.

cal history, and quite properly so: the clash of national interests, the alliances, the military plans, the conferences and confrontations. The rise of nationalism was an obvious cause of the war. Now and again politicians could be heard observing, in a Darwinian spirit, that struggle, competition, and force are the laws of life. Democracy forced officials to take account of a public opinion that was often belligerent and narrow-minded, as well as fiercely nationalist. Diplomacy does not function in a vacuum; politicians are people of their age sharing its prevalent ideas. Historians need to "reconstruct the unspoken assumptions of the men they are studying" and "recreate the climate of opinion in which political leaders operated," James Joll has argued in a thoughtful lecture on *1914: The Unspoken Assumptions.*

These unspoken assumptions of 1914 included a distinct eagerness for war, which the writers and intellectuals shared—something a later generation finds hard to understand, but very much a part of the spirit of the "August Days" at the beginning of the war. The war was extremely popular in all countries at the start. Resisting the war spirit in Britain, Ramsay MacDonald was aware that he was pitted against "the most popular war in British history," a fact to which the incredible rush of voluntary enlistments bears witness. And in the van of these volunteers were the young poets, artists, university students, intellectuals. The story was not different in France, in Germany, in Russia (Hans Rogger has noted the spontaneous enthusiasm for war which swept through Russia in 1914), and soon in Italy. It is difficult to find important leaders of the intellectual community who held out against this martial spirit, and most of them were serving as its cheerleaders. Romain Rolland, one of the few who did try to fight it, cried that "there is not one among the leaders of thought in each country who does not proclaim with conviction that the cause of his people is the cause of God, the cause of liberty and of human progress." The list of "leaders of thought" who did indeed bless the war almost as a holy cause is a lengthy one and includes most of the great individuals discussed in the last chapter, those who were alive in 1914. Bergson, Charles Péguy, Freud (who "gave all his libido to Austria-Hungary"), poets and novelists such as Stefan George, Thomas Mann, were as prominent as historians, sociologists (Durkheim, Max Weber on different sides) and even socialists, who forgot their theoretical antiwar principles and rallied to the cause of their country. This was true of such revolutionaries as Kropotkin, Plekhanov, even some of the Russian Bolsheviks, Lenin being a rare exception; and of the German Social Democrats, the French Socialists, the British Labourites, with only a few exceptions. In England the idol of the hour was the young poet Rupert Brooke, who marched off proudly to die in the war along with so many others who gave their lives as a willing sacrifice to the Moloch of war. To be sure, Rolland exaggerated when he said "not one," for a small minority tried to resist the contagion. But they were all but swamped in 1914 by the rush to jump on the war wagon. As the war wore on and lost its glamor, the situation changed. But it is impossible to escape the conclusion that in the beginning the overwhelming majority of the spiritual leaders of Europe heartily approved of the war.

The reasons for this extraordinary belligerence lead back into some pre-1914 themes. Among the more obvious ingredients in it were (1) a desire for excitement, adventure, and romance, which was associated with the protest against a drab, materialistic, bourgeois civilization; (2) a feeling that the war provided the opportunity for a spiritual renewal through its break with the past and its outpouring of unselfish idealism; (3) an exultation at the healing of a divided society, bridging the gap between classes and between individuals in an organic kind of national unity; and (4) a sort of apocalyptic, Nietzschean mood which saw in this catastrophe both an awful judgment on a doomed civilization and the necessary prelude to a complete rebirth.

Clearly all these attitudes involved prewar intellectual themes. In regard to the protest against bourgeois dullness, the connection is obvious. More interesting is the thrill that people of thought secured from what Karl Vossler (writing to Benedetto Croce) called "the magnificent drama of the exaltation of a nation of 70 million people, all without exception one . . . each one living for all, for the Fatherland." Sophisticated minds such as Max Scheler had come to have as their chief concern "a quest for unity and community in a pluralistic society" and saw in the war a return to the "organic roots of human existence." Barrès's concern about "deracination," the "integral nationalism" of Maurras, and the sociological quest for social solidarity may all be recalled in this connection. A surprising number saw the war as a remedy for modern anomie. The men in the trenches developed feelings of close solidarity in this war, an experience which many soldiers held in high value and hoped to carry into the national life after the war.

Anyone who has studied the mood of 1914 with much care knows that a *mystique* was decidedly present, above all in the young people and those of poetic temperament, the idealists and the restless ones. War, still seen romantically, came as a welcome relief from years of pettiness and greed, triviality and bickering. In France, the period from 1905 on witnessed a sharp revival of what Eugene Weber, who has studied it carefully, sums up as "Discipline, Heroism, Renaissance, *Génie National.*" The conversion of Charles Péguy from socialism to nationalism in 1905 was a landmark; thereafter the former Dreyfusard wrote as a militant patriot, an antipacifist, a fervent prophet of the coming war against Germany. A well-known inquiry into the mood of French university youth in 1913 found that Péguy was the leading influence, along with Barrès and others of the same breed. One of them was Paul Claudel, whose plays and poems radiated heroism and religion and French tradition. In Germany, the years just before the war gave birth to a youth movement whose fierce idealism subsequently was channeled into the war. The *Wandervoegel* of the *Jugendbewegung* were in revolt against their elders, filled with lofty visions of reforming the world, and inclined to a Nietzschean spirit of drastic spiritual renewal accompanied by apocalyptical violence. Poets like Stefan George indulged in visions of a purifying war. That the war would bring "the moral regeneration of Europe" was held by so relatively mild a philosopher as Henri Bergson.

This frenetic preparation for conflict in the mind of the pre-1914 decade and the eager way war was welcomed when it came seemed incongruous later and was therefore somewhat forgotten; it is not well understood today. People soon grew bitterly disillusioned with the war; by 1917 a new mood had set in, which carried through into the despairing postwar years. Yet the spirit of 1914 had existed and had something to do with the coming of the war. Not that the poets and intellectuals deliberately contrived the war, which seemed to come out of the blue, totally unexpected by the vast majority. But when it came they welcomed it almost as a divine omen and gladly marched off to fight in it, thinking that they were redeeming their own lives and rescuing civilization. "Happy are they who die in a just war," Péguy sang before he went off to be killed on the Marne in the early days of the war.

The young Bosnians who killed the Archduke Franz Ferdinand and thus provided the spark that set off the flames were themselves aflame with the restless ideas of pre-1914 Europe. Their idols included Gorki, Andreyev, Whitman, Wilde, and Ibsen. They had learned tyrannicide from 1848 romanticism (Mazzini, "William Tell") and revolution from Ibsen; they lived in an atmosphere of youthful literary romanticism, fed by the exciting writers of the hour, with considerable symbolist and decadent influences. They were in touch with the international anarchist movement.[1]

That the war was a just one was, of course, the almost universal assumption, each side firmly believing itself to have been attacked by the other. The socialists rationalized their support of the war by arguing that if they did not fight, their country would be destroyed and with it their movement. The Germans further held that a victory for Russia would be a victory for the most reactionary of European powers. The French similarly believed that a German conquest would be reactionary, wiping out many social gains already made in France. The working class everywhere tended to be strongly patriotic, and the intellectual socialists were not in fact prepared for the kind of situation that occurred. The Second International had often rhetorically declared that the workers of the world would never fight against each other in a war forced on the people by their wicked rulers; but this war did not happen like that. The great majority knew only that their country was being attacked and must be defended. A small minority of the Socialists in Great Britain, Germany, and Russia thought otherwise but abided by party discipline. Within a fairly short time Karl Liebknecht in Germany, and Lenin, among the exiled Russian Bolsheviks, went into opposition to the war while Ramsay MacDonald resigned the Labour party leadership in England; but these were voices crying in the wilderness for several years. It was dangerous to oppose the war: In England Bertrand Russell was imprisoned, Shaw was snubbed and boycotted, D. H. Lawrence suffered from a feeling of isolation because he could not participate in the *mystique* of the war.

Intellectuals participated in the war to a striking degree. They went off and fought in it, of course, eagerly volunteering in the first rush of battle rapture. They wrote poems to it, hailed it as a regenerating process, celebrated its *mystique*. Many of those who did not serve in the trenches lent their talents to the propaganda side of the war. Arnold Bennett, one of England's leading literary figures, became a di-

---

[1] See among other sources Vladimir Dedijer's article, "Sarajevo Fifty Years After," *Foreign Affairs,* July 1964, and his book, *The Road to Sarajevo* (1966).

rector of British propaganda; distinguished historians fashioned handbooks proving the eternal wickedness of the foe (this happened in the United States, too, after the U.S. joined the war in 1917), and authenticating stories of barbarous atrocities. And of course many died in the war. A sampling of those sacrificed to the war could include the British poets Rupert Brooke, Wilfred Owen, Isaac Rosenberg, Charles Sorley, Edward Thomas; Ivor Gurney went mad. The brilliant Austrian painters Franz Marc and Egon Schiele, August Macke, Raymond Duchamp-Villon, Umberto Boccioni were other slain artists; the poet George Trakl and the sculptor Wilhelm Lehmbruck committed suicide. Of 161 students of the famous *Ecole Normale Superieure* in France from the classes of 1911, 1912, and 1913, 81 died in the war and another 64 were wounded. A French anthology of writers killed in the war contains 500 names, among them Péguy, Alain-Fournier, Apollinaire, Psichari. Such a list might go on and on. The heaviest casualties in the murderous war were among the junior officers, where typically one found educated youth. One is led to wonder what potential earth-shaking achievements were buried with the tens of thousands of brilliant youth killed, what *Ulysses* or Relativity Theory or *Wasteland* was *not* created by some even more talented Joyce or Einstein or Eliot who happened to fall in battle.

Disenchantment soon set it. The reality of war was anything but romantic. "One week in the trenches was sufficient to strip war of its lingering traces of romance," Herbert Read recalled. As the war dragged on and the sickening slaughter mounted, protest against it inevitably arose. In the end, most of those who survived were likely to be ashamed of having been taken in by a romantic view of war. Yet it is well to remember that this was not so in 1914, when a generation of rebels found their great crusade in the war. "We were all flame and fire," Isadora Duncan remembered. Young people lived in fear that the war would be over before they could get into it (it was widely believed that it would be a short one), and of these the educated, university youth were the foremost. It was the hour of Rupert Brooke ("Come and die, it will be such fun"). In the strange story of 1914 the story of the intellectuals is one of the strangest. The student of intellectual history will find much to connect this state of mind with the ferment of ideas in the preceding generation; for the revolutionary message of Nietzsche, Bergson, Jung, Sorel, Baudelaire, Wagner, and all the rest was just making its major impact on the mind of Europe as the war broke out.

The comradeship of the trenches, alas, is apt to remind one of Adolf Hitler, who carried back into peacetime favorable memories of the war's *Gemeinschaft*. The Storm Troopers were a carryover from the war. Still, others than the Nazis entertained a nostalgia for this aspect of the war and hoped that after it was over a more democratic, less class-ridden society might emerge from it. Yet the most obvious results of the war were fascism, followed by nazism; and the communism which had gained control of Russia during the almost total breakdown of the Russian state that occurred in 1917 as a result of the war's intolerable demands. Benito Mussolini, brilliant left-wing Italian Socialist, broke away from the majority of the party on the issue of Italy's entrance into the war in 1915, which he supported. Free to launch ideological ventures of his own after this, he fell increasingly under the influence of Nietzschean and Sorelian ideas and emerged in the troubled days after the war as *duce* of the new movement known as fascism. As for Lenin, few are unaware that he came back to Russia from exile in 1917 following the February Revolution to take charge of Bolshevik strategy and seize power in October, to begin the long dictatorship of the Communist party in Russia.

The prewar socialists were badly split by the war. Though initially the party supported it, a fraction of the German Social Democrats voted against the war in the party caucus, later brought their opposition into the open, and by 1917 created a major split in the party by voting against the war credits. Though Social Democrats took the lead in establishing the new republic which emerged from defeat in 1919, they had to employ armed force against left-wing socialist uprisings and thus threw themselves into the arms of the Right.

POSTWAR PESSIMISM

If the war was initially popular and blessed by the writers, it eventually gave rise to bitter disillusionment. "War is hell, and those who institute it are criminals," Siegfried Sassoon wrote from the trenches. This was the final verdict. The progress of disillusion may be followed in the war poetry—of which this war produced a great deal of high quality. (It remained a writers' war all the way and even in its disappointment produced splendid literature; no other war can compare.) The initial "visions of glory" faded to sorrow and pity and ended in bitterness. The wretchedness, the terror, the nerves tortured by waiting for death, the gassed soldiers, the obscene wounds, even the lice were what the men in the trenches wrote about:

> In winter trenches, cowed and glum,
> With crumps and lice and lack of rum.

Soon they began to scorn the people at home who could have no notion of what the war was really like, and whose knitting of socks or singing of songs seemed a mockery and a sacrilege. A comradeship of suffering and death drew the soldiers close together and sometimes drew them closer to their fellow victims of war in the opposite trenches than to the smug ones at home—or to their own officers. As bitterness developed against the top leadership in this frustrating war which no one could win, soldier-poets wrote of the scarlet majors at the base who "speed glum heroes up the line to death" and would themselves toddle safely home to die in bed. Those who did not die in the first battles but, like Wilfred Owen, lived through almost the whole war (he was killed within hours of the Armistice) could feel nothing but the horror, the pity, and the futility of war. This attitude endured; the romance had gone from war forever and abhorrence of the very thought of war colored the entire postwar era; aiding, ironically, the coming of the next one since a pacifist-minded opinion in the victor countries permitted a revenge-bent Germany to overturn the peace settlement and the balance of power.

The collapse of prewar socialism was not the least of the many interrupted and shattered traditions; discredited by their acceptance of the war, the great majority of its leadership lost control of their own movement from 1917 to 1919. Lenin's Bolshevik faction seized power in Russia and proscribed the Mensheviks along with all other political parties as enemies of the Revolution. In Italy, the ambivalence of social democracy helped pave the way for Mussolini's Fascist dictatorship. The Italian Socialists could not decide whether to be revolutionaries or to defend the democratic constitutional order and ended by doing neither. When the smoke had cleared, Communists looking to Lenin's Russia had greatly increased their following at the expense of the moderate socialists almost everywhere in Europe, though nowhere except in Russia had they been able to seize the state. Their embittered violence frightened the conservative classes into backing extremist regimes in Italy and, within a few years, Germany. In Great Britain, the war wrecked the old Liberal party forever and caused a great increase in the Labour party, which though not Communist had a hyperradical wing and pacifist leadership.

The war years produced a large crop of plans for peace in order to prevent a recurrence of 1914. This was true in all countries. There were League of Nations Societies and Associations, Committees for a Durable Peace, Unions of Democratic Control of foreign policy. These plans were not only at variance with each other but wore an odd air of unreality in most cases; intellectuals struggled in an element alien to them and tended toward utopianism. Most of them were disillusioned with the real League of Nations that struggled to an imperfect birth in the atmosphere of power and hate at the Paris Peace Conference of 1919. The hundreds of tracts and pamphlets written during the war ended as less a contribution to human progress than a curiosity for the historian, a fact which contributed no little to the postwar despair.

Most of the liberals who had so earnestly drawn up blueprints for the postwar world felt that the treaties negotiated at Paris in 1919, along with the League of Nations as adopted, was a betrayal of their ideals and perpetuated old-fashioned "power politics." The postwar years brought a complete revision in ideas about the war's origins. In France, Great Britain, and the United States, nearly everyone assumed it was the Germans who were the criminal unleashers of war; a few combated this notion even during the war, and immediately afterward a momentous investigation into the causes of the war began—with results that were likely to be "revisionist." If scholars did not seek to show that Russia and France were more guilty of the war than Austria and Germany, they at least concluded, typically, that all had been trapped in a circle of fear where one could not well speak of "war guilt." This historical controversy gave rise to a vast and interesting literature, which proved only that no historical event is simple enough to grasp scientifically, but which suggested to millions that their leaders had deceived them in charging all blame on the enemy. At the same time the atrocity stories were radically "debunked," as propaganda ministers ruefully confessed they had manufactured most of these.

Sickened by not only the physical slaughter of millions of Europe's youth but by the moral carnage of a world convulsed by hatred and lies, the postwar generation was the "lost generation."[2] Lost were faith and hope, belief in progress, confidence in the civilization of the West. By way of introducing what was after all a marvelously creative generation too, one may catalog some of these cries of despair that filled the years destined to follow one Armageddon and precede another.

It is difficult to think of any of the great writers of this era—D. H. Lawrence, André Gide, Ernest Hemingway, James Joyce, T. S. Eliot—who did not reject the civilization in which they lived, though it is no less true that this rejection usually antedated the war. They were marked wanderers; the American "expatriates," who joined Gertrude Stein in Paris or Spain, had a counterpart in such as Lawrence, who hated his native England and lived at various times in New Mexico, Mexico, and Italy; or Joyce, a refugee from Ireland who lived in Trieste, Paris, and Zurich. There were, of course, Russian refugees from communism, Italian from fascism, and subsequently German from nazism. Physical flight from the homeland went along with imaginative flight from Western civilization, expressed in Lawrence's admiration for the Etruscans or the Aztecs, in Ezra Pound's importing of Chinese, or what he imagined to be Chinese, literature. "An old bitch, gone in the teeth"—such was Pound's verdict on European civilization, while the usually optimistic, still liberal-socialist H. G. Wells (who coined the phrase "war to end wars" during the war) thought that "this civilization in which we are living is tumbling down, and I think tumbling down very fast." It would be a work of supererogation to reproduce all such comments.

This straying "after strange gods" included a desertion of intellectuals to communism or, less commonly, to fascism. Pound and Wyndham Lewis might be placed in the latter camp, but a larger movement was toward faith in Soviet Russia as a place where a brand-new and hopeful civilization was being shaped, however roughly. This however was much more typical of the 1930s. In the 1920s one mostly believed in art or in sex, if one believed in anything. For the moment, the voice of French critic and commentator Julien Benda held the stage in a book of the hour: *The Treason of the Intellectuals* (1927). The treason that these *clercs* had committed, Benda charged, was deserting the eternal verities to whore after the strange gods of political -isms.

If there was whoring after strange gods, there was also an effort to return to ancestral ones. The neo-Anglicanism of T. S. Eliot, American-born mogul of English letters (another odd case of literary expatriation), had counterparts in the neo-

___

[2] A notable generation effect marked the 1920s; Evelyn Waugh thought it actually the first significant estrangement between old and young in English history. It was in fact a three-way division: between the older pre-1914 "establishment" that had largely not fought in the trenches; those who fought, and managed to survive; and those who having been born about 1900–1905 just missed the military experience. But by all accounts a sharp difference in manners, morals, language, and ideas emerged in the early 1920s between university students and their elders.

T.S. Eliot: A Caricature by David Low. (Cartoon by permission of *The Standard*.)

Thomism of a significant group led by Jacques Maritain in France and the neo-Calvinism and neo-Lutheranism of Karl Barth and Emil Brunner. The return to religion resulted from the collapse of liberal beliefs in secular progress. These theologies in some ways were not orthodox, for they usually "de-mythologized" the Bible, perhaps drew on Jungian conceptions, and regarded Christianity as existentially rather than literally true. But they found in original sin and Christian humility an antidote to the shallow complacency of those prewar liberals and socialists who had believed in rationality and progress. Perhaps old-fashioned Christianity could be a cure for the diseases of a civilization whose sins had been denying its own birthright, succumbing to pride, forgetting the meaning of Christ. Christ was seen less as a preacher of humane ethical precepts than as the apocalyptic or "eschatological" prophet who announced the end of the world and asked people to choose between God and the world. This was especially the bent of Continental neo-orthodoxy, which in the form of the "crisis" theology of Barth came near to Christian existentialism. "It is essential not to have faith in human nature," historian Herbert Butterfield has written. "Such faith is a recent heresy and a very disastrous one." At bottom, the tragic view of life is the true one, asserted many a chastened optimist of the postwar years.

Karl Barth's 1919 *Epistle to the Romans* commentary marked a sharp break with the prevailing liberal and idealist German theology, which had seen the course of history as in large part a fulfillment of God's plan, hence good, a view which could almost blend with the secular idea of progress. The Hegelian influence may readily be seen: God's Reason is immanent in the record of human development, his purposes are realized through Humanity. Regarded quite widely as the greatest theologian of his times, Barth denied as fiercely as possible (in his initial manifestos) that God's kingdom is of this world. There is no synthesis uniting God and Humanity; the two are almost utterly estranged, humanity is incomplete, needing God for fulfillment but unable to find him except in the one tenuous revelation contained in Scripture—the Word. The apparently quite reactionary features of the new theology (variously called "Crisis," "Dialectical," "Kerygmatic")—back to original sin and Luther's hapless human creatures in need of rescuing by divine grace—actually made it seem revolutionary. One rejected a corrupt world and refused to accept a flat, vapid, institutionalized Christianity, demanding life-meaning and relevance in one's faith.

The same general features could be found in Martin Buber's Jewish theology and in N. Berdyaev's voice from the world of Russian Orthodox religion (Berdyaev, initially a communist, fled from Lenin's police state to Berlin and then Paris in the 1920s). These were exciting voices, some of them far less "orthodox" than Barth. Barth's close associate, Rudolf Bultmann, mediated the message for more modernist minds by his "de-mythologizing" idea, which meant that the language with which the Word is expressed in the Bible is a mere husk containing the kernel of essential, true-to-life statements. The neo-orthodox were normally not "fundamentalist" but "modernist" in their view of the biblical text, but they rendered this old debate irrelevant by their insistence that the real message is embedded in the myth.

Whatever the variations in their contours, these postwar theologies were alike in rejecting the old belief in Progress. In a book on the subject in 1920, Dean William Inge, the "gloomy dean," saw the idea of progress as "the working faith of the West for about a hundred and fifty years" and found it a fraud. With hope in social progress shattered, the dream of perpetual onward-and-upward laid in ruins by the hideous facts of the mass slaughter just ended and the moral and political confusion that followed it, the world broken and lost, a personal religion became a tower of retreat in the 1920s. Pessimism was not confined to the religious. Osward Spengler's *Decline of the West* came out of a Germany shattered by defeat, but its message of Western civilization's senility went all over the world and was repeated in varying accents by many others. It was at this time that Arnold J. Toynbee began his even vaster historical study of the rise and fall of civilizations, the first three volumes of which came from the press in 1934. Toynbee has told how, spared from military service by an illness and watching so many of his classmates mowed down in the war, he felt a special duty to devote his life to an inquiry on the causes of such cataclysmic collapses of civilizations. In the same way, the tragedy energized others who had been spared that fate. (Harold Laski, for example, tells a similar story.) Toynbee was led to nothing less than a gigantic comparative analysis of the life cycles of all the civilizations he could find in world history and finished his monumental opus only after another world war made the topic even more timely. But his initial inspiration came during World War I.

The book of the hour right after the war was Spengler's, more hastily written than Toynbee's—though in fact Spengler had begun it before the war—but based on the same premise that civilizations, like people, have life cycles. Needless to say

Spengler found many signs of decay in the contemporary West, whose zenith he thought had come in the later Middle Ages.

The Spaniard Ortega y Gasset's brilliant essay, *The Revolt of the Masses,* conveyed a somewhat similar theme of European decadence from lack of creative leadership. Paul Valéry's famous essay on the European crisis and T. S. Eliot's even more famous poem, *The Waste Land,* might be mentioned in this context. Proust's mammoth novel chronicled the decay of French society. Of course, communists, fascists, and nazis all proclaimed the decadence and imminent death of the old society; that they did so helped eventually to rally some support for traditional European civilization, since these rebels against it so obviously purveyed something far worse. But the 1920s echoed with dirges for the passing of the European age. Eliot's poem said it all: It began with a quotation from Petronius, "we yearn to die." "April is the cruellest month," it no longer brings forth new life, the European world has lost its creativity. Using all the devices of symbolist technique, Eliot, an American-born migrant to England, found images to express the futility of religion, love (it is now known he was registering an acute personal crisis more than he was recording the downfall of the West, but his readers accepted the latter meaning all roo readily):

Here is no water but only rock.

The energizing springs that had fertilized culture in the past had dried up, leaving fear and timidity. "I show you fear in a handful of dust." The great tradition ends not with a bang but a whimper.

A revulsion against popular culture aided this alienation of the intellectuals as the age of the mass media dawned. During the 1920s the "people" seemed more interested in sports events, airplane flights, detective novels, mah-jongg, crossword puzzles, movies stars, and Mickey Mouse than serious ideas or good literature and art. The common man was a sad joke, cultural democracy the last absurdity of an expiring civilization. The mass newspaper and journal with their low intellectual content pervaded society, it seemed. The "shop-girl mentality" and the common man as "boob" (H. L. Mencken) were familiar sneers. Mencken's own United States was a favorite scapegoat: a land without art or culture, home of philistines, prototype of the mindless "ant-world"—*America the menace,* as the subtitle of a French book of the era declared. Europeans eagerly embraced American literature, oddly, for the first time; but it was likely to be Sinclair Lewis's assaults on his own society of Babbits and Gantrys that they relished. Visiting the United States in the 1920s, Bertrand Russell, repeating Tocqueville's point of a century earlier, found it a land without freedom: "It is obvious that, in such a community, freedom can exist only *sub rosa.*" The land of pious peasants was now leavened by a commercial plutocracy. In castigating American civilization, European intellectuals were joined, of course, by young American rebels of the sort who wrote the savagely critical *Civilization in the United States* (1922) and thereafter fled to Paris. Nor did these Europeans like their own cultures much better; America was only an extreme example of the menace that sooner or later threatened everyone.

Contributing to the gray mood of the 1920s were things other than the war and the mess it had left behind, though doubtless the latter contributed the most. What Walter Lippmann once called "the acids of modernity" had corroded belief, leaving behind a cloud of skepticism. These years felt the full force of those deeply subversive ideas developed just before 1914. Freud, for example, now became widely known. Doubtless one can interpret Freudianism optimistically, as many did, particularly in America, regarding it as a new technology supplying medicine for all that ails the mind. But Freud himself was a deeply pessimistic person, especially in his later years, and his books of the 1920s, such as *Civilization and Its Discontents,* express a conviction that the battle between the individual and society can never be ended. Ordered society demands that the id suppress its impulses; "the price of civilization is neurosis." Of course, it is hard not to see Freud as chipping away at the boundaries of the rational mind, pointing to "the cobra-filled jungle of the unconscious" (Chad Walsh) which is the real determinant of human conduct. Freudianism contributed to the iconoclastic mood of the 1920s, to the sexual revolution and the hatred of bourgeois prudery. At times the Freudian message coincided with the return to religion. In an essay on Freud, Reinhold Niebuhr related him to the pessimism of the Barthians; for though Freud was an atheist he agreed with them in seeing the human being as a tragic figure, torn apart by conflicts. Certainly the great psychologist, turned social philosopher increasingly in this latter period of his life, believed that humans are naturally aggressive creatures who will exploit, rob, even torture and kill their fellows if not forcibly restrained. "Who has the courage to dispute it in the face of all the evidence in his own life and in history?" he wrote to Einstein. Freud was extremely skeptical of claims emanating from the Left that a restructuring of society along socialist principles could abolish the essential conflict between individual and society; communism was as much an illusion as traditional religion. With widening fame, and the expansion of psychoanalysis into a great industry particularly in the United States, came a painful illness and further heresies and defections, but Freud continued both amazingly creative and enormously influential until his death in 1939 (driven from Vienna to London by Nazism in his last year). The influences were somewhat ironic: the sexual revolution, the return to religion, the new literature and art all drew on Freud, but he did not think sexual liberation, or religious belief, or art (also an illusion, fantasies created by the neurotic personality) any answer to the tragedy of life. In literature especially, the 1920s swarmed with Freudian influences—Oedipal complexes, illicit love, unconscious motivations (see, as one example, the plays of the great American dramatist Eugene O'Neill). It was said that Freud had restored to modern man the possibility of tragedy, with id and ego standing for the classic powers of fate and free will, the individual against the cosmos.

His onetime colleague and now rival within the psychoanalytical movement, Carl Jung, also extended his reputation. More than Freud, Jung pointed to the psychic need for religion and indeed for a restoration of the holistic, nonintellectual modes of thought of premodern humanity. Nothing more effectively undercut the pretensions of modern civilization with its science to have mastered nature and led

Sigmund Freud. (London, BBC Hulton Picture Library.)

the way to "progress." Civilization had only destroyed man's psychic balance making him an emotional cripple. The use of myth in the literature of the 1920s was at least partly due to the influence of Jung—to whom James Joyce sent his daughter for treatment and who was consulted by many of Europe's cultural elite. T. S. Eliot used myth in his *Waste Land*, Joyce filled his *Ulysses* with it. Eliot saw it as a weapon against chaos, against the fragmentation and confusion of modern life, "a way of controlling, or ordering, of giving a shape and a significance to the immense panorama of futility and anarchy which is contemporary history" (1923).

The disillusionment of the 1920s appeared fashionably and brilliantly in the novels of Aldous Huxley, which were really fictionalized tracts or sermons. One sees in *Antic Hay* (1923) a succession of object lessons in the failure of values. Gumbril, the hero, listens to the clergyman, and then the schoolmaster, and finds both of them useless; the artist fails him, and so does the scientist. Romantic love is a sham, but the amoralist who tries to find satisfaction in perverse or diabolitical behavior is equally absurd. The mordant criticism of all attitudes that try to give life meaning continued in *Those Barren Leaves* (1925) and *Point Counter Point* (1928); these clever, sophisticated studies in pale melancholy hit the decade just right and made Huxley a household word. That he was the grandson of the famous Victorian scientist and believer in progress made his gloom about the human race the more piquant. A search for values always goes on in the astringent Huxleyan way, and in *Point Counter Point* the memorable character gallery of failures—scientists, artists, politicians—turned up one slightly hopeful face in a somewhat Lorenzian philosopher (Huxley was a good friend of D. H. Lawrence). Perhaps by a return to healthy instincts one might make one's way out of the desert. *Brave New World* (1932) carried on Huxley's war with modern civilization. In the 1930s he began to find consolation in withdrawal and mysticism. Not a great novelist, Huxley was a subtle prober of values and a sensitive barometer of the moods of his day among sophisticated Europeans who felt themselves in a dying culture and searched almost in vain for a firm intellectual anchorage for their lives. The same spirit may be found in many another novel, poem, or play of the 1920s and 1930s. Set in a Swiss tuberculosis sanitarium, Thomas Mann's *Magic Mountain* (1924) also contains figures representing types of the modern mind: a scientific rationalist, a Dostoyevskyan irrationalist, a pagan sensualist, and others. And the hope of salvation seems to resemble Huxley's: Hans Castorp almost dies in a snowstorm but rouses himself by a great effort of the will.

It might be noted that the mood was not, really, tragic in the deepest sense. There is a sunset charm about the dying culture; talk is brilliant, personality and ideas both richly abundant, there are always marvelous books to read. What literate person could really be unhappy in a decade that produced Joyce, Lawrence, Proust, Kafka, Mann, and a parade of other stunning commentators on the sickness of civilization? A funeral that attracted so many notable pallbearers had at least its compensations. It remained for World War II to confront Europe with stark tragedy; for the time being, ruminating among the ruins was far from unpleasant. The civilized upper class to which Huxley belonged still existed, if it had gone slightly to seed. If this was not *la belle époque* of pre-1914, neither was it yet the nightmare world of nazism, communism, depression, and war. The 1930s and 1940s brought these things.

Nevertheless the disgust which their civilization inspired in many European writers was both real and ominous. It could lead them to disaster. One example from many: Louis-Ferdinand Céline, in 1932, wrote *Le Voyage au bout de la nuit,* a shocking book, both in style and content, misanthropic much beyond Huxley, scatological beyond Lawrence, a terrible satire on the human race—a book which had a considerable vogue. This talented writer ended an anti-Semite, a pro-Nazi, a collaborator with the German conquerors of France during the war—out of sheer hatred of his native culture, one surmises. He was truly one of those of whom Lawrence wrote in *Kangaroo,* a person driven to defiant estrangement from his fellows. A disgust with the absolute corruption of the world may be found in the brilliantly witty novels of Evelyn Waugh, who converted to Roman Catholicism, and in the subtle psychological probings of French novelist François Mauriac, among others of the great literary names.

THE RENAISSANCE OF THE 1920S

Tinged as it was by despair, the writing and art of the postwar years had a brilliance seldom matched, for it marked the stylistic maturity of the whole modernist movement—shocking, perhaps, but dazzlingly creative. The literary revolution, whose roots lay in the prewar period, burst upon the general public in the 1920s. Graham Hough has placed "between 1910 and the Second World War" a "revolution in the literature of the English language as momentous as the Romantic one of a century before." Perhaps it came earlier in France. But so far as concerned the English-speaking world, such names as Joyce, Pound, Eliot, and Lawrence came to the fore after the war though they had begun their careers just before it. Wyndham Lewis called Ezra Pound, T. S. Eliot, James Joyce, and himself "the men of 1914": This quartet who led the revolution in English literature emerged exactly as the war began. D. H. Lawrence's first major novel, *Sons and Lovers,* was completed in 1913; he wrote *The Rainbow* and *Women in Love* during the war. Joyce had *Ulysses* ready to launch on the world at the end of the war years. Elsewhere, too, buds of the prewar years burst into bloom. Paul Valéry and Marcel Proust in France may be instanced. The latter's great symphony of novels, *Remembrance of Things Past,* appeared between 1913 and 1927, though Proust died in 1922 at the age of 51. The German master Thomas Mann reached the peak of his reputation in the 1920s as did the Frenchman André Gide and the Irish poet W. B. Yeats.

Moreover the new art and music, associated with the names of Picasso and Stravinsky, predated the war in its origins but moved into the limelight once the guns were silenced. The year 1913 had seen those famous riots in Paris that accompanied the first performance of Stravinsky's *Rites of Spring* and also the public tumult aroused by an exhibition of the new nonrepresentational art in the United States. A young American emigré named Gertrude Stein was already buying the paintings of her friend Picasso in Paris—for a song. Picasso was at that time living in poverty among a gloriously bohemian set in the attics of Montmartre. Cubism was born in 1908 and 1910, but the paintings produced by this and other *avant-garde* movements were as yet little more than the obscure eccentricities of certain social outcasts. But after the war, conditions became favorable for the reception of anything new, startling, revolutionary. An embittered "lost generation" of rebels against the purposeless wartime slaughter had no interest in defending the values of their fathers, whether artistic, moral, or philosophical.

In Paris in 1919 writers and artists launched their protest against everything; they named it dada (a nonsense word). Everything seemed nonsense—literature, morality, civilization. Action is vain; art is vain; life is vain. All is absurd. Dada was a combination of literary and intellectual sophistication—all has been said, all ways have been used—with the despair of the years from 1917 to 1919, years of slaughter and stupidity. Dada's activities were expressions of its bitter derision; it held public meetings, well advertised by postfuturist posters, at which people made nonsensical speeches. Tzara, a Hungarian-Swiss who was one of its chief founders, wrote poems by clipping words from a newspaper article, putting them in a sack, shaking them up, and then taking them out one by one.

Needless to say dadaism was a thing of the moment, but its young literary leaders were to be found in the vanguard of other movements of the 1920s. Of these the most important was surrealism. Something of dada's wish to derange meaning deliberately appeared in surrealism, and also some of its violently disruptive political protest, both however made a bit more constructive and coherent. Surrealism borrowed from Freud and Jung the idea that in dreams and semiconscious states the mind is freed from the tyranny of the rational and can produce fresh, authentic symbols. "Psychic automatism" was its method of writing poetry (suspend thought and let the words come). It may indeed be regarded as a continuation of prewar symbolism with Freudian additions.

Underneath such extravagances there was a romantic faith in the autonomy of the realm of art, which the poetic vision might contact beyond the realm of merely rational concepts. It was a kind of mysticism of art, philosophically an idealism. Surrealism long continued to be the dominant force in French poetry. In addition, the surrealists proclaimed themselves political activists and enemies of "bourgeois" society, which they held responsible for the unhappy divorce of art from life. At first they tended to join the communists, who were the most vigorous foes of the "bourgeoisie," but later they grew disillusioned, along with others, with communist tyranny and intolerance. Their sociology, like their politics, tended to be slapdash in the extreme, though occasionally inspired. It was in painting that surrealism, cubism, and related modernist modes had their greatest success. Gertrude Stein's attempt to duplicate in surrealist prose the success in painting of her friend Pablo Picasso did not really come off, though her personality made her one of the most celebrated women of the 1920s. Her mystifying style ("A rose is a rose is a rose"; "How do you do I forgive you everything and there is nothing to forgive") was perhaps not intended to be understood. ("Nobody knows what I am trying to do but I do and I know when I succeed," Gertrude declared.)

The greater writers of a great age of literature were not always incomprehensible. Of the trinity of major novelists, Joyce, Lawrence, and Proust, only the first departed from reasonably straightforward statement, and he only to any marked degree in his last work, *Finnegans Wake*. The novels nevertheless included daring, experimental, and controversial elements. Joyce's *Ulysses* was banned before publication and stirred up one of the chief literary rows of the decade, matched only by Lawrence's *Lady Chatterley's Lover*. The difficulty lay in the frank approach to sex and the use of words heretofore not permitted in polite discourse. To Lawrence, return to a healthy primitive sexuality was important, not in itself but because he thought people who know how to live know how to love. Sex to him was the key to creativity: taproot of all energies, it is the source of beauty, religion, everything wonderful and vital. So far from being a mere hedonism, this resembled romanticism's doorway of the senses to a transcendent realm of truth and beauty; a great deal bolder and buttressed by modern psychology, to be sure. Lawrence castigated the effete intellectualism as well as the timid bourgeois conventionality of the modern world, feeling acutely the need for something more sincere, more intense, more real. This neoprimitivism sent him back to the Etruscans and the Indians, or, if he had to live in the modern world, to Mediterranean peasants. It sent Arthur Koestler and other communist converts to the strong, silent workers.

The integrity and "committedness" of Lawrence, as well as his tremendous creative vitality, made him one of the chief of the modern age's seers. Joyce's *Ulysses,* which then so shocked people, has since received wide recognition as one of the greatest literary achievements of modern times. Its "message," if any, was less clear. A vast allegory on the condition of humanity, a commentary on the futility of human existence, a great symphony in words, an affirmation like Nietzsche and Lawrence of the chaotic abundance of life? It was all of these. Like Eliot's poetry, it made use of startlingly modern techniques to recall modern humanity to its civilized heritage. Whatever else it meant, it was a triumph of art and meant that the artist shapes and gives reality to the world—a message similar to Proust's. These works were testimonies to the autonomy of art and pointed to a withdrawal of the artist—a withdrawal Joyce and Proust made quite explicit—from society, to go it alone.

Unhappy and alienated from the petty bourgeois Irish life around him, the Jesuit-educated Joyce savagely caricatured all this in his pre-1914 stories in *Dubliners,* written in a style not yet experimental. He left Ireland, renounced the Catholic Church, and resolved not to serve a church and a country he said he did not believe in. Living in Paris, Trieste, and Zurich, he worked on the great book which as a portrait of one day in the life of Dublin seems both to revile and admire, laugh at and with the people of the city who represent the entire human race—it is the secret of *Ulysses* that it is as broad and diverse as all of human history. After the success of *Ulysses* Joyce worked from 1922 until 1939, two years before his death, on the vast and enigmatic sequel to *Ulysses* that was finally titled *Finnegans Wake.* It is the dream of the night that follows *Ulysses'* day, in which Joyce virtually invented a new language and revolutionized English literature. A stunning piece of literary virtuosity, it was pronounced a fit companion for Einstein's physics and Kandinsky's painting. Only after a generation of deciphering did the magnificence of this dense piece of writing emerge as an appropriate analog to the great scientist. ("Writing as we know it is unimaginable without him; imagine physics without Einstein!" Hugh Kenner.) If there is any one theme that stands out in Joyce's giant summation, it is the dualism of the artist and the practical man, each flawed—in the end, it is the female life force that prevails.

The excitement of the new literature owed much to its ability to probe the inner world in all its irrational complexities, its occasional nastiness, its vibrant realities. A Lawrence novel takes us immediately into its characters and makes us *be* them as they struggle with their lives and problems; we are engaged with them. In a famous essay Virginia Woolf accused the older novelists, such as Arnold Bennett, of depicting only the external aspects of people; in wanting to see them from within, as their minds actually work almost minute to minute, Woolf was squarely in the center of the new novel.

So there was excitement and creativity in literature, yet also a great sadness, for there is an explicit rejection of the public life. Virginia Woolf's Mrs. Dalloway cannot endure her life as the wife of a leading politician, the whole thing bores her and kills the life of the spirit, found in the cultivation of sensibilities in purely private ways. When Sir Charles Snow, more recently, charged all the literary set with an irresponsible attitude toward politics he had in mind this profound revulsion from the public life that one found in virtually all the great writers of the modern-

A leading figure among the vanguard novelists of the brilliant postwar generation, Virginia Woolf was also an essayist, diarist, critic, and feminist; one of the twentieth century's greatest literary personalities. (National Portrait Gallery, London. Photo by C.S. Beresford.)

ist phase. In the last analysis these artists echoed the decadent view, that in the dying days of a civilization the only consolation lies in art. "I hate politics and the belief in politics, because it makes men arrogant, doctrinaire, obstinate, and inhuman," Thomas Mann wrote in his *Considerations of an Unpolitical Man.* "I have to recognize that I don't care a farthing for political principles," Aldous Huxley exclaimed. Ludwig Marcuse was characteristic, in the 1920s era of political mediocrity, in recalling later that "I don't remember if I voted in those years—certainly not for whom." It was the age of Calvin Coolidge, Stanley Baldwin, and a parade of short-lived nonentities in France and Germany. The Common Man was a sad joke, democracy a farce, politics was the enemy of culture to the Lost Generation's troubled intellectuals.

The interwar years also brought a new architecture and a new music. Le Corbusier (Charles Edouard Jeanneret) led a whole school of architecture that denounced nineteenth-century eclecticism and demanded buildings for the machine age—"functional" and not traditional. Proclaiming that "the past must be destroyed," this architecture had affinities with futurist art and literature. Walter Gropius headed a similar movement in Germany, where the ill-fated Weimar Republic, destined to succumb to Adolf Hitler's Nazis in 1933, experienced a brief renaissance in the mid-1920s. Munich rivaled Paris as a center of modern art, and the Bauhaus architectural and art school, located at Weimar and then Dessau, brought together artists of the caliber of Walter Gropius, Mies van der Rohe, Paul Klee,

Vassily Kandinsky. At once a community, a school, and a place for creative design, the Bauhaus aimed at creating a style suitable for twentieth-century civilization— urban, industrial, technologically modern, yet beautiful. When the advent of Hitler in 1933 forced him out of Germany, Gropius together with Mies van der Rohe brought the new architecture to Britain and then the United States.

Both Le Corbusier and Gropius, as well as the American genius Frank Lloyd Wright, had started their work just before 1914 but reached their creative period after the war. These dates correspond closely with those of the pioneer modernists in painting, music, and literature, and indeed Le Corbusier, who was also a painter, was deeply influenced by cubism and futurism. But almost no one had heard of Le Corbusier, Gropius, the Bauhaus, and "functionalism" before the 1920s, and then they were forced to do battle against outraged traditionalists. One of the larger engagements in this war took place in connection with the League of Nations building at Geneva, supposedly a great symbol of the postwar era, and it is significant that Le Corbusier's modernistic design lost out, even in his native Switzerland, to the sedate neoclassical edifice that still stands there in Geneva. Still, the new style was much discussed and won some triumphs. Dubbed "functionalist," it was in actuality never considered simply as utilitarian by its founders, but was intended to be a modern esthetic. Under cubist influence it tended to be severely abstract-geometrical at first but came to include considerable poetic feeling.

In music, abandonment of tonality was the counterpart of abandonment of perspective in painting and the daring innovations of functionalist architecture. The twelve semitone scale, abandoning the conventional keys, or whole-note scales, represented only one type of musical innovation, reflecting an urgent desire to escape the bondage of the Beethoven century and do something different. Wagner and Débussy had already tampered with the traditional diatonic system; Stravinsky just before World War I caused riots with his violent rhythms and dissonant chords. Arnold Schoenberg's "serialism" invented a new conception of musical structure. There now began a tendency to dispense with thematic development or musical continuity, searching for a "pure" music in a way similar to some of the modernist poets.

There were infinite riches for the eye and ear in these immensely creative years, the years of Picasso, Kandinsky, Gropius, Le Corbusier, and all the others. Though traditionalists might suspect sheer anarchy in their art forms, actually the authentically modern mode in the arts was at work, transforming the way one looks at things and hears them, just as it was at work in Einsteinian physics. It is small wonder that this was a revolutionary epoch in other ways too.

THE CONTINUING SCIENTIFIC REVOLUTION

We have previously mentioned the dramatic observations of May 29, 1919, which "changed the very fabric of the universe" by proving Einstein's new theory of gravity a better one than Newton's. With this timely event, strongly noted if dimly grasped by the entire world, Einstein joined Freud and the new artists among the masters of the unsettled postwar generation. Despite a rash of books trying to explain relativity to the layman, few knew exactly what it portended, but everyone sensed something vastly destabilizing. Another of the seemingly solid props had gone from the cosmos, which became ever less friendly to humankind, less graspable and less "made for man." " 'Tis only one great thought the less," ran the refrain of old Thomas Hardy's "Drinking Song"–lamenting a series of deflations from Copernicus through Darwin to Einstein that had left us "in piteous case." The Spanish philosopher Ortega y Gasset thought the theories of relativity "the most important intellectual fact that the present time can show." There was general agreement on this, but less agreement on just why. A long-familiar picture of the world had been destroyed, creating a sense of confusion and dismay similar to that which had appeared in Europe in the seventeenth century, before Newton came to restore order. The paradoxes of time dilation and other evident violations of common sense were topics of amusement or amazement. But, as Einstein observed, common sense is only the layer of prejudices which our early training has left in our minds; in time the new science might become as familiar as the old. But at first it seemed far more difficult.

If "very little of the nineteenth-century picture of the world remains today," as the editor of a survey of twentieth-century scientific thought observed not long ago, this was due less to Einstein than to the exciting and mystifying riddles of quantum mechanics at the subatomic level. In a somewhat surprising reversal of roles, Einstein himself in the 1920s emerged as an opponent of the more drastic conclusions of atomic physics, which seemed to attack such venerable scientific principles as determinacy and certainty. At a series of international conferences, a new generation of physicists and mathematicians debated new theories. Disciples all, in some sense, of the great Einstein, but now going beyond what the master thought safe, some of those geniuses were amazingly young: Werner Heisenberg was 23, Dirac was 23, De Broglie about the same age when they leaped to the center of the stage. It was the heroic age of modern physics, an era of extreme brilliance. Work on the frontier of "matter," where the unbelievably small atom was now broken into even smaller fragments, flowed in from many directions. As it did, the results challenged the intuition of the great scientists and led to an array of interpretations of unutterably strange phenomena. It seemed that within the atom, the electrons did not behave as particles of matter would be expected to behave; they did not act at all the way "ordinary" objects do in the everyday world. Electrons have properties of *both* particles and waves, being sometimes one and sometimes the other, or being something capable of behaving on occasion like both. Since electrons must be used to observe electrons and exert a disturbing influence, one can never directly observe electrons but can only infer their nature. This, to some, was a disturbing reminder that science has limits beyond which human knowledge can never penetrate. Likewise, the behavior of the subatomic particles can be predicted only within limits of probability, thus striking at that certainty and complete determinacy heretofore claimed and thought necessary for physical science. For example, we cannot know both the position and the velocity of a subatomic particle in the way that we can

know them of larger objects. If an airplane is bound for Boston from Chicago, naturally we can find both its exact position and its speed at any given moment. This cannot be done for an electron bound from one place to another. We *can* get general statistical trends, adequate for most predictive purposes, but the individual electron eludes determinacy and predictability. Heisenberg's "indeterminacy" principle indicated the unsatisfactory situation at the frontiers of physics. In his book *Physics and Philosophy* (1942), Sir James Jeans listed among the consequences of quanta theory: (1) the uniformity of nature disappears, (2) precise knowledge of the outer world becomes impossible, (3) the processes of nature cannot be adequately represented within a framework of space and time, and (4) sharp division between subject and object has ceased to be possible.

Matrix algebra, amazing even Einstein, was introduced to deal with allegedly unobservable electrons as hypothetical "waves of probability." A fifth dimension was hypothesized! Niels Bohr argued that the quantum realm of the atom is so different from our normal experience that we must conceive of its reality as dual— things being both themselves and their opposites. Einstein had contributed greatly to quantum physics but now he shied away from such theories as indeterminacy, probability, and complementarity as disturbing to his sense of cosmic order. "God may be subtle but he is not deceptive," according to the famous Einstein motto. The battle flared at the 1927 Solvay Congress (in Belgium), when Einstein offered objections which Bohr and Heisenberg countered. Most of the top scientific brains at this impressive assembly thought Einstein wrong. One had to accept the limitations of human knowledge, the radically different nature of subatomic behavior, the inability to attain more than theoretical probability (statistical laws only, not prediction of specific events, rather like sociological generalizations).

In 1930 Einstein traveled to California where he dined with Charlie Chaplin and also Upton Sinclair (the great scientist had intermittent and rather simplistic political interests). He visited the Mt. Wilson observatory, biggest telescope in the world, where in 1929 Hubble had observed other galaxies, which are moving away from us with speed relative to distance. Einsteinian relativity had predicted a dynamic universe, just as it predicted atomic energy. Now his theories were being confirmed, mathematical formulas predicting reality. A Belgian priest, the Abbé LeMaitre, theorized about a primeval egg, an incredibly dense and hot object no bigger than an egg that was the universe when it began in an explosion some dozen billion years ago, still going on—indefinitely, or until an eventual contraction back into the egg? In any case, these strange cosmic explosions enhanced the sense of a universe weird beyond the wildest imagination of the fantasists.

Einstein like Freud was to be caught in the political explosions of the times: In 1933 he renounced his German citizenship upon Hitler's taking power in Germany, eventually moving to the United States. The Nazis denounced Einstein as a degenerate Jewish Bolshevik whose theory of relativity was totally wrong. Nor did Stalin's Soviet Union accept these "bourgeois modernist" theories. Science was being politicized in the intolerant political ideologies of a tormented postwar world, spawning "totalitarian" systems.

THE TOTALITARIAN TEMPTATIONS: FASCISM

With Mussolini proclaiming the "lie of universal suffrage" in Italy and Lenin the decadence of bourgeois democracy in Russia, democracy was under attack in the 1920s. It found few defenders among the Western intelligentsia. To Ortega, the Revolt of the Masses was a menace to historic Europe; to Spengler, the Decline of the West began with liberalism and ended with democracy, a soil on which Caesarism, he thought, flourished. Like Georges Sorel, George Bernard Shaw, to whom democracy substituted the rule of the incompetent many for that of the corrupt few, admired both Lenin and Mussolini—any enemy of democracy was his friend. In Spengler's scheme of decline, democracy is the detritus left behind by the decay of organic civilization, a view reminiscent of Plato. Weimar Germany produced whole schools of neoconservatives who lamented *The Rule of the Inferiors,* the title of a 1927 book by the Lutheran romantic reactionary Edgar Jung (later killed by Hitler); Jung was close to the Austrian Catholic advocate of a return to the Middle Ages, Othmar Spann. Many Italian intellectuals were half implicated in fascism, since like the philosopher Benedetto Croce they believed in the rule of superiors. "It is a myth that the Nazi movement represented only the mob," George Lichtheim observed. "It had conquered the universities before it triumphed over society." If this judgment goes too far, reigning intellectual fashions in the 1920s did come measurably close to fascism or nazism and often displayed an initial sympathy toward them.

The poet-turned-nationalist and adventurer, Gabriele D'Annunzio, may well be given credit for inventing the *mystique* of Italian fascism, as the German poet Stefan George provided elitist ideas and symbols to Hitler's movement. The cases of Martin Heidegger, Carl Jung, and Croce, among great leaders of thought, who apparently felt some initial attraction to fascism or nazism, have been much discussed. But antidemocratic ideas were by no means confined to Germany and Italy. H. G. Wells called for a "samurai" class of governing experts, as did the American, Walter Lippmann, in such books as *Public Opinion* (1922) and *The Phantom Public* (1925). The powerfully committed literature and thought of D. H. Lawrence was antidemocratic: "I don't believe in democratic control. . . . The thing must culminate in one real head, as every organic thing must." Though Lawrence never accepted Mussolini as meeting his standards in Caesarism, Ezra Pound did. Evelyn Waugh approved Mussolini and later Franco's right-wing dictatorship in Spain. Robert Brasillach and Drieu la Rochelle joined the older figures Charles Maurras and Maurice Barrès, still active in the 1920s, among French intellectuals who were fascist or semifascist. Fascism was, in fact, an international movement, found almost everywhere in varying degrees. Only in Italy, however, did it manage to lay hold of national power in the 1920s. (Adolf Hitler's German National Socialist movement was then an obscure one.)

A result of the demoralization following the war and a disappointing peace, as well as of frustrated national pride, Italian fascism was hardly a consistent doctrine, but rather a fusion of discontents, successful because of the near collapse of society. It owed something to the fierce strife between socialist trade unions and the industrial capitalists and to the Socialists' paralysis of will in a divided mind, as well as to the continued failure of parliamentary democracy to function well. A mass movement, it appealed to various inchoate emotions. In part it was the nightmare of Ortega, of Spengler, of Lawrence, and of Huxley come true: a revolt of the dehumanized masses, who were then to be enslaved by the totalitarian state. But fascism had its intellectual aspects, and made use of some interesting ideas. Its leader, Benito Mussolini, a man of humble birth, had been a left-wing socialist, and was a journalist with an inquisitive and somewhat intellectual turn of mind. He had absorbed at least superficially the advanced political ideas of the pre-1914 generation—from Nietzsche, Sorel, Bergson, and Pareto. He got from them the need for a complete revolution of values, to replace the decadent ones of bourgeois civilization, but also a contempt for materialistic socialism; a belief in elites rather than democracy; in the superiority of intuition over intellect. Sorel's influence was especially strong in Italy.

Of the Fascist and Communist revolutions, much the same thing may be said as was said of the French Revolution earlier: Ideas did not cause them, but they did guide and shape them. Discontents and the breakdown of order existed, the result of war and postwar problems (economic troubles, demobilization of soldiers). There was a host of other accumulated grievances. Italy had suffered from frustration ever since the rebirth of the nation in 1861, an event which was supposed to lead on to the glory befitting descendants of the Romans but instead brought only a series of humiliations. All this would in any case have brought on trouble, perhaps violence; but ideology helped shape this into a coherent, or more or less coherent, pattern of revolution.

A man of ideas as well as of action, D'Annunzio put himself at the head of some exsoldiers and marched into the disputed city of Fiume in 1919, accompanying his seizure of it with flamboyant gestures of the sort soon copied by Mussolini—the uniformed private army, parades and mass meetings, the leader addressing crowds from the balcony as they roared slogans back at him. Admirer of Wagner and Baudelaire, author of decadent novels, D'Annunzio had been a literary prodigy in the 1890s, after which he turned to the preaching of political adventures. "For Italy's younger generation," writes Ernst Nolte, "he was Nietzsche and Barrès rolled into one." He was a poet who became a national hero. Then he plunged into the world war, became an aviator, lost an eye, was decorated for bravery. No one better symbolized the "Leonardist" and "futurist" spirit which was Italy's version of the Nietzschean will-to-power, the Bergsonian *élan vital*. A Dionysian and a powerful leader of the masses on his own view, he impressed others as an egotist and a charlatan. He was certainly a fertile source of slogans, one of them being the idea that Italy was a proletarian nation which should wage class war—as a united people—against the rich, plutocratic states. The spirit of fascism was very much this spirit of the romantic gesture, action for action's sake, and the mobilization of mass psychology. One may read here the whole mystique of the *avant-garde* movement of the day: the Nietzschean incitement to embrace life and "live dangerously," the rebellion against bourgeois legality, the alienated artist's hatred of respectable society, the socialist and anarchist call to revolt.

Despite the somewhat disreputable character of Mussolini, there were some ways in which fascism was smartly up to date—more up to date than Lenin's Marxism, for it had absorbed the lessons of irrationalism and psychology. It stressed "charismatic" leadership and "superman" activism. The Fascists managed to project an image of dynamic leadership aimed at reviving the Italian nation. Their weakness was the weakness of the new irrationalism: no system or program, just action for the sake of action, belief in belief itself, creation of "myths," whatever they might be.

To supply the element of nationalism lacking in Nietzsche and Sorel, Mussolini invoked Hegelian strains, popular in Italy for some time. He confided the construction of fascist philosophy to the distinguished neo-Hegelian philosopher, Giovanni Gentile. The state represents the ethical ideal and is superior to the individual, Gentile held. Both the individualism of bourgeois liberalism and the divisive class struggle of Marxian socialism are antisocial. Materialism was rejected as ignoble, and an organic conception of society approved. Claiming at first to stand for the individual against the state, Mussolini moved steadily toward more and more statism, a movement of the mind obviously not unaffected by the fact that fascism had seized the state and increasingly subordinated the individual to the community. Fascism represented itself as an answer to the degenerate liberalism of the parliamentary system. The idea of the corporate state, developed in Catholic social thought and carried forward by Charles Maurras, became a part of Mussolini's system. Perhaps its marriage of statism (from Rousseau and Hegel) to the dynamic revolutionary romanticism of Nietzsche and Sorel may be regarded as fascism's most striking achievement.

One may argue with some plausibility that fascism simply grabbed at various bits and pieces of ideas to justify its seizure of power. But it does not seem possible to dismiss its ideological aspects, for these were potent factors. It may be that this was why fascism and nazism had such startling success: Their leaders were aware of the power of ideas, whereas the anemic liberalism of the time was not. Debased as it was, they offered a religion or faith to live by to modern humanity. For a few years Italy's most distinguished philosopher, Benedetto Croce, approved of fascism because it had overcome traditional Italian indifference to politics and the state, revived national morale, and seemingly justified itself by its results. An impressive number of notable Italian writers, artists, musicians, including Papini, Pareto, Pirandello, Puccini, Toscanini, praised the new Italian regime at first. Almost all became severely disillusioned within a few years after 1922. Fascism was in fact no one coherent doctrine but a mixture containing both right and left. On the left some non-Marxist syndicalists whose opposition to capitalism was socialist-anarchist and worker oriented felt in the end that Mussolini had sold them out to the conservatives. As in the case of Hitler's Nazis, discontented elements within the party were something of a threat to Mussolini after he consolidated his power, and he had to suppress them.

Mussolini strove to destroy the "lie of universal suffrage" and parliamentary democracy by substituting a strong, heroic elite; he only succeeded in putting Italy under the heel of a corrupt oligarchy. He broke the power of the trade unions, but his "corporate state" scarcely provided any creative principle of economic cooperation. Fascism as a new religion was stamped on the mind of youth through control of the educational system and the organization of youth movements, but it soon ceased to interest anyone of intellectual quality. Mosca, the old proponent of elites, publicly regretted that he had ever criticized democracy, for the rule of the Fascists was worse yet. In brief, whatever promise there had been of a genuine new creed or spirit in fascism soon vanished with only the old face of state tyranny in evidence, this time backed by the resources of modern technology. It is true that Mussolini for a while put on a reasonably convincing performance of the hero-leader, with some "charismatic" appeal. In many ways he was a genuinely talented man. But he wilted under the demands of the superman role and became rather ridiculous. Quite a few of Italy's better minds fled into exile. Others, like the great writer Ignazio Silone, were turned into Communists who fought the Fascist tyranny as best they could underground.

Fascism, as defined by historian Robert O. Paxton, was "a mass anti-liberal, anti-communist movement, radical in its willingness to employ force and in its contempt for the upper-class values of the time, sharply distinct not only from its enemies on the left but also from its rivals on the right, traditional conservatives." Its leaders, such as the autodidact Adolf Hitler, as well as its support tended to come from well down on the social scale, from "little men" with a pattern of frustrated ambition, often self-taught, "outsider" intellectuals. At the first meeting of the German Workers party that Hitler attended on September 12, 1919, the forty-five members included a doctor, a chemist, a painter, two engineers, a writer, five students, the daughter of a judge, along with artisans, businesspeople, soldiers, white-collar workers—quite a cross-section of society, bound together mostly by a susceptibility to seizure by simple ideas and a profound malaise of spirit, as well as frustrated ambitions. Konrad Heiden called the Nazis "the armed intellectuals." Thomas Mann dubbed them "truants from school." Among the would-be intellectuals in the early Nazi party were an amateur economist (Gottfried Feder), a Wagnerian poet and folklorist (Dietrich Eckhart), the founder of a pagan religion (Alfred Rosenberg)—a weird lot, laughed at initially by the respectable educated. Hitler, with his hillbilly accent and lowbrow anti-Semitism, was nevertheless in his way a man of ideas, fanatically so; ideas which he had accumulated in intensely indiscriminate reading during his down-and-out years after failing to gain admission to the Vienna Academy of Fine Arts in 1907 and 1908 (the academic bureaucrat who turned him down must surely bear a heavy burden of twentieth-century guilt!). From them he shaped his *Weltanschauung,* and no one was more aware of the power of ideas.

Hitler borrowed from Mussolini, whom he admired, but went much beyond the relatively civilized Italian *duce* in the ruthlessness of his methods, where he found Lenin more to his liking. Like Mussolini, Hitler and his group hated democracy, preached a "national" socialism in place of the Marxist sort which they regarded as poisonous, and were fanatically nationalistic and statist. Nazism, too, thrived on defeat, national humiliation, and the disorders of the postwar era, which were very severe in Germany for several years after 1919. It owed a special debt to Richard Wagner and featured anti-Semitism, not conspicuous in Italian fascism. It also opportunistically made appeal to all sorts of emotions. It denounced capitalism, communism, the Jews, the traitors who had allegedly caused the defeat of Germany, the pacifists and liberals who continued to weaken that nation; it demanded a strongly led government capable of voicing the entire national will and leading Germany back to its place in the sun. Its brown-shirted gangs specialized in brutal violence. The party, with its leadership principle, borrowed heavily from Lenin's Russian Communist party in its organization. There were echoes of pre-1914 Pan-Germanism in Hitler's program of German expansion; there was also the "crude Darwinism" which caused Hitler to act consistently on the principle that life is a ruthless struggle in which the weak, the wounded, and the allegedly "biologically inferior" have to perish. Racism came from Wagner and a few other nineteenth-century writers, such as the Frenchman Gobineau, owing something, too, to the fashion for genetics, which sometimes took the form of belief in racial improvement by selective breeding. From Nietzsche (selectively) the Nazis took slogans about supermen, heroic leadership, and the need to purge the old order ruthlessly. Sadly though he may have misunderstood that great tragic seer, Hitler was to make Nietzsche—who hated anti-Semites and despised German nationalism—into the Third Reich's official philosopher.

In the crude thought of the demagogue Hitler, the Jew appears as a scapegoat, blamed for everything: among other things, for capitalism, democracy, socialism, decadent estheticism, modern art and literature, modern skepticism and unbelief. Hitler's taste was severely classical; he shared with Stalin's Communists at least this one trait, a hatred of all modernistic art. In the slightly more sophisticated theorizing of the Nazi "philosopher" A. Rosenberg, the Jew is identified with intellectualism, which is related to internationalism, both to be set off against the sound instincts of a cultural people. Christianity has been corrupted by both Judaic and Mediterranean elements, but there is a sound "Aryan Christianity" which should be encouraged. The decadent phenomena, blamed primarily on Jewish influence, are the internationalist, intellectualist, uprooted, atomistic ones; the sound things are rooted in the soil, national tradition, close group integration, intuition, and custom rather than abstract reason. It is easy to see in this sort of thinking many echoes of German and European thought, from early nineteenth-century conservatism and romanticism, from Wagner and Nietzsche and German sociologists like Frederick Tönnies. They were not all disreputable ideas; perhaps they ought not to be blamed because they fell into the hands of the Nazis. The specifically Nazi contribution was the mysticism of race, which is generally considered to have been complete nonsense. This went so far as to assert that there was an Aryan science and to reject Einstein's theories as Jewish-decadent. In flight from the modernized society, nazism was a desperate attempt to turn the clock back and recreate primitive social solidarity at the level of the nation state. To do so, it invented the myth of racial purity.

Talk about the "Nordic race" and its superiority was quite common and respectable in the later nineteenth and twentieth centuries, as may be seen, for example, in England's Cecil Rhodes, whose Anglo-American scholarships, still awarded annually and considered a high honor in the United States, were established for the purpose of knitting together "the Nordic race"; or in such Americans as Josiah Strong and John W. Burgess, a popular clergyman and a leading professor of political science. The United States rang with laments about the "mongrelization" of the native stock through immigration from "inferior" Slavs and Latins as well as Jews. Anti-Semitism was familiar in Great Britain: A writer has observed that "fifty years ago anti-Semitism was a political force in England that respectable people supported and with which honourable people sympathized" (Henry D'Avigdor-Goldsmid, *History Today,* April 1964). The Dreyfus Case in France in the 1890s brought forth the first major appearance of modern anti-Semitism. Hitler learned his in Austria. There, the Germans as a minority in a sea of Slavs, Hungarians, and Jews developed an often hysterical Pan-Germanism as well as "master race" ideologies. Rosenberg was a Baltic German, again revealing the psychology of the colonist or resident alien. Anti-Semitism had been far more virulent in Russia and Eastern Europe, where vicious mistreatment of the Jew was common practice; in Germany the Jews had apparently become assimilated and there was no "Jewish problem" until the Nazis invented one.

Hitler appropriated ideas from the German conservative writers, a group that included Oswald Spengler, Ernst Jünger, and Moeller van den Bruck, though they did not much approve of him, and after seizing power he persecuted this group as relentlessly as others. These thinkers responded to the defeat and humiliation of Germany in World War I by proposing a Spartan recovery program. Spengler and Moeller wrote of the need for strength of will, national resurgence, and a leader capable of embodying the people's will. All weakening forces, such as democracy (alien to the "Prussian style"), liberalism, and class conflict must be eliminated. These ideologies stemming from the French Revolution were the virus poisoning Germany, which must return to conservative principles to regain unity and strength. Moeller and Spengler were the "conservative revolutionaries" who would use revolutionary means to bring about a conservative, that is, nationalistic, goal. But they were not racists and Hitler to them was a disreputable rabble-rouser. There are some striking affinities between these writers and nazism, but not complete identity.

Ernst Jünger was a spokesman of Germany's restless youth, who just before the war had created a youth movement expressing the urge to get back to nature and renew contact with elemental forces, a protest against the urbanized rationalism of modern life. Something similar existed in France and other countries. After the war, the "fatherless generation" or the embittered exsoldiers were revolutionary in spirit. This youth movement was intensely idealistic, yearning for something much better, earnestly if fuzzily convinced that the existing order—capitalist, mechanical, bourgeois, soulless—was bankrupt. The youth movement with its *Bünde* was separate from the National Socialists but often merged into it. Hitler took advantage of it; in the long run he did not represent its idealism, and it is clear that many young Germans who initially hailed Hitler soon became severely disillusioned with the new slavery his regime introduced. (By that time it was too late.) Radical, revolutionary as it was, young Germany was searching for something to believe in, something exalted and pure. The tragedy was that the figure it thought represented such revolutionary idealism turned out to believe in nothing except himself.

The Nazi and Fascist movements were profoundly anti-intellectual. "When I hear the word 'culture' I reach for my gun," said Joseph Goebbels, Hitler's lieutenant. These movements came to be led by the brutal, the ignorant, and the criminal. They were extremely clever at exploiting the irrationality of the masses, for whom they often expressed great contempt. Keen students of propaganda, the Fascists and Nazis borrowed liberally from all the great mass movements of the past. They employed the language of religious conversion, freely using such words as faith, deliverance, miracle, rebirth, sacrifice. Nineteenth-century nationalism did so too, as one may recall. They took much from the Communists as well as from ritualistic orders such as Jesuits or Freemasons, and from the army; it has been suggested that they also learned a good deal from American advertising. They played on symbols from the national past. Hitler and the Nazis "looked back into the stream of earlier German thinking and selected that which they found of value to them" (Otto Klineberg). There was a deliberate use of "myth," a disparagement of objective truth, a frank acceptance of the need to lead the masses by techniques directed at the irrational mind. All these ideas had been brought forth by such important prewar thinkers as LeBon, Sorel, Wallas. The war itself had exhibited the possibilities of nationalistic propaganda and helped undermine respect for truth, as governments resorted to what amounted to systematic lying. Thus in many ways the Fascist and Nazi movements dredged up all the worst in prewar and war culture. They were the evil spirits of Western civilization, but they did not create the evil so much as exploit it.

It should be stressed that fascism was a Europewide phenomenon. If it emerged first in Italy, with strongly French intellectual antecedents (Sorel, Maurras) under the leadership of an ex-Marxist who held no brief for Italian national traditions, it sooner or later appeared in all parts of Europe (and America). There were Belgian Rexists, and an Austrian Fascist movement, the *Heimwehr* led by Prince Stahremberg (which predated the Nazis and was destroyed by them after Hitler took over Austria). In Rumania the Iron Guard, preaching return to ancestral customs, rejection of modernism, hatred of the Jew as symbol of capitalism and modernism, combined this sort of deep conservatism with a radical, populist program of land redistribution. There were such manifestations everywhere. In Britain, the man regarded as the most brilliant young Labour party leader, Oswald Mosley, imitated Mussolini and tried to create a British Fascist party. If fascism failed to capture power in other countries as it did in Italy and Germany, the reasons were chiefly accidental ones of time and circumstance.

Certainly in France the Fascist movement could not be described as insignificant. In February 1934, 200,000 demonstrators attempted to storm the Chamber of Deputies in Paris and fought police in an all-night battle during which thousands of both police and demonstrators were wounded and a number killed—a melee hard to match even in the long and bloody annals of Parisian street uprisings. These protestors were right-wing followers of the Fascist leagues, seeking to bring down a left-of-center government. The largest of the French Fascist leagues, the *Croix de Feu,* claimed 750,000 members and may have been the largest of all voluntarily recruited Fascist groups. Fascism never won in France, partly because there were too many different Fascist groups—the old *Action Française* now being joined by several other similar factions.

One of France's leading Fascists was a renegade Communist, Jacques Doriot. What, in the last analysis, *was* this post-world war phenomenon that so oddly combined extremes of Right and Left? That it *did* so combine things formerly thought to be unmixable opposites, is indisputable. It appealed to the young and the outcast, demanded drastic change, practiced violent methods. It sought an image of dynamism as well as youth: Mussolini and Hitler made a point of dashing about on motorcycles or in fast cars and otherwise displaying qualities of energy and *élan.* Fascism's specific programs were somewhat anticapitalist, appealing to the "little people" against the monopolists; and it called itself Socialist, though rejecting the materialistic and class-struggle socialism of the Marxists. Its leaders tended to be one-time Marxists—true at least of Mussolini, Doriot, Oswald Mosley, and others. In all these respects it was radical. But in other ways it was deeply conservative. The demand for national unity, cultural integration, what the Germans called *völkisch* qualities was close to the heart of fascism/nazism. Their hatred of Jews and Marxists came to the Fascists from their dislike of things that disrupted organic culture unity and divided the national community. Their extreme intolerance, their contemptuous rejection of democracy and liberalism, their almost insane attempts to create a national ideology—*German* religion, *German* science—along with their racialist fantasies, all this flowed from the impulse to beat back the tides of pluralistic modernism and recreate a truly organic community. The Fascist ideology glorified the country against the city, tried to inculcate blindly obedient patriotism, stressed the family, traditional values, old customs.

In his analysis of the decline and fall of civilizations, published in 1939 (Vols. 4-6 of *A Study of History*), Arnold Toynbee identified among unsuccessful remedies the would-be saviors with a Time Machine (an image adopted from Lewis Carroll and H. G. Wells) who would turn the clock forward or backward—futurists and archaists, both neurotic products of a civilization in crisis. On this view, the fascists and nazis were the archaists, violently trying to stem the tide of modernism and return to some (imagined) simpler and purer age. Their counterparts were the Soviet Russian Communists, with equal violence seeking to leap at one great bound into the future. Of course, much of the rhetoric of fascism represented itself as a bulwark against this barbarism from the East. The Fascists profited from widespread distaste at the bloody methods of Lenin and Stalin in the Soviet Union and their attempts to spread Communism abroad.

This radicalism of the Right was, of course, deeply infused with the irrationalism of the prewar thinkers. An old-fashioned rationalist like Bertrand Russell stood aghast at all this sound and fury, and could only say, "The world between the wars was attracted to madness. Of this attraction nazism was the most emphatic expression." Watching Hitler's parades and mass meetings, listening to his hysterical speeches to roaring, chanting crowds, many others too could only assume that a kind of madness had seized hold of Germany. (In actuality, it would appear, not many Germans paid much attention to the ideology, privately laughing at it; they approved of Hitler because he got things done, restoring Germany to economic health and international success.) But still others pointed out that people, not being rational animals, have need of ritual and romance, a need neglected in modern times, rationalized, bureaucratized, and mechanized as its life had become. Fascism reminded them that modern Western humanity is in search of a religion, to replace a lost Christianity, and found here a substitute. It turned out to be a disastrous one.

chapter 7

The Pink Decade

Who live under the shadow of a war
What can I do that matters?

Stephen Spender

COMMUNISM AND THE INTELLECTUALS

In the 1930s, reaction against nazism provided a rallying point for the shattered morale of European intellectuals. At this time they were precipitated in large numbers into the camp of communism. The "red decade," or at least the "pink" one, had begun.

Quite early, the new Communist government of the Soviet Union received significant support from Western intellectuals. "In this muddy age its ten years shine," wrote the American liberal magazine, *The Nation,* on the tenth birthday of the Russian Revolution in 1927. In that year of the Sacco-Vanzetti agitation,[1] this was probably a representative view on the Left, though during the horrors of the

Displayed quotation from Spender's "What can we do . . ." in *Poems* (New York: Random House, 1934.)

[1] Communists led a worldwide protest against the execution in the summer of 1927 of the two Italian-born American anarchists for a murder they allegedly committed during a robbery in 1920 at South Braintree, Massachusetts. The case became the focus of intense emotions as liberals and leftists charged a frame-up. Decades later, scholars were inclined to think at least one of the "dago martyrs" guilty after all, but for a long time it was an article of the liberal faith that they had been victims of anti-Red hysteria. The irony is that anarchists hated and were savagely persecuted by Communists in Russia after the revolution.

Civil War in Russia, 1918-21, and ensuing confusions amid terrorism and persecution, there had been less sympathy for Lenin's dictatorship; visiting Russia in 1921, Bertrand Russell thought Lenin the most repulsive person he had ever met. Within the next few years, just as Josef Stalin was emerging as the new Soviet leader after a power struggle with Trotsky and others, a wave of pro-Soviet feeling developed.

In 1932 the venerable Fabian socialists, Mr. and Mrs. Webb, who had always stood for political democracy and personal liberty, heaped praise on "Soviet Civilization" in a substantial study; they praised it among other things for "liquidating the landlord and the capitalist." At just that time Stalin's ruthless war on the kulaks was driving peasants to starvation in a way one can hardly imagine the Webbs approving. What became almost a stampede of writers and intellectuals to the Communist bandwagon later appeared inexplicable, even to the people who joined it. There were, however, some reasons for it.

Bolsheviks and left socialists profited, first of all, by having none of the blood of the world war on their hands. Lenin and a few others, for example Ramsay MacDonald in Great Britain, had rejected the conflict from the beginning. As soon as the Bolsheviks fell heir to collapsing Russia in November 1917, they issued an appeal to the workers of the world to lay down their arms. They continued to denounce the whole European state system as an iniquitous capitalist scheme and to cloak themselves in the garb of pacifism. Lenin provided a Marxist explanation of the great war—caused by imperialistic capitalism—and socialists alleged that universal peace would follow the extinction of the capitalist system. The unpopularity of the war, and the hatred of all war, that pervaded these years redounded to the credit of the Communists. A good deal of sympathy for the Russian bolshevist government, also, was aroused by the shocked horror with which respectable circles regarded it; by their efforts to destroy it through military intervention in 1919–20 (though these were feeble and halfhearted), and by their treatment of it as a pariah for some time after 1920.

Perhaps it is not quite possible to explain the pro-Soviet mood in a rational way. It became a symbol for all those who hated the "establishment." The disillusioned and the naturally rebellious, the unhappy young men and women of the "lost generation," saw here a successful revolution, led by a leader of genius and vision, which had overthrown a vicious and reactionary government in Russia. But whatever sympathy the Soviet "experiment" aroused before 1930, it was the impact of the great depression that caused the rush to Marxism. The Webbs, in the study already mentioned, praised especially the Russian "abandonment of the incentive of profit-making, its extinction of unemployment, its planned production for community consumption."[2] The Western democracies struggled almost hopelessly in

---

[2] Fabian socialism was in considerable confusion because its solutions had seemingly not worked. In her diary, Mrs. Webb observed that "we went seriously wrong . . . in suggesting that we knew how to prevent unemployment. We did not." By 1931 there had been two Labour governments in Britain, yet the expected miracles had not come about. "I am beginning to doubt the inevitability of gradualness," Beatrice Webb sighed.

The Webbs visited Russia for only about three weeks, used materials supplied them by the Soviet government, and allowed Stalin's government to read and correct the manuscript.

the mire of economic depression in the 1930s, while in Russia things seemed to go forward with vigor and drive. The first of the great "five-year plans" for the industrialization of Russia was launched in 1929. "There is no unemployment in Russia": The explanation might be that there was economic slavery there, but in the grim atmosphere of the jobless 1930s even that seemed better than unemployment. As a matter of fact, uncritical books by friends of the Soviet Union poured from the press, indicating that something like a paradise for the worker was being created, with all the old vices missing—vices such as greed, selfishness, prostitution, crime, ignorance. "Planned production for community consumption" had replaced the anarchy of capitalism.

The existence of fascism and then nazism polarized political attitudes and diminished the middle position. Mussolini and Hitler excoriated bolshevism, as did all right-wing, conservative people; therefore if you attacked it you could be accused of being a fascist, or as good as one. (Marxist logic featured a method of reasoning by which "objectively" one could be a fascist without even knowing it.) Some very intelligent people admitted that they loved Soviet Russia for the enemies it made (*vide* André Gide). Communists did fight fascism and nazism; they led the way in the famous Spanish Civil War which pitted the two elements against each other. They showed outstanding courage in fighting as best they could the Fascist and Nazi dictatorships in Italy and Germany.

Much aiding this détente with the Communists was the popular front strategy adopted by the latter after 1934. Prior to that the Communist line had been to denounce the moderate Socialists and Social Democrats as "social fascists" and refuse cooperation with them. Some of the fiercest polemics of the 1920s were exchanged between the old Socialists and the new Communists, who had split off from the Second International to establish the Moscow-directed Third International. Recognizing after Hitler's triumph that they had gravely underestimated fascism (in their blindness, the German Communists actually helped Hitler bring down the Weimar Republic, believing, as their dogma taught, that the collapse of "capitalism" must inevitably lead to socialism and communism), the party line shifted and from Moscow came orders to make friends with all shades of left and liberal opinion and form a united front against fascism. It was one of a number of abrupt and sometimes bewildering shifts which earned the Communists the mistrust of others; but at least it meant, in 1935, that the Communists welcomed the friendship of other left-wing elements, no longer denouncing these as "traitors to the working class" because they refused to join the Communist party. Soon there was a Popular Front government in France, headed by the venerable and prestigious Socialist Leon Blum, a Jaurès disciple. It had its troubles keeping so various an amalgamation of doctrinaires together, but for a short time about 1936–37 the Popular Front seemed a success.

An additional attraction that may be suggested in explanation (if not extenuation) of the intellectuals' defection to communism was Soviet literature and art. The arts in Russia had not yet been placed in an official straitjacket, destroying their creativity and interest. They were graced by such names as Maxim Gorki, one of the greatest of living novelists in the 1930s (a holdover from the prewar era, but an enthusiastic convert to the Soviet regime); Eisenstein, the genius of the silent cinema; Prokofiev and Shostakovich, the composers. Culturally, today, the world of communism has virtually nothing to attract the educated Westerner; this was not so true in the 1920s and early 1930s. Stalinization of all artistic and intellectual activity began as soon as Stalin gained complete power, in 1928; the launching in 1929 of the first five-year plan and the violent campaign to force the peasants into collective farms that peaked in 1931 were landmarks in Stalin's drive to use the disciplined military hierarchy of Party and secret police, under his personal control, to transform society by "storming the heavens" in a gigantic campaign of rapid modernization. This was accompanied by moves to force all branches of thought into line, taking their orders from the Party through Stalin; by 1932 the writers and artists were being regimented as soldiers in the class war, required to join Party-dominated organizations and submit to Party control of their work. But this whole astonishing process was not completed until about 1935. After World War II it reached fantastic extremes during the reign of Zhdanov as cultural minister, when even music could be denounced as "ideologically incorrect" and scientists were persecuted for not paying sufficient heed to dialectical materialism. In fact, tension between artists-writers and the Party had developed in Russia fairly early in the revolution. Lenin denounced as "hooligan Communists" some of the high-spirited poetic types who welcomed the revolution. Mayakovsky, most talented of Russian poets, wrote an ode to Lenin but was soon satirizing the new breed of bureaucrats; he killed himself before the decade was out. Many Russian artists and intellectuals joined Sergei Rachmaninoff, Igor Stravinsky, Nicholas Berdyaev, and others in a massive migration to Paris and other Western cities. Nevertheless the Soviet Union maintained its reputation as excitingly creative in the arts, in the main, until the 1930s.

So about 1930 writers grew interested in communism. They had grown weary of the skepticism of the 1920s. Their mood changed sharply with the coming of the great economic depression and the rise of fascism. They wrote off the esthetes of the 1920s as irresponsibles. "But quite suddenly, in the years of 1930–1935, something happens. The literary climate changes. A new group of writers . . . has made its appearance, and though technically these writers owe something to their predecessors, their 'tendency' is entirely different. Suddenly we have got out of the twilight of the gods into a sort of Boy Scout atmosphere of bare knees and community singing" (George Orwell). Writers became serious, political, almost social-messianic in the spirit of 1848. Conversion from gloom and alienation to hope and social purpose seemed a miracle at the time; only later did Orwell, who went through it, see it as he so wryly describes it above. Writers turned to social realism in the 1930s and pinned their hopes on red revolution. "Drop those priggish ways forever, stop behaving like a stone," the poet W. H. Auden admonished his fellow writers. "Start at once to try to live." Come down from the ivory tower and join a picket line.

The intellectuals, it may be noted, had swung to extremes of commitment and withdrawal in alternate generations ever since the earlier nineteenth century. The exalted idealism of 1848 gave way to pessimism and consolation in art and science; then the intellectuals threw themselves into the great crusade of World War I only to fall back in dismay during the 1920s. There now occurred another sudden swing of the cycle. The mood was not unlike 1914 in its structure, though almost diametrically opposite in its content. A final crisis seemed to confront civilization. One must choose (according to C. Day Lewis):

> Singing I was at peace,
> Above the clouds, outside the ring. . . .
> None such shall be left alive:
> The innocent wing is soon shot down,
> And private stars fade in the blood-red dawn
> Where two worlds strive.*

The flight of the intellectuals to communism reflected in substantial measure their own spiritual predicament. Edward Upward wrote that "I came to it [communism] not so much through consciousness of the political and economic situation as through despair." Koestler commented on "the intellectual comfort and relief found in escaping from a tragic predicament into a 'closed system' of beliefs that left no room for hesitation and doubt." Though not proclaimed as such, but rather as an exact science, the Communist ideology clearly functioned as a substitute religion, too, especially appealing to intellectuals. ("The strongest appeal of the Communist party was that it demanded sacrifice," Louis MacNeice recalled. "You had to sink your ego.") Yet, as such, it proved to be—in the words of a famous symposium on the subject—the god that failed.

The artists and intellectuals who rushed into the arms of communism expected to find there greater freedom, greater creativity, a liberating force. Picasso said that he went to communism as to a spring of fresh water. The great irony is that by 1931, communism had become a system of slavery and an intellectual straitjacket, so that the intellectuals who entered it were condemned to frustration. The Communist party was being so organized as to destroy all intraparty democracy in the Soviet Union and also so as to put the various other party units firmly under the control of Moscow. Communists in other countries were required to serve the Stalin-dictated party line blindly. They were led into the role of apologists for whatever might be done by Stalin, and in the middle 1930s this included the astonishing reign of terror that "purged" almost all the old bolsheviks along with literally millions of others as Stalin systematically destroyed all resistance to his dictatorship.[3] In 1939 it included suddenly becoming the ally of Hitler. While a few agreed to submit their individuality entirely to the party and suspend all ethical considerations for the duration of the battle against capitalism, most found the conditions of intellectual servitude imposed on them intolerable and became disillusioned with

---

*From C. Day Lewis, Selected Poems (New York: Harper & Row, Pub., 1967.)

[3] Careful research indicates that no fewer than twenty million people perished as victims of the Stalinist state in Russia between 1930 and 1950, surpassing Hitler's more famous "holocaust" in numbers. See Robert Conquest, The Great Terror (1971).

the USSR. This was the more true when the party line on literature in the 1930s condemned, as "formalism" and "bourgeois decadence," all the modernisms that were most exciting to Western writers. Kafka, Joyce, Eliot, surrealism, everything that had happened since the turn of the century had to be rejected in favor of "socialist realism." Nor was even this realism supposed to be too realistic, by criticizing the Soviet Union or the Communist party.

Arthur Koestler noted that actual entrance into the Communist party on an active basis, which was his experience, choked off literary expression, but that mild contact with Marxism as "fellow travelers" stimulated any number of writers in the 1930s. John Dos Passos and John Steinbeck wrote memorable works of "social realism" in the United States; Barbusse, Romains, and Malraux in France; Brecht and Seghers in Germany. Some of this mock proletarianism later seemed ridiculous. But from the most intellectual circles of Cambridge University in the 1930s emerged Guy Burgess and Kim Philby to penetrate British foreign office and intelligence citadels as long-time spies for the Soviets, down to the 1950s. Well might Karl Radek (soon to be a victim of Stalin in the high ranks of Soviet leadership) boast that "in the heart of bourgeois England, in Oxford, where the sons of the bourgeoisie receive their final polish, we observe the crystallization of a group which sees salvation only with the proletariat." For a time in the mid-1930s it was *de rigueur* for any young person who aspired to be intellectually alive to praise and even to serve the great Soviet Experiment and to admire extravagantly its mighty leader, Joseph Stalin. ("The man whose silhouette on the gigantic posters appears superimposed on those of Karl Marx and of Lenin, is the man who looks after everything and everybody," Henri Barbusse wrote in his laudatory 1935 biography of Stalin.) Poets like W. H. Auden, former surrealists like Louis Aragon in France, announced their conversion to communism. Even Virginia Woolf could be found writing for the *Daily Worker*.

That spectacle of all his heroes abasing themselves before a great tyrant and mass-murderer, in Malcolm Muggeridge's words, caused many a person later to have doubts about the political wisdom of intellectuals. Their hatred of nazism and fascism was worthy of respect; their naiveté in being taken in by Stalin's "guided tours" of the USSR was another matter. Few seemed to want to know much about the real Russia: "I never met any who had the slightest interest in any side of Russia which was not Stalinist propagandist presentation," Stephen Spender recalled of the intellectual Communists. But an exodus from the Party began in 1937, increased in 1939, was somewhat reversed during World War II only to resume during the post-1945 cold war years, when cries of "mea culpa" became a chorus of the Western 1930s generation. They might not abandon their revolutionary or Marxist views in leaving the party; they might claim (plausibly) that Stalin had betrayed the revolution and perverted Marx, as well as Lenin. But the exodus from the party that began about 1937 led most of the converts eventually away from the whole Marxist framework.

Whatever their future destinations, the Left writers departed for them from their Red rendezvous at the end of the 1930s and later treated it for the most part as a mistake. A great deal was written by the one-time Communists about their odyssey in and out of the Party. In his great novel *Darkness at Noon,* Arthur Koestler tried to depict the self-destroying psychology of the Communist who had given over his mind and soul to the Party. Koestler has described his own rather horrifying experience within the Party as a "spiritual discipline" that he would not wish to see expunged from his past, though he came to regard it as an intellectual error. (See *The Invisible Writing.*) A few, like Picasso and Bertolt Brecht, remained; the latter faced and accepted with unusual clarity the decision to lose one's individuality in the Party, to cease thinking and become nameless and faceless, "blank sheets on which the Revolution will write its orders, " prepared to "sink into the mud" and "commit any vileness" in order that the cause might prosper. It was a decision any Communist had to make if staying in the Stalinist party. But it was a singular position for writers or artists to accept, and Brecht was one of the few great ones able to do so. (Brecht's experience suggests the difficulties of the creative writer under communism; for his plays, written in a "modern," *avant-garde* manner, were not performed in Communist countries though he became their most distinguished literary property. In actuality Brecht was never comfortable in the Soviet Union, from which at one time he had fled.)

Leon Trotsky, Lenin's chief lieutenant in the Revolution, who was driven into exile and ultimately assassinated by Stalinists, provided a rallying point for some who wished to remain revolutionary Marxists while repudiating Soviet communism under Stalin. Trotskyites regarded Stalinism as having perverted socialism by the errors of bureaucratization and the cult of personality. They were prone to criticize the lack of intraparty democracy and even the lack of personal freedom in the USSR, yet they remained attached to revolutionary Leninism including the rule of the party as "vanguard" or proletarian elite. On the whole, this group faded out too, after playing some part for a time as the resting place for those disillusioned with events in Russia but not prepared to abandon revolutionary socialism. It would revive a generation later.

An examination of the multitudinous self-analyses of ex-Communists of the 1930s and 1940s leads one to conclude that the chief reasons for disenchantment were the following: the discovery that Marxist ideology is an illusion blinding one to reality; concern about destruction of moral integrity from having to subordinate truth and standards of decency to the Party cause; the Party's ruthless subordination of the individual to its demands; failure to find artistic fulfillment in communism, indeed the opposite, a stultifying effect; and eye-opening discoveries about conditions in Russia, especially the tyrannical treatment of people. Inherently undisciplined, freedom-loving artists were usually quite miserable if they actually entered the Party and were required to submit to its iron discipline. Harold Laski, distinguished left-wing theoretician of the British Labour party who was procommunist in the 1930s, reacted at length against "deception, ruthlessness, contempt for fair play, willingness to use lying and treachery . . . dishonesty in the presentation of facts." Changes in the party line required embarrassing shifts. What one believed depended on the latest word from Moscow. Stalinism gradually destroyed whatever artistic creativity and freedom of thought there had been in Russia and erected a monstrous tyranny which killed and imprisoned millions. This became increasingly obvious to even the most ideology-blinded partisan.

George Orwell's disenchantment with communism came in Spain, where he like so many other intellectuals went in 1936 to fight for the forces of light against those of darkness, for the Spanish Republic against the right-wing rebels backed by Mussolini and Hitler. The future author of *Animal Farm* and *1984,* those devastating satires on Stalinism, saw his friends among a minor socialist party, the POUM, arrested and killed, as well as lied about, by the Republican regime, which had fallen under Soviet Russian influence because only Stalin was sending military aid. Returning from Spain to write about his experiences, Orwell found few on the Left prepared to accept his indictment of the communists, and even had trouble getting his book published, so pro-Communist was the intellectual world at this moment. Orwell wrote as a democratic socialist now convinced that Soviet totalitarianism was the worst enemy of socialism, and filled with disgust at the "smelly little orthodoxies" which bedevilled the world. Of these dehumanizing ideologies, Stalinist Marxism was as bad as Hiterlite national socialism in his view. This was heresy among pre-1939 intellectuals.

During World War II, wartime friendship between the Soviet Union and the Western democracies brought a temporary resurgence of communism within the latter, but the strained relations between Russia and the West after 1945 had the opposite result. Dogmatic Marxism suffered a precipitate decline in Great Britain and the United States. It declined to a lesser degree in Italy and France, perhaps because of a curious affinity between its dogmatic and apocalyptic mood and that of Roman Catholic Christianity. Especially on the Continent, a revival of Marxism lay ahead, but it was another kind of Marx people now discovered—not the Stalinist deformation, the obsolete dogmas, but the ethical protest against capitalism, the denunciation of the workers' alienation from work and from society, which they regarded as the essence of Marx. Of this, more later.

OTHER SOCIAL MOVEMENTS

There were other "progressive" social movements in the decade of depression that were not Marxist but which assailed the existing order of capitalism. The great economic depression caused a searching reappraisal of existing, "classical" economic theory. Among the revisers of economic orthodoxy the Englishman John Maynard Keynes stood out as an acute, penetrating, and incisive mind with a gift of literary expression. Keynes, who had challenged conventional public finance methods in the 1920s, came in the 1930s to put his views in the form of a general theory (1936). Pared down to its essentials, the Keynesian view was that contrary to the old theory there is no automatic tendency toward full employment in the free economy (Say's law); rather, there can be stagnation with unused human resources. This is because, among other things, the community's total savings are not necessarily invested in capital equipment. The interest rate, which is supposed to provide the automatic mechanism for insuring the investment of savings (the rate falling as savings rise), may not function effectively because liquidity preference (desire to keep funds in cash form easily obtainable) causes savers to accept a lower return on their money than they could get. Keynes stressed the propensity to over-save and under-invest in a mature capitalist economy; the result can be economic stagnation. The economy cannot be counted upon to right itself, as the older economics taught. It may have to be righted by the intervention of the government. Formerly the approved policy for dealing with depression was for the government to pare its expenditures and balance its budget, and governments did this during the early stage of the 1930s depression, with apparently ineffective results. The new economics called for an unbalanced budget, the government throwing its overspending into the economic stream to break the logjam.

Thus the new economics, as advocated by Keynes and his followers along with some others (the Swedish school was prominent), encouraged statism though not socialism (public ownership). The private economy can work effectively but it requires regulating with the great fiscal resources of the government used as a balance wheel. Interest rates can be manipulated by government action, the expenditures of the government can be varied, taxes raised or lowered according to the needs of the economy at any given time. The Keynesian view, roughly, prevailed, in that orthodox economic theory soon accepted a modicum of the new economics while governments, even conservative ones, accepted their responsibility to "maintain full employment" by use of a variety of powers such as those mentioned. This was an economic revolution and perhaps by implication a political and social one. It cast the "public sector" of the economy in a new and much more active role. It provided, as some saw it, a democratic alternative to Communist totalitarianism in the area of national economic planning. To others, the "Keynesian revolution" and the "welfare state" were steps on the "road to serfdom" (F. A. Hayek) only slightly less alarming than red bolshevism; they too reflected the coloration of the Pink Decade.

The infatuation of creative writers with social issues in the 1930s left behind remarkable literary deposits, now somewhat out of style but bound to remain as landmarks for the historian to contemplate, some of them awe-inspiring in their sheer magnitude. For example, Jules Romains, the French socialist novelist, wrote ten thousand pages in his mammoth multivolume novel of social realism, *Men of Good Will,* outdoing Marcel Proust in length if not in quality, and intended to rival Balzac's great *Human Comedy* of a century earlier as a picture of the social world. Politicians, capitalists, industrialists, as well as intellectuals seeking to set the world right, fill these pages. The criticism made of Romains and other novels of this sort (the Englishman Robert Briffault and the American Upton Sinclair were among others addicted to it) is, for one thing, that they really had no firsthand knowledge of capitalists and politicians (or workers!) but invented stereotypes of what Marxist or left-liberal theory required them to believe of such individuals. Social realism was often wildly unrealistic. And it was frequently unutterably dreary: sermons flavored with melodrama. It was often enough the fruit of a blind ideological faith. Romains's huge opus is nevertheless a tribute to the moral earnestness of the writers of the 1930s and their desire to bring life back into the scope of art and intellect. Among the curiosities of the 1930s "social realism" was the "Mass Observation poem" poem attempted in England, originating in those who wanted to be both surrealist and communist. Thousands of people all over the country were supposed to send in their literary reports on a single event, the coronation of George VI, from which a composite poem would somehow be created. Predictably, the result was not impressive.

While simple and drastic positions such as Stalinist communism tended to prevail in the anxious 1930s, during which the Western world suffered the ravages of economic depression and watched the drift toward another war, there were subtler variations on the theme of Marxism. The Frankfurt Institute for Social Research to which belonged such German intellectuals as Max Horkheimer, Herbert Marcuse, and Theodor Adorno, specialized in a nondogmatic, more humanistic Marxism. Thrown out of Germany by Hitler in the early 1930s, the Institute ended in New York City as part of that great cultural migration of German scholars, scientists, and intellectuals that so altered American intellectual life. The moment for this critical Marxism, more concerned with the quality of culture than with revolutionary violence, came much later: Marcuse as an old man was to become the sage of the youth movement of the 1960s, in one of the many odd twists of intellectual history. In the interwar period these sophisticated social theorists discovered Marx's unknown early writings, rejected both Stalinism and Social Democracy as simplistic perversions of Marx, experimented in Freudian, existential, or phenomenological graftings onto Marxism. They were an esoteric elite at this time but were later to be seen as pioneers. There were other such left-wing groups in Germany during the Weimar years, all of course destroyed by the Nazi revolution, which did not pause to distinguish between shadings of Marxism, the more so since these circles tended to be heavily Jewish (this was true of the Frankfurt school).

Throughout everything, whatever their other disagreements, writers, intellectuals, political leftists, clergy, and almost everybody else joined in one fervent sentiment: *nie wieder Krieg,* no more war. The war dominated literature. Romains's epic, just mentioned, paused for a whole volume at the battle of Verdun; Ernest Hemingway immortalized Caporetto; the most famous and poignant of all, Erich Maria Remarque's *All Quiet on the Western Front (Im Westen Nichts Neues),* cemented the postwar reconciliation of Germans and French and English on the common sentiment of shuddering abhorrence of the whole grisly event. But a few outstanding examples cannot begin to suggest the extent to which the war provided themes for the novel, memoirs, and likewise serious thought. The huge historical *postmortem* into the causes of the war extended to the popular level. The fashionable radicalism attributed war to the dynamics of the capitalist system or, more naively, to the conspiracies of munitions makers. Such analyses often partook of fantasy more than fact: The widely read book of a British aristocrat turned Communist, John Strachey, *The Coming Struggle for Power* (1932), predicted a war between the United States and Great Britain as the climax of world capitalism's imminent collapse (and also predicted Communist rather than Nazi victory in Germany). But they suited the spirit of the times. Young people took the Oxford Oath, in England, vowing never again to fight for king and country. They repudiated this vow, under the threat of nazism, in the later 1930s. This feeling was in good part responsible for the weakness of the Western democracies in the face of Hitler's post-1935 Nazi challenge; a generation fed on antiwar literature could not admit the thought of war even against the worst of evils. The final tragic irony of this generation was that it had to go back to war, which it hated, in order to destroy fascism and nazism, themselves products of the first war's brutalization of humanity.

Despite its startling modishness, the left-wing socialist or communist position by no means monopolized the 1930s. Apart from the few who followed fascism, a rather distinguished traditional rightism struggled to stem the leftward tide. The Christian revival associated with Karl Barth, Jacques Maritain (neo-Thomism), and Reinhold Niebuhr continued without much interruption. It might sometimes interact with the eschatological visions of the far Left, but in the 1930s, T. S. Eliot announced himself a royalist and a High Anglican and as editor of *Criterion* sought to rally religious humanists to a defense of traditional values against both fascism and communism—which he saw as debased rival religions, successful only if Christian culture failed to assert its message. In France there were many right-wing journals of the intellectuals; Georges Bernanos and Emmanuel Mounier are examples of deeply committed, rather unorthodox, but in some ways highly reactionary leaders of thought. Evelyn Waugh and C. S. Lewis made their way back to "mere Christianity," while Toynbee *A Study of History,* (1939) looked to a religious revival as the only way to recovery. There is something to Evelyn Waugh's complaint that Auden, Spender, et al., "ganged up and captured the decade," leaving behind the impression that everybody had gone far left. This was not wholly so. Auden himself, a great poet who initially was the drillmaster of the Left march—"Wystan, lone flyer, birdman, my bully boy!" as Day Lewis hailed him—by the end of the decade had become a Christian.

THE REVOLUTION IN PHILOSOPHY

A. J. Ayer, the British philosopher identified with "logical positivism" in the 1930s, recalled that "there was a moment when Philip Toynbee almost, but not quite, persuaded me to join the Communist Party. I have to confess that my reason for refusing was not so much that I disbelieved in dialectical materialism as that I recoiled from the idea of party discipline." There was undoubtedly some connection between the mood of this "revolution in philosophy" (self-styled) and the decade of political radicalism. The Vienna Circle tended to be leftish: Otto Neurath had been a member of the brief Spartacist revolutionary regime in Munich in 1919. Logical positivism began life as an iconoclastic doctrine, whatever it may later have become; "the old men were outraged," as Ayer recalls with glee. But its origins went back some years and led to Vienna as well as to the British universities, especially Cambridge.

Logical positivism originated with a group of philosophers and mathematicians active at the University of Vienna from about 1920 until nazism and war dispersed them in the 1930s, whereupon many of them went to Great Britain and the United States and exerted a considerable influence while blending with certain native traditions in these countries. These included Schlick, Carnap, Neurath, and Wittgenstein, the latter going to Cambridge University early. They owed something to the prewar teaching at Vienna of Ernst Mach's "empirio-criticism," a careful analysis of the immediate data of experience based on the neo-Kantian view that only sense data exist and one cannot know the thing-in-itself.[4] In Britain, the influence of Ludwig Wittgenstein (*Tractatus-Logico-Philosophicus,* 1921) blended with a somewhat related movement stemming from G. E. Moore and Bertrand Russell, Cambridge philosophers who broke with the dominant school of idealism beginning about 1900. Their roots were plainly in British empiricism; this was the spirit of Bacon, Locke, and Hume, marked by a tendency to avoid all metaphysical flights, concentrate on careful analysis of actual experience, break problems down into their smallest components, watch out for the loose use of terms, and construct no "systems." The early Wittgenstein joined forces with Russell's "logical atomism"; the later Wittgenstein's keen interest in the logical structure of language reenforced Moore's influence to open up marvelous horizons of subtle inquiry to a generation of "linguistic analysts."

The basic postulate was that philosophical method must be "scientific." Science is not only clear, logical, rational, analytical but also "verifiable by sense experience." The application of these criteria suggested that for philosophy there is no specific end or content; its function must be to help the sciences—which alone can provide knowledge, since empirical investigation is the only sort of knowledge. "The business of philosophy is not to establish a set of philosophical propositions but to make other propositions clear." To clarify the meaning of words and statements might seem a modest goal but it can be most useful. If science experiments and verifies, philosophy defines and clarifies. Many meaningless problems and much nonsense may be removed by the rigorous analysis of words. Indeed the method might be extended to other fields, such as politics or ethics, to clear up confusions by defining terms, thus locating the problems. The early Wittgenstein held that one may by analysis reduce reality to simple, atomic facts (the Viennese had learned from Russell's "logical atomism") and then frame statements which correspond to these facts.

---

[4]Lenin, reading Mach, wrote a furious rebuttal defending Marxist materialism, which he felt to be threatened by this disguised idealism, arguing for a direct-copy realism in which objective reality simply prints itself on the mind without the latter contributing anything substantial (*Materialism and Empiriocriticism*). Philosophers generally found this naive. Lenin accused the phenomenalists or "empirio-critics" of opening the way for reactionary mysticism.

Perhaps this revolution in philosophy may be best characterized by saying that philosophy ceased to be a "search for wisdom" or a quest for absolute answers and became instead just the logic of science or the clarifier of scientific methods and concepts. To those who protested that philosophy was abdicating its chief function and leaving modern humanity, which never so needed help with its values, high and dry, the answer given by philosophers of the new dispensation was that unfortunately this cannot be the philosopher's function. These philosophers were "positivists"; that is, they carried on the tradition, with a greater rigor and clarity, of regarding metaphysics (absolute being and value, transcendental reality) as not a true object of knowledge. One cannot really say anything rational about that. If some, the poets or the seers, want to speak to this question, let them; this is not the realm of clear logical thought which is the philosopher's. Reproducing an argument among the nineteenth-century positivists, some of the new positivists said that statements beyond the realm of verifiable sense experience are merely beyond the competence of the philosopher, while others denied the right to talk about them at all.[5]

The most extreme statement of the new school came from the English philosopher A. J. Ayer in the 1930s. No problems exist, Ayer suggested, except the factual ones of science. All the others can be shown by linguistic analysis to be nonexistent, pseudo problems. Most of the things philosophers and theologians and moralists had been worrying about through the centuries—God, freedom, spirit, purpose, morals, and so forth—were complete wastes of time. They can be shown to be either wrong statements of the problem or else purely personal or "emotive" projections of the feelings of the individual concerned, about which there can be no fruitful argument. Some of them can be reduced to empirical, testable statements, and these in principle can be solved by the scientist (empirical investigator). The rest must be dismissed as so much empty wind.

The shock effect of this position is evident. As someone has remarked, theologians who were accustomed to being told they were wrong found themselves speechless at being told they were not saying anything at all! Applied to morality, logical positivism might be extremely subversive. Statements of value not being empirically verifiable, they become mere expressions of preference. "I think adultery is wrong" is the same sort of statement as "I hate spinach" or "I dislike abstract art." (Though Hume had said something similar in the eighteenth century, he had been willing to fall back on custom and the consensus of humanity; twentieth-century skeptics had scant respect for either.) Strictly speaking, they only pointed out that logical thought can supply no sanctions for behavior; we must look elsewhere for values of this sort. It is open to us to find them in religion or in social utility. At the same time, the frank equation of moral tastes with other kinds of

---

[5] Neo-Kantianism strongly revived in Germany in the later nineteenth century, influencing such social philosophers as Wilhelm Dilthey and Max Weber. Their distinction between the natural and human sciences (*Geisteswissenschaften*), which unlike the natural ones do not seek lawlike generalizations but the understanding of subjective meanings, owed something to this philosophic school, as did also Weber's conviction that empirical science cannot find values, which are the province of religion, leading to his advocacy of a "value-free" social science.

personal taste might be construed as issuing an invitation to moral libertinism. Presumably I should choose my conduct in the same sort of way I choose my neckties—all a matter of personal taste. And if I try to defend one sort of conduct against another by any sort of rational argument, I am talking nonsense.

Language was always a preoccupation of the logical positivist school. To avoid the dread beast metaphysics, one must be careful to use only words such as relate to empirically verifiable facts. Meaningless words, like God, the Idea, the Absolute, have been responsible for metaphysical nonsense. Rudolf Carnap tried to create a logical language, whereby we would use symbols rather than words in the interest of greater clarity. Since languages as they are tend to be untrustworthy guides, disguising and distorting thought, we must purify or clarify them or invent an entirely new, logically sound one. The astringent critique of terminology could lead to such statements as "all philosophy is a critique of language" or "most of the propositions and questions of philosophers arise from our failure to understand the logic of our language." Accused of trivializing the great questions of life by turning them into quibbles about words, philosophers of the linguistic analysis school were convinced that misuse of language is the prime source of confusions in thinking. But in his later years Ludwig Wittgenstein, Austrian-born Oxford professor who was the most colorful and incisive philosopher of his age, changed rather dramatically. Well known only after his death in the 1950s, Wittgenstein's later thinking was marked by skepticism rather than certainty, for we do not, he thought, have any way of knowing whether our language fits external reality or not; we are its total prisoner. In what could we talk about the relationships between language and reality? It would have to be in language—mathematics and logic reduce to words in the end—and so we cannot escape the web of language; therefore, we cannot think about its relationship to the world. Wittgenstein's discovery of this inherent human limitation, tantamount to not being able to jump out of our skin, is analogous to the physicist's discovery in the same period that we cannot be objective observers of electrons since we have to use electrons to observe them.

The later Wittgenstein gave up the Carnapian attempt to devise a new, perfectly logical language. We must make do with the language we have, a rich legacy of thousands of years of human experience. It is a tangled legacy; ordinary language is full of logical mixups which the philosopher can perhaps untangle, thus helping us to greater clarity. Wittgenstein indeed held that most if not all of the philosophical questions that have puzzled people through the ages, the "metaphysical" questions about free will, the meaning of life, and so on, and many other questions as well, disappear when we have properly defined terms and clarified syntax; we see that they aren't really questions at all, simply confusions of language. In a famous Wittgenstein phrase, we let the fly out of the bottle—a kind of philosophical therapy which one might compare to Freud's. The legacy of the later Wittgenstein was "ordinary language" philosophy—often the target of criticism for dealing with the minutiae of speech. But doubtless it is true that many problems are pseudoproblems caused by linguistic confusions, and doubtless it is defensible to argue that we can never get anywhere unless we start by clarifying each individual proposition.

An arid verbalism and a cloistered timidity marked the linguistic school, critics claimed; existentialists and analysts stared at each other uncomprehendingly at philosophic conferences, in one of the many little wars of knowledge characteristic of recent times. But "the absence of any dogma or jargon, any universal method, any claim to finality" together with the keenness and closeness of its thought impressed other observers of English philosophy. In the 1920s and 1930s, logical positivism's astringency, skepticism, and almost nihilistic tendencies recommended it. And in this respect it bore some resemblance to such other phenomena as the prose of Ernest Hemingway. One has only to read the first sentence of Ayer's "manifesto," *Language, Truth and Logic* (1935), to sense this mood: "The traditional disputes of philosophers are, for the most part, as unwarranted as they are unfruitful."

But the giant figure of this group, Ludwig Wittgenstein, was far from a pedestrian personality. The Vienna-born philosopher, scion of a remarkable family, had been an accomplished aeronautical engineering student before swinging to philosophy under Russell's influence. After publication of *Tractatus*—the only book he ever published in his lifetime—having reached the celebrated conclusion that we cannot say anything about ultimate values and so had better be silent about them, he became a village schoolteacher; a visit to the Soviet Union evidently disillusioned him with that path. He interested himself in Oriental philosophy. He returned to philosophy at the end of the 1920s and became a famous figure at Oxford and then Cambridge; the dimensions of his revised thought only struck the public after his death, when his *Philosophical Investigations* were published in 1953. Clearly Wittgenstein was a deeply committed, even mystical person; that he said nothing about the "great questions" was because he thought them beyond the reach of formal thought, not because he disdained them. "When all scientific questions have been answered, the problems of life remain untouched." He retired to an Irish fishing village in 1947 where the natives found him charming the birds. Now widely recognized as one of the three or four greatest twentieth-century philosophers, his lode of wisdom is still being mined; it was wisdom in concrete specifics, for he gave up any attempt to formulate a "system." And it was profoundly caged within our mental structures: language tells us nothing about the world, only about itself.

The astringent and analytical spirit appeared also in English literary criticism. The magazine *Scrutiny,* edited by Oxford professor F. R. Leavis, founded in the 1930s and published until 1953, encouraged what its title suggested, a meticulous line-by-line examination of poetry, in reaction against both the chatty sort of armchair talk about literature that had passed for criticism in Victorian times and against lack of clear literary standards. The scrutinizers thought of themselves as cutting away large husks of sentimentality with a keen razor of critical analysis, in order to get down to the solid core of real literary value. Like the analytic philosophers, they were to be accused of aridity and pedantry; in 1945 a fairly strong reaction against them set in. But they succeeded in introducing what seemed like a scientific expertness in the examination of the arts. Somehow this was bracing.

For science commanded great respect. Progress went on in numerous areas of science, though sometimes it seemed rather gloomy progress. It was at this time that genetics became a fashionable study. Psychology, in the universities, lay more under the influence of J. B. Watson, the behaviorist, and the Russian, Pavlov, than of the more speculative theories of Freud and Jung. Eschewing any attempt to analyze interior states of mind as unsuitable for the scientific method, the behaviorists stuck to measurable observations of external behavior. This was an American school but for a time found considerable international favor. In its more dogmatic moods it was inclined to insist that human nature is determined by its environment in a mechanical sort of way, that life is made up of a series of conditioned reflexes, and that mind, as such, does not exist, there being only a pattern of electric reactions in brain tissue. Very positivist, even eighteenth century.

"Scientific humanism" was a term much in use; what it meant, roughly, was the possibility of raising humanity to new heights by the use of science alone, with heavy overtones of hostility to traditional religion. But to many the march of science threatened dehumanization. In his *Brave New World Revisited* (1959), written twenty-seven years after his famous depiction of what might be the fate of humanity in a few centuries when it had been totally organized in accordance with scientific techniques, Aldous Huxley noted the use of Pavlovian theories in the brainwashing techniques practiced by the Chinese Communists. His *Brave New World,* he felt, had all but come true in a mere quarter of a century. Freedom and individuality would be sacrificed to the demands of the machine, large-scale organization, and technological progress. In the years since 1920 there has always gone on a lively controversy between those who hail science and technology as the liberator and savior of humanity and those who fear it is being enslaved and spiritually destroyed by these terrible servants. With the spectacular advances in science and technology of these years, the issue became an urgent one.

EXISTENTIALISM

The triumph of severely analytical, rational, scientific modes of philosophizing in England, Austria, the Scandinavian countries, soon in the United States (carried there directly by Rudolf Carnap and other Austrian refugees after 1938 as well as by British influences and offshoots of native pragmatism) was, strangely enough, completely reversed in much of the rest of continental Europe, where a highly nonrational sort of philosophy came into prominence in the 1930s.

Born between the wars chiefly in the writings of the German philosopher Martin Heidegger, "existentialism" did not become well known until just after World War II, when it leaped into international prominence largely owing to the brilliance of one of the outstanding writers and thinkers of modern times, Jean-Paul Sartre. Sartre has been novelist, playwright, editor, essayist, and political activist as well as philosopher (author of the long and difficult *Being and Nothingness*)—a combination of talents that, given the quantity and range of his writings and his role as moral and intellectual leader of a generation, made him something of a modern Voltaire. He was seldom out of the limelight for forty years between his sensational first novel of 1938 and his death in 1980. His fellow Frenchman, the Algerian-born essayist and novelist Albert Camus, killed in an accident in 1960, joined Sartre in leadership of the "second lost generation" after 1945. With all gods really dead now, nothing to believe in, the existentialists quite remarkably turned to humanity itself to find new values.

Though the experiences of the war are often regarded as decisive in the shaping of existentialism, the fact is that Sartre's mind was formed in the 1920s and 1930s, and his bitter alienation as well as his ambivalent attachment to Marxism came out of that epoch. After graduating from the super-elite Ecole Normale Superieur with a dual interest in philosophy and literature—a key to his whole subsequent achievement—Sartre was still searching for what he wanted and found it in Berlin in 1933-34 where at the suggestion of Raymond Aron he went to study Edmund Husserl and Martin Heidegger. To a significant degree, Sartre took his key ideas from these philosophers; but he put his own original stamp on them and cannot be regarded as merely a popularizer of the two great Germans. Among these three thinkers there was a pattern of mutual rejection as well as influence, for Husserl rejected his pupil Heidegger and both repudiated Sartre, who in turn did not like Heidegger chiefly because of the latter's political stance. Yet all three share certain basic very striking postulates of what had begun as the Phenomenology of Husserl, was carried on in Heidegger's *Existenzphilosophie,* and emerged as the Existentialism of Sartre.

Jean-Paul Sartre, shown in a December 1974 photo taken during his 70th year. (UPI/Bettman Archive.)

Husserl's initial publications on what he called Phenomenology (a term found earlier, it will be recalled, in Hegel) date from 1901. Since this German-Jewish philosopher, born like Freud in Moravia at about the same time (1859), was influenced by the Viennese philosopher Franz Brentano, it is tempting to associate Husserl's explorations of the inner self with Freud's, although they took somewhat different forms. Husserl sought a science of inward states. What lies in the consciousness as pure receptivity, if we could pare away or put on one side ("bracket") all content? What is in the mind, we might put it, before anything specific is in it? Consciousness must have objects, it is that very different form of being that responds to or "intends" objects. A thirst for the deepest form of reality that lies behind all ideas, all theories, not subject to any preconceived categories, marked Phenomenology. Husserl initially hoped to be able, by the exercise of bracketing out all objects, to find and classify these original states of consciousness—rather like Kant's categories of the understanding, but far deeper (for our Logic like other ideas is an invention of the mind which becomes an object.) This proved impossible; how can consciousness stand outside consciousness? This is like Wittgenstein's discovery that there is nothing in which we can talk about language. Husserl in his later thought (he lived until 1938), again rather like the Viennese-born philosopher Wittgenstein, retreated to more specific, concrete approaches to the phenomenological "life world," abandoning systems ("the day of systems is over").

In time Phenomenology became one of the most widely taught modes of modern philosophy. In 1927, the brilliant Heidegger put it on the map with his *Sein und Zeit* (Vol. I; the second volume never was published). For young Germans eagerly looking for new answers amid the postwar wreckage of values,[6] Heidegger added moral relevance to the austere scientism of Husserl: Inside consciousness lurks that Being with which modern humanity has lost touch, through an excess of abstractness, and must rediscover on pain of extinction. Heidegger succeeded to Husserl's chair at Freiburg University in 1928. In the Nazi years, he fell silent after an initial sympathy with Nazism which was to compromise his standing for a long time among Western intellectuals. Like Wittgenstein, Heidegger's reputation soared in his later years, especially after his death in 1976. Many would now rank him with Wittgenstein as among the greatest philosophers of the century.

Sartre's special contribution was to take Husserl and Heidegger off the academic shelf, giving them sharp relevance to contemporary life, and to make their abstractions vividly real with the aid of his powerful literary imagination. In Sartre's hands, Phenomenology became bitterly pessimistic though tinged with a dash of desperate hope. Sartre's first major work was the extraordinary novel *Nausea* (1938), which was a dramatization of his own phenomenological existentialism. Its central figure had indeed been stripped down to bare existence; he has no job, no home, he loses his girl and is friendless, and he has only the task of finishing his historical doctoral dissertation, which he abandons as meaningless. Roquentin was

[6] See the striking passage in Hans-Georg Gadamer, *Philosophical Hermeneutics,* transl. David E. Linge (1976), pp. 133–39.

an alienated hero for his time. Reduced to pure consciousness, he experiences the anxiety and despair that comes from realizing the absurdity and contingency of existence and the basic nothingness of our selves. Sartre radicalized Heidegger's concept of the self by depriving it of any essence or transcendence; consciousness is nothing but a series of responses to objects, it has no core of identity unless we artificially manufacture one.[7] The hero of *Nausea* experiences nausea (at his own body, his own face in the mirror), he loses his ability to participate in life, even to prevent a crime. (The famous New York City episode of a few years ago in which scores of people stood aside and failed to intervene as a grisly crime was being committed suggests that the modern megalopolis is filled with dehumanized Roquentins.) But in the end, he seems to be saved by the realization that his nothingness-consciousness is radically free to invent meaning for the world. Roquentin finds himself through a literary project—which Sartre soon came to think inadequate. But he made a commitment. The human situation is an almost impossible one because we want to have objective being, grounded in some necessity, yet are condemned to be the other kind of being that has no objectivity or necessity. In Sartre's vocabulary, ultimately derived from Hegel, the *pour-soi* or for-itself is human consciousness; *en-soi* or being-in-itself is other being. It is the dilemma of human existence that we yearn for solidity of objective being but cannot find it except at the cost of doing violence to our *pour-soi* selves—as when we are *constituted* in the eyes of other people, who make objects of us, assign us our roles. In sum, people are condemned to try to reconcile two radically different and irreconcilable modes of being. "Man is a useless passion"; "a being who is what he is not and is not what he is."

The masterly, disturbing philosophical novel *Nausea* was followed by Sartre's philosophical treatise *Being and Nothingness* (1943) and by a series of plays during the war which stamped him as the intellectual leader of his generation. The German occupation of France after humiliating defeat in the *blitzkrieg* war of 1940 forced stark choices on Frenchmen: to collaborate or to resist. Sartre became active in the resistance movement as editor and writer, was imprisoned by the Nazis yet had his play *The Flies* presented in 1943: It was interpreted as a disguised anti-Nazi message. Upon the liberation of Paris in 1944, Sartre's most famous play, *No Exit,* was the first to be performed. He had become a remarkable kind of national hero and even world intellectual hero. The war experience changed Sartre into a believer in the need for action, not just writing, as the existential choice one must make to discover "authentic" being. Choose, act, be "committed," and in so doing bestow meaning and dignity on an absurd world—such was the message emanating from Paris at the end of the terrible war. The ethic of existentialism was that no one can choose for us, we cannot find the answers in any prescribed code, to do so is "bad

---

[7]This may be expressed by saying that to Husserl Ego and consciousness are the same, whereas Sartre sees the Ego as an idea made up by the consciousness, an object. To Sartre, there is only consciousness which has no structure, though it evidently has the ability to invent reality, via imagination. Heidegger thought "Ego" a term too suggestive of objectivity and spoke of the "Da-Sein," the being-there, a piece of consciousness "thrown" into the world.

faith," inauthentic being. I must understand that the choice is mine alone on the basis of my own unique situation.

Existentialism drew on earlier ideas and indeed one of its attractive features was its absorption of much of the gropings of European thought and expression since 1800, or perhaps even earlier, into one structure; there is something here of a *philosophia perennia*. In one sense it is the ultimate Nietzscheanism. Sartre once wrote that "existentialism is . . . an attempt to draw all the consequences from a consistent atheist position." "Dostoyevsky has written that if God did not exist, all would be permitted. That is Existentialism's starting point." If we really grasp the meaning of modern godless man's plight, we are at first reduced to nausea and despair. We must pass through the awful sense of depression that accompanies a real insight into man's condition. He is alone, for he cannot really communicate with others. He finds himself in a world to which he is utterly alien and which has no purpose or meaning. Society, too, is at work trying to depersonalize him, make him into a cog in the machine, make him play a role that crushes his individuality. But on the far side of this abyss (existentialism is a "philosophy of the abyss," Emmanuel Mounier said) there is one message of salvation, one ground of hope: man, the human consciousness, is after all left. He is somehow here, able to react; even in feeling despair, he shows the possibility of bestowing value on the meaningless world. As Camus noted, the world is absurd; but then it could not be absurd unless men judged it to be so; this feeling of the absurd itself is the start of philosophy.

For man, "existence is prior to essence," Kierkegaard had already asserted. This striking idea found reenforcement in the naturalistic outlook of Darwin, as well as in the psychology of Freud. Reason does not precede and determine man, but vice versa; man exists, and his will to exist leads him to invent "rational" systems, which are thus not ultimate but are a product of his drives, instincts, fears, hopes. It is of the nature of the human being to be unique, a concrete particular not to be understood by membership in a class or group, like other objects. True, insofar as a man is flesh he is the usual kind of being; moreover society is always at work trying to make him into a stereotyped object.

My own past, insofar as I look at it as something vanished and dead, is being of this sort. But human consciousness, as it exists in our minds every moment, *now,* is a radically different kind of thing. The *pour-soi* is actually not being at all, but a kind of "hole in being." This striking analysis of human consciousness owed a great deal not only to Husserl but to Hegel's *The Phenomenology of Mind.* Thus there is an undercurrent of thought here reaching back to the earlier nineteenth century, as in the case of Freud.

If Sartre's analysis of this elusive substance is sometimes a bit fuzzy, it is a remarkably stimulating effort to examine what seldom has been examined. It provided him with the basis for both his pessimism and his optimism. There can be no God, for our consciousness-being submits to no generalization, there can be no being-in-general. And there cannot really be any happy relationships between people. The other person is an object to me, and I to the other person. We try to reject the other person's reducing us to an object. The realm of interpersonal relationships is to Sartre condemned to frustration, at best. "Hell is other people," as one of the most famous of his plays points out. The individual could only be happy if able to structure the entire universe to fit his ego, and this of course is impossible.

"This world is without importance, and whoever recognizes this fact wins his freedom," one of Camus's characters observes. When we realize that with each choice and act we not only make ourselves but give the whole universe what value it has, we have discovered the dignity of being human. Then we must be "committed," we must believe nothing that is merely idle opinion—what we believe must be for life. Like Nietzsche we must grasp it with our whole heart and soul, not merely with the "cold prying tantacles" of conceptual thought.

The rational is *not* the real, as Hegel taught. Existence is not rational, but even absurd; it simply is, and we cannot possibly reason about it—being it ourselves. Only some superhuman being could do that. Existence is a brute fact. We come to realize that people have invented reason to hide their fears or rationalize their desires. Baffled by this knowledge, we must nevertheless choose and act. As Yeats wrote, "We cannot know the truth but we can live it."

Sartre went on to further adventures of the mind, most notably his interaction with communism in the postwar years. Unlike most intellectuals, Sartre showed relatively little interest in Marxism in the 1930s. His teachers were Descartes, Kant, Hegel, Husserl, Heidegger; he was also absorbed in literature. But the war taught him that "one must be engaged, committed." The French Communists were outstandingly courageous in the wartime underground, and Sartre learned to respect them. He found existing Marxism, then closely identified with Stalinism, to be woefully inadequate as a philosophy and notably lacking in any understanding of the subjective element. Mechanical Marxism was an inadequate revolutionary theory because it totally failed to shed light on the individual revolutionary. Revolutions are made by living beings; robots will not rebel, the subjective element is all important. Criticizing the Party for its obsolete metaphysics, for its hierarchical rigidity, and above all for its total lack of "a sense of what man is," Sartre offered to add his existentialism to Marxism to create the perfect revolutionary theory. It was an offer the Party indignantly refused, branding Jean-Paul—he who so despised the "bourgeoisie" from which he sprang[8]—a decadent bourgeois thinker! This story belongs to the postwar years. Sartre continued for many years a vibrant, embattled force in the realms of European politics, literature, and thought.

Existential psychology was often superbly insightful. Sartre's analysis of the frustrating interrelationship of subjectivities in the game of love, or Heidegger's discussion of the anxiety that arises when the individual feels loss of contact with the grounds of his being, or seeks to escape into the false being of inauthenticity—letting others dictate one's choices—became modern classics and gave rise to a new branch of psychoanalysis. Sartre's criticism of Freud was basically that Freud had falsely attempted to impose methods of positivistic science in areas where they do

---

[8] In his 1964 *Les Mots (The Words),* Sartre wrote a masterpiece of autobiography narrating the psychic development of his early years.

not belong; the *pour-soi* is a radically different kind of being. The criticism resembles D. H. Lawrence's charge that Freud had created a kind of technology of the soul which was monstrous. Existential psychiatry, whether derived from Heidegger, Sartre, or Karl Jaspers, spoke of "identity crisis" and "ontological insecurity" and gave rise to a number of notable practitioners who might combine existentialism with Freud or Jung. Among these were Ludwig Binswanger and Medard Boss, later Erik Erikson and R. D. Laing.

So a new and exciting set of ideas about human nature entered the arena to interact with older ones, whether Christian, Marxian, Freudian, or other. The existentialist impact on literature was as strong as Freud's had been. Sartre's own plays and novels led the way. There arose a Theatre of the Absurd.

We will return to existentialism, for it persisted and indeed came into its own after 1945 as a major theme of contemporary thought. There were other forms of Sartre's atheistic variety. The religious form went back chiefly to the obscure nineteenth-century Danish Lutheran, Kierkegaard, a major rediscovery of the twentieth century (translated into German, 1909, Italian 1910, French 1929, English 1938). "The Kierkegaard renaissance is one of the strangest phenomena of our times," F. Heineman has remarked. But the time had at last become ripe for the "lonely thinker" who lived between 1813 and 1855 and died at age 42, a poor unknown. Criticizing Hegel's deterministic system, as he construed it, Kierkegaard declared that "existence is prior to essence," the individual person precedes every abstraction. He complained that Hegel's system was not "for life" and demanded a faith that was. (Careful students of Hegel complain quite properly that this is unfair, for at times Hegel himself could be quite "existential." Still, the contours of his main system as widely understood doubtless conform to Kierkegaard's indictment.) This was the same thirst for absolute commitment, for a creed related to one's life situation, that one finds in Nietzsche, who never read or heard of the obscure Danish parson. But Kierkegaard, unlike Nietzsche, was deeply religious, though his intense personalism caused him to attack the Church as a menace to real faith. Through anxiety and despair, individuals must make their own way to God. The Dane's intense suspicion of conformism, the crowd, institutions, phony external substitutes for inward experience, are somewhat reminiscent of certain of the esthetes, and it may be significant that he was a contemporary of Baudelaire (who in the end turned to religion himself). But Kierkegaard, a pastor of the Lutheran Church, also pointed back to the great founder of his church, who demanded a faith based on personal experience and denounced sacramentalism along with the moralism of salvation via good works.

The "return to orthodoxy" in Continental theology after World War I, previously discussed, owed something to Kierkegaard. Nicholas Berdyaev, a Russian of the Orthodox Church; Martin Buber, a Jew; Jacques Maritain, French Catholic; and the Protestants, Lutheran and Calvinist, respectively, Karl Barth and Emil Brunner were influenced by Kierkegaard though they might disagree with him in particulars (see Martin Buber's well-known essay on Kierkegaard in which, from the viewpoint of Jewish Hasidic communalism, he reproached the Dane for being too antisocial, while testifying to the importance of *Fear and Trembling* in his own development).

Buber's *I and Thou* appeared in 1923; Berdyaev, who had known exile under the tsar and had drifted close to Marxism before the war, hailed the Revolution of 1917 but found himself arrested and exiled by Lenin's dictatorship in 1920, after which he taught, lectured, and wrote in Berlin and Paris. Buber was born in 1878, Berdyaev in 1874, Maritain in 1882; all these men grew to intellectual maturity before World War I but then had their lives sharply altered by that event. They became the greatest of modern theologians.

Christian existentialism touches closely on these imposing figures who attempted to revive a somnolent religion in refutation of Nietzsche's and Sartre's claim that "God is dead." Maritain tried to reconcile his neo-Thomism with existentialism. The "crisis theology" of Barth comes close to it, as does the I-Thou experience described by Buber (a distinction between a person's relation to other persons and to things, with God as the "eternal Thou" to be encountered in a dialogue). Paul Tillich and Gabriel Marcel from the Protestant and Catholic camps, respectively, were close to existentialism. The trend was decidedly away from a rationalized religion, a polite and moral one, an easy and conventional one. In dread and anxiety the soul realizes its dire predicament and then makes the "leap" to faith. The individual chooses and wins his existence by reaching out to a transcendent Being who is not "understood" but is encountered, addressed.

Certainly not all modern theologians accepted existential ideas, but it is significant that an earnest revival of theology centered on such doctrines as Original Sin, the nature of Christ, and atonement. Relegated at one time virtually to the scrapheap of vanished dogmas, these issues once again became important in an era when human pride leading to self-destruction appeared as historic fact. Christian or Judaic thinkers pointed out that one does not need to desert our basic Western traditions and embrace an anarchy of strange beliefs; it is possible to come to terms with the modern experience through the medium of an enlarged but basically traditional religious outlook. The Bible, in the words of Rudolf Bultmann, has been "de-mythologized"; the assaults of the higher criticism have become irrelevant, for it is not the literal truth but the existential truth of this spiritual record that matters. Without God, or some transcendent source of value, humanity is condemned to destroy itself. Modern Christian thinkers have tended to see in the totalitarian regimes and world wars of the unhappy twentieth century a consequence of the despiritualization of humanity through de-Christianization.

Martin Heidegger's quest was broadly religious, though it did not involve a personal God, and in 1946 (*Existentialism Is a Humanism*) Sartre situated Heidegger's existentialism with his own as an atheistic and humanist sort. The two thinkers were actually very different, diverging from a common set of ideas (the two different modes of being, the interest in human subjectivity, the crisis of *angst* or despair at the world's chaos, authentic and inauthentic being). There is a religious aura about Heidegger's reverence for Being—not God, but something transcendent that is the root of all meaning, from which man has been cut off, and with which he must try to regain contact. Sartre sees no such transcendent Being, only the ideas invented and acted upon by individual human consciousnesses. The styles of the two were very different, Heidegger being quietist, conservative, hostile to modern technology, profoundly archaist, fleeing to the forest and listening to nature— eventually becoming a hero of the environmentalist "Greens" of a later day. The search for lost Being leads us to rethink all our words and categories, going back to an ancient time when language—"the house of being"—was in close contact with Being. With Nietzsche, who deeply influenced him, Heidegger would return to the pre-Socratic philosophers of ancient Greece, before intellectualism caused our words to lose their original magic. Art, especially poetry, is a means of regaining this contact with Being. Heidegger, a notable interpreter of literary works, offered an exciting esthetic that saw art as not just an imitation of the world but as a drawing out of deeper meaning, a partial revelation of Being. There are affinities to Oriental mysticism in Heidegger's "listening to the music of Being." (But at least one great scientist, Weizsaecker, found value in this: Scientists should listen rather than appropriate.) "Man is the shepherd of Being." Heidegger's vocabulary teems with metaphors of tending, shepherding, caring, listening, always in reverent search of that transcendent mystery that lies beneath the phenomenal world.

The other German philosopher associated with "existentialism" (though like most of them he eventually denied that he was an Existentialist), who also believed that we may have glimpses of a transcendent Being in authentic life experience, was Karl Jaspers. Jaspers began his career in medicine, moved to psychology, and hence to philosophy; influenced by Nietzsche and Max Weber, his path crossed those of Husserl, Freud, and Jung. His early (1913) book on psychopathology pioneered a kind of phenomenological psychiatry. After World War I, he secured a philosophy chair at Heidelberg with some difficulty, was ridiculed by more traditional philosophers until in 1932 his *Philosophy* stamped him out as an exciting proponent of the *Existenzphilosophie.* The violent politics of the 1930s cut across Jasper's life too. Married to a Jewess, he was forced out of teaching by the Nazis and narrowly escaped the extermination camp in 1945. He lived in Switzerland after the war until his death in 1969; he was a tremendously prolific writer and a popular one. Millions in many lands (his works were translated into 16 languages) learned their existentialism from Jaspers, especially from his most famous work *Man in the Modern Age* (1931), with its call for a recovery of essential selfhood in an era in which the ground shakes under our feet.

Existentialism has been introduced at this point because it was definitely born between the wars, when Martin Heidegger and Karl Jaspers were at work, and Heidegger's student Sartre began his literary career; when the revival of religion with overtones of an existentialist nature took place, through Buber, Maritain, Barth, Niebuhr, Berdyaev. But during that feverish decade of political alarums and excursions, the 1930s, which began with the economic hammer blows of the Great Depression, moved on to Hitler's Nazi conquest of Germany, then to the war brought on by Nazi hatreds and aggressiveness, with Stalin's five-year plans and purge trials a part of the picture, little else gained much attention except these economic and political questions. Then came a war more dreadful than the last one, and more inhumane: the terror bombing of European cities by the Allies, the murder of the Jews by the Nazis, incredible and untold suffering, great and some-times unrecorded heroism. This traumatic experience helped make relevant the insights of the existentialists, and after the war this "philosophy" achieved large popularity.

In the epoch of the world wars European intellectuals lived in a state of shock, in a nightmare world, such as one finds metaphorically projected in the fantasies of Franz Kafka (*The Trial, The Castle*). If unlucky enough, one might have watched the mass slaughter at Verdun, seen the bolshevik terror in Russia, observed the black-shirted and brown-shirted hysteria in Italy and Germany, the riots of starving workers during the Great Depression, fought in the Spanish Civil War, noted the appalling drift to world war again in the 1930s, and perhaps ended in a Nazi con-centration camp, after having destroyed whole German or Japanese cities from the air. It was seemingly a world of terror and inhumanity, marked by the almost total breakdown of civilized processes and political rationality. On the other hand, one could have observed extraordinary wonders, too, not only scientific and technologi-cal but literary, philosophical, scholarly, suggesting a fund of creative energy in Western civilization that might yet save it. Evidently the chief problem was one of values: something in which to believe that sophisticated modern humanity *could* believe in, something to serve as a directing principle for the aimless power of scien-tific technology, something to teach to the hundreds of millions of democratic citizens who, now "free," were slaves in their freedom for want of such values.

Linking the world of high theory and the world of nightmare reality was the atomic bomb; its landmarks neatly parallel, chronologically, the political events of the era. As World War I ended, in 1919, Ernest Rutherford, working in Cambridge, managed to transmute atoms, something not thought possible (like Darwin and the transmutation of species). The violent collision of helium and nitrogen changed them into hydrogen and oxygen, but Rutherford's experiment did not attract much attention at the time. In 1932, again at the Cavendish Laboratory, James Chadwick discovered the neutron, which unlike the negatively charged electron could ap-proach an atomic nucleus without being repelled and thus could be used to bom-bard and split it. The Hungarian scientist Leo Szilard filed a patent for a chain reaction in 1934, the same year in which Enrico Fermi in Italy caused a uranium atom to split by bombarding it with neutrons, though he did not then realize what he had done. In 1938, an old friend of Einstein's, Otto Hahn, repeated this. Europe was in turmoil, on the road to another war. Lise Meitner and her nephew Otto Frisch, in Austria, were among the first to realize that Einstein's $E = mc^2$ was now a reality. Exiled along with Freud after the Nazi seizure of Austria, they came to the United States as did Fermi and Szilard. Einstein of course was already there. With Einstein's letter to President Franklin Roosevelt in August 1939 (prodded by Szilard), the process was begun by which the Ultimate Weapon was to be created. These European scientists provided the theoretical knowledge for the atomic bomb.

The day before Pearl Harbor, President Roosevelt ordered the launching of the project to build an A-bomb. It would be ready in time to terminate the war that had begun in 1939. In 1942, the first atomic "pile" or reactor, showing the reality of nuclear fission with its release of enormous energy, supervised by "the Italian explorer" Fermi, was placed under the football field at Chicago University, today commemorated by a plaque near what is now the university library.

chapter 8

Contemporary Ideas in the West

Trends in Thought Since 1945

*We live in a moment of history where change is so
speeded up that we begin to see the present only when
it is already disappearing.*

R. D. Laing

EUROPE AFTER THE WAR

As Europeans awoke from the nightmare of World War II to stand amid the ruins
that assured them that the horrors had really happened, they were understandably
tempted to reject all the old and start anew. If World War I damaged the respect felt
for ancestral tradition, the second such cataclysm twenty years later seemed likely
to destroy it. Gabriel Marcel, to quote but one example, has written of "the more
than physical horror and anxiety I experienced in walking among the ruins of inner
Vienna in 1946, or more recently in Caen, Rouen or Würzburg." Almost any European city between the English Channel and the Dnieper could be qualified, though
German cities suffered most, as a result of the incessant allied aerial bombings. He
went on to note that for many the corollary was a total rejection of the European
heritage (*The Decline of Wisdom,* 1954). These physical ruins were manifestations
of the moral ruins displayed in Hitler's ghastly extermination of the Jews; the gas

Displayed quote from R. D. Laing, *The Politics of Experience* (New York: Pantheon
Books, a Division of Random House, Inc., 1967).

chambers of Auschwitz and Dachau brooded over a European atmosphere heavy with the smell of death.

Apart from the sheer physical and moral damages of the war, there had occurred what one historian phrased in the title of a book, *The Passing of the European Age,* or as the distinguished German, Alfred Weber, brother of Max, titled a little book of 1946, *Abschied von der Bisherigen Geschichte,* translated as *Farewell to European History.* In 1946, H. G. Wells, who had preached progress toward utopia for half a century, wrote *Mind at the End of Its Tether,* in which he decided that the end of civilization, of humanity, and perhaps of life on earth was rapidly approaching. A shattered and exhausted Europe was occupied by American and Soviet soldiers, both of whom most Europeans looked upon as barbarians from outside. Before long it became evident that the Russians, at least, intended no liberation but a new enslavement to communism. The Americans were to be looked upon as allies against the menace of Soviet power, and many Europeans were glad to clasp hands with the democratic land of the New World. The fact remains that quite a few bearers of the European culture continued to regard "Russia and America as the same," basically; as Martin Heidegger put it, "the same dreary technological frenzy, the same unrestricted organization of the average man" (*An Introduction to Metaphysics,* 1959).

For those who had expected brighter days with the Allied victory over Hitlerism, the coming of peace and the establishment of the United Nations, the years just after 1945 were deeply disappointing. As economic ruin engulfed Europe, a quarrel between the Soviet Union and the Western powers threatened a renewal of war—another war in the apparently self-perpetuating cycle of "wars in chain reaction," as a French writer (Raymond Aron) titled a book. The war had ended with the ghastly explosion of the atomic bomb over Hiroshima, wiping out an entire city; by 1954 far more destructive nuclear weapons carried by intercontinental missiles were available to guarantee that the seemingly inevitable next war would put a finish to much of the world. Pending this last apocalypse, the world was far from at peace, for there was war in Korea (1950-53), in Indochina, in Palestine, and elsewhere.

Whoever controlled Europe, Europe and the West no longer held the same monopoly of world power, prestige, and influence as formerly. The world had shrunk and yet enlarged, as Weber noted: Smaller because of modern transportation and communications, it was filled with all kinds of peoples formerly almost beyond the fringes of Europe's consciousness. For the peoples of Asia and Africa, too, in addition to the powerful United States of America, had arrived on the scene. They had gained or were about to gain their independence, they were "out of control" and demanding a place in the sun, and though as yet not powerful states they could no longer be ignored. Loosely united in attitudes shaped by their former vassalage to the West, they were a "third force" in world politics, of vast significance. Suddenly Europe became aware that it was after all a fairly diminutive peninsula on the huge land mass of Eurasia, and that what happened in Iran or the Indies, or in the Congo and Algeria, was of some consequence. This was a revolution in geopolitical perspectives that announced a new epoch of world history, perhaps the first one since the fall of the ancient Oriental empires.

The other radically new perspective was a technological-scientific one, signaled by the explosion over Hiroshima. What the atomic age meant no one could foresee— whether the passing of the human race or its ascent to incomparably higher levels of material civilization. For the time being, it meant assuredly that military power rested overwhelmingly with those who held the capacity to make and deliver nuclear weapons, which included only the Americans and, soon, the Soviets. Apart from this confirmation of weakness and dependency, atomic energy drastically transformed basic thought processes about the material world, driving home to all some of the implications of the new physics heretofore appreciated by only a few.

On the other hand, there were countervailing tendencies working against the picture of bleak despair. The terrible war had at least purged Europe of much: of nazism, of anti-Semitism, and even, to a degree, of nationalism. The need to rehabilitate a culture drew people together. Survivors of the terrible experiences of the war, whether living under the nightly threat of terror and death from the skies, or in the hell of a Nazi concentration camp, or as fighters in the "underground," often testified to the strange kind of value in such experiences. Life was given more value by being precarious; simple objects acquired value. Such situations were at least a cure for empty complacency, a reminder of the tragic and serious nature of life, a precipitant of elemental human values. To come up against and face the absolute worst is a kind of purgative; this is the message that emerges from much of the postwar European writing.

It is clear that in many ways the shock of adversity was good for Europe; from the enormous evil of World War II much good was to come—an example, no doubt, of that law of compensation in human affairs which many thinkers have noticed—*ex malo bonum*. To take the case of France, its defeat and occupation by the Germans, bitterest humiliation in French history, provided a stimulus and an opportunity for economic modernization. The war visited physical destruction so that railroads and plants could be rebuilt and modernized, but it also shattered old political alignments, brought former enemies together, raised up new leaders, altered attitudes. A new unity and a new vision of France, "competing in growth, vigor, and material power with her neighbors," as Robert Paxton writes in his history of the Occupation, emerged from the trauma of the war. Karl Marx's remark that war is the midwife of revolution was exemplified in a veritable revolution of opinion leading to France's economic modernization and, in its social policy, a creative combination of free enterprise *with* "planification." For Germany, too, the war even more drastically was a challenge to rebuild on sounder foundations, wipe out the stain of Hitlerism, show the world that German culture was capable of creative democracy. A flood of exiles from former German regions in Eastern Europe brought to the new Germany soon to rise from the ashes of defeat the vigor of competent people who were forced to rehabilitate themselves by hard work Throughout Western Europe, the wartime experience in economic planning encouraged an optimism about being able to steer the economy toward greater abundance and equality by the use of state power, without sacrificing individual liberty. It was during the war that the foundations were laid for Great Britain's "welfare state," which the victorious Labour Party was to install between 1945 and 1951. People like William Beveridge in Britain, author of the highly important study of "Full Employment in a Free Society," and Jean Monnet, in France, were technocrats concerned with creative *planification* within the framework of "a free society." Add a substantial number of technical and medical advances that might be attributed to the war, and one can make a case for the uses of adversity here, the evils of war engendering some good things. Traumatic shocks can jolt societies out of long stagnation, as happened to France; sheer military necessity bred innovation and experimentation.

Standing together against the Soviet threat and then building a new Europe from the ashes, a Europe that might at last have learned to unify itself in a federation—these were goals that gave the common life some meaning. Europe began to make a spectacular economic recovery which swept on through much of the 1950s and brought to birth a unified European economy, the Common Market, that resulted from the Rome Treaty of 1957 and was expected to lead on by stages to full political federation. Hope returned with the development of the NATO alliance between North America and the states of Western Europe, and with the avoidance of major war. Though life as always was filled with problems, many Europeans saw the light breaking through in the second decade after the war, with prospects even of Europe again assuming its place in world affairs—no "passing of the European age," despite the power of Russia and of America, and the arrival of the non-European peoples. The change between 1945 and 1963 was summed up by Raymond Aron: "In 1945, Western Europe was a mass of ruins; today it is one of the most prosperous regions of the world."

Just ahead lay worse times; the later 1960s brought student riots all over Europe, a new malaise, and the beginning of a sharply reduced rate of economic growth. The conservative 1950s gave way to the radical 1960s. It was by no means clear whether the rally of the postwar years, which had brought spectacular recovery from the ashes of destruction, was a momentary flicker of the flame before final extinction or an almost epochal surmounting of the long crisis that had begun in 1914, continued during the Great Depression, and climaxed with the horrors of World War II. One thing was certain: There was a crescendo of books, ideas, consciousness. Intellectually at least, it was with a bang and not a whimper that the world was ending, if it was ending. This explosion of thought accompanied an educational revolution, enlarging Europe's charmed circle of the higher literacy at least tenfold. It is a difficult task to take stock of the human condition today as reflected in philosophy, literature, and religious, social, and political ideas, for never were there so many. Trends become harder to establish; the river of history has perhaps ended "in a sea where all waters mingle confusedly together."[1] Nevertheless, a sharp general change can be noted between the 1950s and the 1960s.

---

[1] Roland N. Stromberg, *After Everything: Western Intellectual History Since 1945* (1975), p. 105.

THE END OF IDEOLOGY

Unquestionably the postwar climate of opinion was overshadowed by the sense of catastrophe and disaster, because of war, power, and the bomb. J. M. Cohen, in the concluding statements to his book *Poetry of This Age,* remarked that "events have dwarfed all possible comment" on public affairs and driven the poet to purely personal statement. "All that he can hope to rescue from an ever-imminent disaster will be a moment of love or insight or a clear conception of truth, which, having once been, can never be destroyed." It is possible to wonder whether this contingency of life is really so new. Every person's life is contingent every moment and always has been. Apart from that, earlier generations lived under the threat of starvation, disease, and other afflictions from which many moderns are by comparison almost free. In terms of the totality of human life, the modern world with its massive and longer-lived populations would be far ahead of any previous age even if it experienced a thermonuclear war. (The greatest world problem, today, according to many, is *over*population.) Nevertheless, the reminder of one's contingent being, one's constant confrontation with death, the possibility of centuries of progress being extinguished in a few moments (which might even be the result of an accident)—all this undoubtedly further undermined nineteenth-century beliefs in a secular utopia or the progress of humanity toward perfection. The "boundary situations" about which existentialists talk seem all too real in the world as it exists today.

Thus the turn to "personal statement," to an insight of the moment and away from the ideologies or total faiths. The retreat from ideologies was a prominent theme after World War II. The political activism characteristic of the 1930s fell to low ebb in the 1950s. "Outside the Communists," a French writer observed in 1952, "French youth is almost totally disinterested in politics today." The same could be said for British youth, German youth, Italian youth. Strong at the war's end in France, communism weakened badly during the cold war years, when the behavior of Stalin destroyed it in Germany. There was a profound reaction against Soviet Russia under the Stalinist dictatorship, a regime which sent millions of people to prison and labor camps without fair trial, showed itself willing to employ every sort of iniquity in the crudest "means justified by the end" credo, and threw international relations into chaos, while also destroying creative Russian thought and literature by a straitjacket of political control. In the sight of Western intellectuals, who had once seen it through a veil of illusions, the last of these was torn from the ugly face of Soviet communism by the enslavement through military force of the peoples of Eastern Europe.

To some extent, too, the "end of ideology" has been facilitated by the failure of ideology in the Soviet Union itself. In Stalin's era the high priests of the Communist party, charged with the zeal and dogmatism of the Marxist faith, made decisions. In the Khrushchev era (1953-64) and afterward this power tended to gravitate toward bureaucracy, a process summed up by one authority as a "transition from charismatics to mathematics." In general, the element of breathless, apocalyptic exaltation in the Soviet Union, that was a legacy of the great Revolution and was perpetuated in the Party, tended steadily to wane as rationalization and normality took over. Not even the charisma of Lenin is safe from the corrosions of time and life. If Stalinization debased it, the post-Stalin era completely destroyed it; the New Jerusalem of Marx and Lenin became just another managerial and bureaucratic society.

For some, the moment of final disenchantment was 1948, when the suicide of Jan Masaryk marked the end of Czechoslovak independence; for others, it was 1956, when, even after the death of Stalin and the disclosure of some of the enormities committed during his reign by the new bolshevik leaders themselves, Russian tanks poured into Budapest to put down a Hungarian uprising against Soviet rule. The blood shed in the streets of Prague in 1968 was only a dismal postscript to the story of Soviet oppression in all the countries of Eastern Europe, most especially in those countries for whose liberation from Nazi power the war had originally been fought—Poland and Czechoslovakia. Meanwhile in Russia itself those who had predicted a humanizing and liberalizing trend following the demise of the terrible Georgian were proved wrong by the subsequent treatment of critics of the Soviet regime. A brilliant and courageous group of young writers who claimed a right to do something else than parrot the official government line was imprisoned or sent to mental institutions. The story of the trial of Daniel and Sinyavsky and the proscribed writings of Solzhenitsyn and Pasternak, became known in the West. At the same time exhaustive research by Western scholars, exemplified in Robert Conquest's *The Great Terror,* stripped the last veils of illusion from the picture of a benevolent Soviet Union, revealing an inhumanity that surpassed even Hitler's. The fiftieth anniversary of the Revolution, in 1967, provided an opportunity for reappraisal, and it is significant that even those from the Left were overwhelmingly unfavorable. A bureaucratic society with a bourgeois culture and a reactionary foreign policy, not altogether converted from its nasty habit of killing off anyone who dissented in the slightest from a mindless orthodoxy—the Soviet Union was Orwell's nightmare of *1984* come true.

Influenced by Max Weber, social theory now strongly reiterated the point that a modern industrial society has essential features of bureaucratic, rationalized organization whether it is "socialist" or "capitalist." Whether the managers work for the state or a large corporation, whether the machine-tenders receive their paychecks from the government or the private company makes relatively little difference. Alienation is a function of the process, not the technicality of ownership. If anything, socialism is likely to be even more bureaucratic and alienating than capitalism, since the administrative units are larger. The European socialist tradition had based its indictment of the capitalist socioeconomic order on its alleged inefficiency; socialism promised more machines, more production, more and larger cities—all the things for which there was now a revulsion. Salvation, if any, would have to come from a different direction.

When in the 1960s a more radical political mood returned, it found world communism divided as never before; one might choose to follow the Chinese brand, more highly emotional and aggressively ideological, or the Cuban brand, none of them in agreement with the others. Communist parties in the West were released from rigidity and freer to develop in different directions. But this meant an end to the onetime god, now fragmented in a host of minor deities, and in fact the new leftists of the 1960s were gloriously anarchic, quite undisciplined, wholly unlike the old Communists, though some of them might pay passing respects to Castro or Mao or Ho Chi Minh simply because they were enemies of the West. It was a highly existentialized, extremely unorthodox Marxism that inspired these younger rebels, grown up since the 1930s and no longer knowing its idols.

Let that story be postponed for a moment. The 1950s was by and large a conservative decade and even its despair was quiet. If Marxism was generally rejected, any other fervent sort of political mystique was equally suspect. There was little enthusiasm for democracy—two cheers for it, as E. M. Forster wrote, but not three; it is the worst of all forms of government except for all the others, as Winston Churchill had put it; one accepted it as the elimination of ideologies, not as an ideology. In France, the Fourth Republic set up immediately after the liberation of 1944 to 1945 was more democratic than the Third had been, but gave way in 1958 to the considerably less democratic (or at least less parliamentary) Fifth, headed by national leader Charles de Gaulle, hero of the war. The Gaullist state was in some ways progressive, for it aimed at modernizing France technologically. But it proposed to do this chiefly by a Saint-Simonian expertise of government administrators, bypassing the old game of party politics and operating beyond the old ideologies. De Gaulle hoped to restore a national community in a semifascist way, though without the harsh and tyrannical methods of the Nazis. The great writer André Malraux was foremost among the intellectuals who, in their disillusionment with the failed god, Stalin, found in the war hero an authentically great historic personality, offering a fresh vision of France and of Europe reborn to greatness. But in the end, despite impressive achievements in modernizing France, extricating it from imperialism, and restoring national morale, de Gaulle offered little that was new. He was himself rather characteristic of the low-key 1950s in his disabused realism, his skeptical antiutopianism. "I am like Hemingway's Old Man of the Sea, I have brought back a skeleton," he sighed in the end.

Something similar happened in Britain in that the Labour party, elected to office in 1945 on a tide of socialist idealism, was voted out in 1951 in an atmosphere of considerable disenchantment with its policies. It tended thereafter to become much less ideological. The Conservative party held office from 1951 to 1964. In place of total solutions, political theorists suggested piecemeal solutions (Karl Popper). "Rationalism in politics" is a snare (M. Oakeshott); the art of politics is an adjustment of differences in pragmatic ways. After experiencing all those "cruel or fierce political ideologies [which] have played havoc with human welfare," wrote famed British historian L. B. Namier, the mature political community learns to do without them altogether. Namier gave his approval to the condition described with some degree of alarm by philosopher Stuart Hampshire: "There is a tired lull in English politics, and argument on general principles has largely died. . . . Both political parties are now in this sense conservative, tied to day-to-day expedients." While a modernized Conservative party accepted the welfare state, Keynesian economics, and the managed economy, the Labour leader of the 1950s and early 1960s, Hugh Gaitskell, asked his party to stop being dogmatically socialist and appeal to a wider public than the doctrinaires. Someone coined the word "Butskellism," joining the liberal Tory R. A. Butler to the moderate Socialist Gaitskell—there was not much difference between the parties, "consensus" was the word. The model of the successful economy, a mixture of free enterprise and government direction, was almost the same for a majority of both political parties. Labour theorist W. Arthur Lewis opted for a more vigorous kind of entrepreneurial capitalism.

Political writing took the form of close analysis of actual political behavior (such as voting), which often left few romantic illusions about the rationality and responsibility of "the people," or ordinary citizens. Analyses in any wider sense were apt to bypass ideology, too. Bertrand de Jouvenel, writing *On Power (Du Pouvoir)*, found the most significant aspect of political evolution to lie not in the forms of government, aristocratic or democratic, but in the steady growth of the apparatus of coercion, regardless of forms—the growth of power.

Similarly in economic thought, argument and analysis were likely to transcend the old issues between capitalism and socialism. For example the discussion of economic growth, carried on in such books as those of W. Arthur Lewis, Colin Clark (*The Conditions of Economic Progress*), and W. W. Rostow, who subtitled his *Stages of Economic Growth* "a noncommunist manifesto," noted among other things that ownership of property is not as such a vital factor. Neither David Ricardo nor Karl Marx is very relevant to twentieth-century economic problems, whether they are those of the "affluent societies" of the Western democracies or the youthful near-primitive economies of new African and Asian nations trying to find a shortcut to affluence. Even in the Soviet Union, realism began to prevail over Marxist dogma. Economic reforms of the sort associated with Evsei Liberman in the Soviet Union and Ota Sik in Czechoslovakia, brought forward as a remedy for a decidedly unsatisfactory economic performance under the rigidly centralized Stalinist system, asked for a greater role for individual enterprises in the planning process, and for profit incentives in a quasi-market economy. Khrushchev encouraged such new ideas, which the Chinese Communists called "a restoration of capitalism"! Those who talked about the "convergence" of the two systems, capitalism and socialism, thought that each would approach a middle ground from opposite directions—the mixed economy of public and private sectors together, the only workable one for a modern industrial society.

The study of power was an outstanding feature of postwar political and social thought. "We have all become intensely aware of power as the major phenomenon in all societies," Raymond Aron wrote. In addition to Jouvenel's brilliant book, the works of the Heidelberg sociologist A. Rüstow, writing in the shadow of Max Weber, may be instanced among the general theoretical studies. The theme comes through in any number of more specific studies of foreign policy and international relations.[2] George Orwell's *1984* gave expression to the frightening possibilities of

---

[2] See also the studies of "power elites" within nations by such sociologists as Theodore Geiger and C. Wright Mills, or such historians as Sir Lewis Namier and his disciples (a very important school in England), or, in France, Jean Lhomme (*La grande bourgeoisie au pouvoir*); also political scientists who dwelt on "pluralism" and a competition of elites in a "polyarchical" order of power.

power in the modern state to enslave its citizenry. This popular fantasy-satire described a condition in which the government disseminates all knowledge. Technology enables the state to control everything, even to read thoughts; "Big Brother" is everywhere. Thought control has become accomplished so thoroughly that people have ceased to think, they have been brainwashed into automatons by their governments. This fear for liberty under the conditions of modern life ran counter to pre-war progressivism in that the latter, whether Marxist or Keynesian, tended to be statist. The new political thought, whether Left or Right, showed greater mistrust of the power of the state, whoever may be in charge of the state. It returned to Lord Acton's motto that all power tends to corrupt and absolute power corrupts absolutely.

"The mighty invasion of government into economic life," it has been often noted, constitutes "one of the most fundamental contrasts between the twentieth century and the nineteenth." The depression of the 1930s frightened people into accepting large measures of government regulation, a trend aided by the new economic theories of Keynes, while World War II brought total war and with it, of necessity, total organization under government control. Since 1945, a continuing vast military defense program and a "space" program of gigantic dimensions have meant an expanding role of government in most countries. This increasing statism, while ardently defended by a variety of collectivists, including neoliberals as well as socialists, aroused protests against it in the name of the sovereign individual, of spiritual autonomy, and of esthetic and moral values opposed to the reign of bureaucracy and the rule of the machine. Orwell's *1984* may be regarded as representative of such protests. (See also Huxley's *Brave New World Revisited*.)[3] And, indeed, students of "dystopias" noted the appearance in recent times of a whole category of such literature, contrasting with the utopias of the nineteenth century. (One of the first, which influenced Orwell, came from a disillusioned Russian Communist as early as 1920—see Yevgeny Zamyatin's *We*.) Utopia had turned into nightmare.

Many continued to fear more than anything else the eclipse of liberty and of the free personality under the exorbitant encroachment of statism and mass society. "Personality is losing all along the line against power," J. B. Priestley wrote in 1955 ("The Gentle Anarchists"); the popular British author added that the younger generation "takes regimentation for granted," having become accustomed to the loss of liberties which everyone enjoyed until a few decades ago.

SARTRE AND EXISTENTIALISM

Existentialism, emanating from Paris, continued to be the world's leading fashion in ideas for some years after 1945. To realize fully that the world had no meaning, to know loneliness and dread, to reject conventional morality and religion, and then,

---

[3] In his acute book *The Liberal Mind* (1963), Kenneth Minogue pointed out that liberalism suffers from, among other things, the contradiction of wishing both to enlarge the individual's freedom by diminishing state action and to promote welfare by increasing state action. Basically individualist, the liberal seeks to harness the state to serve individual purposes, yet sanctions an ever-growing network of statist restrictions on personal liberty.

"on the far side of despair," to affirm one's freedom to act and thus create value—the existentialist recipe was known to every undergraduate of the 1950s. Meanwhile Sartre, the leading existentialist, continued his brilliant career as philosopher, dramatist, editor (of the leading journal of ideas, *Les temps modernes*), and would-be activist, now convinced, as we know, that the intellectual must commit himself to a political cause. He had offered to help a philosophically backward Communist party develop a truly revolutionary theory, with the aid of existentialist ideas. Sartre's conversion to Marxism coincided with the discovery of another Marx, represented in previously unknown writings, who might be rescued from Kremlin dogmatism; but it also coincided with the grim years of late Stalinism when repression reached a climax and all modernist literature and thought were rejected. There were ferocious attacks on Sartre, including some from major figures such as Henri Lefebvre and George Lukacs who later broke with Moscow and apologized to Jean-Paul. Sartre's popular play *Les mains sales* (*Dirty Hands,* 1948) appeared to pillory the cynicism and stupidity of the Party bureaucrats—though it might also be read as a criticism of the bourgeois intellectual who is too pure for the real political world. In 1950-51 Sartre moved closer to the Party under the impact of the cold war (he blamed the Korean emergency on the United States which he accused of practicing germ warfare.) He soon broke with his fellow existentialists, Maurice Merleau-Ponty and Albert Camus, on this issue, as Sartre went so far as to say one should not criticize the Party even if it is wrong, for does it not represent the proletariat? His long 1951 play, *The Devil and the Good Lord* (which Sartre regarded as his best) seemed to reverse the lesson of *Dirty Hands*: The toughminded bully boys who know how to act are right.

A typical product of the cold war, Sartre's violent swing to the Communist side ended abruptly in 1956 on the occasion of the Hungarian revolution crushed by Soviet tanks. Sartre denounced the repression and was disgusted with the French Communist party for seeking to defend it. He never trusted Communists again, though he later said that if he were Italian he would join the CPI, which led the way toward emancipation of Western Communists from Soviet Russian domination. He continued to think of himself as some sort of Marxist, rescuing Marx from the Kremlin, as others were also doing. The Hungarian revolt of 1956 brought wholesale resignations from the French Communist party and brought Lukacs over to Sartre's side; from this hour, followed closely by the breach between Russian and Chinese Communism, dates the breakup of the Marxist monolith as wholesale reinterpretation of Marx began. This was usually in a "humanistic" direction, stressing the early Marx of alienation theory rather than the economic determinist of *Das Kapital* (which the Italian, Gramsci, called a bourgeois book). Sartre's own reaction was to attempt a massive work of social theory begun in 1957, the first volume of which was published in 1960 as *The Critique of Dialectical Reason.* The second volume never appeared, though fragments of it were printed after Sartre's death. In the end, Sartre ceased to think of himself as a Marxist, remarking that Marx was all right for his own day but not relevant to the present. The *Critique de la raison dialectique,* such of it as appeared, was a tribute to Sartre's vitality and intellectual energy, but in the end perhaps it failed. In a tortuously difficult work, he sought to evolve a true Marxian theory of history that would deal with real human beings not with abstract conceptualizations.

The work contains some interesting concepts such as the "practico-inert," the body of reified alienated institutions which, born of human needs, has become ossified and now, as "worked matter," frustrates these needs and escape human control: a contribution to neo-Marxian alienation theory with some Bergsonian overtones. "Seriality" is the mechanical, artificial form of human association—like the bus queue, an accidental grouping of people. Beginning in scarcity, feeding on the struggle for existence, seriality and the practico-inert have prevailed through human history, frustrating *praxis* or true, creative interaction between individual and group. The "group in fusion," a spontaneous and organic community found especially in revolutions, overcomes this conflict between individual and society. A good deal of rather pretentious theorizing of this sort does not seem to take us much farther than some familiar notions such as the coldness of bureaucracy, the weight of entrenched interests, the way "things" can dominate us, and the tendency of revolutionary unity to give way to institutionalization (everything begins in *mystique* and ends in politique, Péguy had observed.) Some sociologists, however, have found Sartre's theory illuminating. He himself gave up in the end. "I cannot see how it is possible to resolve the problems which are brought about by any institutionalized structure," Sartre remarked in 1972. Yet the revolutionary stuudents in one glorious moment of *mystique* in 1968, hailing Sartre as their prophet, thought you could.

The abandoned second volume of the *Critique* contains a concrete historical examination of how the Russian Revolution went wrong, separately published in good part as *The Ghost of Stalin*. It seems that Sartre floundered and faded out in this attempt to encompass all human history in a theory, as well he might, "The day of systems is past." The tireless Jean-Paul, whom his faithful companion and co-existentialist Simone de Beauvoir pictures as staying up all night with pills and coffee working on the book, turned to write another play, perhaps his greatest, *The Condemned of Altona*—which seems a reversion to his earlier, pure existentialism of *No Exit,* redolent of the "useless passion" that man is. But in the public mind, this play was a commentary on the alleged use of torture in the Algerian revolution then going on (1960). Sartre still was a great public commentator.

Sartre, then, as the leading intellectual of his time kept up what was on the whole a losing battle to be both a thinker and effective activist. After his break with the Communists he moved not to the right, but farther to the left. While his friendly rival Raymond Aron wrote of "the end of the socialist myth," Sartre became one of the prophets of a new wave of radicalism in the 1960s. Of this, more in a moment. Meanwhile other existentialist philosophies flourished. The Kierkegaard renaissance continued, and there was a Nietzsche renaissance; the great German thinker was rescued from the Nazi appropriation of him and, with the aid of new materials as in the case of Marx, seen as a mighty prophet of the modern godless predicament and an insightful critic of all manner of false dogmas. Edmund Husserl left behind a large corpus of manuscripts which were rescued from the Nazis during the war and smuggled into Belgium, where they remain, at Louvain. Husserl's last major work, *The Crisis of European Sciences and Transcendental Phenomenology,* made it clear that he disapproved of Heidegger and of existentialist irrationalism; phenomenology must be "a rigorous science of philosophy," even if a different kind of science than the positivistic sort.

As a "hermeneutical" inquiry into unique, concrete human meanings, phenomenology in practice blended with existentialism, with the poetry of private states of mind, in brief with the introspective, personalist humanism so characteristic of the 1950s. System making in the older philosophic way has no place in phenomenology. The nonrational categories of the mind turn out to be numerous, ambiguous, not reducible to any order. Phenomenology bears some relationship to the school in literature which describes itself as *chosiste,* or thing-ist: dedicated to the full exploration of objects *qua* objects, the thing for its own sake, not seen as a symbol of anything or as part of any logical scheme. One remains content, in both *choisisme* and phenomenology, with concrete existents, experienced and described as they are, just because they are.

Those philosophers who belonged to the very different tradition of logical positivism, which was described as dominant in England and Scandinavia, tended toward some of the same conclusions the existentialists reached, even if they arrived by a different route. The later Wittgenstein is readily classified as a kind of phenomenologist: His "language games" are a form of life. "The desire to understand the world is an outmoded folly"; we simply accept it in all its tangled diversity, gently untangling it where we can, helping people out of their confusions. The Oxford philosophers of the "ordinary language" school followed in Wittgenstein's footsteps—to the great disgust of old Bertrand Russell who said that this sort of philosophizing was only concerned with "the different ways silly people can say silly things."

The Oxford philosophizers of the analytical school continued to feel that philosophy has no great messages to deliver, being a method and not a creed—its job, to help clarify thoughts. Under the influence of Wittgenstein II it tended in the 1950s to become ever more absorbed in linguistic word games. It drew back in horror from any suggestion that philosophers might construct systems, or assert truths, or discover values. Like the phenomenologists, the analysts took things as they found them, preferring concrete particular problems, tending to deflate all abstractions and generalizations. The modesty, or perhaps false modesty, of this school was reflected in J. L. Austin's characterization of his work as "something about one way of possibly doing one part of philosophy"! "Doing" philosophy, the fashionable way of putting it, connoted the limited goals—no finding or making of great truths—as well as the brisk professionalism of an academic exercise. To those who occasionally complained that philosophers were supposed to offer more help than this to beleaguered modern humanity, these Anglo-Saxon professors answered, in effect, "Sorry, old boy, not our job." In which, of course, they differed much from the existentialists, and there were the famous uncomprehending confrontations of the two groups at international congresses in the 1950s. But this mistrust broke down somewhat, and books began to appear pointing out that analytical and phenomenological philosophy had after all some points of contact.

Professional philosophy as well as other disciplines was increasingly cut off from the larger public to be immersed in the specialized subculture, with incentives to be original, invent a new thesis, be clever. It proliferated all sorts of combinations during the 1960s and 1970s in the burgeoning universities. A glorious but confusing eclecticism set in. There were phenomenological sociologists (Schütz, Gadamer), linguistic psychoanalysts, and so forth. Based on linguistics structuralism arose as an important new tendency. (See the further discussions that follow.) Sociologists complained that more than half a dozen different schools—functionalists, structuralists, phenomenologists, behavioralists, Marxists, existentialists, Symbolic Interactionists—disputed the mastery of their terrain in complicated methodological quarrels that left students bewildered before they could begin. Much the same thing was true in psychology. A 1975 assessment of philosophy[4] found such diversity—from Zen Buddhists to Logical Positivists, from revolutionary activists to austere purists—as to defy the judgment that this is a single subject. This, perhaps, was one cause of the student uprising of the later 1960s: Learning, the enraged students complained, had become irrelevant to life.

THE NEW RADICALISM

While the 1950s were politically quiet, they were hardly complacent. As the cold war between the rival power blocs of Russia and the West threatened to erupt at any moment, in a decade punctuated by international crises (Korean war, Berlin crises, Suez/Hungarian joint crisis in 1956, Cuban missile crisis in 1962), the development of the nuclear hydrogen bomb and intercontinental missiles kept humanity cringing under the threat of annihilation. Among the most widely read serious books of the decade were Orwell's *1984* nightmare of total war between totalitarian slave states and Neville Shute's picture of the horrors of atomic war, *On the Beach,* to which one might add William Golding's parable of boys reduced to savagery, *Lord of the Flies.* Such highly esteemed novelists as François Mauriac, Graham Greene, Angus Wilson, Evelyn Waugh presented a gloomy view of human nature derived from traditional Christianity, as did the older T. S. Eliot, whose brilliant modernist delineation of *The Waste Land* now gave place to the Christian humility of *Four Quartets.* The decade was not revolutionary, since it had ceased to believe in Marx's romantic epic of history and had seen his disciples end by establishing a new tyranny. In literature, the decade had turned away from socialist realism, whose tracts seemed unutterably dreary. It also turned away from the path blazed by Joyce—what could you possibly do to follow *Finnegans Wake*? The

[4]Charles J. Bontemps and S. Jack Odell, eds., *The Owl of Minerva: Philosophers on Philosophy* (1975).

British novel tended to return to traditional forms,[5] away from an extreme modernism which seemed a dead end, leading to incessant, ever more bizarre searches for novelty. It followed Existentialist leads with the *nouveau roman* of Robbe-Grillet and Sarraute in France, with plays like Samuel Beckett's *Waiting for Godot* or the Theatre of the Absurd of Ionesco and Sartre's friend Jean Genet. The Swiss dramatist Friedrich Dürrenmatt, considered by some the greatest German language playwright of his generation, radiated the religious intensity of neo-orthodox Lutheranism.

Signs of discontent began to appear toward the end of the decade. Curiously, the discrediting and then the splitting up of world communism opened the way to a freer development of the Left. After 1956 some of the Communist parties, for example the British, cut loose from Moscow's moorings altogether and sailed off on their own toward some kind of neocommunism. The Italian Communist party moved far away from the rigid dogmatism of Stalin's day to become almost an open-minded party of the Left, willing to discard old shibboleths and seek fresh formulations. In Italy and France a "dialogue between Catholicism and Communism" began, receiving encouragement from new currents in the Catholic Church, expressed in Pope John XXIII's extraordinary 1963 encyclical "Pacem in Terris," which issued a call to liberal thought and social action in the Church. With the fragmentation of the world Communist movement, which began in the late 1950s and carried on into the 1960s, Chinese Maoist and Cuban Castroist versions of the revolutionary faith became live options for leftists; there was a good deal more charisma and mystique in these than in the old, tired Moscow version, which still hopefully presented its lives of Lenin but was now run by bureaucrats in gray flannel suits. New revolutionary heroes such as Che Guevara appeared. Or, if one preferred milder brew, some of the East European satellites of the Soviet Union produced revisionist Marxism which tried to soften the harsh Leninist variety by administering doses of Kantian ethics or other humanizing ingredients. In France a *Union de la Gauche Socialiste,* created in 1957, experimented in a more eclectic socialism drawing on Proudhon, Jaurès, and the Christian socialism of Lamennais and Sangnier. It dreamed of defanaticizing the Communists and undogmatizing Marx, in order to fit them into this "Popular Front." In brief, the demise of historic Soviet communism as a world revolutionary faith allowed fresh breezes to blow through the dried-up landscape of the Left and inaugurated a period of confusion but considerably greater vitality there.

Another cause of the new radicalism was a new generation, as usual rebelling against the attitudes of its parents. The 1950s were still dominated intellectually by the generation that had matured between the wars, had known Hitler and Stalin and the Red Decade, had experienced the gigantic trauma of World War II, and had ended disillusioned with all ideologies, unable to believe in any utopias. A younger generation, to whom these events were but faint memories, began to find a voice, at first hesitantly, in the later 1950s. In Britain, John Osborne's play *Look Back in*

[5]Cf. Rubin Rabinovitz, *The Reaction Against Experiment in the English Novel 1950–1960* (1967).

Anger (1956) came to seem a curiously significant landmark. Other writers and critics asked for more commitment and social relevance; a debate about this, initially between critic Kenneth Tynan and veteran dramatist Eugene Ionesco, enlivened the later 1950s. Few mature writers in the 1950s dared to say a word for social realism, which raised memories of the dreary propagandist tracts of the 1930s. The Angry Young Men now demanded action. It was not altogether clear what they were angry at—at Britain's declining power, at the "caste system" of a still somewhat snobbish society, or just angry, with the natural rebelliousness of youth. By comparison with the rock-throwing militants of a decade later they were quite mild, and many of them, like Kingsley Amis and John Braine, later became conservative. But their somewhat incoherent protests together with their demand for a less quietly resigned voice in literature marked a certain turning point.

With France somnolent under de Gaulle and communism in disarray, the British writers commanded the center of the world stage for a time. But in West Germany, where the student rebellion was to begin early and with extreme bitterness, "angries" quickly arose in imitation of the British. Let us be sand rather than oil in the world's machinery, one of them said. Activism coalesced momentarily in a strong pacifist campaign, influenced among others by the nonagenarian philosopher Bertrand Russell (always a maverick), which culminated in the Campaign for Nuclear Disarmament along with attacks on American foreign policy and demands to take Great Britain out of the North Atlantic alliance. The decade of the 1960s began with the first of many protest marches, organized by the C.N.D. in behalf of its demand for Britain unilaterally to abandon her nuclear weaponry. In the *New Left Review,* those impatient with the Labour party's caution and pragmatism tried to discover new roads to socialism. The "establishment" came under attack from satirists. The new spirit was mocking, irreverent, and impatient.

The irrepressible Sartre assailed the French authorities who were attempting to put down Arab nationalist rebellion in Algeria, a rehearsal for the denunciation of American warfare in Vietnam later. He had previously led opposition to the French attempt to hold onto Indochina, terminated in 1954. President de Gaulle's 1962 decision to grant Algeria its independence scarcely diminished Sartre's dislike of the Gaullist Fifth Republic. In 1960 he visited Cuba and enthusiastically approved the new revolutionary regime of Fidel Castro; and in 1961 he wrote a preface to the West Indian psychiatrist Frantz Fanon's *Wretched of the Earth* which was destined to considerable notoriety. In this writing Sartre went violent with a vengeance: The oppressed people of the Third World must kill the Europeans in order to win their self-respect (as Fanon argued in this widely read tract). An almost hysterical anti-American during the Vietnam war, Sartre implored the Soviet Union to use nuclear bombs against the United States, against "this hell of hatred and blood called the free world." He joined with Bertrand Russell in an attempt to stage a trial of the Americans for war crimes. At about this time, too, the veteran existentialist Karl Jaspers wrote a long and bitter polemic against the West German Republic, charging that it was plotting new wars and leading the way to another Nazi dictatorship. (*Where Is the Federal Republic Heading?* 1965).

So a stream of ideas emanating from lofty intellectual sources was fed into the student uprisings that marked the later 1960s. The causes lay as usual partly in the realm of ideas and partly in social circumstances. Among the latter must be included the revolution in higher education which sent far more students into institutions of higher learning, many of them new. In England, for example, the virtual monopoly of university education and of intellectual life by the two ancient universities, Oxford and Cambridge, with a place made for the University of London in certain subjects, had never been challenged and ensured the supremacy of a small intellectual elite steeped in the classical literary traditions of Western civilization. Now a considerable number of new universities served tens of thousands who would formerly never have gone to college. In 1970 there were some 450,000 university students in Great Britain, with talk of another doubling in the next decade. A hundred years earlier, the most advanced country in the world in this respect, Germany, had but 14,000, with considerably fewer than this in Britain. The number of French university students increased from 60,000 just before the war to around 600,000 by the late 1960s, a tenfold growth mostly since 1950. This educational explosion occurred all over Europe.

The new universities were taught by a kind of intellectual middle class, less prestigious than Oxbridge but more receptive to nontraditional studies: Sociology flourished there in England, experiencing a remarkable boom in a land which heretofore had almost neglected it. The students were less subtle and perhaps less able but often intensely interested. The immense expansion in numbers of university students clearly bore some relationship to student radicalism; students might complain of the mass effect, feeling unrecognized and "processed" rather than educated. In many universities, a critical situation due to dreadful overcrowding obviously existed. There may also have been an overproduction of degree recipients in such fields as sociology, leading to frustration.

But other factors entered also. A widespread *malaise* among the young at the sheer dullness of contemporary life lay behind their restless, often aimless protests. A spirit something like that of 1914 might be detected; not that the young wanted this time to march off to war, for their protests were likely to be directed *against* war. But they craved excitement, demanded romance, and took to violence in their marches and protests. Their bitter complaints, directed vaguely against "the system," "the establishment," or other whopping abstractions, more often reproached the quality of life in a society ever more technological, ever more specialized, ever more organized. It was Max Weber's "iron cage" of "rationalization" that closed in on them; they echoed Ruskin's complaint about people being fragmented by the division of labor, while art and adventure and spontaneity disappeared from life. They looked for some Great Adventure. They faced a long list of exhausted options: no more wars, no more revolutions, no great crusades, no more great movements in the arts, no more undiscovered lands or exotic places. Whether destined for the factory or the office, they found the prospects of work unexciting.

Whatever one's preferences in a list of the causes of the "youth rebellion"— and many would wish to include the factor of affluence, of enough wealth to permit the spoiled children of yesterday's bourgeoisie to indulge all their fantasies of a world without work—it is obvious that ideas entered in. There were special intellectual currents abroad in this period that shaped the contours of radical thought.

An article in 1973 in the Soviet Union, whose Communist orthodoxy criticized the "New Left" radicalism of the students and was in turn rejected by them, named all the following as "revisionist" misleaders of youth: Scheler, Husserl, Unamuno, Heidegger, Jaspers, Camus, Garaudy, Adorno, Horkheimer, Marcuse, Fromm. The well-informed student will recognize here most prominently the existentialists along with members of the Frankfurt school (critical Marxists). Well might the essay have added Chairman Mao Tse-tung and the Chinese Communists, much more popular with youth than Moscow's old-fashioned Reds; the student attempts to take over the universities were indeed modeled after Mao's Great Cultural Revolution in China. It should have mentioned Jean-Paul Sartre, who had transferred his existentialist *engagement* to the cause of total, violent revolution. This intoxicating ferment of ideas stemmed from neo-Marxism, nourished on the discovery of the master's long unpublished early writings and on wholesale reinterpretations of his thought, freeing Marx from bondage to boring Kremlin "diamat"; from existentialist and Freudian amalgamations with Marxism; from Third World champions of revolt in Cuba, Vietnam, Algeria; from the Maoist model; and from other sources as well. The sexual revolution was well underway. (A much discussed event of the year 1960 which may prove to be a landmark of cultural history was the British court case which adjudged D. H. Lawrence's *Lady Chatterley's Lover* not obscene. The decision opened the gates to a flood of pornography.) The word was "liberation." The black flag of anarchism was as much in evidence as the red one in student demonstrations; and the new Marxism talked less about economic exploitation than about the alienation of the individual in a false society. Herbert Marcuse, in fact, accused capitalism of producing not too little but too much, thus corrupting the working class. Affluence, more than poverty, was the target of criticism; even more so was bureaucracy, the whole industrial society, the technological society—shades of Max Weber, as well as Marx and Bakunin.

The necessary revolution against a culturally impoverished, "one-dimensional" capitalism cannot be led by the workers, the New Left gospel taught, for they have become a part of the system, seduced by bourgeois values. But Lenin's vanguard party has also proved to be a terrible delusion, leading only to bloody tyranny without cultural progress. The revolution must be the work of those completely outside the system, such as students, dropouts, and the guerrilla bands in the colonial world. Seizing university buildings in campus uprisings, the revolutionary students hoped to set off further revolts throughout the society, which they held to be linked together indissolubly in a single system. Total negation, rejecting the society *in toto,* was seen as the key to drastic social change, after which all would live freely in sexual and esthetic fulfillment. Both Marcuse and the Sartre of *Critique of Dialectical Reason* seemed to reject any kind of group organization on a permanent basis; all "structures of authority" must be abolished, the self-motivating individual left free to find self-realization. This *mélange* of fantasy, utopia, and negation, as can be seen, contained echoes of almost every strain of European social thought from the past two centuries—not only Marx and Freud and Nietzsche and Weber but the early socialists, the anarchists, Trotskyists, existentialists. It all came to a glorious explosion in the period of campus revolt during 1967 and 1968, climaxed by the great Paris Spring of May 1968, when for a moment it looked as if the students would indeed bring down the established order.

VARIETIES OF MARXISM

Some moments of revolutionary ecstasy in the late 1960s, corresponding perhaps to Sartre's "group in fusion" which manages to achieve solidarity without alienation, proved ephemeral, ecstasy being a perishable commodity. A public reaction against student disruptions was not a greater cause of New Left failure than its own vagueness, utopianism, and incurable divisions. And of course for most of the students this adventure had to be a rite of passage; most of the would-be campus Lenins, the Dutschkes and Cohn-Bendits and Tariq Ali, either dropped back into obscurity or found new interests after leaving school. A rage for occultisms and new religions in the "counterculture" soon supplanted guerilla warfare in the classrooms as the next trend.

Student militants frequently claimed to be rejecting all "ideology," all programs and positions. The editor of a compilation of revolutionary materials from this era comments that the movement "owes more to Marinetti, Dada, Surrealism, Artaud, the Marx Brothers, than to Lenin or Mao." Belief in action for action's sake and a mistrust of all intellectualizing led to charges that the New Left was "left-wing fascism"—charges indignantly denied, needless to say. In fact, youth had been deeply if confusedly moved by ideas. The *Thoughts of Chairman Mao* were in every student pocket, Regis Debray's book about Che Guevara sold a million copies as did Fanon's *Wretched of the Earth.* At the height of the Paris student revolt in 1968, Jean-Paul Sartre addressed ten thousand students; an almost equal number showed up for debates about the Marxist dialectic between Sartre, Louis Althusser, Roger Garaudy.

From the furor of the 1960s the most significant theme to select for brief comment was this revival and transformation of Karl Marx. The discovery of a large body of previously unpublished and largely unknown Marx-Engels writings as a factor in this process has been mentioned; also the effect of emancipation from Stalinism in freeing the Marxist mind for new interpretations. In the 1960s several older revisionisms received full recognition, as if their time had come. Long at work seeking to rescue Marx from the dogmatists, the Frankfurt school, which had migrated to New York in the 1930s where its scholars worked in (and with!) considerable obscurity, gained fame with the popularity in his later years of Herbert Marcuse, who died in 1979, an idol of the student revolutionaries. Also belatedly acclaimed were the works of Italian Communist theoretician Antonio Gramsci, written in prison in the 1920s but published only after the war; likewise George Lukacs, Hungarian literary critic and philosopher, who like his friend Bertolt Brecht had clung with leech-like adherence to the Communist party while attempting to save it from Stalinism. Paris professors, concerned that Marxism was "dying of boredom," tried to revivify it by injections of Freudianism, phenomenology, and other stimulants. Most significant of all, Sartre turned his existentialism more pointedly toward Marx, announcing that as the essential and unavoidable doctrine of our time, Marxism must be rescued from the dead hand of "official" Kremlin dogma. To the humanizing of Marx East European philosophers such as the Pole Kolakowski also contributed; the "socialism with a human face" ideology of the 1968 Czech movement drew on Karl Kosik's 1963 *Dialectic of the Concrete.* As boldly as they dared, these East European Marxists used Marxist humanism as a weapon against the Soviet model. A less dogmatic Marx who saw man making his history with no predetermined outcome could support such views as (1) there is no one socialist system that fits all peoples, each country should work out its own model; (2) the alienation of labor, even the class struggle, has not been ended in the Soviet Union; (3) there should be greater freedom and diversity in socialist literature.

Far from the simple sloganizer once dismissed by serious scholars, Marx as fully revealed was a profound and subtle thinker, his new interpreters claimed. Though Marx had turned away from Hegel, the trend now was to re-Hegelianize him (Lenin himself had begun this during the period from 1914 to 1916), which meant less economic determinism, less historical necessity. "Who sees in ideologies the mechanical, passive product of ... economic processes," Lukacs declared, "understands absolutely nothing of their nature and growth, and holds not Marxism but a caricature of it." The Chinese Communists added their voice to the charge that Russian "dialectical materialism" had distorted Marx and led to an elite dictatorship. Lukacs, Gramsci, and the Frankfurt school all broadly agreed that the true Marx was no system maker who created an objective science of history or society. Like most interpretations, this one took what it liked from Marx, excluding the rest; it preferred the early Marx. It startled older Marxists in talking less of economic impoverishment than cultural oppression. Indeed, the neo-Marxists tended to admit what was obvious, that "capitalism" was all too successful in material terms; it had bought off the workers (evidently all too willing to be seduced) with automobiles and television sets, but at the cost of cultural values. The real "contradictions of capitalism" were cultural: Its very material success breaks down social discipline, leads to an extreme enhancement of individual consciousness, yet at the same time demands a straitjacket of corporate conformism and bureaucratic regulation.

The new Marxists were almost all critical of Soviet society as well as Soviet Marxism, which they saw as linked. A monstrous state bureaucracy, suppressing dissent and dehumanizing labor, was clearly not what the founding fathers of communism had intended. Stalinism had debased Marxism into a crude mechanical determinism which led to an elite ruling stratum, in effect a new ruling class. The Soviet Union's alleged Marxism-Leninism was a sad misunderstanding of both Marx and Lenin. From Lenin, the Lenin of *State and Revolution,* one might salvage something—a decentralized society run by the workers, not the bureaucrats.

Drawing heavily on modern psychology or phenomenology and criticizing

Soviet Marxism for having no knowledge of human nature, Western critical Marxism was typically subjectivist and at times almost irrationalist. Some of the Frankfurt school writings assailed "science" as a product of bourgeois culture. Lukacs's "reification" of consciousness, allegedly a product of capitalism, is a result of too much of what Max Weber had called "rationalization." Influence from Weber and Heidegger crept in, though Marxists found much to reject in these thinkers whom they accused of fascistic tendencies. Walter Benjamin, in a well-known Frankfurt essay, shuddered at mass production of art objects, as Adorno deplored jazz and Marcuse despised "one-dimensional" popular culture—a strain of cultural elitism in these thinkers, which allowed the Kremlin to brand them "bourgeois decadents." But Moscow, condemning rock music, long hair, drugs, and sexual freedom, was very much out of it among college youth in the 1960s, while Marcuse, rejoicing in "bodies unsoiled by plastic cleanliness," had their ear for a while.

Some stressed the democratic side of Marx, who had seldom sanctioned revolutionary conspiracies after 1848. Gramsci declared that before the working class makes a revolution it must first conquer in the cultural domain. "Politics is only the means, the end is culture," Lukacs agreed. When, in the 1968 Prague Spring, Alexander Dubcek declared that "it is not possible for a small minority to introduce and maintain socialism"—a heresy which quickly earned him armed intervention from Moscow—he reflected the influence of the new breed of humanist Marxists. And the Soviet suppression of the Czech movement, which sundered a world Communist movement already shaken by the quarrel between China and the Soviet Union, was a watershed beyond which most Marxist waters ran steadily away from the long admiration for Russia as the land of the first great proletarian revolution. The Communist parties of the West, above all in Italy but also in France and Spain, now began to repudiate violent revolution and dictatorship, to talk of appealing to groups other than the "proletariat" and of reaching power by democratic means. They were reevaluating their whole heritage in the light of conditions both in the Soviet Union and in the West. Euro-Communism was now mature enough to stand on its own feet, no longer needing to lean on Moscow, said the leader of the Spanish Communist party. If some disgruntled *gauchistes* accused the party of selling out to the bourgeoisie, other people took heart at the absorption of an alienated minority into the body politic.

These were permanent changes, and in the long run even Soviet Marxism would feel the impact of liberalizing influences. Courageous reformers within Russia such as the Medvedev brothers paid for their efforts with imprisonment or deportation, but the thaw which Khrushchev had begun in 1956 with his "secret speech" denouncing Stalin went on, if with what seemed glacial slowness. The new Soviet establishment did not shoot dissidents without trial, as Stalin would have done, but repressed much more hesitantly. Theorists of "modernization" thought that sooner or later, both being modern urban-industrial societies, the capitalist and Communist regions would "converge" toward a similar social order.

The student uprising foundered on its inconsistencies, contradictions, and divisions, most basically perhaps the contradiction of complete outsiders claiming to lead a democratic, "power to the people" movement while at the same time eschewing elitist dictatorship and claiming the right of a tiny minority to totally revolutionize society. (If the existing society is as corrupt as they claim it is, how can a better one come from it?) As for existentialized Marxism, the laws of neophilia condemned it to come under attack soon from a fresh generation. Louis Althusser led a movement back to Marxist objectivism and scientism, back to *Das Kapital* and away from Hegel, away from "humanism," even if not a return to Stalinism. Academic Marxist disputes became so involved that few except the experts could follow them; Althusser was pronounced incomprehensible. (British Marxist scholar David McLellan complained of Althusser's *Reading "Capital"* that "large parts of the book are virtually unintelligible.") Marxism had become an arcane science mastered only by professional philosophers or social theorists, with almost every point in interminable dispute—light years away from the simple faith of those earlier Marxists now scornfully dismissed as "vulgar." Revolutionaries took to acts of terrorism, mindlessly, while intellectuals frequently confessed to despair at their inability to contribute anything helpful to practical politics. Whether or not Marx had been "embourgeoisfied," he had certainly been mystified.

In his last years Jean-Paul Sartre apparently succumbed to pessimism about the political situation. "No political party offers any hope at all," he sighed, almost a decade after the dissipation of the 1968 moment of ecstasy.[6] His Chinese friend had proved another false prophet; the Vietnam war had ended, leaving less to abuse the Americans about. Still advocating a rather utopian "libertarian socialism," he found no revolutionary potential any longer in a proletariat which had let itself be "serialized." He retracted the view that existentialism is only an enclave within Marxism and returned to purely psycholiterary studies, especially his mammoth, unfinished biography of Gustave Flaubert, whom he saw as the primeval and archetypal modern bourgeois writer-intellectual. He was also busy up until his death being a celebrated world figure, being interviewed and appearing on television. He no longer sold anarchist tracts on the street to get himself arrested. The age of revolution was over, and even Existentialism had grown bourgeois.

STRUCTURALISM

Althusser's Marxism received influences from a new school of thought, rising to prominence in the late 1950s and early 1960s to reach a peak in the later 1960s; whether a passing fancy of the neophiliac age or a permanent contribution to the intellectual landscape of Europe, it might be too early to judge. As a fashion in French ideas it was the successor to existentialism. Structuralism as expressed by anthropologist Claude Levi-Strauss issued an explicit challenge to Sartre. Its mood was cool, detached, objective; it was antihistorical and specialized in mathematical analysis—a new Cartesianism, in some ways, opposing the rather frenetic subjectiv-

[6] See *Situations X*, transl. as *Life/Situation* (1977).

ism and romanticism of the existentialists. The roots of structuralism were in linguistics; Levi-Strauss applied it to anthropology (myths, kinship systems); it soon
became a tool in literary criticism, sociology, psychology, Marxism; a mode of
thought, or a method, that could be used almost anywhere and, as such, able to
transcend narrow specialization and exert a general intellectual appeal.

Unquestionably the brilliant Levi-Strauss, of a French-Jewish family, was the
person who put structuralism on the map. It is true that he borrowed the idea from
the linguistic scholar Roman Jakobson, who had migrated from Moscow via Prague
to the United States, bringing with him the insights of Russian "formalism." And a
younger scholar, Noam Chomsky, influenced by Jakobson, made something of a
sensation in 1957 with his book *Syntactic Structures.* Chomsky found a "deep
structure" underlying the surface forms of sentences, a structure expressible in
mathematical symbols: some kind of built-in human capacity to understand basic
grammatical principles and convert these—generating or transforming them—into
language as it exists. It was a kind of linguistic Kantianism. Wilhelm Dilthey, Max
Weber's teacher, had called his work a "critique of historical reason." Sartre had
written his *Critique of Dialectical Reason.* Chomsky might have titled his book the
critique of linguistic reason. The transcendental *ir*rational had been the object of
Husserl's quest. Immanuel Kant lived on in all these modern projects; but the
structuralists did away with the subject. People, they declared, do not count; the
structures which determine language and, by extension, all culture, are determinants
which use individuals, as Hegel's "cunning of reason" had done. Hegel's agent had
been the World Spirit, working through human history. Structuralism's was a hidden
harmony of things, generating languages, patterns of culture, ideologies, and institutions.

Structuralism was a rationalism: One does not discover the hidden harmonies
or patterns by amassing empirical studies but by means of abstractions, mental
constructs. A homely analogy might be taken from the daily newspaper: It is its
"layout" that the structuralist is interested in and which is found to be arranged in
a grammatical manner, like a sentence. The content would be less interesting; Levi-
Strauss affected to be uninterested in the content of the hundreds of North American myths which he classified, tabulated, and found to be logically related according
to their components.

It is easy to read into structuralism the last stages of a "decadent" weariness.
All ideas have been expressed, all novels written, it only remains to play games with
their elements. Levi-Strauss was a passionate advocate of the "cool" world of the
primitive, to which he had turned (going to Brazil to find the last ones unspoiled by
contact with "civilization"). Roland Barthes, French structuralist critic, found only
"untiring repetition" in literature; the same components used over and over. An
ultrasophistication was evident in the structuralist manner, which tended to be
excruciatingly difficult; the complaint about Althusser's forbidding prose applied
also to Barthes, Jacques Lacan (who applied structuralism to Freudianism, as
Althusser applied it to Marxism), and other high priests of the new arcana. They
were extremely alienated. Lacan was described as "Freud crossed with structural

linguistics and strained through some of the most harrowing French since Mallarmé." A fabulous showman as lecturer, Lacan became a cult figure in the strange world of intellectual high fashion. His role in the 1968 insurrection was to provide the sportive, prank-playing side a status in high theory—for to Lacan the unconscious, realm of the outrageous and absurd as well as obscene, must be unleashed—Marxism of the Harpo variety, a type of insanity later translated onto the television screen by "Monty Python."

The structuralists' most scandalous aspect, the ultimate shocker of the good bourgeois, was their antihumanism. Humanity has been abolished; it was an invention now seen through. History is a process without a subject, its formations imposed on people by a "hidden mechanism," just as language forces one to think in certain ways. The author is irrelevant to the study of a work. *Escape from the Self*—the title of a book said it all.

Whence come these hidden mechanisms, these deep structures that underlie and determine? This is a mystery one can never resolve. Structuralists joined the later Wittgenstein, and perhaps even Heidegger in his later years, in seeing people as ultimately prisoners of language, which one cannot get outside of, no more than the physicists can find an observation point outside nature. Structuralism was however a fascinating new way of looking at everything human and cultural, with which clever people could play complex games. But in some ways it offered a new principle of certainty. It was an answer to historical relativism, since it gives us "a science of the permanent," as Levi-Strauss claimed. Overriding the boundaries of the various academic disciplines or departments of knowledge, a fragmentation which threatens the intellectual disease of tunnel vision, structuralism provided a unifying perspective, tying together not only all the social sciences but all the human studies, including literature, art (*The Hidden Order of Art* was a notable structuralist title), popular culture. Perhaps the ultimate mathematical order, indeed, is the same for all of nature. This logic printed into the human mind—all human minds—may be akin to that which the mathematical mystics, from Pythagoras on down, have viewed as the key to the riddle of the universe. "The penetration of mathematics, mathematical methods, and above all the mathematical way of thinking, into areas which previously appeared to be closed to it," Johannes Weissinger marked as one of the most extraordinary of recent intellectual trends.[7]

Levi-Strauss, when all is said, was the charismatic figure of the Structuralist vogue. His dazzling demonstrations of the hidden order behind kinship systems and myths among primitive peoples subsequently came under much attack, for leaving out some of the data, as perhaps every grand social theory in the end must—Marx

---

[7]In Thomas L. Saaty and F. Joachim Weyl, eds., *The Spirit and the Uses of the Mathematical Sciences* (1969); the same idea is frequently expressed throughout this volume. Structuralist approaches also entered from the side of "organismic" biology, Gestalt psychology, and other "holistic" methods, which stress the need to look at the whole system first, rather than at the parts.

For a debunking of some of these fashions, see David Berlinski, *On Systems Analysis: An Essay Concerning the Limitations of Some Mathematical Models in the Social, Political, and Biological Sciences* (1976).

and Spencer and Freud had suffered the same fate. The French-Jewish anthropologist had begun like Sartre as a discontented Sorbonne philosophy student; born in 1908, he was just three years younger than Sartre, and his life was molded in the same year as Sartre's, 1934, when Levi-Strauss went not to Germany to study philosophy but to Brazil to teach anthropology and fall in love with some of the last unspoiled tribal cultures in the world. He used these delightful savages as a stick to beat modern civilization, and he was at bottom, some have thought, a surrealist poet more than a scientist; certainly he wrote with a beautiful mastery of style. His friend and inspirer, the linguist theorist Roman Jakobson, also was a modernist *litterateur* who had been close to the poet Mayakovsky and others of the pre-1917 Russian *avant-garde*. It was this literary and ideological component that gave structuralism its fighting edge in the 1950s and 1960s when it was in high vogue, influencing the novel and film. But by the same token, its claims to scientific precision were to be called into question.

As a major fashion in thought, challenging if not replacing existentialism, structuralism in turn was to be challenged or modified by the post-Structuralists or deconstructors. The deconstructors, led by the brilliant Jacques Derrida, retained and even intensified the Structuralist abolition of the person, unmasking the "metaphysics of presence" that causes us to assume a person behind the text. No such essential author exists; we have only the text. When we write, we do not "express" ourselves; we enter a domain of words dominated by the modes of language and by an impersonal culture of public discourse. In holding this, the post-Structuralists agreed with structuralism. (Lacan held more or less seriously—it was always difficult to tell—that individuality dated only from the invention of the full-length mirror in the sixteenth century!) But the post-Structuralists took delight in showing that logical structures are illusions, which may be shown to rest on some unproven assumption, some tautology or contradiction. (They tacitly assume that which they reject.) To "deconstruct" is to show that this is so of some system, unpacking it to reveal that at bottom it is no more than rhetoric. (An exercise comparable to Wittgenstein's opening of the fly bottle, it might be noted.) Derrida and other post-Structuralist critics usually held, too, that *texts* have no implicit meaning, whereas the Structuralists had thought that the text, if not the author, may be placed firmly within some logical structure. Not only is there no "real" Marx, or Kafka, there is no real *Capital* or *Castle*, for every reader will take the work differently, it changes its meaning according to time and place, and it is vain to ask which of these numerous interpretations is the "true" one. In the end we have only the irrational realm of language, a magnificent disorder in which, with Nietzsche or Joyce, we may bathe ourselves, rejoicing in life's plenty, without thought of plan or unity in it all.

None of this was perhaps very new. Derrida acknowledged a large debt to Nietzsche. But of the rich ingredients lying about in the storehouse of modern ideas, from Nietzsche, Freud, and the post-Freudians, Existential and Phenomenological philosophers, the poets and novelists and schools of literary criticism, ingenious minds made bewildering mixtures. (Some noted that the structuralist elimination of individuality was only theoretical; it did not prevent some considerable egos from seeking fame; Derrida did not efface his name from the title pages of his books.) Almost anything went; the sanction for highly subjective readings of texts found in Heidegger "hermeneutics" and post-Structuralist criticism put a premium on startlingly *outré* interpretations, provided only that they were adroitly and knowledgeably handled. (For such outrages, one group of American academic literary critics won the appellation "hermeneutical mafia.") In all this might be seen the fine hand of professional academic competition, rewarding novelty and subtlety, granting the posts and the prizes to the innovators and the technicians.

The reigning doctrine of the intellectuals became that no intellectual construction is to be trusted. That this could hardly exclude their own was a point seldom fully appreciated in the glee of exposing other, rival intellectuals as gulls. To take at face value anything affirmed by a writer became a mark of naiveté; one must "unmask" it, reveal its real meaning, show its secret roots in situations social or personal, economic or psychological. Determinism of ideas by forces outside individual control was preached in varying ways by Marxists, Freudians, Structuralists, and others—to the point that an idea might be "overdetermined" ludicrously, subject to five or six interpretations. (What I have written in this book may be explained as a product of my abnormal childhood, my petty bourgeois background, my generation, my reading, etc.)

A common tension or controversy in all the human studies was that stated in the title of a book of readings in psychology: *Without/Within.* Psychologists were polarized between the mechanists—the behavioralists, studying conditioned reflexes and looking upon the human being as a lower animal, subject to social engineering, as B. F. Skinner thought—and on the other hand depth psychologists—existentializing psychologists, "humanistic" ones (following A. Maslow), who were indignant at such reductionism. The most emotional dispute among historians was between the "quantifiers," with their computerized methods and their pages of statistics, and those more traditional historians, who sought the concrete experiences in all their uniqueness. Sociologists were divided into several schools among which a line was evident between phenomenologists and "symbolic interactionists" on the one side and objectivist, behavioralist schools on the other. It seemed impossible to capture both the richness and inwardness of specific reality and the universality of law-like generalizations. The generalizers produced statistical tables and "laws" so abstract, or tautological, as to be meaningless. The particularizers described endless numbers of actual cases but lost track of the larger meanings. Within Marxism, the two strains have fought from the beginning, down to Sartre versus Althusser, and were present in Marx himself.

In this perennial antinomy, which Kant had indicated in his unresolvable dualism of phenomenal and noumenal realms, the structuralists seemed to come down heavily on the objectivist side. Alienated from the excessively "hot" twentieth century with its chaos of individual egos, they would wipe out the subject and abolish consciousness. Yet their own principle of organization was an inward one: Structures derive from that logic printed in each mind, the world has meaning because we endow it with such. In this they would seem to agree at bottom with their foes, the existentialists.

THE FRAGMENTATION OF THOUGHT

Despite yearnings for wholeness, themselves an indication of its loss, the trend of Western thought was toward ever less unity, ever more fragmentation of knowledge. The old dream of the *totum scibile,* the sum of the knowable, which might be mastered by a single mind, was doubtless always an unobtainable ideal, but it had existed as a goal.[8] Now it had to be given up, along with the quest for some absolute system of values. One might endow chaos with the less opprobrious name of "pluralism" and gradually learn to live with it. "This situation does not bother me," a recent writer on the theater remarks, the situation being one where "there exists in the West no set of artistic, cultural or social standards so sacrosanct that they are not constantly under attack nor any standards readily at hand to replace them."[9]

Among the leading dilemmas of modern humanity is the factor of sheer size. It is not less a factor in the realm of ideas than it is in social life generally; in fact, it is above all a problem here. Consider the quantity of writing. It has been estimated that more books have been published since 1945 than in the entire preceding 490 or so years since the birth of printing. A hundred thousand or so books are published each year in Western Europe and the United States, not to count the thousands of periodicals. Scholarship and criticism have proliferated with the multiplication of university posts; a vast number of people have been brought somewhere near the region of serious thought and expression as mass higher education spreads. This region was, as recently as the earlier part of this century, inhabited by a small intellectual elite, numbered probably in the low thousands for Western Europe. That number has now swelled to millions. Never were so many books read by so many. Encouraging, no doubt; and yet bringing with it, as the inevitable price of quantity, fragmentation, loss of unity, and intense specialization. "Literature today is fragmented. . . . Scholarship is fragmented too; so is life." Thus was the recent (1968) lament of a distinguished British scholar.

Specialization, with technical competence in a high degree but compensating losses in range, depth, and linkage with other fields, is found wherever one looks. It has infected philosophy itself, no longer monarch of the intellect but largely content to be a specialized branch of experimental science. Economics, also, has fallen victim to specialization, as has sociology, in that the grand classical syntheses have been abandoned in favor of microanalysis, the examination of particular situations

---

[8] For a note on this ideal as a nineteenth-century scholar felt it, see John Sparrow, *Mark Pattison and the Idea of a University* (1967). In his last, unfinished novel, *Bouvard et Pecuchet,* Flaubert records the efforts of two retired office workers to make an inventory of all human knowledge.

[9] John Elsom, *Erotic Theatre* (1973), p. 193.

rather than the whole of society. It would be impossible to find a branch of learning not afflicted with this sort of crisis. There is far more knowledge; it is far less meaningful because less integrated. This dilemma has also appeared in other disciplines formerly more humanistic. Much literary criticism in recent times has spurned the historical, biographical, or moral aspects for close verbal or structural analysis of the work of literature itself—a sort of literary linguistic analysis. The branches of creative literature themselves have shown a similar pattern. A distinguished contemporary English literary critic (Graham Hough) has spoken of the enormous gains in "technical competence, sheer skill in handling the tools" since 1935 or so—of the conquering, among other things, of a whole new realm, the unconscious—and yet accompanying this a "loss of authority," a loss also of range and substance, a tendency to deal with the "ripples on the surface" of life.

Widely noted in the 1960s was the crisis in the arts, with the apparent playing out of the "modernist" movement in a paroxysm of fads. While thousands of "little magazines" flourished, and public poetry readings testified to an urgently felt need, the net effect was aimlessness and sterility. The modernists—in the age of symbolists and expressionists, of Eliot, Yeats, Joyce, the surrealists, all that dazzling exhibition of virtuosity and audacity that lay between Rimbaud and Pound—had played with the fire of extreme subtlety and subjectivity—statements personal, elliptical, complex, multileveled. They were often aware that after them, almost nothing else could be except chaos. In the words of Stephen Spender, himself a great modern poet, "to go further would lead to a new and completer fragmentation, utter obscurity, form (or rather formlessness) without end." Nietzsche had foreseen the "dissolution of art" once it had cut loose completely from the discipline of the classical rules and bounds. Rimbaud, Verlaine, the surrealists, and the dadaists did it once; but one cannot add to them, one can only repeat them in ever more violent and therefore feebler ways. Writing of the contemporary *avant-garde,* Ken Baynes remarks that "the artist's brave cry of freedom has turned into the shout of a buffoon." Among recent *avant-garde* trends, theater of cruelty, merging the grotesque and shocking, drew on surrealism, Kafka, the Marx brothers, the Lacanian dream world of buffoonery, with elements of sadism in which people are often eaten, tortured; sexual perversion—these are just the cheerier parts. The London stage in the 1960s was enriched by spectacles of babies being stoned to death, soldiers burned alive. The diminutive Spaniard, Fernando Arrabal, whose childhood had been traumatized by the Civil War, became a Parisian favorite in the 1970s; his themes included "sadism, masochism, matricide, necrophilia, scatology, perversion, and stage nudity" (Francis Donahue)—necessary now to secure a shock effect. (The rage of the younger generation was that of those who wanted to break the rules but found no rules left to break.) The equivalent of these trends in drama could of course be found in all the other arts.

In the more institutionalized areas of knowledge, technique has brought precision, has eliminated much untidiness, and cleared up errors, but it would seem to have entailed a loss of vitality and to have fragmented thought and culture into unrelated pieces. Historical writing today takes the form of well-researched, technically accomplished studies, making use of archival material—the sacred emblem of the historian's guild—but lacking the literary skill, the grand manner, the sweep of older historians. To the archives were then added statistical data analyzed by computers. Any publishable or attention-drawing monograph had to come equipped with charts, graphs, content analysis, and some psychohistory, whether it needed it or not. The new, or supposedly new, "social history" made use of both arcane records and computer-based statistical analysis to shed light on the masses of common folk heretofore approached by novelists and antiquarians more than by historians; or at least they exposed the quantifiable aspects of their behavior, an exercise often standing in arid contrast to the needs for more subjectivity. Similar frontiers of highly esoteric methodology invaded literature departments, rendering what used to be the mere "appreciation" of the great writers one of the most forbidding disciplines this side of nuclear physics. In both literary and historical (as well as archeological[10]) studies, the influence of Freud, or of Freud blended with structuralism, was notable; few major figures and events escaped being reduced to an offshoot of neuropathology. Similar innovations invaded other of the traditional subjects like economics and political science, while whole new ones were invented. It then became necessary to establish "interdisciplinary" methods, which only added more to the load of specialized pedantry.

If the arts offered less scope for Western humanity's spirit, the same could perhaps be said for science. A considerable chapter in the history of recent thought can be written around the theme indicated in C. P. Snow's widely read and discussed book of 1959, *The Two Cultures*. Sir Charles, a novelist of note as well as a public administrator with a keen interest in science, charged the entire literary-humanist camp with a disregard for and ignorance of science, as well as with a general irresponsibility toward all public affairs. Since the dawn of modernism the novelist and poet had cultivated a domain of private sensibilities, scorning the area of "normal" life where dwelt such hopelessly philistine souls as politicians and businesspeople. (If they turned to politics, they hoped to revolutionize it completely and were quite unrealistic.) It was a function of their profound alienation from modern society. Science, needless to say, was one of the West's grand intellectual traditions, if not *the* grand tradition, and the realm of Galileo and Newton remained central through the Enlightenment and into the age of Darwin and Pasteur. Educated, enlightened people normally expected it to lead the march of progress toward a better, more decent life for all. Even if, like the socialists, they rejected the way modern industrial society is organized, they expected a better organization to release the beneficial effects of scientific technology. In the 1970s and 1980s, the antinuclear, environmentalist Greens enlisted more support among discontented youth than any other cause. If "for them, politics is hardly the practice of the possible," as one of their ex-leaders observed, this was because they had little inter-

---

[10]The "new archeology" sought to impose theoretical models to "decode" (a code word) the scattered evidence dug up by unimaginative field workers; it included some angry young American Leftists of the 1960s whose work the more traditional archeologists regarded as wildly speculative and pseudoscientific.

est in or comprehension of the mainstream goals of a technological society. Particularly strong in Germany, these rebels against the values of *both* capitalist West and communist East often looked to strains in serious philosophy (Heidegger) or literature, those that were most agrarian, reactionary, or mystical.

Science itself as an arena of thought and activity was exciting yet frightening. The dramatic discoveries in genetics raised prospects of "biological engineering" while laser technology's military potential threatened to destabilize the nuclear "balance of terror." Intellectual synthesis in post-Einstein physics remained elusive. A pluralistic universe, as we recall, had been indicated in the failure to find a single kind of force. Einstein, clinging to his faith in an orderly cosmos, spent his last years (he died in 1955) working on a unified field theory, attempting to unite his special and general relativities, electromagnetism and gravity, by postulating that ultimate physical reality consists not of particles but of fields, that is, areas of influence, like knots in a string. In 1945 Einstein published a general theory of this sort, but few scientists accepted it. The disarray got rather worse in ensuing years. The number of subatomic particles that scientists identified reached 200, their classification uncertain. The protons and neutrons that make up the nucleus of atoms were themselves smashed by giant cyclotron accelerators to reveal their subunits—in a never-ending cycle of the infinitely small?—to which some literate scientist—a true reconciler of the two cultures war—gave the name of "quarks," borrowed from *Finnegans Wake.* There now appeared to be not two but four basic forces: added to electromagnetism and gravity were the "strong force" binding together atoms and molecules—the awesome force of nuclear energy—and a "weak force" that held together the protons and neutrons. Hope was held out for an eventual formula that might link at least some of these forces, but no one was sure. In one type of theory the five dimensions had increased to eleven! Some of the subatomic particles lived less than a billionth of a second, others apparently occupied no space at all. At the other extreme, literally billions of galaxies (each containing billions of stars like our own solar system) were revealed by radio telescopes, which also turned up quasars, pulsars, black holes—the gravitational collapse of large stars leading to a sensational confirmation of Einstein in the trapping of light. Those who tried to keep up with these amazing frontiers of physics might suspect a total divorce of language from reality, confirming Wittgenstein: One should not confuse these instrumental words and formulas with ontological reality, with which they have no connection. Or they might find that science as human perception of reality constantly changes, like the arts and like the fads and fashions which sweep through urban populations ever more rapidly. Science never reaches final truths, it overthrows yesterday's theory with a new one which will also last but a short time—and so *ad infinitum,* or as long as a precarious civilization endures. No stable fulcrum could be found in science. The new physics was more bizarre than any science fiction.

The myth of science appeared to fade as it was increasingly identified with the kind of society intellectuals hated. The technological society looked uncivilized as well as polluted. Science meant technology. Its crowning achievement of the 1960s was a trip to the moon, much heralded and looked toward; but when it happened the thrill did not last. The real frontiers for contemporary humanity lie within the human heart and must be crossed with the help of studies quite other than the rational science for which Western civilization had long been famous. Such was the burden of many a book and essay. There were complaints that an excess of products and wastes upsets the balance of nature and corrupts air and water. Here was an ambivalence: Science went on, technology went on, not only because there was no way of stopping them but because many of the things they created could not be rejected. Not even intellectuals appeared to want to do without the comforts offered by modern technology. Yet there was a serious questioning of the values of "more and more," of material goods for their own sake, questions Carlyle and Ruskin had raised long before but which now spread widely throughout society.

The Soviet Union had conducted ever since 1917 an experiment in a monist or monolithic society built on a single ideology. The cost was ghastly persecution of dissent under Stalin, and costly mistakes in appraising the status of the sciences. Yet the Soviet Union survived, largely because Russia had been accustomed through centuries of misfortune to endure a great deal. It modernized and industrialized; but the contradiction was that the modernized, urban, technological society is inevitably pluralistic and attempts to suppress dissent from Marxist-Leninist-Stalinist orthodoxy by force are increasingly futile.

The thaw in the Soviet Union of the Stalinist ice-block of dogmatism and isolation might seem agonizingly slow, but it went on steadily. Defiantly refusing to accept in principle any equation of the two "industrial societies," and continuing to insist that socialism leading to communism must replace and supplant "capitalism" as the highest and last historic form of society, the aging leaders of the Soviet Union in fact watched the dissolution of their utopian dreams. Their society was neither more efficient nor more enlightened nor more moral than the West, if anything less so, and was becoming steadily more open, more modernized, less distinctive. Students of Soviet intellectual life noted the convergence as often as did those who looked at the economic system or the popular culture: The attempt to mark off a Marxist science and philosophy and literature which differed from and was superior to that of the corrupt and decadent capitalists failed at point after point and was quietly abandoned, except in public rhetoric. In both societies, a range of problems was similar. While even the Western communists gave up their belief in "Soviet civilization" and young radicals looked elsewhere for their inspiration if they looked anywhere, the only excitement coming out of Russia concerned the courageous dissidents, the Solzhenitsyns and Medvedevs and Sakharovs, who dared to denounce the cancer wards of an ugly repression and to point to the moral bankruptcy of an order that revealed the horrors of Stalin's tyranny but did not dare repudiate it. The collapse of communism as a viable alternative to capitalism spread over the world, until revolutions in non-European countries directed against Western influence denounced *both* Moscow and Washington, seeing them as much alike. The Age of Lenin died in 1968, with the flagrant armed intervention to prevent Czechoslovakia from adopting a democratic socialism—at the same time as the student revolutions in the West signaled the crisis of *its* order.

The world watched the drama of Soviet dissent, whether in the Soviet Union itself or in the Eastern European satellites. If a battery of courageous dissidents were left with little to show for their efforts, the chief ones eventually being expelled, their ineffectiveness owed less to suppression, perhaps, than to their own disunities—some offered a reformed socialism, others like Solzhenitsyn would retreat to conservative religion, while the distinguished physicist Andrei Sakharov recommended liberal freedoms. And even more to the fact that the Soviet Union in unacknowledged ways actually was becoming a pluralistic if not democratic society. There was a clandestine free enterprise segment of the economy. The *samizhdat* or self-published, illicit books and magazines appeared in profusion; reforms in the direction of "market socialism" rather than completely centralized planning were installed in the satellites. Hungary, her revolution crushed in 1956, quietly liberalized under a Communist dictatorship that became adept at hiding pragmatic reforms behind a facade of public orthodoxy. The heroic Polish workers' movement known as Solidarity exploded in 1980 to be suppressed by a Polish regime that tried to prevent the even worse fate of Russian intervention by a relatively humane terror. Cynicism was the outstanding feature of attitudes within the Communist bloc. It seemed likely that the leaders themselves had lost all ideological faith though the legitimacy of their tattered authority rested on the pretense of maintaining it.

"Monolithic social ends," Karl Popper writes, "would mean the death of freedom: of the freedom of thought, of the free search for truth, and with it, of the rationality and dignity of man." The case for European liberalism rests on the value of the "open society" as well as on the hatefulness of persecution for conscience's sake. It rests on the belief that only through the free inquiry of many minds working in many ways can we hope to find solutions to our manifold human problems, still so numerous as almost to stagger the mind. The retreat to an island of dogmatism enforced by the sword is a shallow, superficial, erroneous answer—really an abdication.

But the pluralism and sophistication of the Western intellect create difficulties, though they are a source of strength. It now finds it difficult to believe in anything; it tries, but it is too self-conscious, it knows that its faith will be a myth. Contemporary culture lacks unity and lacks faith; yet people want and seek these things.

The postwar years witnessed some valiant attempts at integration of knowledge. Arnold J. Toynbee's vast tapestry of universal history with its sweeping claim to unearth the laws governing the rise and fall of civilization was not favorably received by most professional historians. Yet the literate public eagerly bought and read it, indicating a thirst for "philosophical" history, not assuaged by most historical writing today. With vast erudition and an appropriately grave and classical style, Toynbee set forth on the somewhat romantic quest of finding in history the secret of the sickness of Western civilization. He offered a study in comparative civilizations, identifying twenty-one different civilizations in human history and seeking to show the common pattern of their inception, growth, decline, and disintegration—some, in his view, having perished completely. A meditative if sometimes platitudinous style, a deeply spiritual outlook, an awareness of an amazing range of ideas as well as historic facts, lent to Toynbee's leisurely *Study of History* (altogether in twelve volumes, the substance of it abridged by D. S. Somervell in two volumes) a great appeal. His conclusions were not regarded by most of his competent critics as having much validity. "Laws" turn out to be truisms; there is doubt about the neat isolating of civilizations as separate units; comparisons mean little when stripped of Toynbeean rhetoric. A landmark of these times, Toynbee's massive work testified to the global perspective and to the technical resources of the modern historian—the historian of no previous generation could have assembled so much knowledge from all over the world—and to the perennial interest in the great question, whither mankind? But it scarcely provided an answer.

Toynbee protested against too much narrow specialization but fell afoul of specialists. Most historians seem content to plough well their own narrow furrow, each building his own separate tunnel to the past, as one historian has recently put it. (J. H. Hexter). This is the tendency in all branches of knowledge. Martin Heidegger wrote in 1929, in one of his searching criticisms of modern civilization, that "the scientific fields are far apart. Their subjects are treated in fundamentally different ways. Today this hodgepodge of disciplines is held together only by the technical organization of the universities and faculties and preserves what meaning it has only through the practical aims of the different branches."

Overspecialization is a particular danger because it may cut off that crossfertilization of the disciplines that has so often proved stimulating in the past. Darwin received vital stimulation and critical ideas from Malthus, Kant from Rousseau, Kepler from Pythagorean mysticism, Freud and Marx were masters of the literary tradition. If the disciplines—or even worse, small sections within each discipline, as seems to be the case today—are cut off from each other and from a matrix of general ideas common to all, we have a formula for scientific desiccation. Our sciences as well as our general culture will dry up, humanity itself will shrivel, the human personality lose itself in a wilderness of jargon and pettiness. The individual in modern specialized society loses the human personality to become "an agglomeration of functions." This destruction of a sense of whole being seems to be what the existentialist psychotherapists (such as the German Binswanger) have in mind as the basic cause of neurosis and psychosis in the individual.

It may be noted that this complexity and specialization defeats the dreams of the individual's mental power and thus ends a long epoch in modern history. The realm of knowledge becomes far too vast for any one mind to grasp, even in the most general terms, and one gives up the quest, resigning oneself to being at the most a cog in some incomprehensible machine. People of the Renaissance, Enlightenment, and romantic era thought it possible to understand everything. In the sixteenth century, Walter Ralegh observed casually that he bought *every* book that was published! In the eighteenth, a Voltaire, a Hume, a Jefferson kept abreast of just about all branches of knowledge, also without impeding their numerous other activities. The last of those who still sought omniscience were the great nineteenth-century synthesizers, Hegel, Marx, and Spencer, but their schemes broke down. Synthesis is beyond the grasp of anyone today, evidently. Such virtuosi of erudition as Toynbee and Teilhard reach toward it, but even these are far from achieving it. This dream must be abandoned; and if so, the failure would seem to entail a fundamental alteration in Western humanity's outlook: a defeat for individualism, for rationalism in the older sense. The assault on what David Knowles calls "a single reasoned and intelligible explanation of the universe on the natural level, and a single analysis of man and his powers . . . valid for all men and final within its sphere" came under attack as early as the fourteenth century with the skepticism of Ockham and was further eroded in the Reformation. And yet, as Knowles adds, this skepticism "was never wholly victorious, and never finally accepted": European humanity clung to its dramatic belief in an ultimate knowledge accessible to the enlightened mind. Doubtless both Hegelianism and Darwinism in their different ways undermined it; doubtless no one had ever really been omniscient; and yet the great Victorians did continue to believe in the unity of knowledge and the individual's ability to grasp in a general way this unity. If we are driven to complete fragmentation, we are at the end of rational individualism. Perhaps we are at the end of personality as well as philosophy—condemned to be interchangeable with computers or to be intellectual drones who heap up useless knowledge.

Thus the "dissolution of man," the abolition of the subject in a sea of self-generating discourse, proposed by the Structuralists, seems most appropriate to the modern situation. Contributing to this dehumanization is that "consciousness of life's increasing depreciation" (Erich Heller) which is a product of earth's steady dethronement from center of the cosmos to an obscure speck of dust. Likewise, the disintegration of human ties amid the hurry and impersonality of vast cities which causes people to look to the State for all manner of "social services" once provided personally; which in turn furthers social disintegration.

Another consequence of overspecialization, or at least a related cultural phenomenon, is the gulf between the average person and the expert or adept. There is no audience, no common ground. The complexity and diversity of thought, breeding a situation in which a few experts in any area communicate only with each other, leaves a vacuum in the popular mind which must be filled largely by rubbish. While the popular market for fiction and nonfiction alike is mostly satisfied by low-quality journalism, serious thought and advanced expression go on among isolated and esoteric minorities. Cultural distance between popular and advanced thought has always existed and perhaps always will; but there have been cultures wherein a general consensus or forum was closer to a possibility than in the vast democratic nations of today. This is sometimes blamed on their being vast, or their being democratic; but the true culprit, in the main, would seem to be the intellectual fragmentation that has been discussed.

THE QUEST FOR VALUES

A major dilemma of modern humanity obviously is its need for life-giving values, which can evidently come only from some sort of religious faith (religious in the widest sense), while its heritage of skepticism prevents any such belief. This dilemma is substantially that expressed by a Shavian character who cried that "we have outgrown our religion, outgrown our political system, outgrown our strength of mind and character. The fatal word NOT has been miraculously inscribed in all our creeds."[11] "I've been looking for something to believe in," says Alan Squier in Robert Sherwood's *Petrified Forest* (1936). "I've been hoping to find something that's worth living for—and dying for." Modern poets, novelists, dramatists, philosophers, preachers have now and again found things worth living and dying for. They found it in the 1930s and 1940s in the struggle against nazism and after that possibly in the fight against communism. These were negative crusades—against something evil that had appeared, something itself the result of modern spiritual illness—and it is not clear that they provided the basis for a positive structure of value. Plainly many people believe in and struggle for such things as social justice, racial equality, honest government, the elimination of extreme poverty, national self-government for peoples who do not have it, and so forth. The questions remain, freedom for what? (Georges Bernanos, *La liberté pour quoi faire?* 1953). A higher standard of life to what end? Can liberty, equality, and democracy really be ends in themselves, or are they not rather the means through which humanity can achieve some goals and values of life? If so, does not achievement of the former without the latter lead only to an ignoble materialism, an affluent society with vulgar tastes, the spiritual deserts of suburbia so often seen today in the United States?

In this dilemma there were signs of a yearning to return to traditional creeds. The great Italian writer and former communist, Ignazio Silone, has declared that "the rediscovery of a Christian heritage in the revolution of our time remains the most important gain that has been made in these last years for the conscience of our generation" (1946). Both world wars quickened interest in religion. Silone joined the late W. H. Auden, the late T. S. Eliot, Graham Greene, the late François Mauriac, and many another distinguished elder representative of the literary world in embracing a Christian creed, sometimes after having followed strange gods earlier. The Oxford and Cambridge scholar C. S. Lewis, one of the most brilliant men of his generation, had earlier found his way to "Mere Christianity." Appalled by his intellectual friends abasing themselves before a great tyrant, the British writer and TV personality Malcolm Muggeridge wrote of *Jesus Rediscovered* (1969). Christian Socialist or Christian Democrat political parties had emerged from World War II, the result of the stark choices facing people under tragic conditions; the same forces that bred existentialist commitment encouraged a return to traditional religion. (The great German resisters of Hitler were Christians, like the martyred Dietrich Bonhoeffer.) Though the French Christian Party (M.R.P.) failed to live up to its early promise, the Christian parties in West Germany and Italy almost dominated the politics of their respective countries through the postwar decades. Toynbee concluded his massive and widely read study of civilizations with the advice to return with a contrite heart to the bosom of religion; he saw a higher religion as the leading *telos* of the historical process and speculated about a future world religion

[11] *Too True to Be Good* (1934).

to be synthesized from the present international crisis. Via a series of popular lectures and books drawn from *A Study of History,* the last four volumes of which appeared in 1954, Toynbee became a well-known public figure.

Sixty years of atheist rule in the Soviet Union had not destroyed the Russian churches, which persisted underground despite all persecutions, and the great Alexander Solzhenitsyn in his crusade against Stalinist society reaffirmed the Orthodox creed. The Roman Catholic Church was a bulwark against total communization in Poland during the widespread protests of 1980–83. Among many other signs of a persisting religious thrust was the thriving study of theology, producing great figures like the Heidegger-influenced Karl Rahner (d. 1984). Sartre's atheist existentialism, as we know, was not the only brand; Gabriel Marcel and Paul Tillich were among those described as Christian existentialists, while Martin Buber was a tremendously prestigious Jewish one. In the 1960s there was a lively Marxist-Christian dialogue in Europe, marked among other things by the passage of a leading French communist theoretician, Roger Garaudy, over to the Christian side. Others than Toynbee explored the possibility of a higher religious synthesis between East and West. Jung directed attention to the universal symbols or archetypes underlying all religious experience. Zaehner, Kerenyi, Eliade, and others engaged in a massive exploration of the domain of comparative religions. Never was there greater interest in historical and theological studies of the Christian past.

Unfortunately all this religious spirit was as fragmented as the rest of thought. There was a much publicized "ecumenical" movement in the Christian world aimed at breaching the walls between sects and churches, which gave rise to many a conference and book, but in the end it seemed to do little to halt the fissiparous tendencies. There were all manner of new Christians.

Some of the dilemmas confronting a Christianity that wishes to adjust to the modern age were illustrated by "secular theology" which in its earnest desire to make the Church "relevant" virtually bracketed out any Christian content. The position popularized in England by the Bishop of Woolwich (*Honest to God*) prided itself on being liberated from anything specifically Christian in the way of formal creed or liturgy. Leaning on "situation ethics," the Church could bypass conventional Christian morality; it could even talk of atheist or religionless Christianity. Muggeridge wondered whether there would be anything left of "institutional Christianity" within a few years. Even the Roman Church was shaken by a series of crises marked by bold criticism of the Church from left-wing theologians like the Swiss Hans Küng; in surrendering to a degree to demands for "modernization," including church services in the vernacular, the Church risked alienating its traditional membership. The Latin American wing led one portion of the Roman Church toward alliance with radical political causes. One obvious danger in all this was losing anything recognizably Christian, as in those split-level Unitarian churches satirized by the American novelist Peter De Vries, indistinguishable from pinkish political clubs. To take the Church down the road of Karl Marx rather than John D. Rockefeller might do it some good, but it was equally dissolvent of Christianity as such. While "Jesus freaks" among the youthful held to little recognizable in the old orthodoxy, learned theologians "de-mythologized" the Word (though to be sure there were some countervailing tendencies, for example in the school of Professor Pannenberg of Mainz); any specific content of Christian doctrine seemed in danger of disappearing.

It is evident that the whole period we have dealt with in this book has had as one of its underlying long-term movements that aspect of modernization called secularization: that is, a steady decline in the religious aspects of life as function after function is transferred to nonreligious, secular, "lay" institutions. Once upon a time not so long before 1789, religion was virtually the same thing as society; not only philosophical and ethical teaching, but art, music, and architecture were focused on the Church and its creed, and in addition all manner of social services including health care and care of the poor came from the clerics. Education of course had been a monopoly of the only literate class, the clerics or clerks; and so late as the nineteenth century the transformation of clergymen into professional lay teachers, "professors" or "dons" was just underway in the universities.[12] This vast process has continued relentlessly, grinding away every bit of what once permeated all of life, and there is no reason to suppose so massive a trend can be checked; the very nature of modern society is nonreligious.

Clearly there were startling signs of a yearning for faith in the profusion of often weird spiritual phenomena among the young and the alienated.

A host of cults ranging from scientology and astrology to the Unification Church and other sometimes bizarre sects eloquently registered the need for faith. All sorts of mixtures of Eastern and Western religions, neosuperstitions and pseudo-scientisms were available, especially if one lived in California. Harvey Cox, trendy-religious holder of a chair of theology at Harvard University, testified in his 1978 *Turning East* that "within twenty blocks of the intersection of Massachusetts Avenue and Boylston Street, forty or fifty different neo-Oriental religious movements thrive" in Boston. A wave of religious fundamentalism swept in from the Islamic world in the 1970s. The mixture of peoples in the increasingly polyglot cities of the world made for an amalgamation of all creeds as never before.

In London as much as in San Francisco there were visionaries like John Michell who received messages from beyond the earth portending the end of an age and the beginning of another marked by a new "expansion of consciousness"—code words in the anticities where dropouts from the conventional society explored alternative life-styles. (A famous one appeared inside Copenhagen, staid Danish capital that emerged astonishingly as the porn capital of Europe for a time in the early 1970s.) Here evidently was the counterpart of that religious ferment which had marked the declining days of the ancient world. Apocalyptic themes appeared everywhere, and even children's literature, according to a German report, changed from the traditional happy optimism to preoccupation with "psychic catastrophes, violence, injustice, unmerited destruction" (*Stimmen der Zeit,* November 1976.) Apocalyptic themes abound in science fiction, that most popular of literary genres,

---

[12] See, for example, A. J. Engel, *From Clergyman to Don: The Rise of the Academic Profession in the Nineteenth-Century Oxford* (1983).

whose celebration of scientific marvels now turned toward visions of the extinction of this planet, or this galaxy, or this universe—"waiting for the end."

The children of affluent French, Swiss, German, Italian parents could be found along with Americans roaming the roads of India in search of salvation in Hinduism or hashish. Meanwhile in West Germany another report indicated that 10 to 12 percent of all people would at some time or another in their lives seek psychiatric help, while the widespread use of tranquilizing drugs by respectable Americans accompanied a flourishing trade in books offering advice about how to "cope," to handle stress, and so forth.

All this is familiar; anxieties are as obvious as liberations, the "expansion of consciousness" as evident as the troubles it brings along with its pleasures. An increasing number of people find that, paradoxically, the most affluent of societies is the least endurable. Quite often a chiliastic hatred of the great Babylon of the world, accompanied by ecstatic visions of a future perfect state, resembled nothing so much as early Christianity. And perhaps the children living in communes as hippies were engaged in bringing forth a second Jerusalem. Certainly many of them see visions and believe in signs and portents. They predict the end of the world and cultivate witchcraft. Such a strange variety of spiritual phenomena has not been seen since the age of the Reformation.

But this "new religious consciousness," about which much was said, in the end seems to mean little except that modern humanity is uprooted, intermingled, disturbed. The indices of divorce, mental illness, suicide, crime, drug addiction point alarmingly to such symptoms of anomie and anxiety. If the function of religion is to provide a core of values that all can share, uniting and stabilizing the community, then these numerous crazes flitting through the heated urban world do not serve the function of religion, but are rather a sign of its absence. They are akin to the fervid worship of ephemeral pop music and film stars and sports heroes. They bear comparison to art fashions among the more cultivated. They compete with various secular ideologies, remnants of nineteenth-century socialism or anarchism.

Of these, feminism is a notable one. Born during the French Revolution like all other ideologies (apart from some faint earlier anticipations), the cause of women's rights and liberation was represented prominently in the George Sand generation; John Stuart Mill was its Liberal spokesman, as we recall; then Ibsen and the *fin de siècle* artist-intellectuals presaged a great upsurge in Edwardian England when the "suffragettes" endured martyrdom and practiced terrorism in their demand for voting rights.[13] Winning the right to vote (though not until after World War II in France), women entered the work force in increasing numbers and divorce laws were liberalized; it was possible for a woman to declare in 1956[14] that women's emanci-

---

[13] Despite the clamorous nature of recent feminism with claims that it really was the first important such movement (one ardent feminist dated the modern calendar from 1968), the Edwardian women would seem to bear away the prizes. A quarter of a million women attended some of their mass rallies, over 100 women were arrested at one 1910 demonstration in front of Parliament; they broke windows, slashed art works, tied themselves to railway tracks, threw themselves under horses, perfected all the devices of "civil disobedience" practiced by later protestors. The core of the support came from middle- and upper-class women, not lower class.

[14] Marjorie Tait, *The Education of Women for Citizenship* (1956).

pation was all but completed. If nevertheless an outburst of radical feminism in the late 1960s brought with it claims that female slavery had existed without alleviation since time immemorial, this was because this cause served quasi-religious purposes. (It was also because women who took part in the youth revolt of the 1960s discovered "male chauvinism" among their revolutionary partners. Fidel Castro, Stokely Carmichael, and all manner of sexually liberated New Leftists saw women's role in a somewhat nonliberated light. This contradiction between the sexual and the class struggle somewhat repeated the experience of women in the pre-1914 Socialist movement.) The Liberationist surge related also to educational expansion and the new scholarship: A veritable intellectual revolution was contained in looking at old issues in the light of women's participation. "Everything one looks at assumes a different appearance," a feminist scholar rightly observed.

Against the imperatives of faith, the critical reason of modern humanity stood ready to aim its deflating shafts. British empiricism as represented by Lord Russell and others remained unconvinced of the merits of anything not founded on experimental verification and the critical reason. "As soon as it is held that any belief . . . is important for some other reason than that it is true, a whole host of evils is ready to spring up," Russell remarked. And it is more than doubtful that he would regard the truths of Jung, of the existentialists, and of the crisis theologians as demonstrable. "Scientific humanists" like Julian Huxley combined a strong dislike of Christianity and others of the classic "religions," such as Buddhism, with a conviction that Western humanity desperately needs some sort of substitute for religion, some kind of integrating and orienting idea-system, rooted in science yet able to supply values. This feeling bears some relationship to the Russian-American social theorist P. A. Sorokin's call for an "integral" philosophy, to combine the best of all of his alleged sociocultural modes, the idealist, sensate, and ideational—in other words to get the best of the religious, philosophical, and scientific worlds. So Huxley's humanism looked very much like Comte's religion of humanity, asking us in effect to worship human nature. In the view of existentialist and religious critics, Sir Julian's man-worship leads to those very totalitarian systems he most abhors, to nazism and communism, which are the fruits of godlessness and "titanism." But this vigorous scientist, who became the first director of UNESCO, would say that only through the scientific reason can one find the way to sanity in an age of irrationality.

If religious need is, as C. E. M. Joad has written, "a product of man's consciousness of his loneliness and helplessness in an alien and indifferent universe," then this need has never been greater than it is today; for with all its technological apparatus, modern humanity must realize as never before how frightening are the cosmic forces it confronts. "The spirit of man in the present age has been under a gray pall of uncertainty, insecurity, skepticism," a well-known British philosophical writer, Lord Samuel, remarked a few years ago. In the present age, it has also exhibited unconquerable vitality, defying a hostile universe to assert new values, in a truly Promethean gesture. But there remains a deep schism in the soul of the West which it is hard to see being altogether cured, so long as it retains the knowledge and subtlety of which skepticism is the natural fruit. This dilemma has haunted the

Lasting almost a century, Bertrand Russell's life stretched from the Edwardian to the Atomic era and was involved at almost every stage with controversy. The notable philosopher ended as a militant political activist especially famed for his leadership of the Campaign for Nuclear Disarmament. (Caricature of Bertrand Russell by Jack Rosen, caricaturist of World Figures. Courtesy of the Bertrand Russell Archives, McMaster University.)

most sensitive and creative minds of the twentieth century. And this dilemma may explain why intelligent non-Westerners have been puzzled by the West's apparent lack of faith in itself. Dr. Malik, the Arab philosopher, remarked a few years ago that "the Western mind . . . has been softened and undermined from within and without. The effect of this softening has been for this mind to lose faith in itself. . . ."

A study of André Malraux by William Righter finds the clue to that extraordinary Frenchman in a restless search for a cause. In turn revolutionary, novelist, art critic, and politician, this modern Chateaubriand, child of Nietzsche, Spengler, and Pascal, with a sense of modern humanity's tragic predicament tried to escape it by finding a worthy goal to pursue. Though he tried many, it is not clear that Malraux ever settled on one. Like his political foe, Jean-Paul Sartre, Malraux was the protean consciousness constantly remaking itself.

Pervasive criticism deflates all constructions, seeing them as "myths." Disenchantment with the mainstream society of bureaucracy and business was a century or more old; but now there was disenchantment with all the political revolutions against this bourgeois order, which whether Right or Left had sadly, often grimly, failed. There was disenchantment too with the artistic free spirit whose proud myth had degenerated into market-oriented buffoonery. The identity crisis grows ever worse. Widely noted by political analysts was the increasing volatility of voters, who retain less loyalty to a party, switch rapidly and unpredictably, demand more and more of government, and find any regime intolerable after a short time—"the ungovernable in pursuit of the unattainable." Meanwhile rapid technological change moved toward the "postindustrial" society in which electronics, biochemistry, and other tertiary industries replace the old smokestack and blue-collar factories, demanding more brain power of a certain kind. Those prepared to specialize in computers could get well-paid jobs and by all accounts were highly bored with them. The affluent professionals became the most restless, often alienated, element: not Marx's proletariat, which had never been revolutionary, but the educated technocracy formed the nucleus of possible revolution. "Revolution to what end?" remained the unanswered question.

THE NEXT STAGE?

Having pointed out some notable areas of tension afflicting common civilization today—between technology and humanism, reason and faith—and some signs of decadence, it would be wrong not to add that every civilization confronts similar conflicts, along with others, and that Western civilization possesses terrific resources of vitality with which to encounter them. Western civilization has revealed powers of renewal and regeneration many times before. Its history is a history of renaissances, of which *the* Renaissance, the postmedieval renewal based on rediscovery of the ancient classics, was only one. Battered by the terrific crisis of the Reformation, Europe came up with the scientific and intellectual renaissance of the seventeenth century, a renewal based on the creative use of older materials. Shaken by the French Revolution and its wars, Europe integrated this revolution into its traditional culture in the nineteenth century. Mass democracy, specialization, and industrial technology today present a challenge that Western civilization may be able to meet.

The historian is inevitably uncertain in the present. Tomorrow is necessary to understand today. That is the very reason for writing history: With the passage of time, the past falls into perspective—into various perspectives, indeed—and events or ideas which then seemed chaotic reveal their meaning. The historian is at a loss to predict the future. "Historicisms" of the past which claimed that they had found the key to all history, past, present, and future, stand forever discredited; we can no longer believe in this particular brand of theology disguised as science. Evolution creates ever fresh forms which are outgrowths of the past but could not have been predicted; lucky guesses are possible, but systematic prediction and control are not. If one knew only the seed one could hardly foretell the plant. In history, too, we are in the position of not knowing what the final result, if there is any, will be. Of all people, indeed, the historian is probably most aware of diversity and contingency in humanity's affairs. (This has not prevented the growth recently of "futurology," the intense and solemn study of the future, as if the most pressing problem confronting modern humankind was prognostication.)

One guess which seems very nearly a certainty is that the West must and in-evitably will continue its contacts with non-Western peoples, including not only the richly developed Oriental civilizations but also peoples much closer to the primitive than ourselves. Asia and Africa have entered into history, and the world has taken on new dimensions for European humanity. A typical comment is this one by Mircea Eliade: "Western culture will be in danger of a decline into a sterilizing provincialism if it despises or neglects the dialogue with the other cultures. . . . The West will have to know and to understand the existential situations and the cultural universe of the non-Western peoples. . . . Furthermore, this confrontation with 'the others' helps Western man better to understand himself."[15] Professor Eliade, a lead-ing student of comparative religions, adds that some recent developments in Western thought have prepared us for this task. Depth psychology, including Jung's interest in the world of myth as related to the dynamism of the psyche, is one; and in gener-al that discovery of the unconscious irrational which came to Europe in the age of Nietzsche and Freud, and of the symbolists in art. This encounter between the European West and Africa and Asia began in small ways long ago but has only recently reached the stage of a true syncretization of cultures, enhanced by the spatial mobility of the modern age.

There is a great deal of mixing and mingling going on today, as everyone knows. Americans assist in the founding of African universities; people from all over the world come to American, British, French, and Russian universities; thou-sands of scholars annually exploit the lavish subsidization of international intel-lectual exchange. Refugees from Palestine, Vietnam, dissidents fleeing Soviet perse-cution, all kinds of other displaced persons swell the cities of the free world which become almost homogeneous, from Singapore to Sao Paulo and Lagos to Los Angeles—all melting pots of "cosmic man."

The outcome of all this is most problematical; but no one would deny that it must eventually entail some sort of a revolution in the mental outlook of all human-kind. What sort, it is impossible to predict. Wyndham Lewis spoke of "cosmic man," denationalized and made into a common mold; he thought that the Ameri-cans represented this process, having no particular national culture but being products of the modern machine age, and that the rest of the world would sooner or later be "Americanized." It is a fate many European intellectuals would regard as worse than death, yet there may be something in it. Their own lands are in fact being to a degree "Americanized" by the penetration of modern technology and its by-products and of cultural democracy. (One of the most widely read serious books of recent years in France was *The American Challenge,* by the brilliant politician-journalist Jacques Servan-Schreiber.) Neither machine technology nor democracy was invented by the Americans; they only arrived at their full fruition earliest in the United States. Television and the cinema are "cosmic" cultural forces, along with the business and industry of a world increasingly knit together commercially. The "international style" in architecture may be as depressing as most motion pictures

---

[15] See his *Myths, Dreams, and Mysteries: The Encounter Between Contemporary Faiths and Archaic Religions,* (1975).

made on the French Riviera by American producers using Italian actresses; it may be equally depressing to some to watch Tokyo change from a Japanese city to a kind of exotic imitation of New York. Fads for Zen or for African art may seem the shallow pretensions of pseudointellectuals. But all this happened once before in history, at the time of the Alexandrian and then Roman Empire. And perhaps out of this vast process of syncretization will emerge new civilizations, as Western Europe emerged from the decay of the ancient world.

For better or worse, ideas seem to become more important in the postmodern world. Leisure time increases apace with more education in postindustrial society. At the same time the decay of traditional social institutions leaves the individual seeking more of his or her amusements elsewhere than in custom; in books, records, movies, sports, television. Most of this, no doubt, is not very intellectual and indeed from a traditional perspective is appallingly crude. Yet for a growing minority, serious art, literature, music, and thought are increasingly important. These are all big businesses, whether we look at symphony orchestras paying star conductors salaries not too incommensurate with those earned by football players and rock musicians, the sale of paintings for millions of dollars, or the vast royalties earned by a successful novelist who may well be a Mailer or Bellow with pretensions to advanced culture. A great many people today obviously live in the worlds created by such as Joyce, Marcel Proust, William Faulkner. (Some years ago Virginia Woolf had remarked that "the life which is increasingly real to us is the fictitious life.") In 1982 thousands of people from all over the world descended on an amazed Dublin to celebrate Joyce's one-hundredth anniversary year, by enacting scenes from *Ulysses* on "Bloomsday," which to them were obviously more real as well as more interesting than anything in real life. In France you can take tours revisiting the places important in Proust's great novel. Television productions of *Sons and Lovers, Buddenbrooks,* Wagner's *Ring,* Dickens's *Nicholas Nickleby,* and many other classics of modern literature reach millions of viewers. Meanwhile academics make major industries of all these figures, of Marx and Nietzsche, Sartre and Wittgenstein, as well as the creative writers. Taken all in all, it is impossible to deny that with all its anti-intellectual crassness, contemporary mass society also omnivorously consumes Culture, as humanity never consumed it before.

John Locke long ago claimed that "in truth the ideas and images in men's minds are the invisible powers that constantly govern them." This is the realm of what Father Teilhard de Chardin has named the "noösphere," the realm of the mind and all its products. Here, as Julian Huxley has written, man finds "floating in this noösphere . . . for his taking, the daring speculations and aspiring ideals of men long dead, the organized knowledge of science, the hoary wisdom of the ancients, the creative imaginings of all the world's poets and artists"—all this and much more too. The organization of the noösphere, both these great modern biologists suggest, is the great task of the future and one which has scarcely yet begun. Huxley has noted how much of the vast amount of knowledge presently being accumulated, in the various special branches of learning, is "lying around unused" because "not integrated into fruitful concepts and principles, not brought into relevance to human life and its problems" (*The Humanist Frame*, 1961).

If the most urgent task confronting us is the organization of our ideas that they may be creatively used, and if these ideas indeed are "the invisible powers that govern men," then the systematic study of ideas, in relation to life, that is, the social and historical context, would seem to be not the least important of the many studies currently pursued.

Suggested Readings

This listing of books recommended for further reading is highly selective. There is a large literature on almost every particular subject. For the student doing research, some aids to locating additional sources are given at the end of this bibliography.

The Enlightenment and the French Revolution

Franco Venturi, *Utopia and Reform in the Enlightenment* (1970); Alan C. Kors, *D'Holbach's Coterie* (1976); Douglas W. Johnson, ed., *French Society and the Revolution* (1976); Robert Darnton, *The Literary Background of the Old Regime* (1982); Joan McDonald, *Rousseau and the French Revolution* (1965); Richard Cobb, *Reactions to the French Revolution* (1972); Marilyn Butler, ed., *Burke, Paine, Godwin and the Revolution Controversy* (1984); John P. Clark, *The Philosophical Anarchism of William Godwin* (1977); Carl B. Cone, *The English Jacobins* (1968); Gerald W. Chapman, *Edmund Burke: The Practical Imagination* (1967); Colin Bonwick, *English Radicals and the American Revolution* (1977); J. L. Talmon, *Origins of Totalitarian Democracy* (1960); Christopher Herold, ed., *The Mind of Napoleon* (1955), and *Mistress to an Age: Mme. de Stael* (1958); Claire Tomalin, *The Life and Death of Mary Wollstonecraft* (1974); J. F. C. Harrison, *The Second Coming: Popular Millenarianism 1780–1820* (1979).

Kant and German Philosophy

Frederick Copleston, *History of Philosophy* Vols. VI, VII (1960, 1963); Arnulf Zweig, ed., *The Essential Kant* (1971); W. H. Walsh, *Kant's Critique of Metaphysics* (1975); J. M. Mahanty and R. W. Shahan, ed., *Essays on Kant's Critique of Pure Reason* (1982); Robert P. Wolff, ed., *Kant: A Collection of Critical Essays* (1968); H. J. Paton, *The Categorical Imperative: A Study in Kant's Moral Philosophy* (1967); Gordon S. Brittan, *Kant's Theory of Science* (1978); Karl Jaspers, *Kant* (1962); René Wellek, *Kant in England* (1931); John Herman Randall, Jr., *The Career of Philosophy*, Vol. 2, *From the Enlightenment to the Age of Darwin* (1965); Tom Rockmore, *Fichte, Marx, and the German Philosophical Tradition* (1980);

F. M. Barnard, *Herder's Social and Political Thought: From Enlightenment to Nationalism* (1965); George A. Kelly, *Idealism, Politics, and History: Sources of Hegelian Thought* (1969).

Romanticism

Geoffrey Grigson, ed., *The Romantics* (1962); Walter Jackson Bate, *From Classic to Romantic* (1946); Meyer H. Abrams, *The Mirror and the Lamp* (1953); Maurice Bowra, *The Romantic Imagination* (1961); Hugh Honour, *Romanticism* (1979); Northrop Frye, *A Study of English Romanticism* (1968); Northrop Frye, ed., *Romanticism Reconsidered* (1963); Harold Bloom, ed., *Romanticism and Consciousness* (1970); Geoffrey Hartman and David Thorburn, ed., *Romanticism: Vistas, Instances, Continuities* (1973); Peter L. Thorslev, *The Byronic Hero* (1962); G. P. Thompson, ed., *The Gothic Imagination: Essays in Dark Romanticism* (1974); Robert T. Denommé, *Nineteenth Century French Romantic Poets* (1969); S. S. Prawer, ed., *The Romantic Period in Germany* (1970); D. O. Evans, *Social Romanticism in France 1830-1848* (1951); Kenneth N. Cameron, ed., *Romantic Rebels: Essays in Shelley and His Circle* (1973); Fred Kaplan, *Thomas Carlyle: A Biography* (1984).

Political Ideologies

René Remond, *The Right Wing in France from 1815 to De Gaulle* (1965); Hans Rogger and Eugen Weber, ed., *The European Right* (1965); R. A. Lebrun, *Throne and Altar: The Political and Religious Thought of Joseph de Maistre* (1965); David P. Calleo, *Coleridge and the Idea of the Modern State* (1966); W. F. Kennedy, *Humanist versus Economist: The Economic Thought of Samuel Taylor Coleridge* (1958); John Stuart Mill, *On Bentham and Coleridge* (reprinted 1950); Klaus Epstein, *The Genesis of German Conservatism* (1966); Donald Read, *Cobden and Bright* (1968); William D. Grampp, *The Manchester School of Liberalism* (1960); Walter M. Simon, ed., *French Liberalism* (1972); Jack Lively, *The Social and Political Thought of Alexis de Tocqueville* (1962); James J. Sheehan, *German Liberalism in the Nineteenth Century* (1978).

Political Economy and Utilitarianism

Mary P. Mack, *Jeremy Bentham: An Odyssey of Ideas* (1962); Bhiku Parekh, ed., *Bentham's Political Thought* (1973); David P. Crook, *American Democracy in English Politics 1815-1850* (1965); Mary Thale, ed., *The Autobiography of Francis Place* (1973); William Thomas, *The Philosophical Radicals* (1979); D. H. Hodgson, *Consequences of Utilitarianism* (1967); A. Sen and B. Williams, ed., *Utilitarianism and Beyond* (1982); Marc Blaug, *Ricardian Economics* (1958); D. P. O'Brien, *The Classical Economists* (1975); Thomas Sowell, *Classical Economics Reconsidered* (1974); H. B. Acton, *The Morals of Markets* (1971); Warren J. Samuels, *The Classical Theory of Economic Policy* (1968); William Peterson, *Malthus* (1979); Gertrude Himmelfarb, *The Idea of Poverty: England in the Early Industrial Age* (1984); Harold Silver, *The Concept of Popular Education: A Study of Ideas and Social Movements in the Early Nineteenth Century* (1965).

Early Socialism

George Lichtheim, *Origins of Socialism* (1969); R. B. Rose, *Gracchus Babeuf* (1978); Elizabeth Eisenstein, *The First Professional Revolutionary: Buonarroti*

(1959); J. F. C. Harrison, *Quest for the New Moral World: Robert Owen and the Owenites in Britain and America* (1969); Frank E. Manuel, *The New World of Henri Saint-Simon* (1956); G. G. Iggers, *The Cult of Authority: Political Philosophy of the Saint-Simonians* (1958); N. Riasonovsky, *The Teaching of Charles Fourier* (1969); Jonathan Beecher and Richard Bienvenu, ed., *The Utopian Vision of Charles Fourier* (1983); Robert L. Hoffman, *Revolutionary Justice: The Social and Political Theory of P. J. Proudhon* (1972); Peter Stearns, *Lamennais: Priest and Revolutionary* (1968); Christopher H. Johnson, *Utopian Communism in France: Cabet and the Icarians 1839-1851* (1974); J. T. Ward, *Chartism* (1973); W. J. Fishman, *The Insurrectionists* (1971); James T. Billington, *Fire in the Minds of Men: Origins of the Revolutionary Faith* (1980); Martin Malia, *Alexander Herzen and the Birth of Russian Socialism* (1961); Albert S. Lindemann, *A History of European Socialism* (1984).

Hegel and Hegelianism

Peter Singer, *Hegel* (1983); Raymond Plant, *Hegel* (1973); Herbert Marcuse, *Reason and Revolution: Hegel and the Rise of Social Theory* (1941); Walter A. Kaufmann, *Hegel: A Reinterpretation* (1965); J. N. Findlay, *Hegel: A Reexamination* (1957); B. M. G. Reardon, *Hegel's Philosophy of Religion* (1977); Shlomo Avineri, *Hegel's Theory of the Modern State* (1973); Walter Kaufmann, ed., *Hegel's Political Philosophy* (1970); Bernard Cullen, *Hegel's Social and Political Thoought, An Introduction* (1979); George D. O'Brien, *Hegel on Reason and History* (1975); Charles Taylor, *Hegel and Modern Society* (1979); Burleigh T. Wilkins, *Hegel's Philosophy of History* (1979); William J. Brazill, *The Young Hegelians* (1970); David McLellan, *The Young Hegelians and Karl Marx* (1969); Sidney Hook, *From Hegel to Marx* (1950); Edward J. Brown, *Stankevich and His Moscow Circle 1830-1840* (1967); Marilyn Chapin Massey, *Christ Unmasked: The Meaning of "The Life of Jesus" in German Politics* (1983). (See also under *Marx.*)

Victorian Thought

Walter E. Houghton, *The Victorian Frame of Mind* (1957); Gordon Haight, ed., *The Portable Victorian Reader* (1972); Gertrude Himmelfarb, *Victorian Minds* (1968); B. M. G. Reardon, *Religious Thought in the Victorian Age* (1980); Ian Bradley, *The Call to Seriousness: The Evangelical Impact on the Victorians* (1976); Trygve Tholfsen, *Working Class Radicalism in Mid-Victorian England* (1977); Angus Wilson, *The World of Dickens* (1970); Marghanita Laski, *George Eliot and Her World* (1973); John D. Rosenberg, *The Darkening Glass* (1961), and *The Genius of John Ruskin: Selections from His Writings* (1963); Edward Alexander, *Matthew Arnold, John Ruskin, and the Modern Temper* (1973); Michael St. John Packe, *Life of John Stuart Mill* (1954); John M. Robson, *The Improvement of Mankind: The Social and Political Thought of John Stuart Mill* (1968); Shirley Letwin, *The Pursuit of Certainty* (1965); Pedro Schwarz, *The New Political Economy of John Stuart Mill* (1973); Alice Rossi, ed., *Essays on Sex Equality by John Stuart Mill and Harriet Taylor Mill* (1970); Martha Vicinus, ed., *Suffer and Be Still: Women in the Victorian Age* (1972).

Comte and Positivism

John Stuart Mill, *August Comte and Positivism* (reprinted 1961); D. G. Charlton, *Positivist Thought in France 1852-1870* (1959); Walter M. Simon, *European Positivism in the Nineteenth Century* (1963); Gertrud Lenzer, ed., *Comte's Essential Writings* (1975); Christopher Kent, *Brains and Numbers: Elitism, Comteanism and Democracy in Mid-Victorian England* (1978); H. W. Wardman, *Ernest Renan: A Critical Biography* (1964); M. A. Crowther, *Church Embattled: Religious Controversy in Mid-Victorian England* (1970); Anthony Symondson, ed., *The Victorian Crisis of Faith* (1970); U. C. Knoepflmacher, *Religious Humanism and the Victorian Novel* (1965); A. O. J. Cockshut, *The Unbelievers: English Agnostic Thought 1840–1890* (1966); Donald Thomas, *Swinburne: The Poet and His World* (1979); Harry Levin, *The Gates of Horn: A Study of Five French Realists* (1963); J. Hillis Miller, *The Disappearance of God* (1963).

Darwin and Darwinism

Philip Appleman, ed., *Darwin* (1979); Bentley Glass, ed., *Forerunners of Darwin* (1959); G. G. Gillispie, *Genesis and Geology* (1951); Roy Porter, *The Making of Geology: Earth Science in Britain 1660–1815* (1977); Peter L. Brent, *Charles Darwin* (1981); David Hull, *Darwin and His Critics* (1973); Peter J. Vorzimmer, *Charles Darwin, the Years of Controversy 1859–1862* (1971); Michael Ruse, *The Darwinian Revolution: Science Red in Tooth and Claw* (1979); Neal C. Gillespie, *Charles Darwin and the Problem of Creation* (1979); Basil Willey, *Darwin and Butler* (1960); D. F. Bratchell, *The Impact of Darwinism* (1981); Stephen J. Gould, *Ever Since Darwin* (1977), and *The Panda's Thumb* (1980); J. R. Moore, *The Post-Darwinian Controversies* (1977); Brian Leith, *The Descent of Darwin: A Handbook of Doubts about Darwinism* (1982); William Irvine, *Apes, Angels, and Victorians* (1955).

Herbert Spencer, Social Darwinism

Robert C. Bannister, *Social Darwinism: Science and Myth in Anglo-American Thought* (1978); J. W. Burrow, *Evolution and Society: A Study in Victorian Social Theory* (1966); Bernard Semmel, *Imperialism and Social Reform* (1960, 1968); Greta Jones, *Social Darwinism and English Thought* (1980); Linda L. Clark, *Social Darwinism in France* (1984); Frank M. Turner, *Between Science and Religion: The Reaction to Scientific Naturalism in Late Victorian England* (1974); Alfred Kelley, *The Descent of Darwin: The Popularization of Darwin in Germany 1860–1914* (1981); J. D. Y. Peel, ed., *Herbert Spencer on Social Evolution* (1972), and *Herbert Spencer: Evolution of a Sociologist* (1971); J. G. Kennedy, *Herbert Spencer* (1978); Murray J. Leaf, *Man, Mind and Science* (1979); George W. Stocking, *Race, Culture, and Evolution: Essays in the History of Anthropology* (1968, 1982); Michael P. Banton, *The Idea of Race* (1977); Michael D. Biddiss, ed., *Images of Race* (1979).

Marx and Marxism

David McLellan, ed., *Karl Marx: Selected Writings* (1977), and *Karl Marx, His Life and Thought* (1973); L. Kolakowski, *Main Currents of Marxism*, Vol. I. (1978); S. Avineri, *Social and Political Thought of Marx* (1969); R. H. Hunt, *The Political Ideas of Marx and Engels* (1974); Robert C. Tucker, *Philosophy and Myth in Karl Marx* (1961); S. S. Prawer, *Karl Marx and World Literature* (1976); Paul Thomas, *Marx and the Anarchists* (1980); Norman Levine, *The Tragic Deception: Marx contra Engels* (1975); Karl Federn, *The Materialist Conception of History, A Critical Analysis* (1971); Frank Parkin, *Marxism and Class Theory: A Bourgeois Critique* (1979); Marshall Cohen et al., eds., *Marx, Justice and History* (1980); G. H. R. Parkinson, ed., *Marx and Marxisms* (1982); M. C. Howard and J. E. King, *The Economics of Marx* (1976); George Lichtheim, *From Marx to Hegel* (1971); Lucio Colletti, *Marxism and Hegel* (1973); Anthony Giddens, *Capitalism and Modern*

Social Theory (1971); Z. A. Jordan, *The Evolution of Dialectical Materialism* (1967); Dick Howard, *The Marxian Legacy* (1978).

Other Socialism: Second International Marxism

Kolakowski, *Main Currents of Marxism*, Vol. 2 (1980); Leslie Derfler, *Socialism Since Marx* (1973); Gary P. Steenson, *Karl Kautsky 1854-1938: Marxism in the Classical Years* (1978); Peter Gay, *The Dilemma of Democratic Socialism: Bernstein's Challenge to Marx* (1952); J. P. Nettl, *Rosa Luxemburg* (1966); Harvey Goldberg, *Jean Jaurès* (1962); George Lichtheim, *Marxism in Modern France* (1966); F. F. Ridley, *French Syndicalism* (1970); Patrick H. Hutton, *The Cult of the Revolutionary Tradition: The Blanquists in French Politics 1864-1893* (1981); Paul Avrich, ed., *Bakunin on Anarchy* (1972), and *The Russian Anarchists* (1967); Temma Kaplan, *Anarchists of Andulasia, 1868-1903* (1976); Willard Wolfe, *From Radicalism to Socialism: Foundations of Fabian Socialism 1881-1889* (1975); Norman and Jeanne MacKenzie, *The Fabians* (1977); J. W. Hulse, *Revolutionists in London: A Study of Five Unorthodox Socialists* (1970); Peter D'Arcy Jones, *The Christian Socialist Revival in England* (1968); Lillian P. Wallace, *Leo XIII and the Rise of Socialism* (1966). (For Russian socialists and revolutionaries, see under *Lenin*.)

Nationalism

Eugene Kamenka, *Nationalism: The Nature and Evolution of an Idea* (1976); Salo W. Baron, *Modern Nationalism and Religion* (1947); Anthony D. Smith, *Theories of Nationalism* (1971, 1983); Friedrich Meinecke, *Cosmopolitanism and the National State* (transl. 1970); M. B. Petrovich, *The Emergence of Russian Pan-Slavism* (1956); N. Riasanovsky, *Russia and the West in the Teaching of the Slavophiles* (1952); Leonard Schapiro, *Rationalism and Nationalism in Russian Nineteenth Century Thought* (1967); Eugen Weber, *Peasants into Frenchmen: The Modernization of Rural France 1870-1914* (1976), and *Action Française* (1962); Robert Soucy, *Fascism in France: The Case of Maurice Barrès* (1973); Peter Brock, *The Slovak National Awakening: An Essay in the Intellectual History of East Central Europe* (1976); George Barany, *Stephen Szechenyi and the Awakening of Hungarian Nationalism 1791-1841* (1968); Oliver MacDonough, W. F. Mandle, and Pauric Travers, eds., *Irish Culture and Nationalism 1750-1950* (1983); Rosalind Mitchum, ed., *The Roots of Nationalism: Studies in Northern Europe* (1980); David Vital, *The Origins of Zionism* (1975), and *Zionism: The Formative Years* (1982).

Nietzsche

Walter Kaufmann, ed., *Basic Writings of Nietzsche* (1968) and *Nietzsche: Philosopher, Psychologist, Antichrist* (4th ed., 1974); F. C. Lea, *The Tragic Philosopher* (1957, 1973); R. J. Hollingdale, *Nietzsche, the Man and His Philosophy* (1965); Arthur Danto, *Nietzsche as Philosopher* (1967); Malcolm Pasley, ed., *Nietzsche: Imagery and Thought* (1978); J. P. Stern, *The Study of Nietzsche* (1979); Martin Heidegger, *Nietzsche* (1961, 1979); Karl Jaspers, *Nietzsche: An Introduction to the Understanding of His Philosophical Activity* (1965); R. H. Thomas, *Nietzsche in German Politics and Society 1890-1918* (1983); Freny Mistry, *Nietzsche and Buddhism* (1981); Herbert W. Reichert, *Nietzsche's Impact on Modern German Literature* (1975); William D. Williams, *Nietzsche and the French* (1952); Patrick Bridgwater, *Nietzsche in Anglosaxony* (1972), and *Nietzsche and Kafka* (1974); Rudolph Binion, *Frau Lou: Nietzsche's Wayward Disciple* (1968); William J.

McGrath, *Dionysian Art and Populist Politics in Austria* (1973); Bernice G. Rosenthal, *The Artist as Prophet: D. S. Merezhkovsky and the "Silver Age"* (1975).

Bergson, Sorel

Thomas Hanna, ed., *The Bergsonian Heritage* (1962); A. E. Pilkington, *Henri Bergson and His Influence* (1976); S. K. Kumar, *Bergson and the Stream of Consciousness Novel* (1963); P. A. Y. Gunter, ed., *Bergson and the Evolution of Physics* (1967); I. J. Gallagher, *Morality in Evolution: The Moral Philosophy of Henri Bergson* (1970); Gerhard Masur, *Prophets of Yesterday* (1961); Jack J. Roth, *The Cult of Violence: Sorel and the Sorelians* (1980); J. H. Meisel, *The Genesis of Georges Sorel* (1951); Michael Curtis, *Three Against the Third Republic* (1959); I. L. Horowitz, *Radicalism and the Revolt Against Reason* (1961); Richard Vernon, *Commitment and Change: Georges Sorel and the Idea of Revolution* (1978); John and Charlotte Stanley, ed., *From Georges Sorel: Essays in Socialism and Philosophy* (1976); David D. Roberts, *The Syndicalist Tradition and Italian Fascism* (1979); Isaiah Berlin, *Against the Current: Essays in the History of Ideas* (1980); John Stanley, *The Sociology of Virtue: Political and Social Themes of Georges Sorel* (1981).

Freud

Ronald W. Clark, *Freud: The Man and the Cause* (1980); Marthe Robert, *The Psychoanalytic Revolution: Sigmund Freud's Life and Achievement* (1966); Harry F. Ellenberger, *The Discovery of the Unconscious* (1970); Jonathan Miller, ed., *Freud* (1972); Paul Ricoeur, *Freud and Philosophy* (1970); Robert Bocock, *Freud and Modern Society* (1978); Frederick J. Hoffman, *Freudianism and the Literary Mind* (1957); Edwin R. Wallace, *Freud's Anthropology* (1983); Martin G. Kalin, *The Utopian Flight from Unhappiness: Freud Against Marx on Social Progress* (1974); H. J. Eysenck and Glenn D. Wilson, *The Experimental Study of Freudian Theories* (1973); B. A. Farrell, *The Standing of Psychoanalysis* (1981); Gerald N. Izenberg, *The Crisis of Autonomy: The Existentialist Critique of Freud* (1976); Erich Fromm, *The Crisis of Psychoanalysis* (1970); David E. Stannard, *Shrinking History: Freud and the Failure of Psychohistory* (1961); Lucy Freeman and Herbert S. Strean, *Freud and Women* (1981); Morris Lazerowitz, *The Language of Philosophy: Freud and Wittgenstein* (1977).

Jung, Other Psychoanalysts

Robert S. Steele, *Freud and Jung* (1982); Walter Kaufmann, *Freud versus Adler and Jung* (1980); *Freud-Jung Letters* (1974); Anthony Storr, ed., *The Essential Jung* (1983); Paul J. Stern, *Jung: The Haunted Prophet* (1976); Ira Progroff, *Jung's Psychology and Its Social Meaning* (1969); Peter Homans, *Jung in Context* (1979); James Olney, *The Rhizome and the Flower: Jung and Yeats* (1980); Bettina L. Knapp, *A Jungian Approach to Literature* (1984); Charles B. Hanna, *The Face of the Deep: The Religious Ideas of Carl Jung* (1967); Carl G. Jung, *Man and His Symbols* (1964); Paul Roazen, *Freud and His Followers* (1971); Anthony Clare, *Psychiatry in Dissent* (1979); T. S. Szasz, *Karl Kraus and the Soul Doctors* (1976); Phyllis Grosskurth, *Havelock Ellis* (1980); J. E. Rivers, *Proust and the Art of Love* (1980).

The Beginnings of Modernism in the Arts

Malcolm Bradbury and James McFarlane, ed., *Modernism 1890–1913* (1976); Herschel B. Chipp, *Theories of Modern Art: A Source Book* (1968); Roger Shattuck, *The Banquet Years: The Arts in France 1885–1918* (1958); Roy Pascal, *From Naturalism to Expressionism: German Literature and Society 1880–1918* (1973); Carl Schorske, *Fin de Siècle Vienna* (1980); Samuel Hynes, *The Edwardian Turn of Mind* (1968); Carl and Ellendra Proffer, *The Silver Age of Russian Culture* (1971); Edmund Wilson, *Axel's Castle* (1936); Anna Balakian, *The Symbolist Movement: A Critical Appraisal* (1977); Holbrook Jackson, *The 1890's* (1913); Mario Praz, *The Romantic Agony* (1954); Philippe Julian, *Dreamers of Decadence* (1971); James West, *Russian Symbolism* (1970); Vladimir Markov, *Russian Futurism* (1969); Marianne W. Martin, *Futurist Art and Theory* (1968); Paul Raabe, ed., *The Era of German Expressionism* (1974); Peter Paret, *The Berlin Secession: Modernism and Its Enemies in Imperial Germany* (1980); John Golding, *Cubism: A History and Analysis* (1968); Wilfred Mellers, *Caliban Reborn: Renewal in Twentieth Century Music* (1967).

Sociology and Social Thought

H. Stuart Hughes, *Consciousness and Society: European Social Thought 1890–1930* (1958); Raymond Aron, *Main Currents of Sociological Thought*, Vol. 2 (1967); Robert A. Nisbet, *The Sociological Tradition* (1966); Arthur Mitzman, *Sociology and Estrangement* (1973); Anthony Giddens, *Studies in Social and Political Theory* (1977); Philip Abrams, *The Origins of British Sociology 1834–1914* (1968); Reinhard Bendix, *Max Weber: An Intellectual Portrait* (1965); Wolfgang Schluchter, *The Rise of Western Rationalism: Max Weber's Developmental History* (1981); S. Andreski, ed., *Max Weber on Capitalism, Bureaucracy, and Religion: A Selection of Texts* (1983); Robert A. Nye, *The Anti-Democratic Sources of Elite Theory: Pareto, Mosca, Michels* (1977); George Simmel, *Essays in Sociology* (ed. Kurt Worff) (1959); Steven Lukes, *Emile Durkheim: His Life and Work* (1973); Robert A. Nye, *The Origins of Crowd Psychology: Gustave LeBon and the Crisis of Mass Democracy in the Third Republic* (1975); William Logue, *From Philosophy to Sociology: The Evolution of French Liberalism 1870–1914* (1983); Rudolf A. Makreel, *Wilhelm Dilthey, Philosopher of the Human Studies* (1975); Fritz Ringer, *The Decline of the German Mandarins* (1969).

The Intellectuals and World War I

Roland N. Stromberg, *Redemption by War: The Intellectuals and 1914* (1982); Paul Fussell, *The Great War and Modern Memory* (1975); Robert Wohl, *The Generation of 1914* (1979); Eugen Weber, *The Nationalist Revival in France 1905–1914* (1959); Walter Laqueur, *Young Germany* (1962); J. D. Ellis, *French Socialists and the Problem of Peace 1904–1914* (1967); Georges Haupt, *Socialism and the Great War: The Collapse of the Second International* (1972); Jon Silkin, *Out of Battle: The Poetry of the First World War* (1977); George Panichas, ed., *Promise of Greatness* (1968); Bernard Bergonzi, *Heroes' Twilight* (1964); F. L. Carsten, *War Against War: British and German Radical Movements in the First World War* (1982); Paul Delany, *D. H. Lawrence's Nightmare: The Writer and His Circle During the Years of the Great War* (1979); Frank Field, *Three French Writers and the Great War* (1975); Jo Vellacott, *Bertrand Russell and the Pacifists in the First World War* (1981); Charles S. Doty, *From Cultural Rebellion to Counter-Revolution: the Politics of Maurice Barrès* (1976); William T. Starr, *Romain Rolland and a World at War*

(1956); John Cruickshank, *Variations on Catastrophe: Some French Responses to the Great War* (1982).

Lenin and the Russian Revolution

Philip Pomper, *The Russian Revolutionary Intelligentsia* (1970); Franco Venturi, *Roots of Revolution* (1970); James H. Billington, *Mikhailovsky and Russian Populism* (1958); A. Walicki, *The Controversy over Capitalism: Studies in the Social Philosophy of the Russian Populists* (1969); Vera Broido, *Apostles and Terrorists: Women and the Revolutionary Movement in the Russia of Alexander II* (1977); Samuel H. Baron, *Plekhanov: The Father of Russian Marxism* (1963); L. H. Haimson, *The Russian Marxists and the Origins of Bolshevism* (1955); Tibor Szamuely, *The Russian Tradition* (1974); A. B. Ulam, *Lenin and the Bolsheviks: The Intellectual and Political History of the Triumph of Bolshevism in Russia* (1965); Leonard Schapiro and Peter Reddaway, ed., *Lenin: The Man, the Theorist, the Leader* (1967); Rolf H. W. Theen, *Lenin: Genesis and Development of a Revolutionary* (1973); Robert C. Tucker, ed., *The Lenin Anthology* (1975); Stephen F. Cohen, *Bukharin and the Bolshevik Revolution* (1973); Curtis Stokes, *The Evolution of Trotsky's Theory of Revolution* (1982); Alain Besançon, *The Rise of the Gulag: Intellectual Origins of Leninism* (1981); Robert C. Williams, *Artists in Revolution: Portraits of the Russian Avant-Garde 1905-1925* (1977).

The Continuing Literary and Artistic Revolution
Post-World War I

Graham Hough, *Image and Experience: Studies in a Literary Revolution* (1960); Herbert S. Gershman, *The Surrealist Revolution in France* (1968); Leon Edel, *Bloomsbury: A House of Lions* (1979); Alan Bance, ed., *Weimar Germany: Writers and Politics* (1982); Hans M. Wingler, *The Bauhaus* (1970); Hugh Kenner, *The Pound Era* (1971); Germaine Bree and Margaret Guiton, *An Age of Fiction: The French Novel from Gide to Camus* (1958); Peter Blake, *The Master Builders* (1960, 1976); Joseph G. Brennan, *Three Philosophical Novelists* (Joyce, Gide, Mann) (1964); Ronald Bush, *T. S. Eliot: A Study in Character and Style* (1984); Roger Kojecky, *T. S. Eliot's Social Criticism* (1971); J. I. M. Stewart, *Eight Modern English Writers* (1963); George Stade, ed., *Six Modern British Novelists* (1974); Quentin Bell, *Virginia Woolf* (1972); Harry T. Moore, *D. H. Lawrence: The Priest of Love* (1974); J. M. Cocking, ed., *Proust: Collected Essays on the Writer and His Art* (1982); Richard Ellman, *James Joyce*, 2nd ed., (1984); Angel Flores and Homer Swander, ed., *Franz Kafka Today* (1958).

Einstein and the New Scientific Revolution

Ronald W. Clark, *Einstein: Life and Times* (1971); G. J. Whitrow, ed., *Einstein: The Man and His Achievement* (1967); A. P. French, ed., *Einstein: A Centenary Volume* (1979); Abraham Pais, *"Subtle Is the Lord": The Science and the Life of Albert Einstein* (1983); L. S. Swenson, *The Genesis of Relativity* (1979); Bertrand Russell, *The ABC of Relativity* (1958); Albert Einstein, *The Meaning of Relativity*, 5th ed. (1955); Max Planck, *The New Science* (1959); Werner Heisenberg, *Physics and Philosophy* (1959); Louis de Broglie, *Physics and Microphysics* (1955); George Gamow, *Thirty Years That Shook Physics* (1966); Robert M. Wald, *Space, Time, and Gravity* (1977); Isaac Asimov, *Understanding Physics: The Electron, Proton, and Neutron* (1966); R. Harré, ed., *Scientific Thought 1900-1960: A Selective*

Survey (1969); Roger B. Stuewer, ed., *Symposium on the History of Nuclear Physics* (1977).

Fascism, Nazism

Ernst Nolte, *Three Faces of Fascism* (1967); Renzo de Felice, *Interpretations of Fascism* (1977); Stanley G. Payne, *Fascism: Comparison and Definition* (1980); A. James Gregor, *The Ideology of Fascism* (1969); George L. Mosse, *Masses and Man: Nationalist and Fascist Perceptions of Reality* (1980); Hannah Arendt, *The Origins of Totalitarianism* (1966); Adrian Lyttleton, ed., *Italian Fascisms from Pareto to Gentile* (1975); George L. Mosse, *Toward the Final Solution: A History of European Racism* (1977); George L. Mosse, ed., *Nazi Culture* (1966); Walter Struve, *Elites Against Democracy* (1973); Eberhard Jäckel, *Hitler's Weltanschauung* (1972); Werner Maser, *Hitler: Legend, Myth, and Reality* (1974); James B. Whisker, *The Social, Political, and Religious Thought of Alfred Rosenberg* (1982); William R. Tucker, *The Fascist Ego: A Political Biography of Robert Brasillach* (1975); Robert Soucy, *Fascist Intellectual: Drieu La Rochelle* (1979); W. F. Mandle, *Anti-Semitism and the British Union of Fascists* (1968); Frederic Jameson, *Wyndham Lewis: The Modernist as Fascist* (1979); A. D. Beyerchen, *Scientists Under Hitler* (1977); Robert R. Taylor, *The World in Stone: The Role of Architecture in National Socialist Ideology* (1974); J. M. Ritchie, *German Literature Under National Socialism* (1983).

Soviet Communism; Stalinism

Robert A. Maguire, *Red Virgin Soil: Soviet Literature in the 1920s* (1968); Edward J. Brown, *Mayakovsky: A Poet in the Revolution* (1973); Alexander Erlich, *The Soviet Industrialization Debate 1924-1928* (1961); Joel Carmichael, *Trotsky* (1975); C. Vaughan Jones, *Soviet Socialist Realism: Origins and Theory* (1975); Stephen F. Cohen, *Bukharin and the Bolshevik Revolution* (1973); Robert C. Tucker, ed., *Stalinism: Essays in Historical Interpretation* (1977); G. R. Urban, ed., *Stalinism: Its Impact on Russia and the World* (1983); Vera Dunham, *In Stalin's Time: Middle Class Values in Soviet Fiction* (1976); Victor Serge, *Memoirs of a Revolutionary 1901-1941* (1965); Robert Conquest, *The Great Terror: Stalin's Purge of the Thirties* (1971); Nadezhda Mandelstam, *Hope Against Hope* (1970); Alec Nove, *Stalinism and After* (2nd ed., 1981); Lee Congdon, *The Young Lukacs* (1983); George Lichtheim, *George Lukacs* (1970); Eugene Lunn, *Marxism and Modernism* (1982); Robert C. Tucker, *The Soviet Political Mind* (1971).

Communism and the Western Intellectuals in the 1930s

David Caute, *The Fellow Travellers* (1972); Neal Wood, *Communism and British Intellectuals* (1964); R. H. S. Crossman, ed., *The God That Failed* (1950); Raymond Aron, *The Opium of the Intellectuals* (1952); Irwin Wall, *French Communism in the Era of Stalin* (1983); Arthur Koestler, *The Invisible Writing* (1954); Samuel Hynes, *The Auden Generation* (1977); Humphrey Carpenter, *W. H. Auden: A Biography* (1981); Bernard Crick, *George Orwell: A Life* (1980); Stanley Weintraub, *The Last Great Cause* (1968); Frederick R. Benson, *Writers in Arms: The Literary Impact of the Spanish Civil War* (1967); Daniel Brower, *The New Jacobins: The French Communists and the Popular Front* (1968); John T. Marcus, *French Socialism in the Crisis Years 1933-1936* (1958); David Pike, *German Writers in Soviet Exile 1933-1945* (1982); G. L. S. Shackle, *The Years of High Theory* (1967); Richard F. Kahn, *The Making of Keynes' "General Theory"* (1984).

Logical Positivism and Linguistic Philosophy

Leszek Kolakowski, *Positivist Philosophy* (1972); Osward Hanfling, *Logical Positivism* (1981); Arne Naess, *Four Modern Philosophers* (1965); David F. Lindenfeld, *Alexius Meinong and European Thought 1880-1920* (1980); Michael Dummett, *Frege, Philosopher of Language* (1973); A. J. Ayer, *Philosophy in the Twentieth Century* (1982); Paul Levy, *G. E. Moore and the Cambridge Apostles* (1979); Gustav Bergmann, *The Metaphysics of Logical Positivism* (1967); J. O. Urmson, *Philosophical Analysis: Its Development Between the Two World Wars* (1956); Gerd Brand, *The Essential Wittgenstein* (1979); Allan Janik and Stephen Toulmin, *Wittgenstein's Vienna* (1973); Renford Bambrough et al., *Understanding Wittgenstein* (1974); Garth Hallett, *A Companion to Wittgenstein's "Philosophical Investigations"* (1977); David Pears, *Ludwig Wittgenstein* (1969); Fr. Waissman, *Wittgenstein and the Vienna Circle* (1979); Bertrand Russell, *My Philosophical Development* (1959); *The Basic Writings of Bertrand Russell,* ed. R. E. Egner and L. E. Denom (1961); J. L. Austin, *Philosophical Papers* (1970); C. W. K. Mundle, *A Critique of Linguistic Philosophy* (1970).

Sartre

M. Contat and M. Rybalka, eds., *The Writings of Jean-Paul Sartre* (1974); Paul Schilpp, ed., *The Philosophy of Sartre* (1980); Istvan Meszaros, *The Work of Sartre* (1979); Axel Madsen, *Hearts and Minds: The Common Journey of Simone de Beauvoir and Jean-Paul Sartre* (1977); Joseph F. Fell, *Heidegger and Sartre* (1979); Germaine Bree, *Camus and Sartre* (1972); Jean D. Kellogg, *Dark Prophets of Hope* (1975); Mark Poster, *Existential Marxism in Postwar France* (1975); James F. Sheridan, *Sartre: The Radical Conversion* (1969); Ian Craib, *Existentialism and Sociology* (1976); Raymond Aron, *History and the Dialectic of Violence: An Analysis of Sartre's "Critique de la Raison Dialectique"* (1974); Douglas Collins, *Sartre as Biographer* (1980); Hazel E. Barnes, *Sartre and Flaubert* (1981); Alfred Stern, *Sartre, His Philosophy and Existential Psychoanalysis* (1967).

Other Existentialists and Phenomenologists

Martin Faber, *The Foundations of Phenomenology* (1968); J. J. Kockelmanns, *Introduction to Husserl's Phenomenology* (1967); Zygmunt Bauman, *Hermeneutics and Social Science* (1978); Hans-G. Gadamer, *Philosophical Hermeneutics* (1976); Thomas Sheehan, ed., *Heidegger: The Man and the Thinker* (1981); John Sallis, ed., *Radical Phenomenology: Essays in Honor of Martin Heidegger* (1978); Edward N. Lee and Maurice Mandelbaum, ed., *Phenomenology and Existentialism* (1967); Karl Jaspers, *The Philosophy of Existence* (1971); Rudolf Bultmann, *Existence and Faith* (1960); Alden L. Fisher, ed., *The Essential Writings of Maurice Merleau-Ponty* (1969); John O'Neill, *Perception, Experience, and History: The Social Phenomenology of Maurice Marleau-Ponty* (1970); Leonard H. Ehrlich, *Karl Jaspers: Philosophy and Faith* (1975); David E. Roberts, *Existentialism and Religious Belief* (1963).

World War II and the Intellectuals

Robert Hewison, *Under Siege: Literary Life in London 1939-1945* (1977); José Harris, *William Beveridge: A Biography* (1977); George Orwell, *Collected Essays, Journalism and Letters,* ed. Sonia Orwell and Ian Angus, Vols. 2 and 3 (1968); James D. Wilkinson, *The Intellectual Resistance in Europe* (1981); H. R. Kedward,

Resistance in Vichy France: A Study of Ideas and Motivation in the Southern Zone 1940-1942 (1978); Jean Monnet, *Memories* (1976); Gerhard Ritter, *The German Resistance: Carl Goederler's Struggle Against Tyranny* (1958); Ian Kershaw, *Popular Opinion and Political Dissent in the Third Reich: Bavaria 1933-1945* (1983); Wilhelm W. Schütz, *Pens Under the Swastika* (1971); Ilya Ehrenburg, *The War 1914-1945* (1964); Donald Fleming and Bernard Bailyn, eds., *The Intellectual Migration: Europe and America 1930-1960* (1969); H. Stuart Hughes, *The Sea Change: The Migration of Social Thought 1930-1965* (1975); Lawrence L. Langer, *Versions of Survival: The Holocaust and the Human Spirit* (1982); Sidra G. Ezrahi, *By Works Alone: The Holocaust in Literature* (1980).

Neo-Marxism, Critical Marxism

Dick Howard, *The Unknown Dimension: European Marxism Since Lenin* (1972); Wolfgang Leonhard, *Three Faces of Marxism* (1974); M. M. Drachkovitch, ed., *Marxism in the Modern World* (1965); Raymond Guess, *The Idea of Critical Theory* (1981); Martin Jay, *The Dialectical Imagination* (1973); John O'Neill, ed., *On Critical Theory* (1976); David Held, *Introduction to Critical Theory: Horkheimer to Habermas* (1980); Gillian Rose, *The Melancholy Science: An Introduction to the Thought of Theodor Adorno* (1979); Thomas W. McCarthy, *The Critical Theory of Jürgen Habermas* (1978); Julius Sensat, *Habermas and Marxism: An Appraisal* (1979); Alastair Davidson, *Antonio Gramsci: Toward an Intellectual Biography* (1977); Walter L. Adamson, *Hegemony and Revolution: Antonio Gramsci's Political and Cultural Theory* (1980); Maurice Cranston, ed., *The New Left* (1971); Neil McInnes, *The Western Marxists* (1972); Annie Kriegel, *Euro-Communism: A New Kind of Communism?* (1978); Rudolf F. Tökes, ed., *European Communism in the Age of Detente* (1977); Klaus Mehnert, *Moscow and the New Left* (1976).

Soviet Dissidents, East European Marxism

Robert Conquest, *The Politics of Ideas in the USSR* (1967); R. L. Tökes, ed., *Dissent in the USSR* (1975); Abraham Rothberg, *The Heirs of Stalin: Dissidence and the Soviet Regime 1953-1970* (1972); Peter Reddaway, *Russia's Underground Intellectuals* (1970); David Joravsky, *The Lysenko Affair* (1970); Alexander Solzhenitsyn, *The Oak and the Calf: Sketches of Literary Life in the Soviet Union* (1975); Gerson S. Sher, *Praxis: Marxist Criticism and Dissent in Socialist Yugoslavia* (1977); N. Markovic and Robert S. Cohen, *Yugoslavia: The Rise and Fall of Socialist Humanism* (1978); A. Hegedus, A. Heller, N. Markus, and M. Vajda, *The Humanization of Socialism: Writings of the Budapest School* (1976); Vladimir Kusin, *Intellectual Origins of the Prague Spring* (1971); Marc Rakovski, *Toward an East European Marxism* (1978); Timothy G. Ash, *The Polish Revolution: Solidarity 1980-1982* (1984); Geoffrey Hosking, *Beyond Socialist Realism: Soviet Fiction Since "Ivan Denisovich"* (1980); Michael Meerson-Aksenov and Boris Shagrin, eds., *The Political, Social, and Religious Thought of Russian "Samizdat": An Anthology* (1977).

Structuralism

Howard Gardner, *The Quest for Mind: Piaget, Levi-Strauss, and the Structuralist Movement* (1981); Edith Kurzweil, *The Age of Structuralism* (1980); John Sturrock, ed., *Structuralism and Since: From Levi-Strauss to Derrida* (1980); E. Nelson Hayes and Tanya Hayes, ed., *Claude Levi-Strauss: The Anthropologist as Hero*

(1970); Alex Callinicos, *Althusser's Marxism* (1976); Fredric Jameson, *The Prison House of Language: A Critical History of Structuralism and Formalism* (1972); Roland Barthes, *Mythologies* (1972); Michel Foucault, *The Order of Things* (1970); Jacques Derrida, *Margins of Philosophy* (1983); Geoffrey H. Hartman, *Saving the Text: Literature, Derrida, Philosophy* (1981); Jonathan Culler, *On Deconstruction: Theory and Criticism After Structuralism* (1983); Sherry Turkle, *Psychoanalytic Politics: Freud's French Revolution* (1978); Stuart Schneiderman, *Jacques Lacan: The Death of an Intellectual Hero* (1983); John Sturrock, *The French New Novel* (1969).

Other Books about Recent Thought and Culture

Robert A. Nisbet, *The Twilight of Authority* (1975); M. Ashley Montagu and F. Watson, *The Dehumanization of Man* (1983); Henry Jacoby, *The Bureaucratization of the World* (1973); Raymond Aron, *In Defense of Decadent Europe* (1979); Judith Shklar, *After Utopia: The Decline of Political Faith* (1959); Roland N. Stromberg, *After Everything* (1975); Arthur Koestler, *The Roots of Coincidence* (1972); Christopher Booker, *The Neophiliacs* (1970); Malcolm Bradbury, ed., *The Novel Today* (1977); George Stade, ed., *Six Contemporary British Novelists* (1976); G. Santoni, ed., *Contemporary French Culture and Society* (1981); Irving Howe, ed., *1984 Revisited* (1983); Ronald Hayman, *Theatre and Anti-theatre: New Movements Since Beckett* (1977); R. J. Reilly, *Romantic Religion: A Study of Barfield, Lewis, Williams, and Tolkien* (1971); Daniel Cohen, *Waiting for the Apocalypse* (1983); Warren Wagar, *Terminal Visions: The Literature of Last Things* (1982); Hans Küng, *Does God Exist? An Answer for Today* (1980).

Note on Finding Additional Sources

The foregoing list of books is a highly selective one and does not contain articles in scholarly journals, where some of the most important research in any field will be found. If you are interested in developing a fuller bibliography on some subject, you can search your library's card catalog, or the subject catalog of the *National Union Catalogue* published by the Library of Congress, available in most university libraries. Or you may consult a bibliography of bibliographies, such as *Bibliographical Index* (periodical). You will also want to know the scholarly journal most appropriate to the subject, which usually is a source of bibliography. And, to keep up with the periodical literature, you should know the guides to that literature, some of which include abstracts of the articles.

There are many special bibliographies of works by or about major individual figures or schools. The numerous works now devoted solely to bibliography are an indication of the magnitude of scholarly publications in recent years. For example, I recently read a Ph.D. dissertation that consisted of an annotated list of writings about Thomas Hardy in the 1970s, which turned out to embrace some 40 books and 900 articles! If the English departments excel all others in the production of books and articles (there being more academics employed there), there is no shortage in other fields. Thus the student may find an extensive bibliography already prepared on his or her subject.

The following are useful bibliographies: Modern Language Association, *Annual Bibliography;* English Association of London, *The Year's Work in English Studies,* annually; *Bibliography of Studies in Victorian Literature,* edited by William D. Templeman, Robert C. Slack, and others, several volumes since 1945; *Philosopher's Index: A Retrospective Guide 1940-1976,* and annually; National Library of

Medicine, *Bibliographical Guide to the History of Medicine,* periodically (actual scope much beyond its subject narrowly conceived); *Repertoire internationale de litterature et d'art* (periodically, in English; especially useful for the fine arts); Dagmar Laytved, *A Bibliographical Guide to Women's Studies* (1981); *Bibliographical Guide to Soviet and East European Studies,* annually; *Comprehensive Dissertation Index; Isis* (the journal of the history of science), *Critical Bibliography in the History of Science,* annually.

The Garland Reference Library publishes numerous volumes of annotated bibliography, among them William J. Wainwright, *Philosophy of Religion in the Twentieth Century* (1978), and Diane L. Hoeveler, *English Prose and Criticism in the Nineteenth Century* (1979). Northern Illinois University Press's series of *Annotated Secondary Bibliographies on English Literature in Transition 1880–1920* includes James L. Cowan, *An Annotated Bibliography of Writings about D. H. Lawrence* (1984). Some other bibliographies on individual authors or special subjects are Francis Lapointe, *Jean-Paul Sartre and His Critics: An Introductory Bibliography,* 2nd ed., (1981); Dan H. Laurence, *Bernard Shaw: A Bibliography* (1984); Alistair Davies, *An Annotated Critical Bibliography of Modernism* (1983); Paul Raabe, *Index of Expressionism* (1974); John E. Stoll (aptly titled) *The Great Deluge: A Yeats Bibliography* (1971).

Useful for keeping up with articles are these periodical publications: *Historical Abstracts* and *Twentieth Century Abstracts; Sociological Abstracts; Psychological Abstracts; Journal of Economic Literature; Recently Published Articles,* an adjunct to the *American Historical Review; Index to Religious Periodical Literature; Philosopher's Index; Women's Studies Abstracts.* Scholarly journals preeminent in their fields which provide bibliographical service include *Isis, Studies in Romanticism, Victorian Studies, Signs, Women's Studies, Canadian Review of Studies in Nationalism, Soviet Studies, French Historical Studies, Journal of Religion.*

Other research tools worth mentioning include Henry and Mary Garland, *Oxford Companion to German Literature* (1976); *The Pelican Guides to English Literature,* in several volumes (Boris Ford, ed., *From Dickens to Hardy,* 1983, is Vol. 6); Richard T. DeGeorge, *The Philosopher's Guide* (1980); *Subject Guide to Books in Print,* published annually by the Publishers' Trade List; *Book Review Digest* (see what critics had to say about the book you may have chosen to report on).

Those who have access to computerized "on-line" bibliographic service and are willing to pay for it will find professional areas such as medicine (MEDLINE) and law (LEXUS) better developed than the humanities, but there are some available services in the latter; consult the specialist at your library.

Index

CONCEPTS INDEX